fashion design techniques

by zeshu takamura

Table of Contents

Foreword 3

Gallery 4

Chapter 1: The Body 9
[1] Proportions of the Body 10
[2] Method of Creating Beautiful Poses 21
[3] Method of Drawing Body Parts 47

Chapter 2: Technical Drawing 53
[1] Shirts and Blouses 55
[2] Jackets and Blazers 58
[3] Jumpers (Short Jackets) 60
[4] Knitwear 61
[5] Vests (Waistcoats) 62
[6] Coats 63
[7] Pants/Trousers 64
[8] Dresses 66
[9] Skirts 67

Chapter 3: Fashion Drawing 69
[1] Dressing 70
[2] Color Application 84
  (1) Mechanisms of Color 84
  (2) Artist's Materials for Coloring 85
  (3) Coloring Method 86
[3] Textile Rendition 94
[4] Warp Lines of A Garment 108
[5] Fashion Drawing Step-by-Step 112
[6] Stylized Fashion Drawing 120
[7] Proportion by Age 122

Chapter 4: Computer Graphic Techniques 125
[1] Using Photoshop 126
  (1) How to Create A Fashion Drawing 129
  (2) Creating Textiles 133
[2] Using Illustrator 147
  (1) Technical Drawing 150
  (2) Color Variation for Technical Drawing 153
  (3) How to Create An Original Pattern 155

Postscript 159
Author's Biography 160

Foreword

I would like to address the subject of this book from the point of view of the origin of the words fashion design technique. Fashion has the sense of a temporary popularity, and the popularity with the fastest turnover is in garments, so that in recent years fashion has come to mean garments (clothing and accessories).

Design can be divided into 'de' and 'sign'. Since the prefix 'de' indicates completeness, and a sign is a symbol, design can be interpreted as a way of turning an idea into a full symbol by giving it a distinct form.

The technique of presenting (designing) ideas about garments (fashion) to people in a readily understandable way involves representing pictorially the shape, material, pattern, color, and other elements and is known as design drawing.

Apparel manufacturers manage the series of processes involved in creating clothes through division of labor. The designer takes the ideas, concepts, colors, and textiles or materials planned by the merchandiser and designs the clothes by making design drawings. In this way, concrete decisions are made on design points such as the outline of the garment and the detail. The patterner carries out pattern-making on the basis of these design drawings, and this pattern becomes the basis for the sewing which leads to the finished product. The finished products are then arranged in shops where we the consumers can access them.

It is very important not only for people who are to become designers but also for those who undertake other tasks in the work of clothes making to have the ability to understand and interpret design drawings. If patterners are able to grasp the meaning of design drawing at a deeper level, the patterns they create will be more stylish. If one has experienced the difficult task of actually drawing something oneself, one naturally acquires the ability to interpret other people's drawings. If one is to sell clothes, one needs the ability to interpret the technical drawings used for catalog lists. If one perceives clearly which are the design points of each product, one will be better able to recommend to customers products that meet their needs.

In the uniform industry, there is competition between a number of companies to obtain the rights to planning and production. Each company makes a presentation. To do this they prepare comps (planning and editing mock-ups) in which fashion illustrators elevate design drawing to the level of fashion illustration as a way of helping to create comps that beat the comps of other companies. In this way, design drawing is a central pillar of fashion design and constitutes the very essence of fashion design technique.

In recent years, enterprises have sought human resources who are of immediate value. In response, vocational schools, colleges and universities are making their teaching more practically oriented and are introducing teaching based on computer use. Against this social background, the present book, which draws together a diverse content ranging from the basics of design drawing to computer-based applications, has been edited so as to serve as a textbook not only for students but also the professionally active. Work hard and remember: practice makes perfect.

Gallery There are various styles of design drawing depending on the purpose, for example, in addition to so-called "design drawing", which is simply concerned with the design of garments, there are also "fashion drawing", which places priority on image and "fashion illustration", which is elevated to the level of art including a background. It is advisable to be aware of the fact that there are such different styles, rather than categorizing.

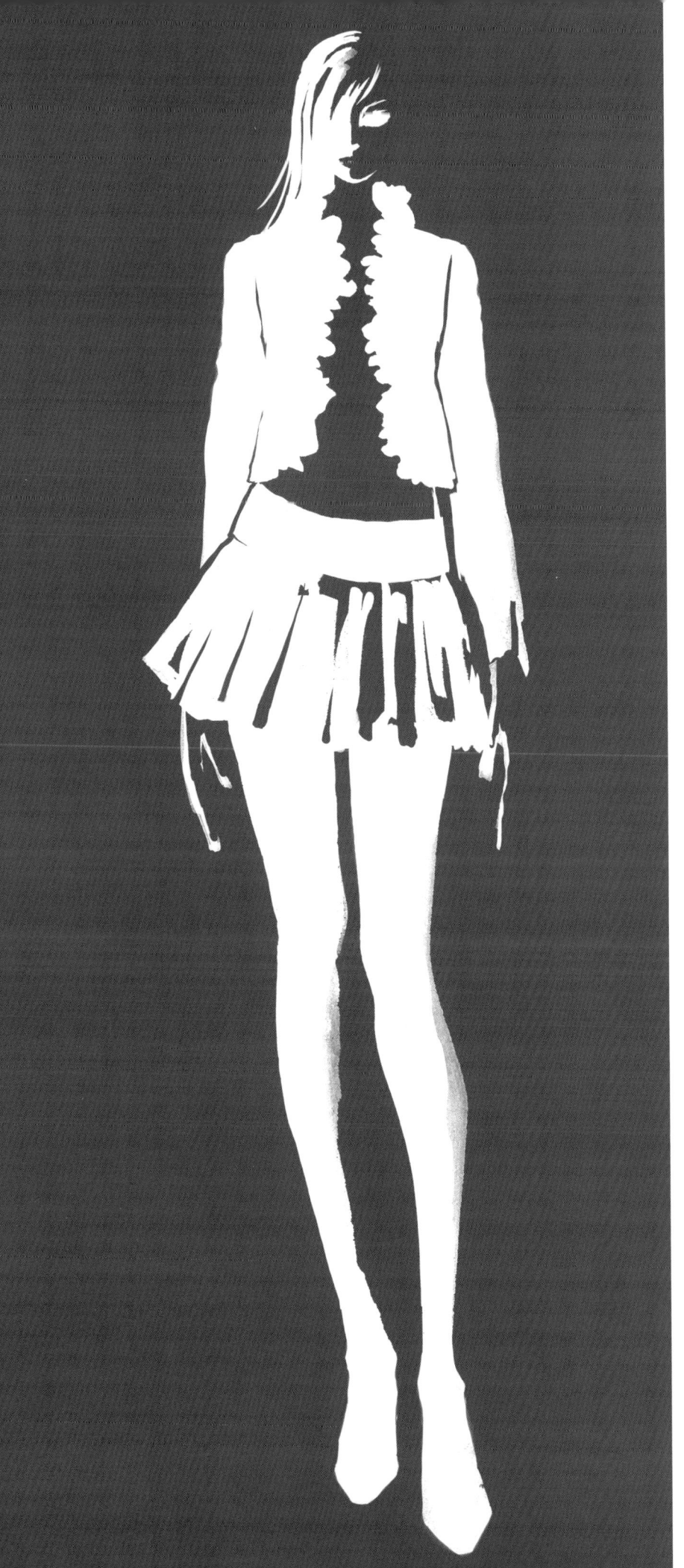

Chapter 1
The Body

We will first study the body that is to be clothed. The aim is to acquire the ability to draw figures, which consistently have the same proportions. The balance between different items of clothing is rather delicate, as their length and sense of volume constantly change with the times.

The starting point of 'fashion design technique' is to be able to draw the body from all angles, with the same proportions, in order to clearly express the design points in each case.

[1] Proportions of the Body

Necessary materials:
- Ruler at least 35 cm in length
- B4-size sketchpad
- Pencil or mechanical pencil with B or softer lead. (If the lead is too hard, it tends to damage the paper.)

(1) Balance of the Body

First let us study the human body which will be clothed. The aim here is to draw a steady standing pose. To draw a pose that has a sense of gravity, it is important to be able to discern on which leg the weight is being supported. Since human existence is still relatively recent compared with other animals, there is little difference between the species. For example, if we compare the Doberman, chihuahua and bulldog, their skeletal structures have entirely different proportions. In contrast, although the skin and hair color of Caucasians, Africans, Asians and people of mixed blood differ, their skeletal structures have approximately the same relative proportions. Such a species, i.e. the human being with few individual structural differences can be drawn by studying certain fixed principles.

Let's look more closely at those principles.

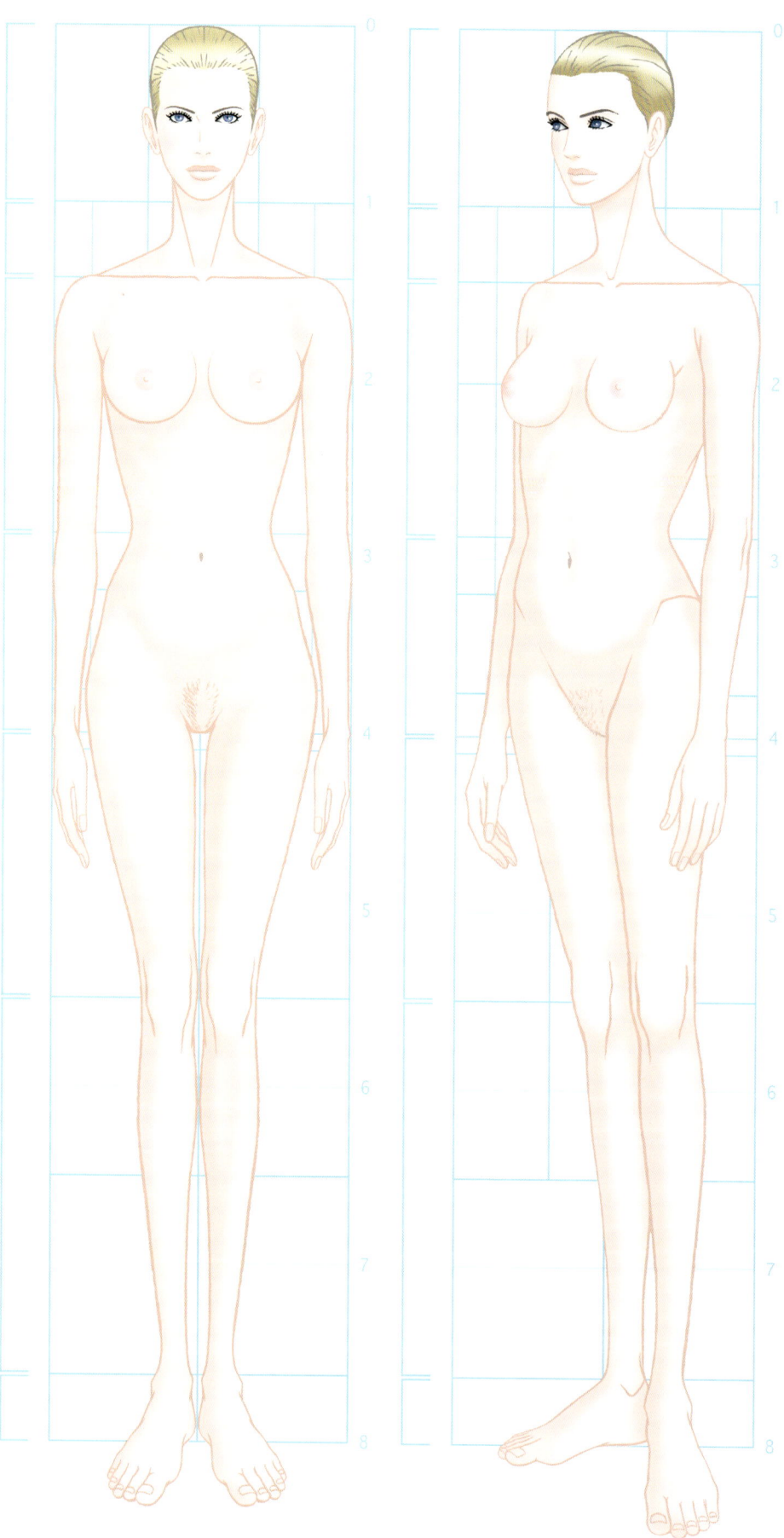

Female Erect Frontal View

Female Erect Diagonal View

Male Erect Frontal View **Male Erect Diagonal View**

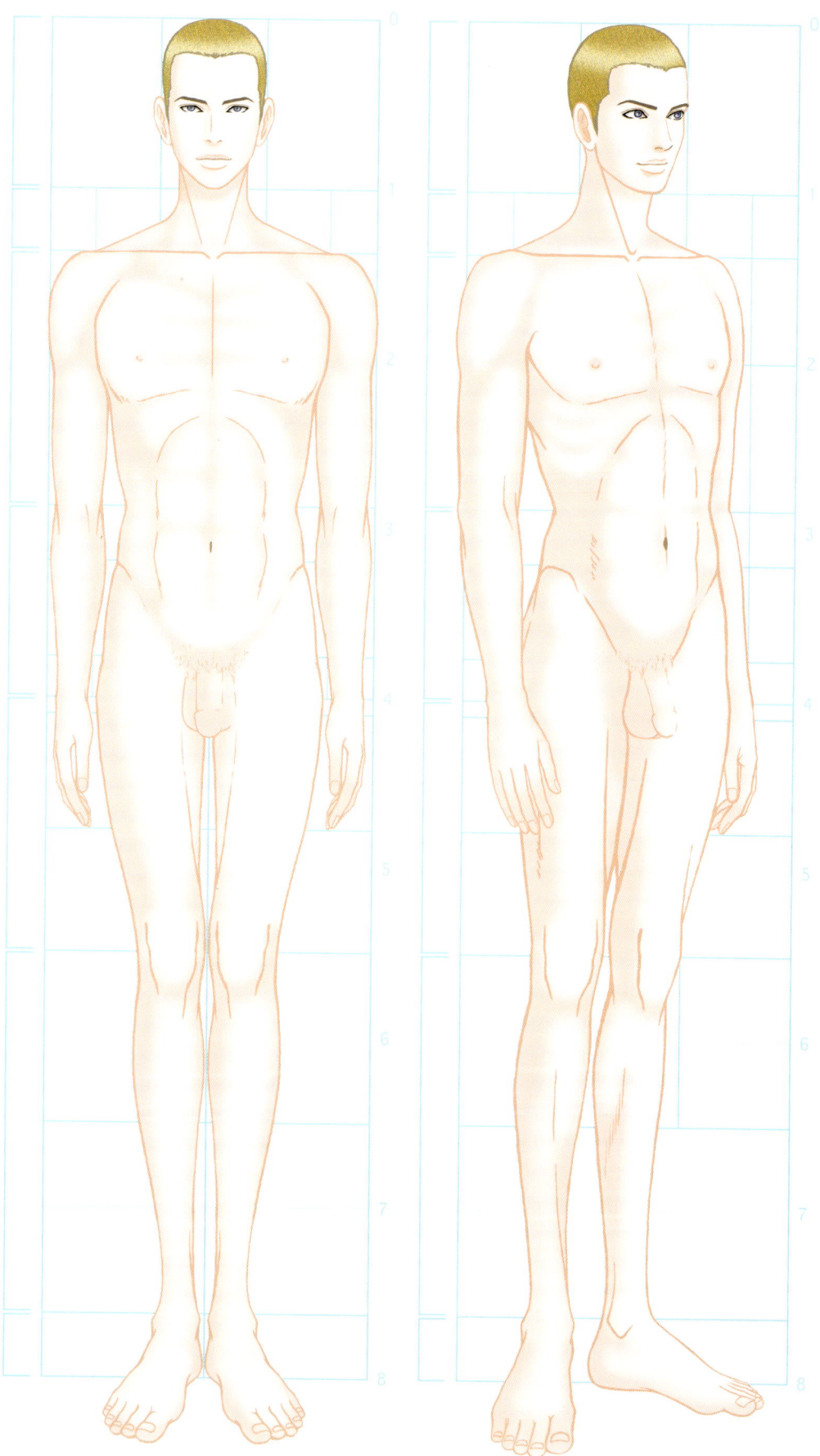

Chapter 1 : The Body

Male Erect Side View **Male Erect Diagonal Back View** **Male Erect Back View**

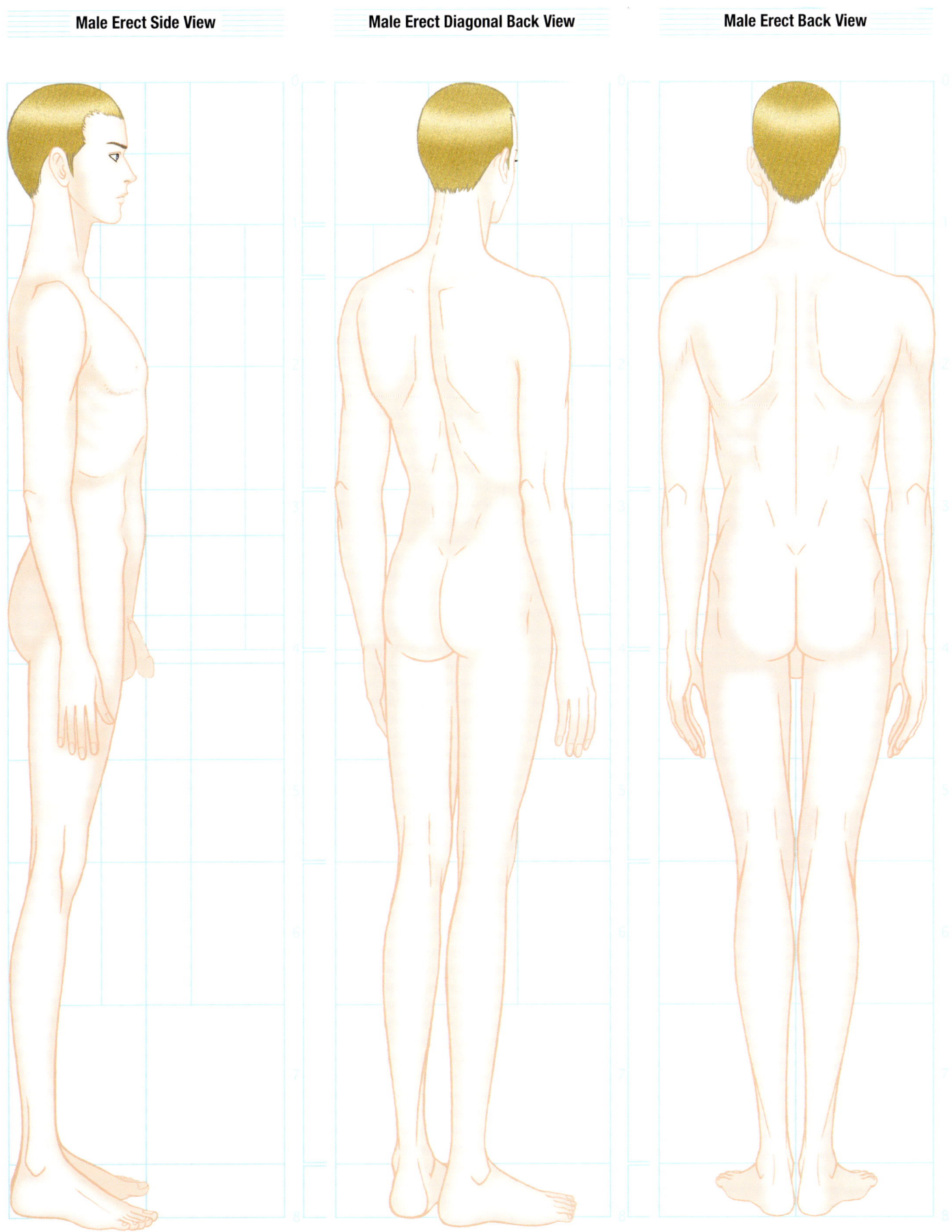

(2) Principles of Body Proportion

Let us base the ideal height of the female and male on between 175 - 180 cm and 185 - 190 cm respectively. The length is described based on a unit of head length and width. One head width is two thirds of the head length. Based on these, the principles are shown as below. Actual sizes in the case of drawing on B4 paper are also provided, as this size of paper is commonly used.

1) **The total body height is equal to eight head lengths. (32 cm with a 4 cm head length)**

2) **The total body width of the full frontal view is slightly under two head lengths (7 cm) for the female and two head lengths (8 cm) for the male.**

• Allocate numbers from 0 to 8 between the top of the head and the heel, and designate the position of each body component, based on its joint, as the length of bones will be known when the distance between the joints is known. Let's go over this from the top.

3) **Top of the head: 0**

4) **Chin: 1**

5) **Collarbones: Between 1 and 2 (1.7 cm below position 1 for the female, 1.5 cm below position 1 for the male)**

6) **Bust point: 2**

7) **Waist line: Slightly higher than position 3 (by 0.5 cm)**

8) **Crotch: 4 (so that the legs represent half the body length)**

9) **Knee center: The median of 5 and 6**

10) **Ankle: 1.5 cm higher than position 8**

11) **Heel: 8**

12) **Elbow: Same position as the waistline**

13) **Wrist: Same position as the crotch**

14) **Shoulder and hip widths: Two head widths (5.2 cm)**

15) **Waist and knee widths: Slightly wider (by 2 mm each on both the left and right sides) than one head width (3.1 cm)**

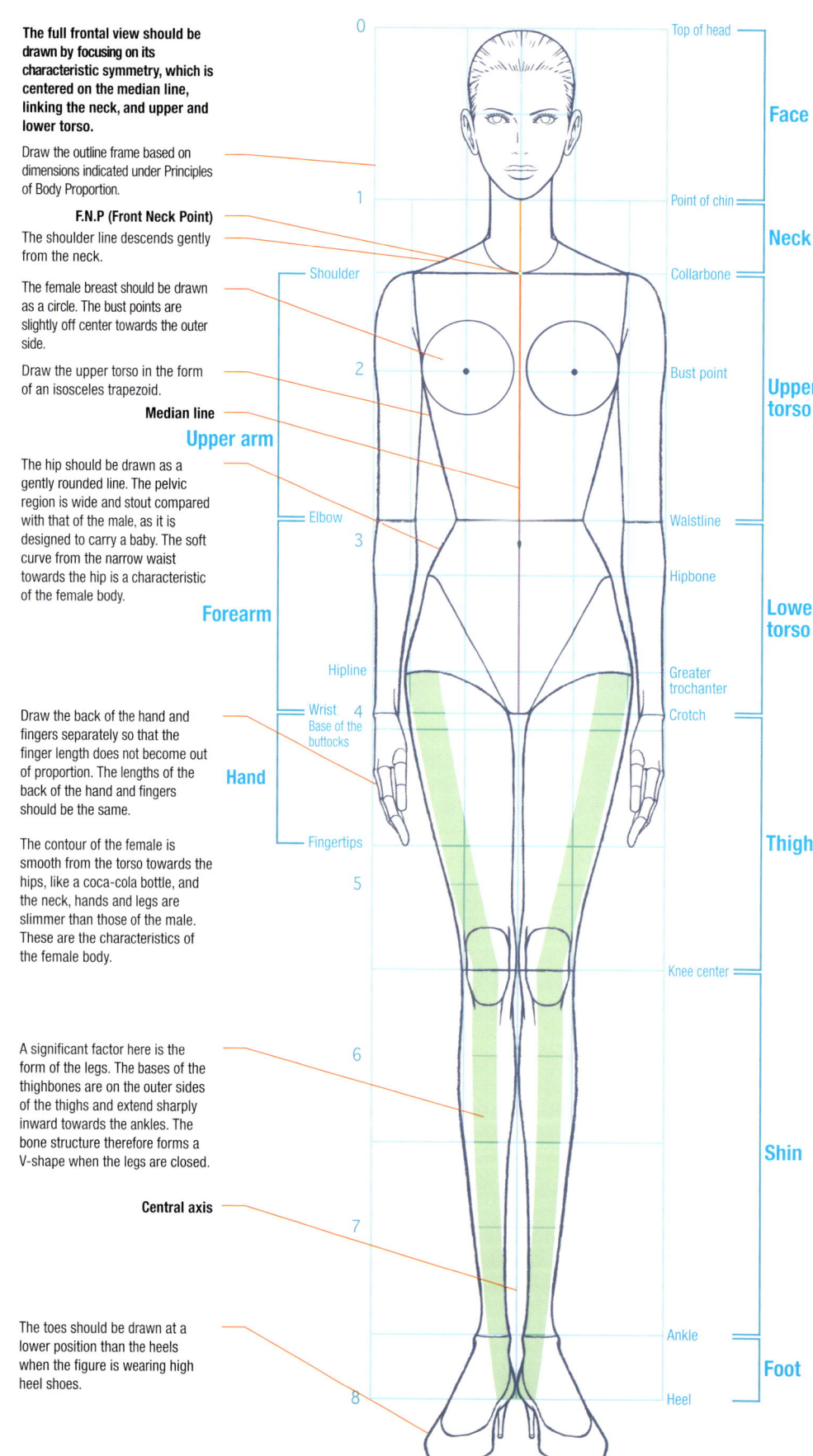

Erect Frontal View (Female)

The full frontal view should be drawn by focusing on its characteristic symmetry, which is centered on the median line, linking the neck, and upper and lower torso.

Draw the outline frame based on dimensions indicated under Principles of Body Proportion.

F.N.P (Front Neck Point)
The shoulder line descends gently from the neck.

The female breast should be drawn as a circle. The bust points are slightly off center towards the outer side.

Draw the upper torso in the form of an isosceles trapezoid.

Median line

The hip should be drawn as a gently rounded line. The pelvic region is wide and stout compared with that of the male, as it is designed to carry a baby. The soft curve from the narrow waist towards the hip is a characteristic of the female body.

Draw the back of the hand and fingers separately so that the finger length does not become out of proportion. The lengths of the back of the hand and fingers should be the same.

The contour of the female is smooth from the torso towards the hips, like a coca-cola bottle, and the neck, hands and legs are slimmer than those of the male. These are the characteristics of the female body.

A significant factor here is the form of the legs. The bases of the thighbones are on the outer sides of the thighs and extend sharply inward towards the ankles. The bone structure therefore forms a V-shape when the legs are closed.

Central axis

The toes should be drawn at a lower position than the heels when the figure is wearing high heel shoes.

Enlarge this page by copy and trace the drawing many times to acquire the body proportion.

Chapter 1 : The Body

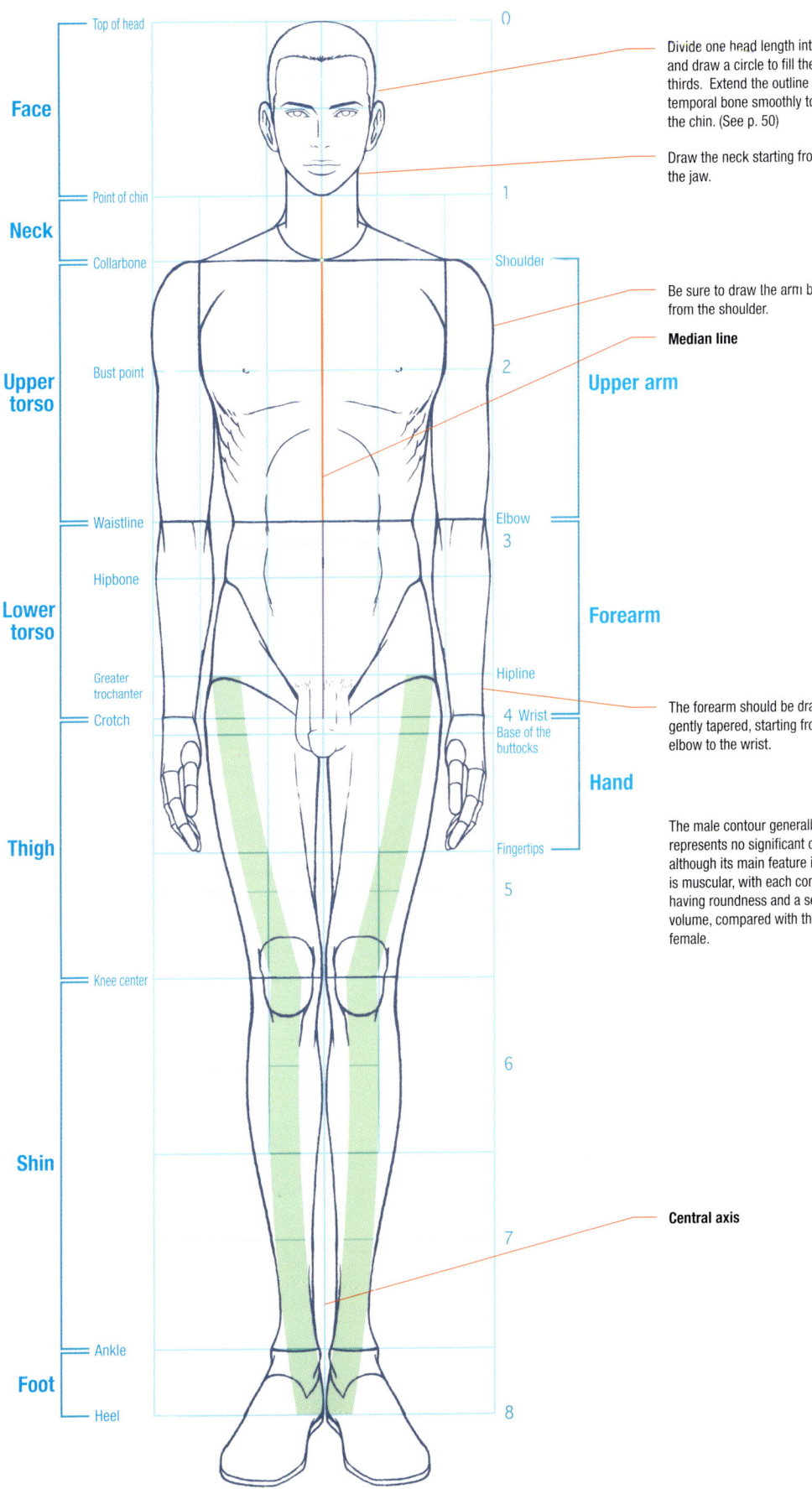

Erect Frontal View (Male)

(3) Method for Drawing the Body

When drawing the human body, it is advisable to start with a mannequin, rather than a nude figure. The reason is that unless you draw while being strongly conscious of the forms and characteristics of each component, as well as the movable parts, you will not be able to draw various poses.

[Key points]

1) Draw the body thinner than the actual size: When drawing an actual three-dimensional figure on a two dimensional piece of paper, it will appear fatter, unless you draw one size thinner by eliminating the shading of the outline, due to the difficulty of rendering perspective or depth of the figure. The fact that celebrities on TV screens appear fatter than they are in reality also results from the flat surface, which lacks depth.

2) Draw the figure part by part using the grid as a guide: Make sure to fully understand the length and width of each component, as the position of the joints is important when creating poses.

3) Pay attention to the volume of each component: The bones which protect the inner organs such as skull, ribs and pelvis each have a certain volume, and the form of the bone represents the contour, while the movable bones such as neck, arms and legs have muscles around them and have a stick-like form.

15

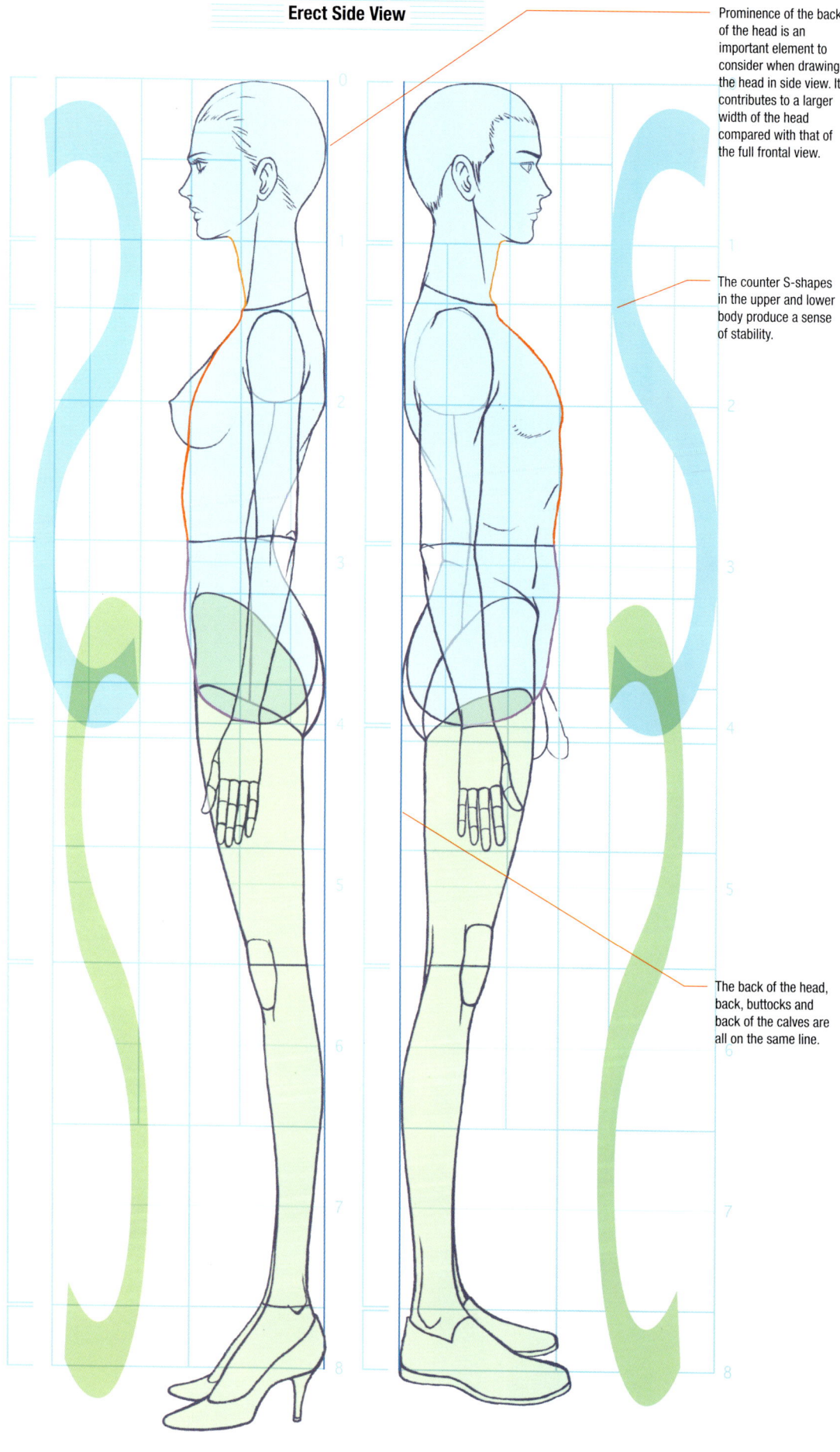

Erect Side View

A characteristic of the body's side view is that the median line (centerline of the body) which is straight when seen from the full front, becomes an S-shape. When human beings evolved to bipedal animals, they succeeded in alleviating the gravity load by cleverly using this delicate curve. The legs however have a reverse S-shape contrary to the median line. The thickness between the bust and back is a little less than one head length (3.5 cm) for the female and one head length (4 cm) for the male.

Prominence of the back of the head is an important element to consider when drawing the head in side view. It contributes to a larger width of the head compared with that of the full frontal view.

The counter S-shapes in the upper and lower body produce a sense of stability.

The back of the head, back, buttocks and back of the calves are all on the same line.

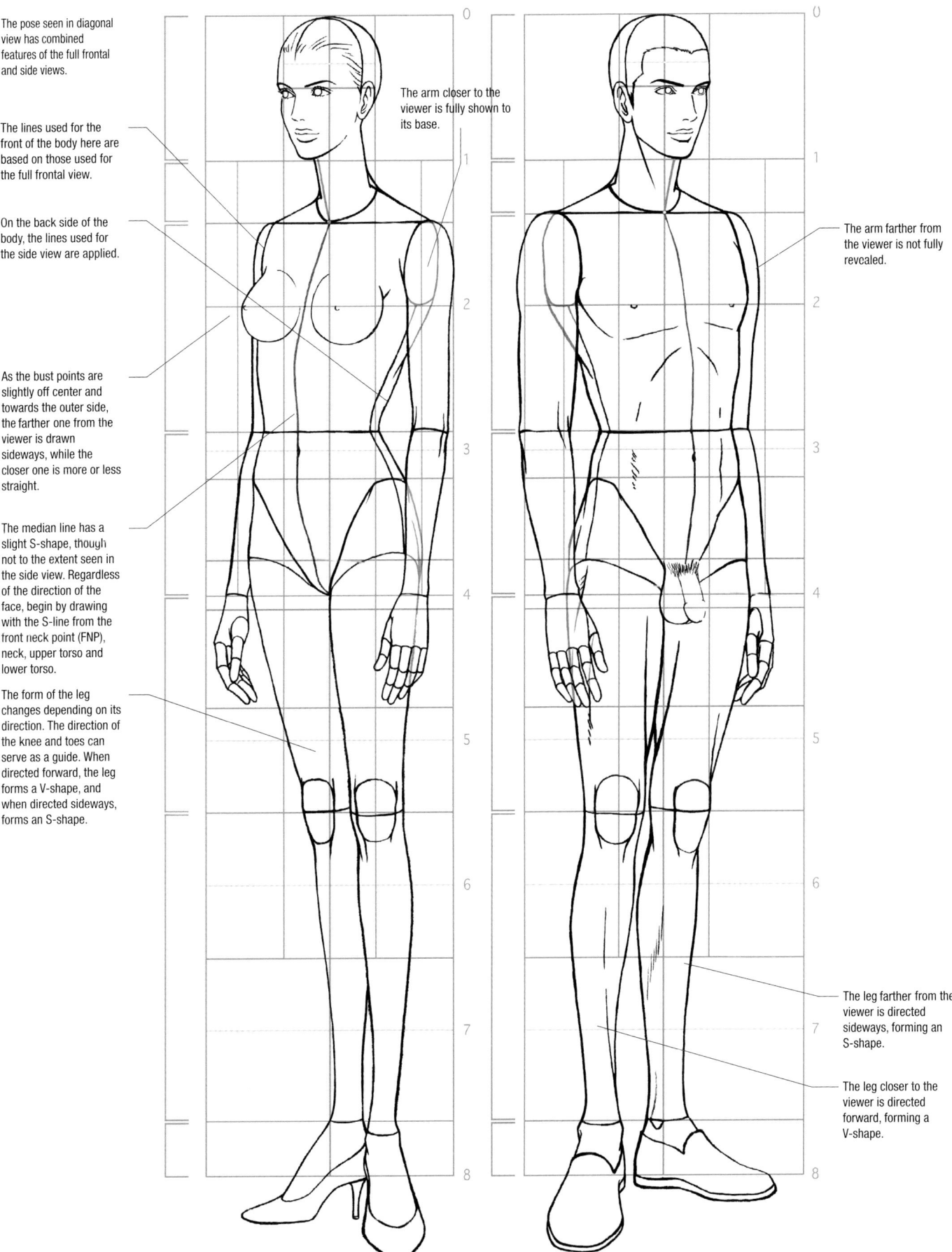

Chapter 1 : The Body

Erect Diagonal View

The pose seen in diagonal view has combined features of the full frontal and side views.

The lines used for the front of the body here are based on those used for the full frontal view.

On the back side of the body, the lines used for the side view are applied.

As the bust points are slightly off center and towards the outer side, the farther one from the viewer is drawn sideways, while the closer one is more or less straight.

The median line has a slight S-shape, though not to the extent seen in the side view. Regardless of the direction of the face, begin by drawing with the S-line from the front neck point (FNP), neck, upper torso and lower torso.

The form of the leg changes depending on its direction. The direction of the knee and toes can serve as a guide. When directed forward, the leg forms a V-shape, and when directed sideways, forms an S-shape.

The arm closer to the viewer is fully shown to its base.

The arm farther from the viewer is not fully revealed.

The leg farther from the viewer is directed sideways, forming an S-shape.

The leg closer to the viewer is directed forward, forming a V-shape.

17

Erect Back View

The contour of the back view is the same as that of the full frontal view.

The key is to carefully draw components which cannot be seen from the front, such as the back of the neck, shoulder blades, buttocks and heels.

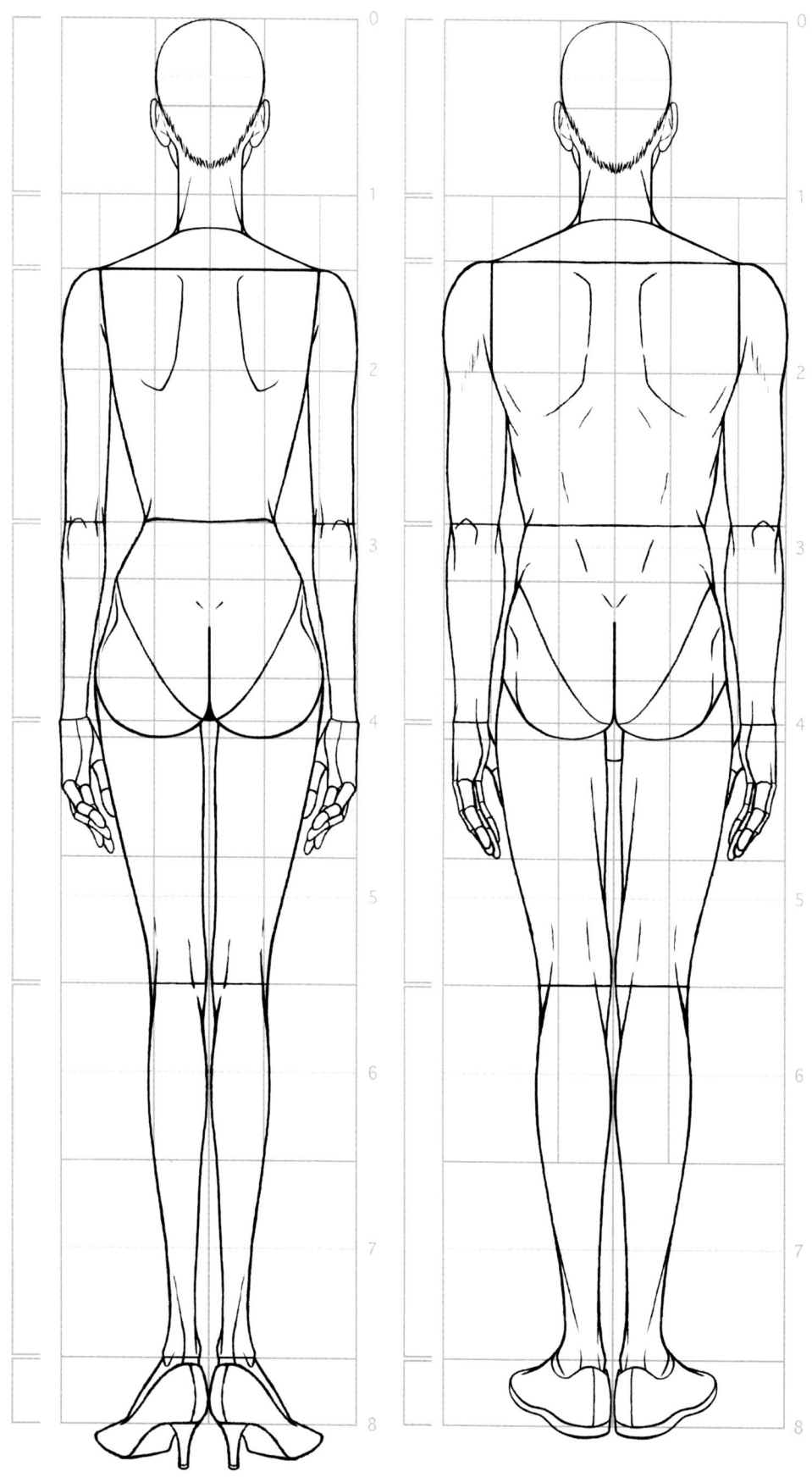

Chapter 1 : The Body

Erect Diagonal Back View

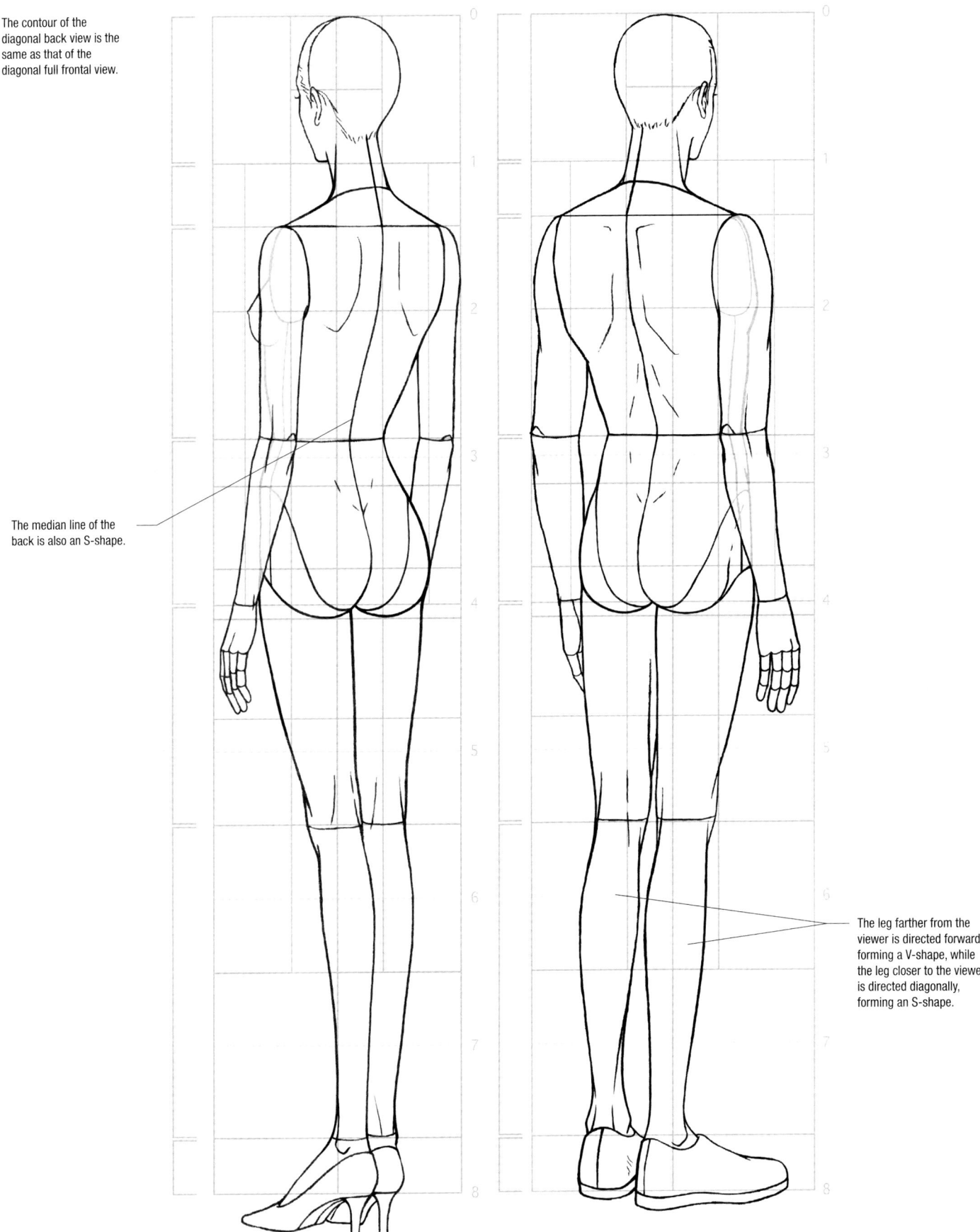

The contour of the diagonal back view is the same as that of the diagonal full frontal view.

The median line of the back is also an S-shape.

The leg farther from the viewer is directed forward, forming a V-shape, while the leg closer to the viewer is directed diagonally, forming an S-shape.

[Perspective]

In the case of the diagonal view, a sense of perspective will be given. Place the eye level at around the front neck point to obtain a good balance.

Vanishing point: It is better for design drawings not to have too much perspective, by establishing the vanishing point in the far distance. Make sure not to set the eye level too low or too high, as this will hinder correct rendition of the outline and configuration of the garment.

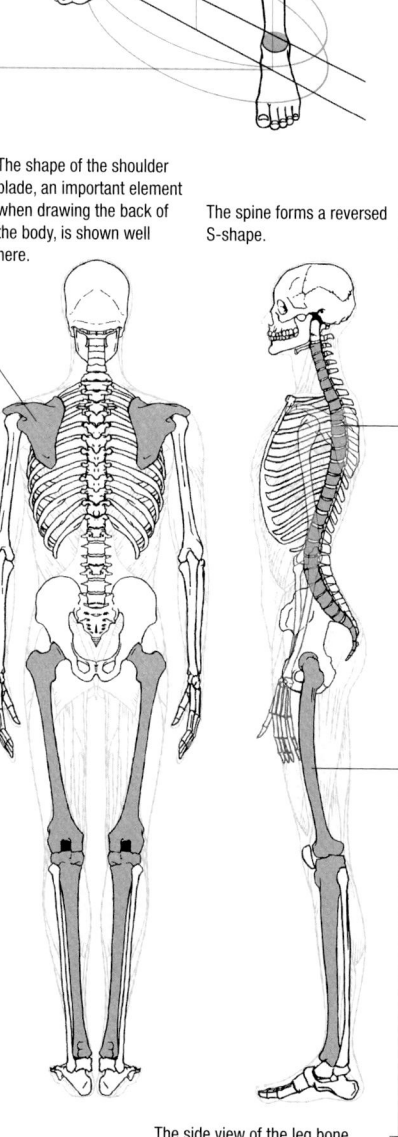

* Eye level

The feet opened apart sideways should be on the same perspective lines. The foot closer to the viewer, in this case the left foot should be drawn lower than the right.

Muscle

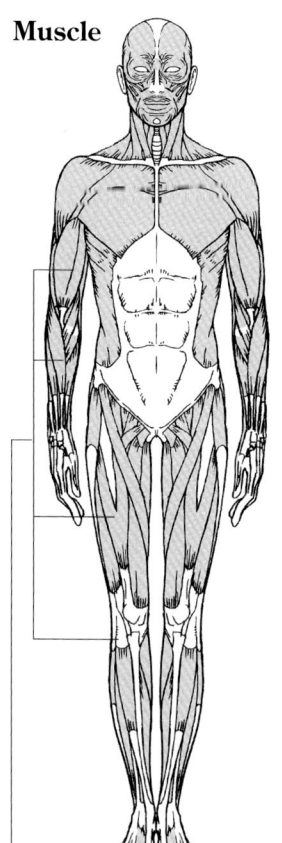

The bones of movable parts (arms and legs) are covered with multiple and complex muscles.

Bone Structure

Pay particular attention to the spine and structure of the leg bones.

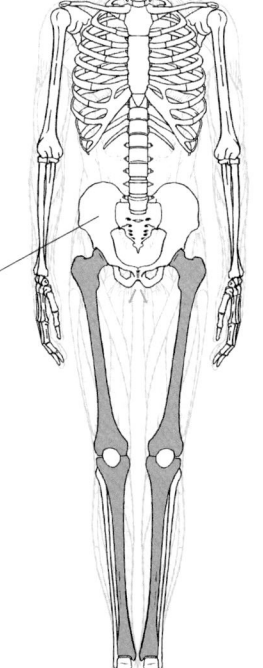

The pelvis shows the most remarkable difference between the male and female. The male pelvis is in the shape of a heart with the base of the pubis forming an acute angle, while the female pelvis is wider with the base of pubis forming a wide angle.

The shape of the shoulder blade, an important element when drawing the back of the body, is shown well here.

The spine forms a reversed S-shape.

It is clearly seen here that the full frontal view of the leg bones forms a V-shape.

The side view of the leg bone forms an S-shape, while the spine forms a reverse S-shape.

Chapter 1 : The Body

Frontal Pose with Weight on One Leg (Female)

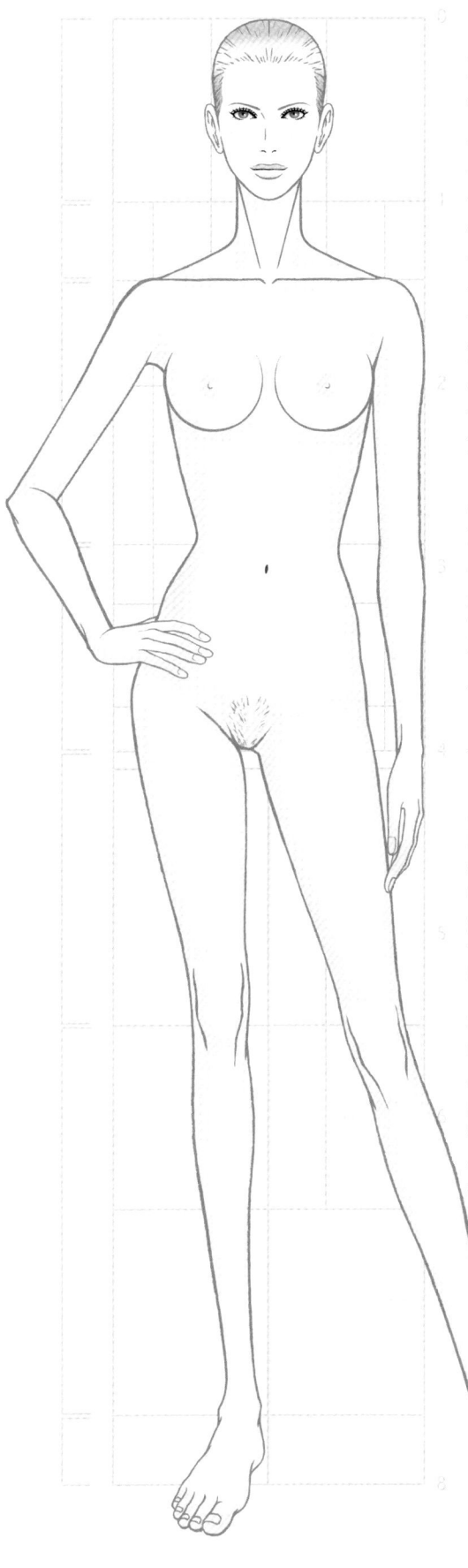

Frontal Pose with Weight on One Leg (Male)

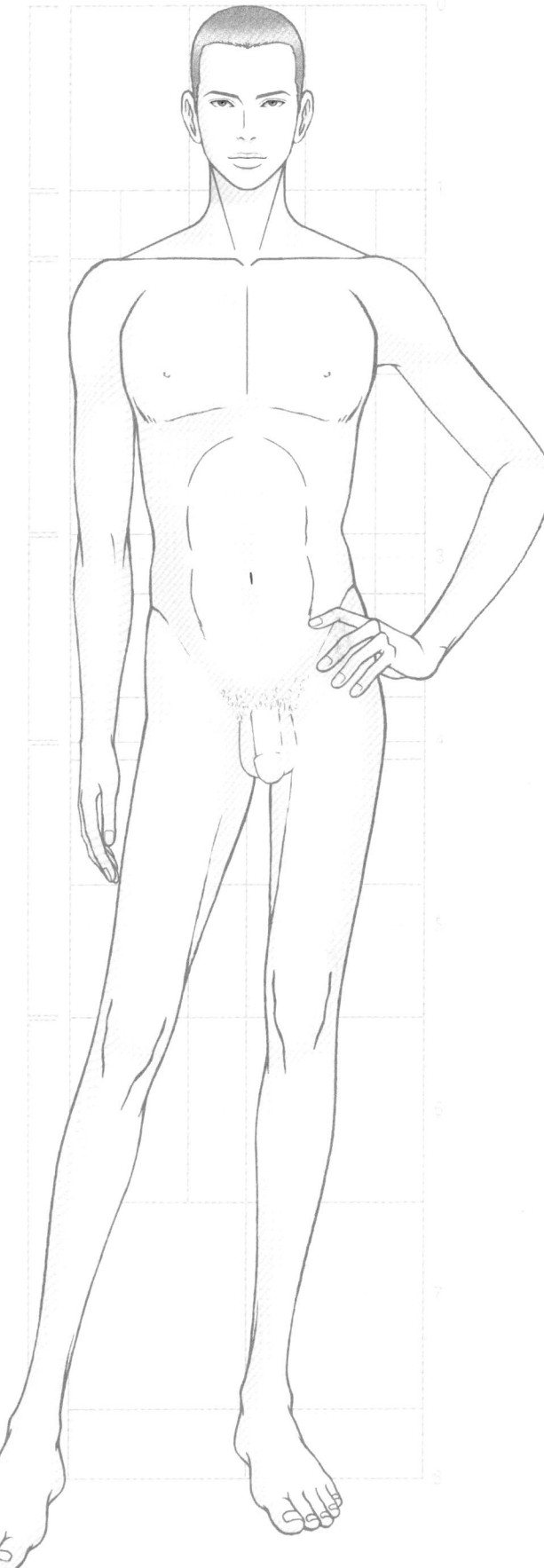

[2] Method of Creating Beautiful Poses

There are two types of erect pose; one with the weight positioned equally on both legs which is called the "erect pose" and the other with the weight positioned on one leg which is called the "pose with weight on one leg". A pose should be created by moving the head, hands and legs as necessary, based on the erect pose. A correct understanding and rendition of how the weight is supported in a standing position is the key for the creation of beautiful poses. The human bone structure consists of curved lines, creating a very rhythmical impression. Here, we learn the drawing process of the beautiful pose, mainly focusing on the lower body.

(1) Principles of the Pose with Weight on One Leg

1) When shifting from the erect pose to the pose with weight on one leg, only the lower body will be affected as the weight is shifted. The upper torso remains unchanged from the erect pose.

2) The leg supporting the weight is called the "pivotal leg (supporting leg)" and the leg without the weight is called the "bracing leg (idle leg)".

3) The hip of the pivotal leg is rotated and raised.

4) The ankle of the pivotal leg is near to the point where the central axis descends straight down from the front neck point.

5) The lines connecting both knees and ankles are parallel with the waistline.

Let's begin by following these principles.

Necessary materials:
- Ruler at least 35 cm in length
- B4-size sketchpad
- Pencil with B or softer lead
- Sketches of the erect pose (pages 14 and 15)

[Drawing Method]
Prepare a copy of an erect pose. Enlarge the drawings of the erect full frontal view on pages 14 and 15 by copy to size B4. Calculate the rate of enlargement so that the head length becomes 4 cm. (1.45 times = 145%)

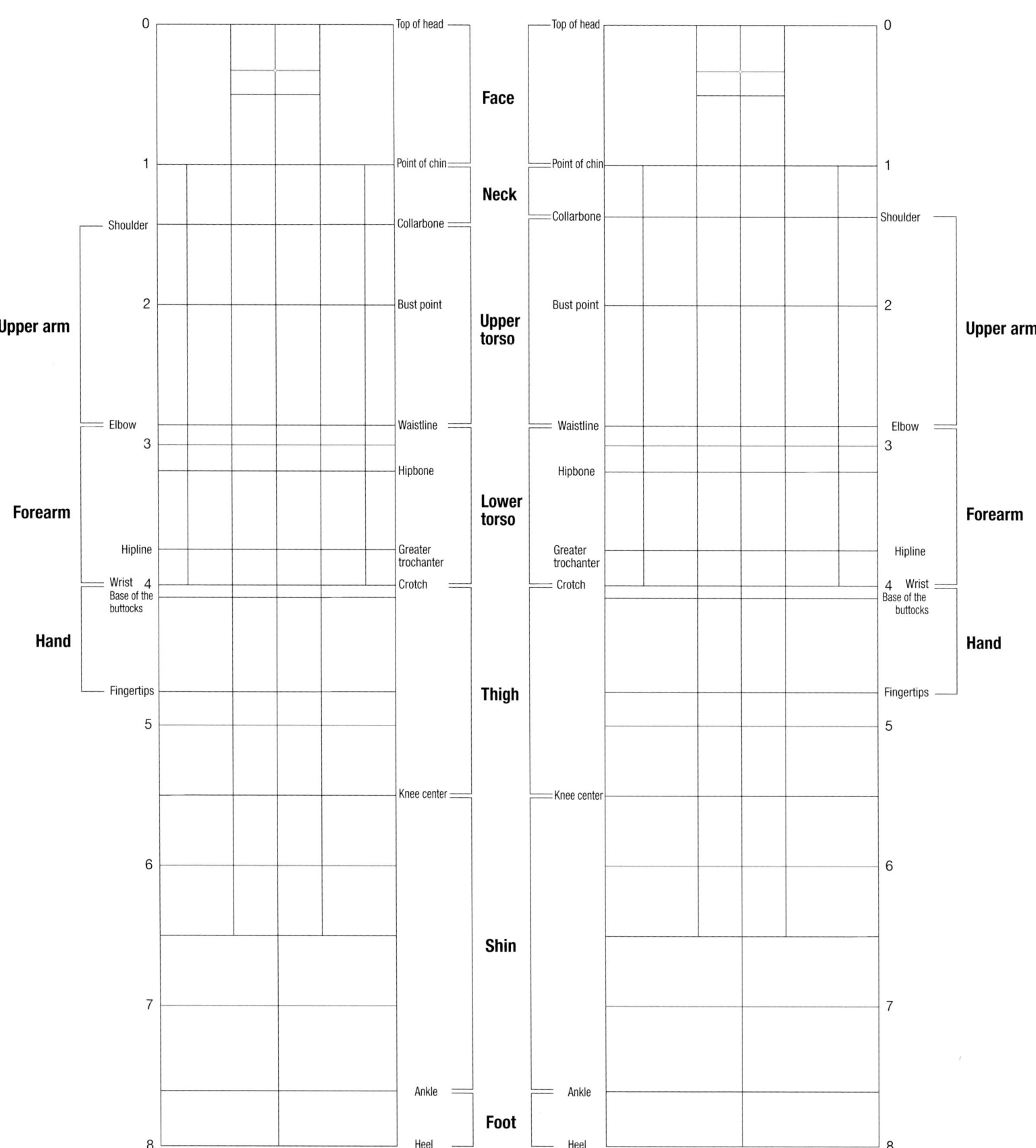

Chapter 1 : The Body

Place a thin sheet of paper (e.g. a page from the sketchpad or tracing paper) on top of the copy print for drawing.

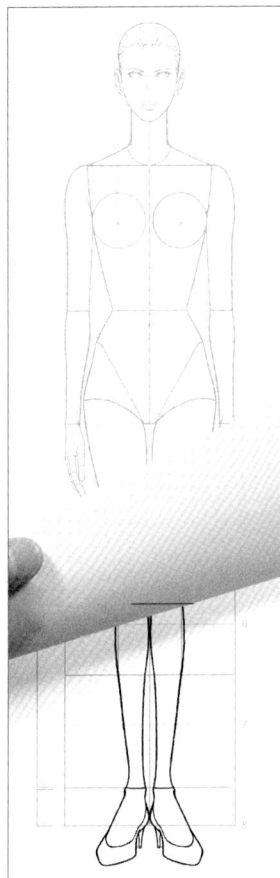

①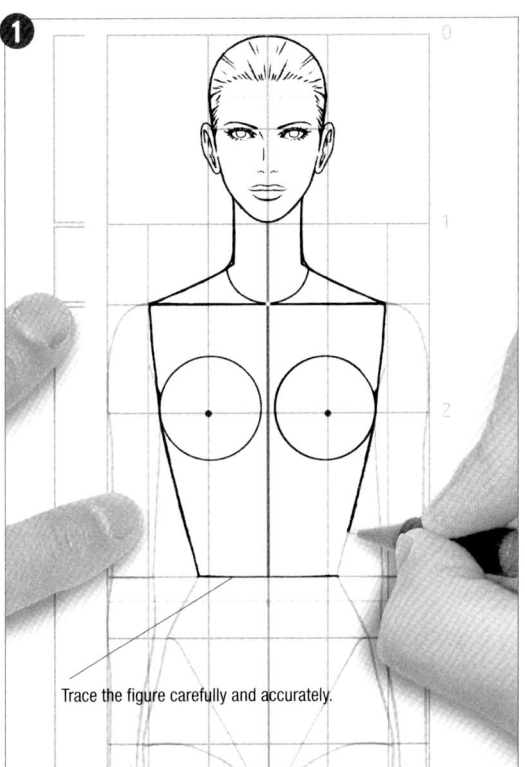

Trace the figure carefully and accurately.

As the upper part of the body remains unchanged, draw it as is once you have completed the proportion framework diagram.

②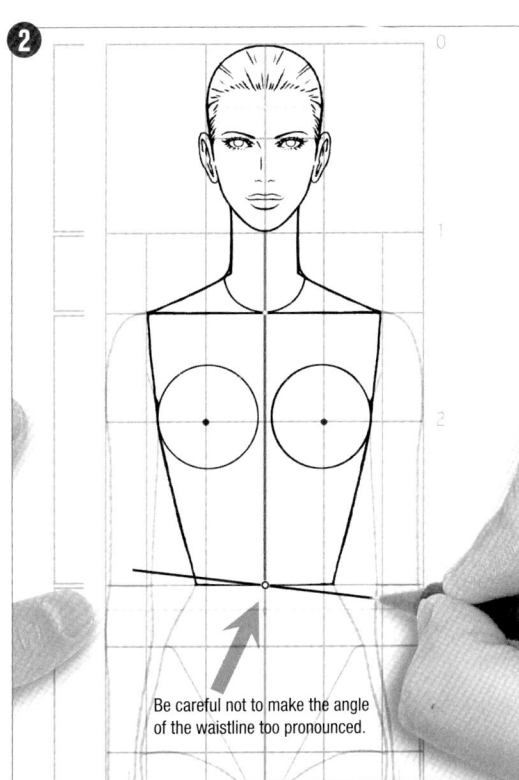

Be careful not to make the angle of the waistline too pronounced.

Since the hip on the pivotal leg side turns and rises, and the waistline inclines, draw the waistline at an angle centering the point where the waistline and the centerline intersect.

③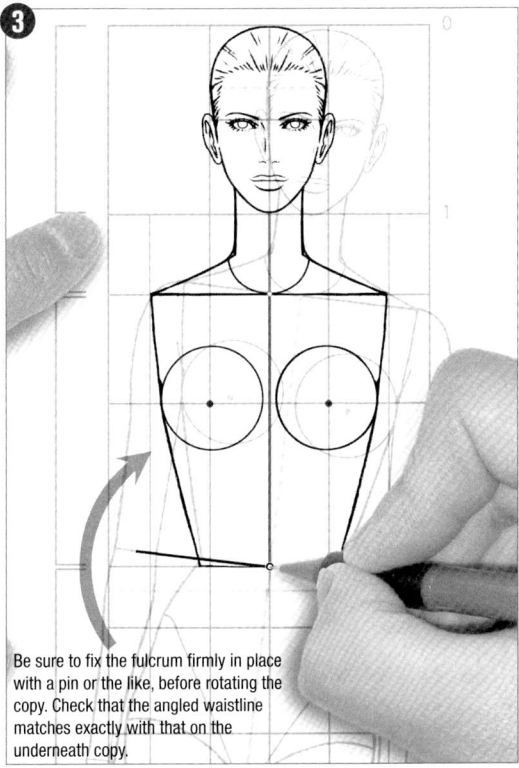

Be sure to fix the fulcrum firmly in place with a pin or the like, before rotating the copy. Check that the angled waistline matches exactly with that on the underneath copy.

Fix the point marked with a small circle as the fulcrum. Rotate the copy underneath and match up the waistlines.

④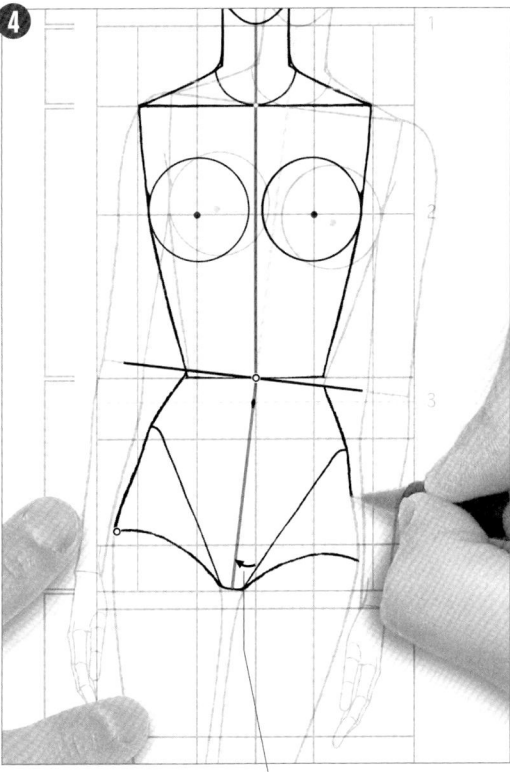

Trace the lower torso area.

If you trace it correctly, you will see that the groin has shifted to the pivotal leg side.

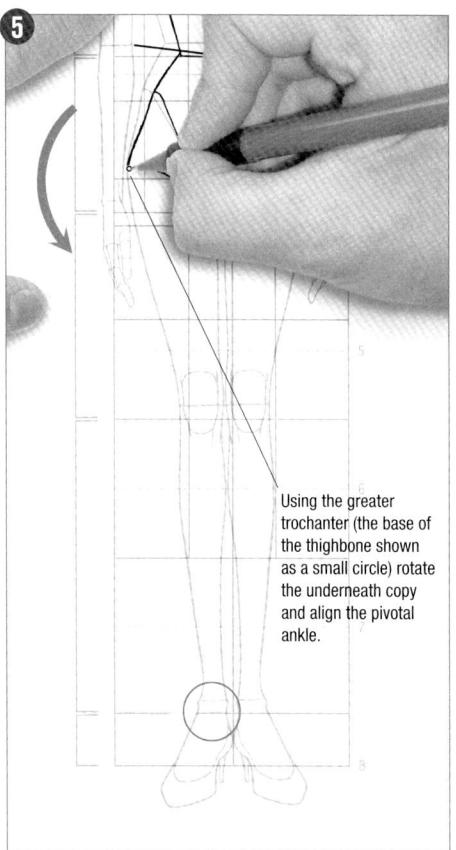

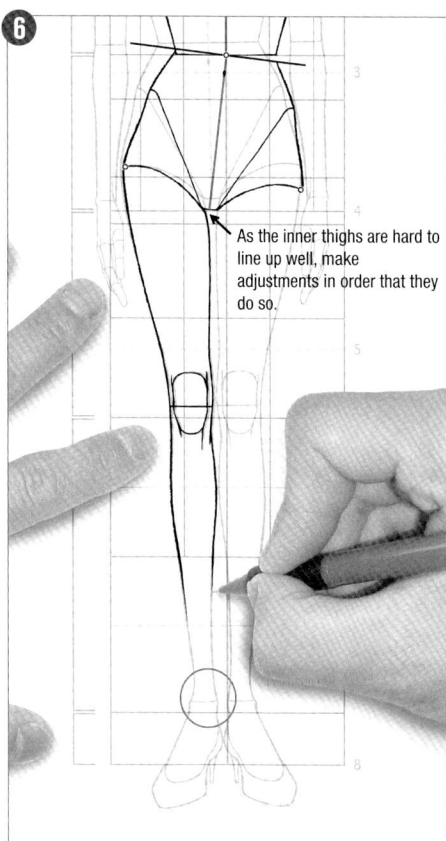

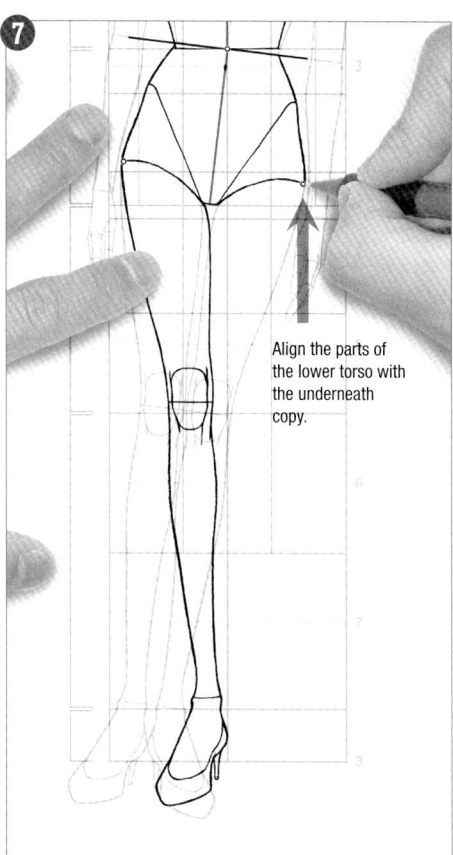

Position the ankle of the pivotal leg where the center of the gravity line descends straight down from the front neck point. Using the greater trochanter as the fulcrum, rotate the copy underneath until the pivotal ankle lines up, and trace it.

Draw the pivotal leg, while correcting minute differences. In this pose, the subject could almost stand on one leg, so draw it sharply and powerfully.

For the non-weight bearing leg (bracing leg), use the greater trochanter as the fulcrum to pivot from.

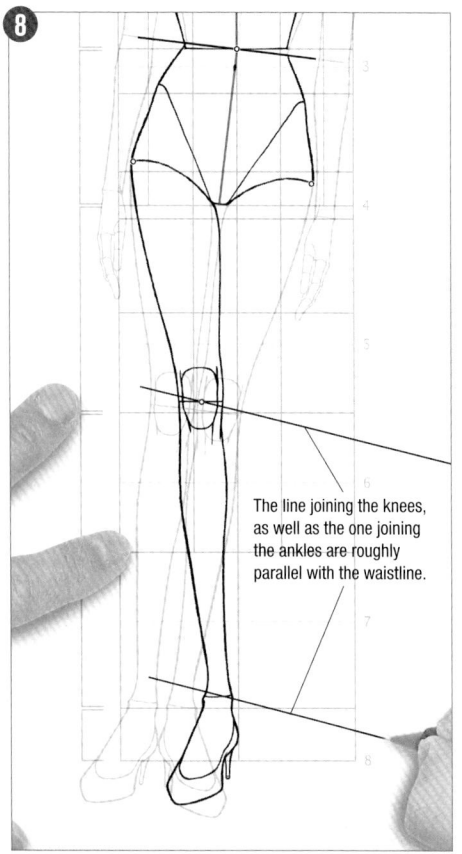

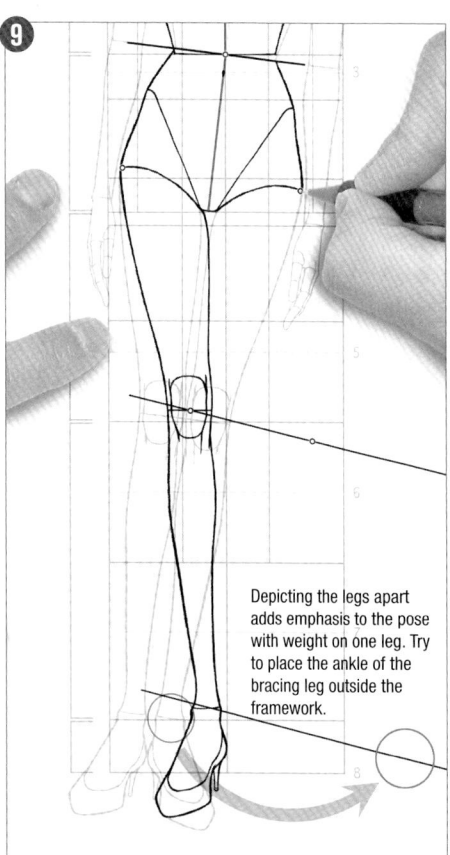

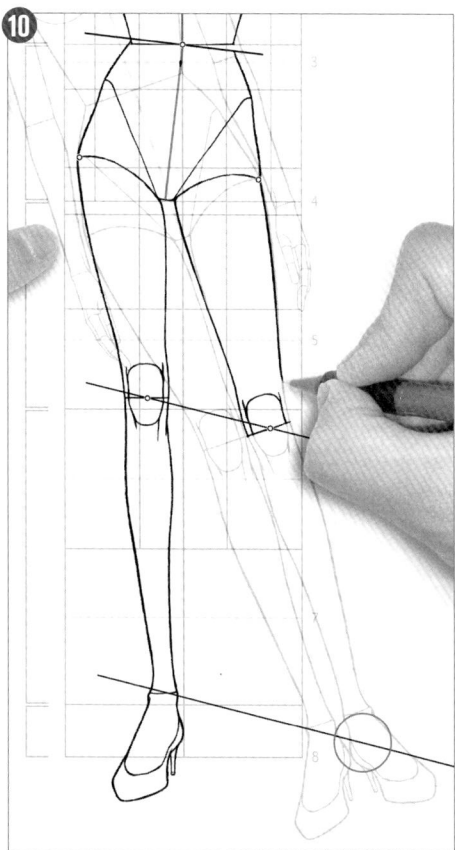

As the angle of the line joining the knees and the one joining the ankles are the same as that of the waistline, draw a slanting line with the pivotal ankle as the starting point.

Set the position of the ankle of the bracing leg on the slanting line extending from the ankle of the pivotal leg.

With the greater trochanter of the bracing leg as a fulcrum, rotate the underneath copy and align the ankle of the bracing leg.

Chapter 1 : The Body

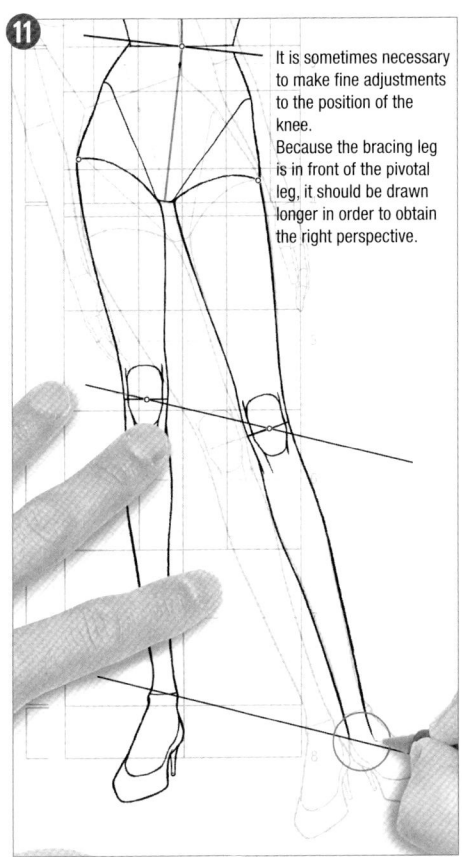

⑪ It is sometimes necessary to make fine adjustments to the position of the knee.
Because the bracing leg is in front of the pivotal leg, it should be drawn longer in order to obtain the right perspective.

Draw the bracing leg while making fine adjustments so that the ankle is in the same position.

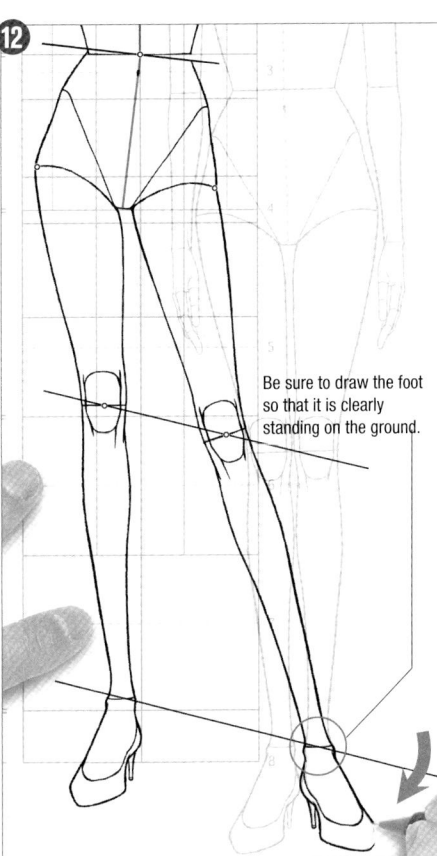

⑫ Be sure to draw the foot so that it is clearly standing on the ground.

Draw the feet.

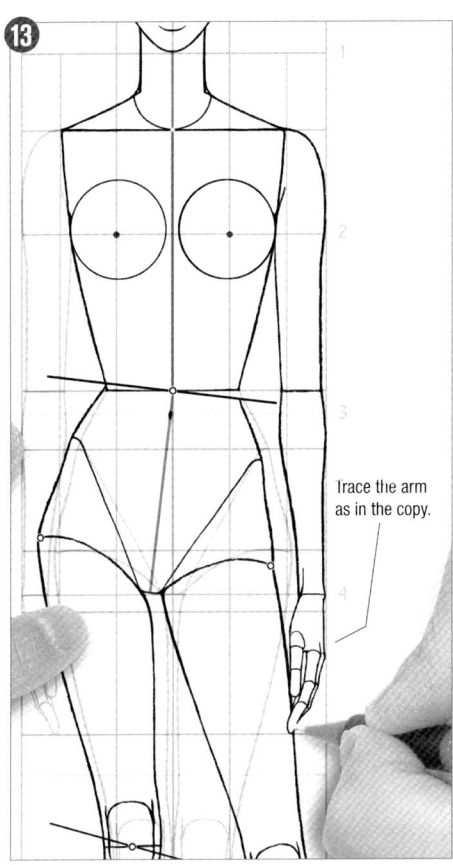

⑬ Trace the arm as in the copy.

Make the left arm hang straight down.

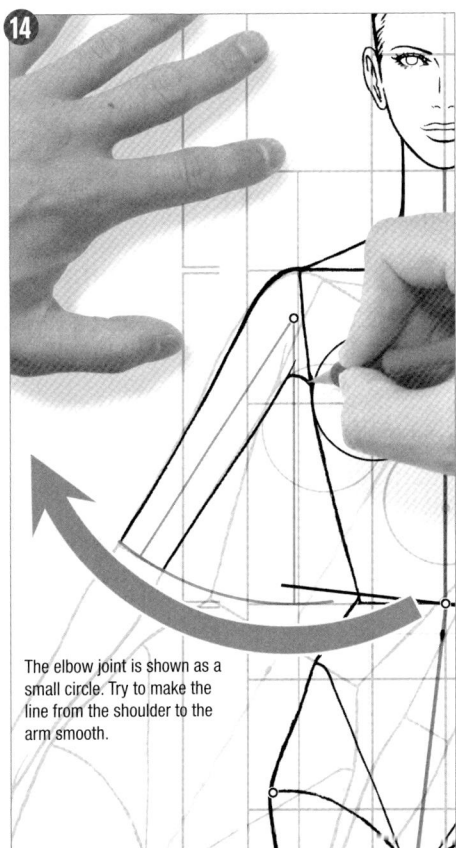

⑭ The elbow joint is shown as a small circle. Try to make the line from the shoulder to the arm smooth.

Try drawing the right arm with the hand on the hip. First rotate the upper arm using the shoulder joint (shown as a small circle) as the starting point, and trace the underneath copy.

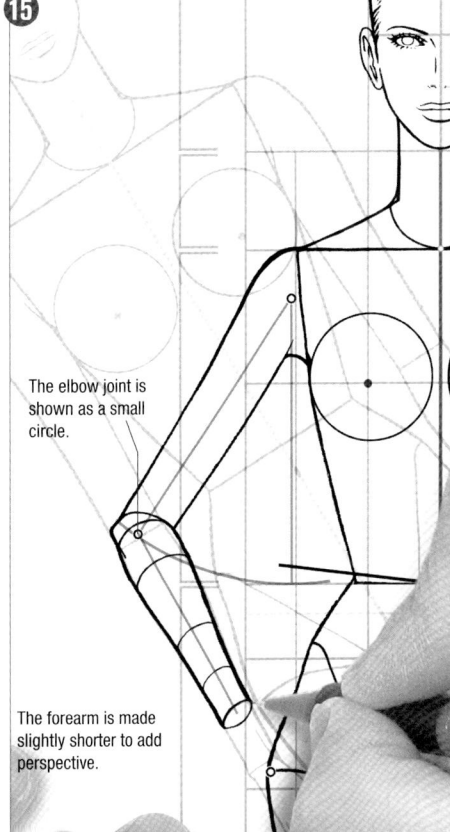

⑮ The elbow joint is shown as a small circle.

The forearm is made slightly shorter to add perspective.

Using the elbow joint as the fulcrum, rotate the forearm and trace the underneath copy.

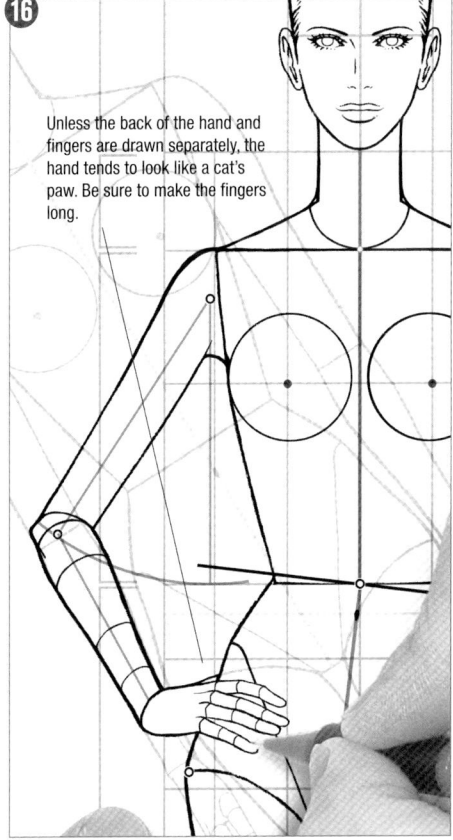

⑯ Unless the back of the hand and fingers are drawn separately, the hand tends to look like a cat's paw. Be sure to make the fingers long.

Draw the hand.

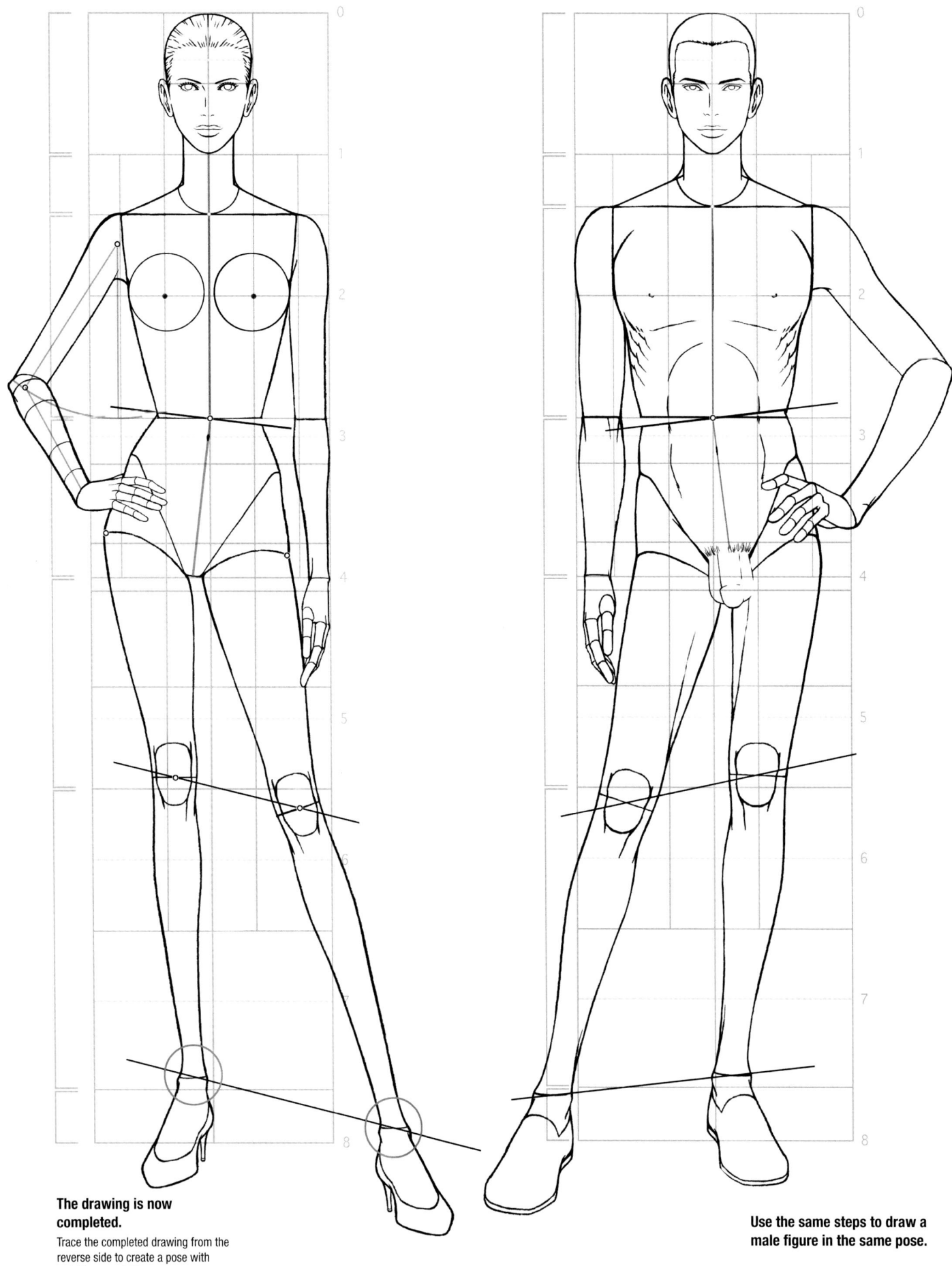

The drawing is now completed.

Trace the completed drawing from the reverse side to create a pose with weight on one left leg.

Use the same steps to draw a male figure in the same pose.

Chapter 1 : The Body

Basic parts for the full frontal pose with weight on one leg

Since the face, hands and the bracing leg are not supporting the body, various poses can be created by moving them as preferred. Copy the bodies on the right, and try producing their variations.

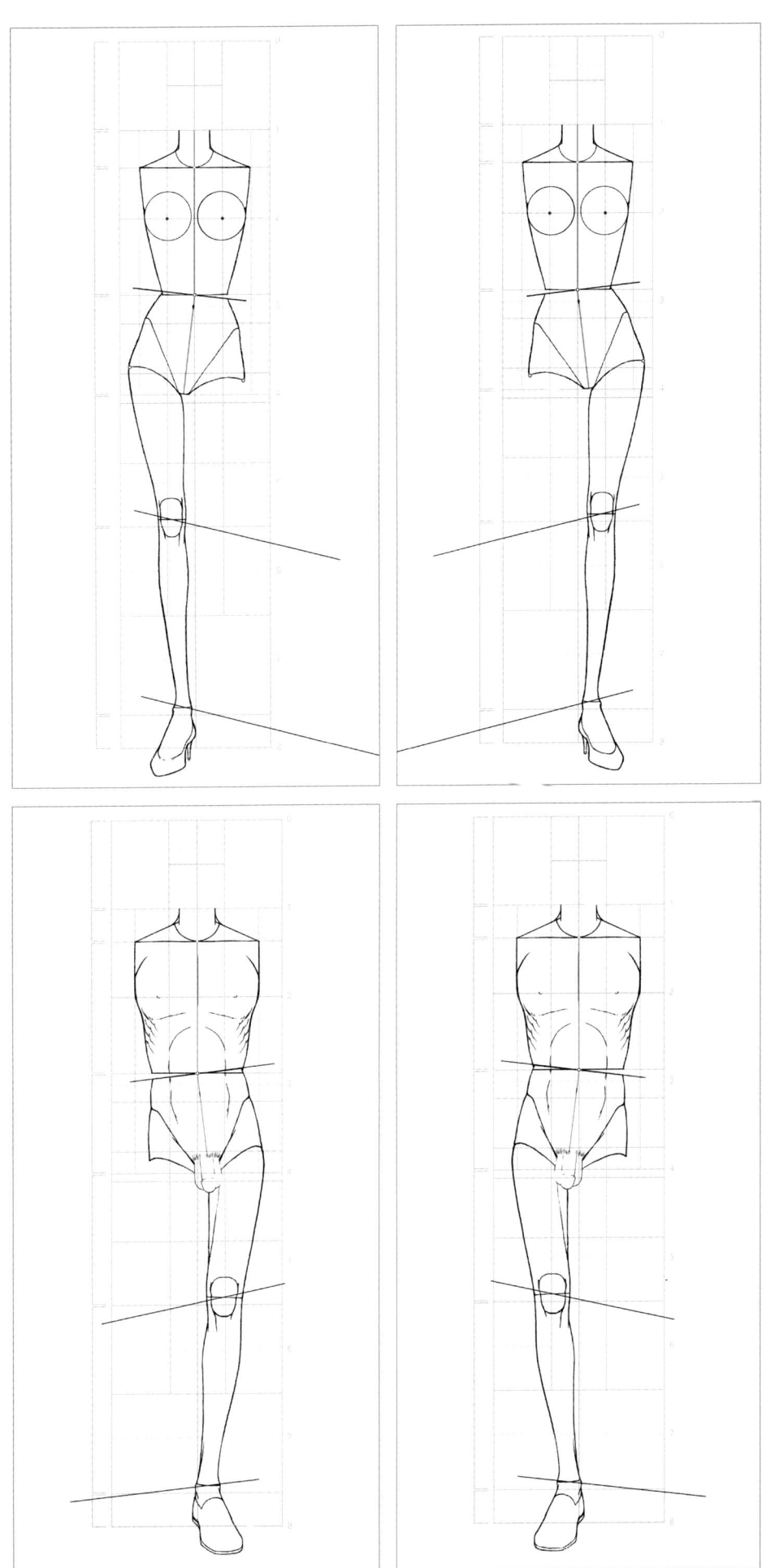

The bracing leg can be moved as long as it stays on the slanting line. Try moving it.

(2) Frontal Pose with Weight on One Leg — Variations

With respect to how to move the head and hands, please refer to detailed information given on pages 41 and 42.

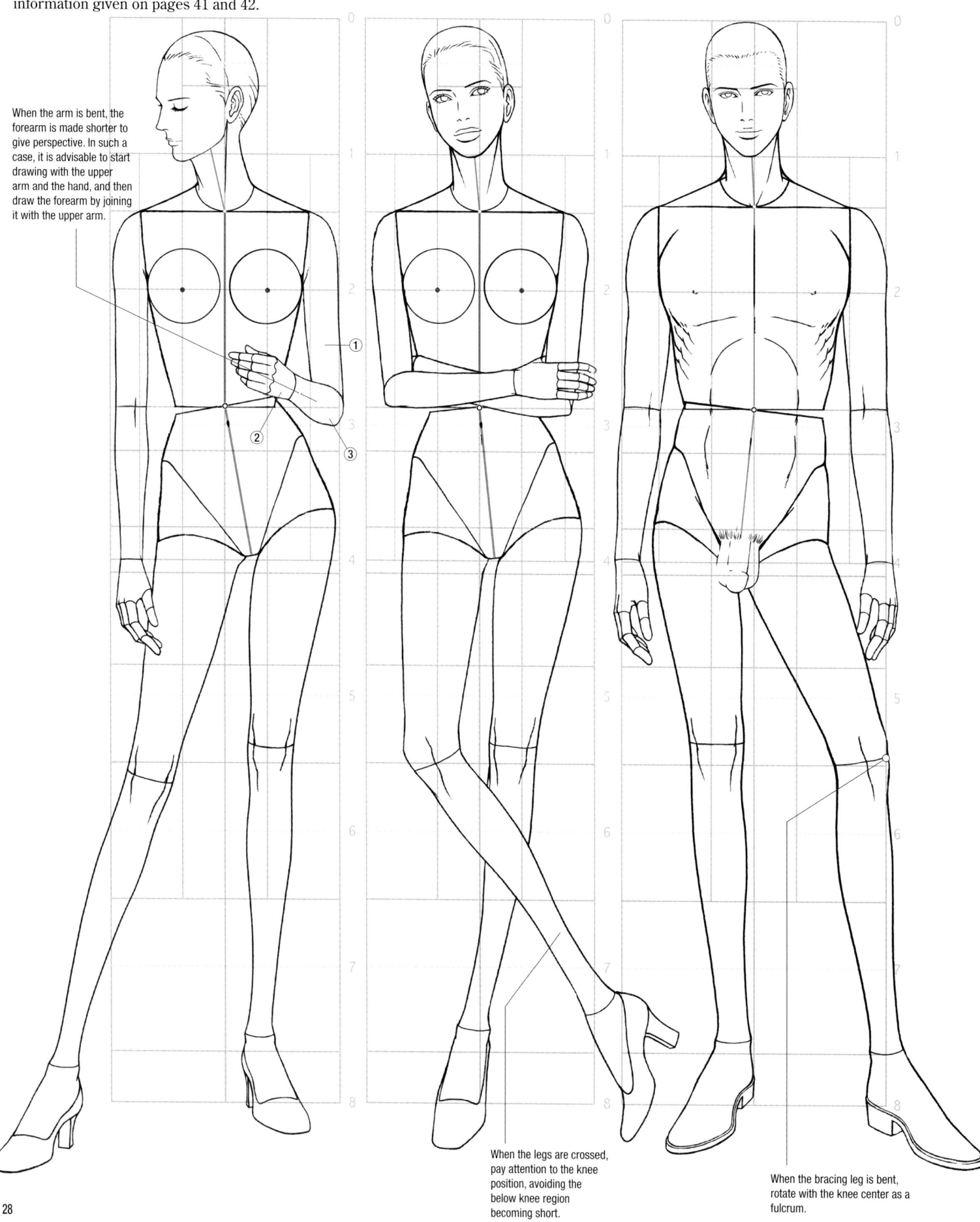

When the arm is bent, the forearm is made shorter to give perspective. In such a case, it is advisable to start drawing with the upper arm and the hand, and then draw the forearm by joining it with the upper arm.

When the legs are crossed, pay attention to the knee position, avoiding the below knee region becoming short.

When the bracing leg is bent, rotate with the knee center as a fulcrum.

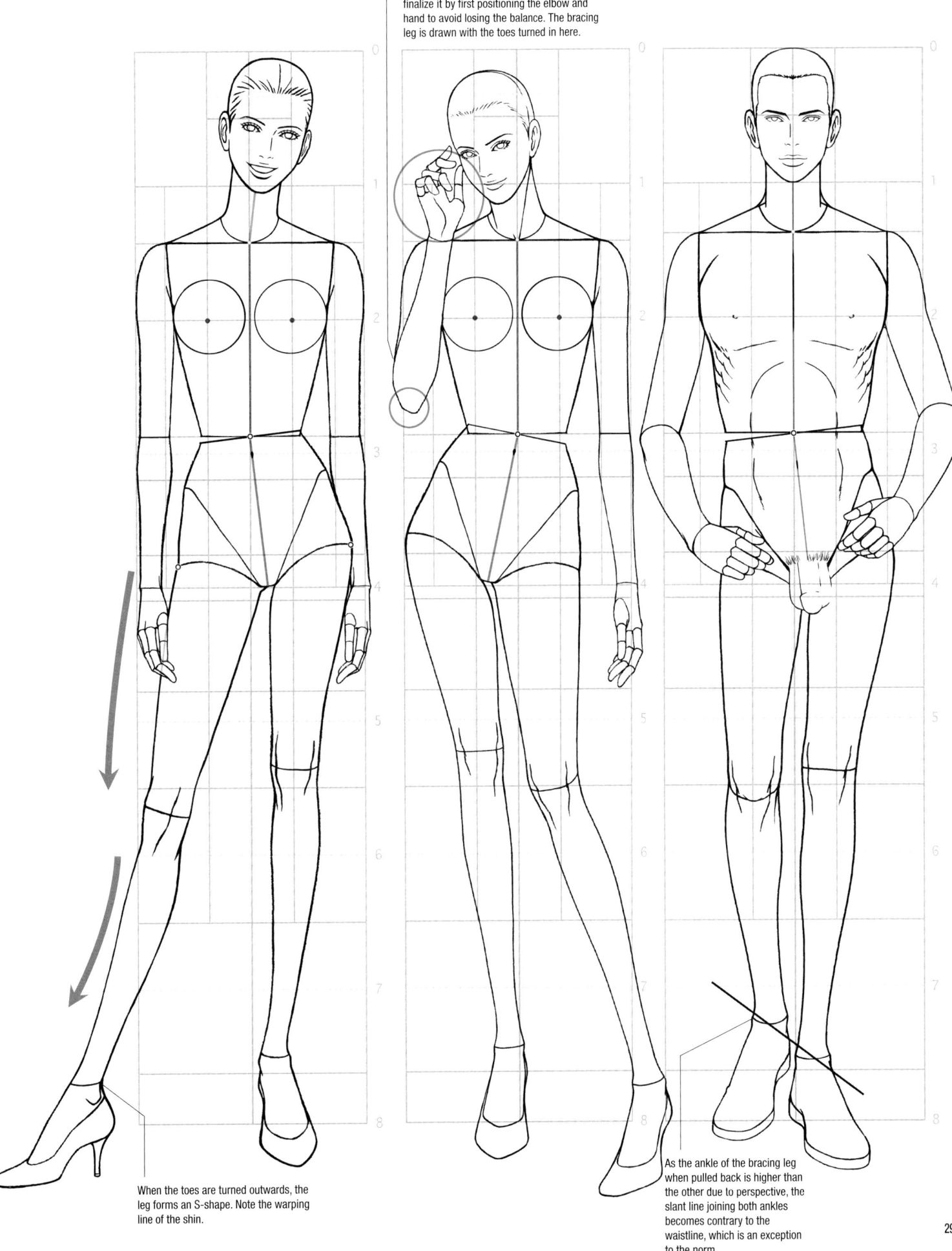

(3) Diagonal Pose with Weight on One Leg

We draw this pose using the erect diagonal pose. The procedure is exactly the same as that for the erect full frontal pose, except that there are two examples of diagonal pose with weight on one leg; the pivotal leg behind and in front.

Diagonal Pose with Weight on One Leg (Pivotal Leg Behind)

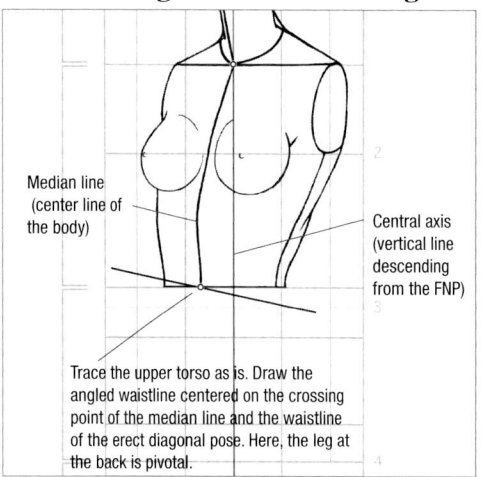

Median line (center line of the body)

Central axis (vertical line descending from the FNP)

Trace the upper torso as is. Draw the angled waistline centered on the crossing point of the median line and the waistline of the erect diagonal pose. Here, the leg at the back is pivotal.

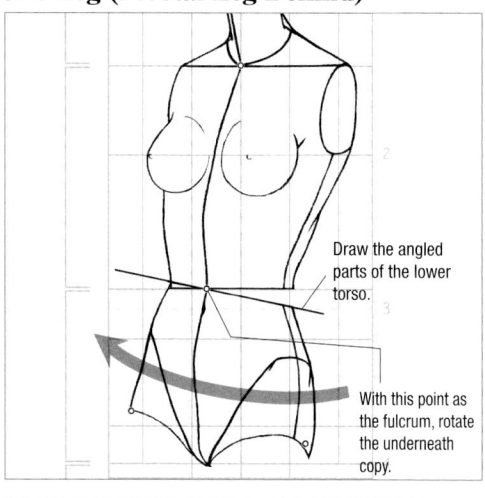

Draw the angled parts of the lower torso.

With this point as the fulcrum, rotate the underneath copy.

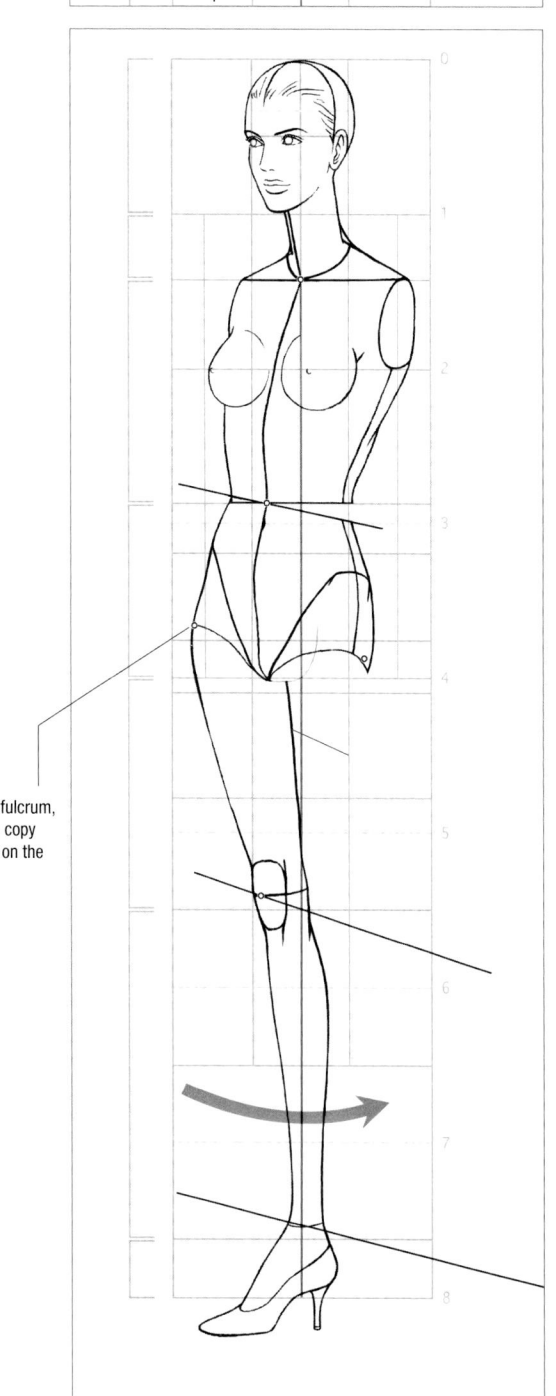

With this point as the fulcrum, rotate the underneath copy until the pivotal leg is on the central axis.

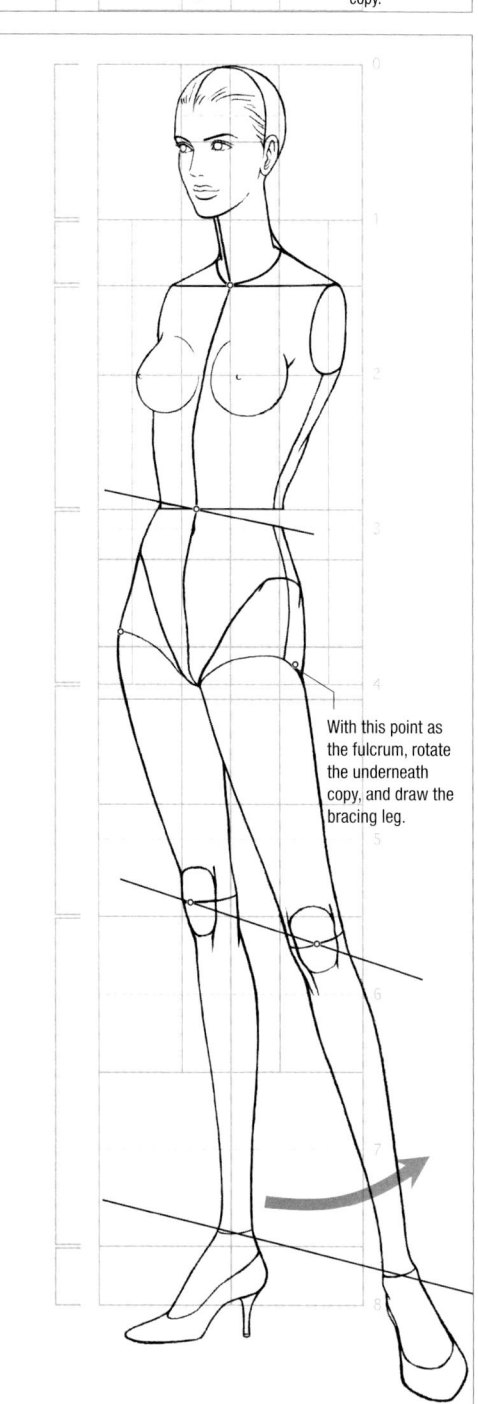

With this point as the fulcrum, rotate the underneath copy, and draw the bracing leg.

Chapter 1 : The Body

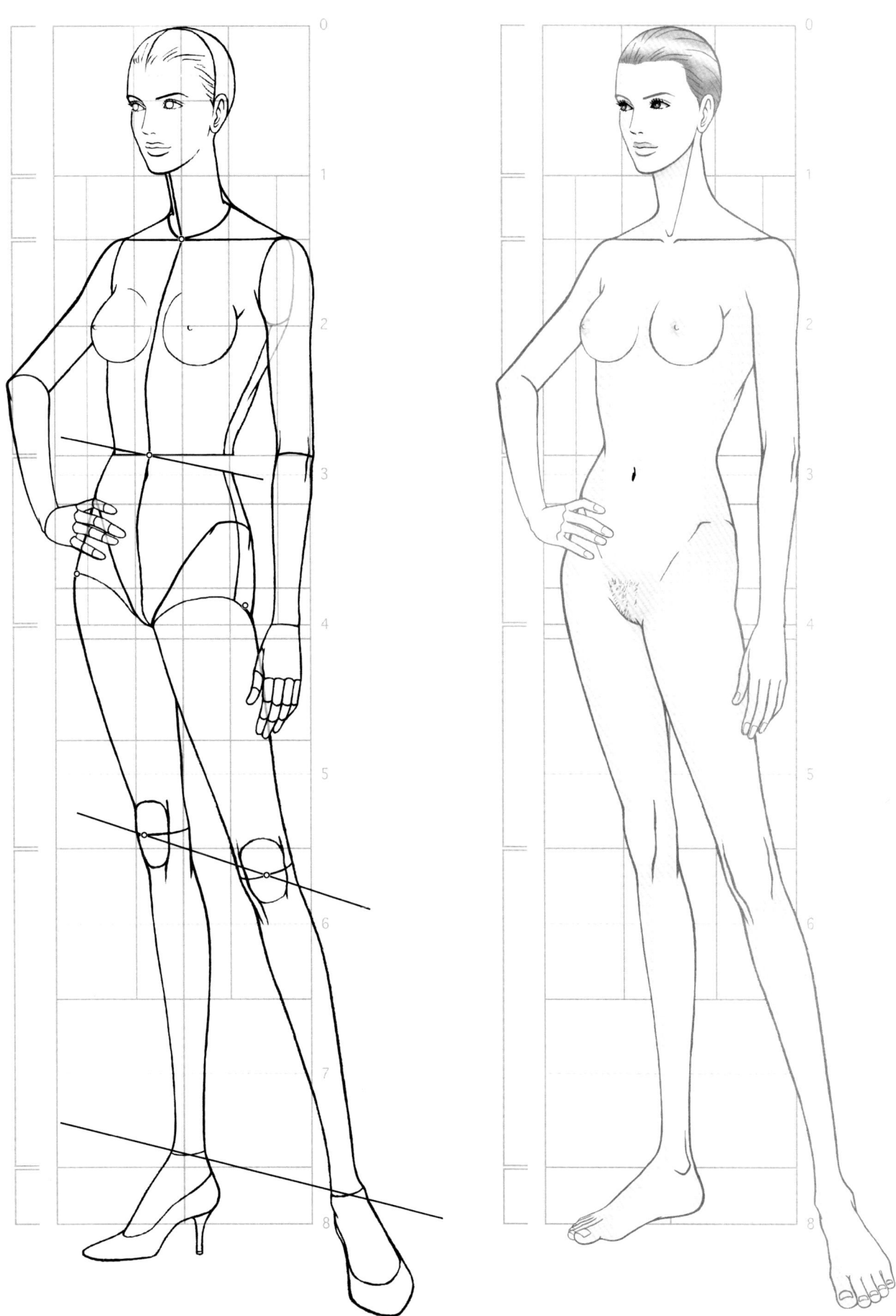

Draw the arms and hands to complete the pose.

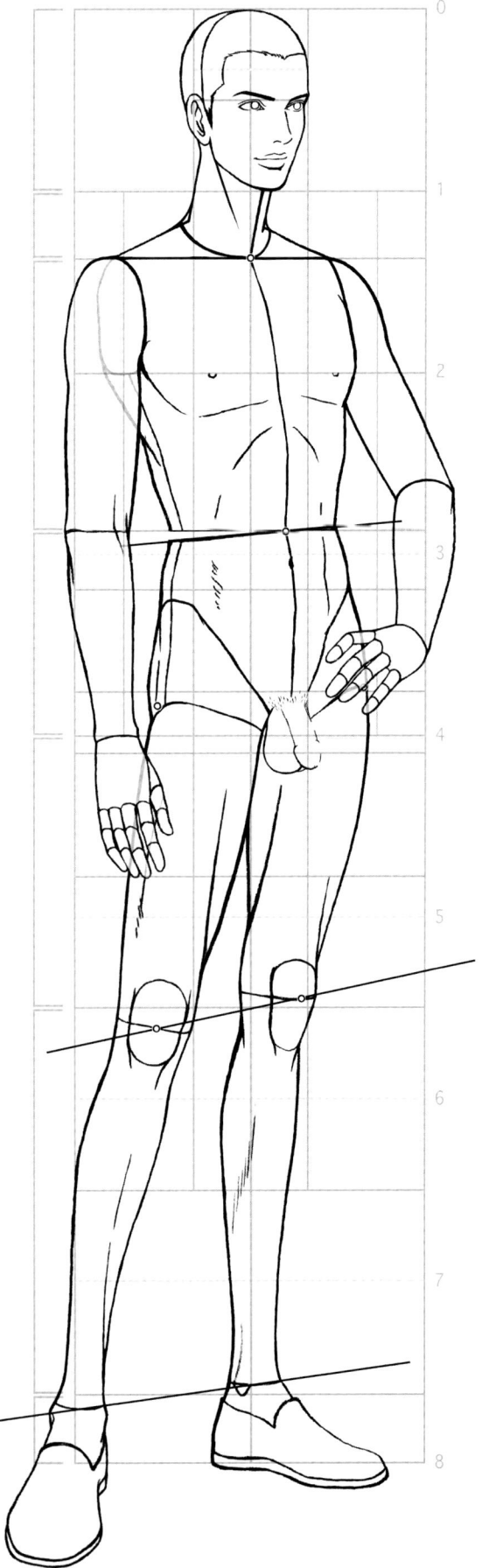
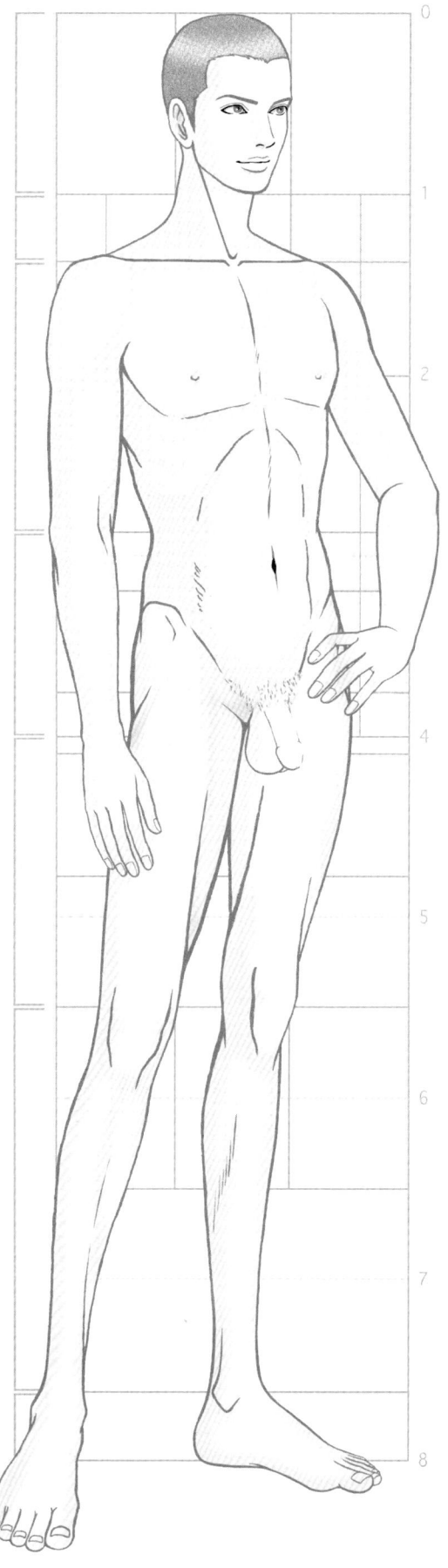

The same method can be applied to the male pose.

Chapter 1 : The Body

Diagonal Pose with Weight on One Leg (Pivotal Leg in Front)

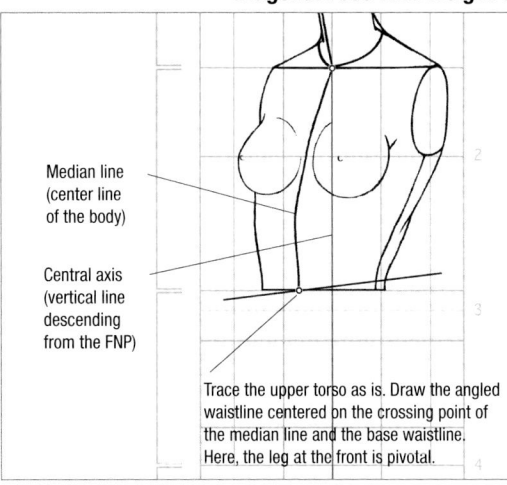

Median line (center line of the body)

Central axis (vertical line descending from the FNP)

Trace the upper torso as is. Draw the angled waistline centered on the crossing point of the median line and the base waistline. Here, the leg at the front is pivotal.

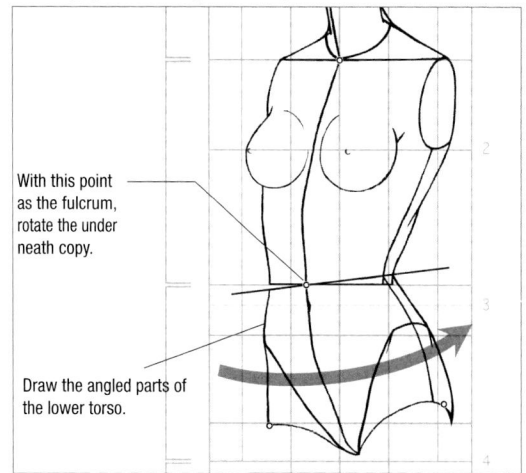

With this point as the fulcrum, rotate the under neath copy.

Draw the angled parts of the lower torso.

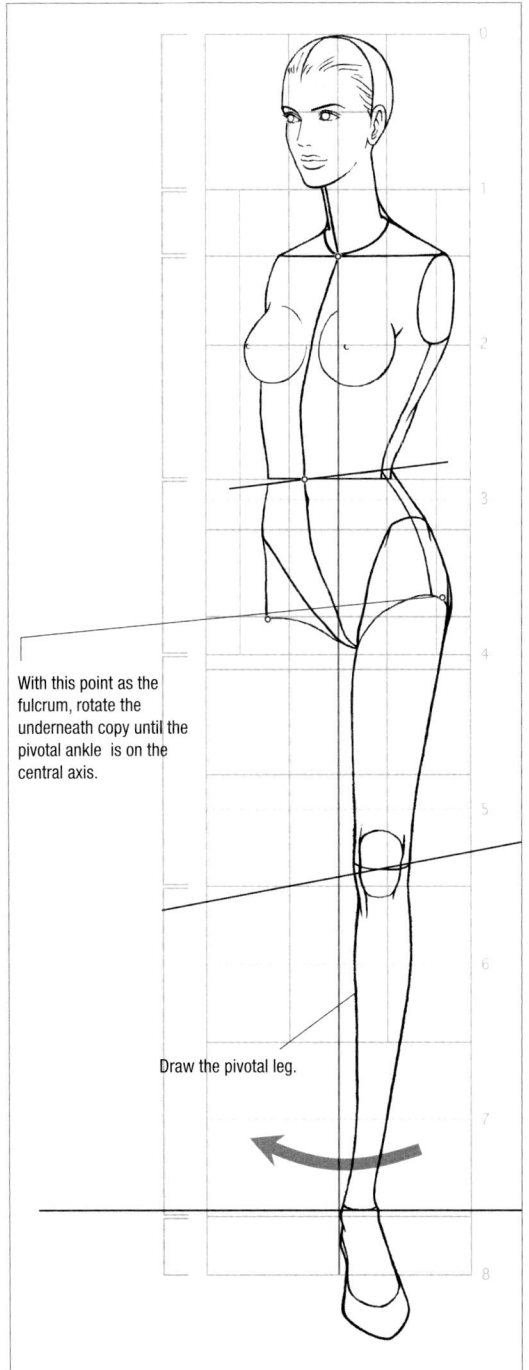

With this point as the fulcrum, rotate the underneath copy until the pivotal ankle is on the central axis.

Draw the pivotal leg.

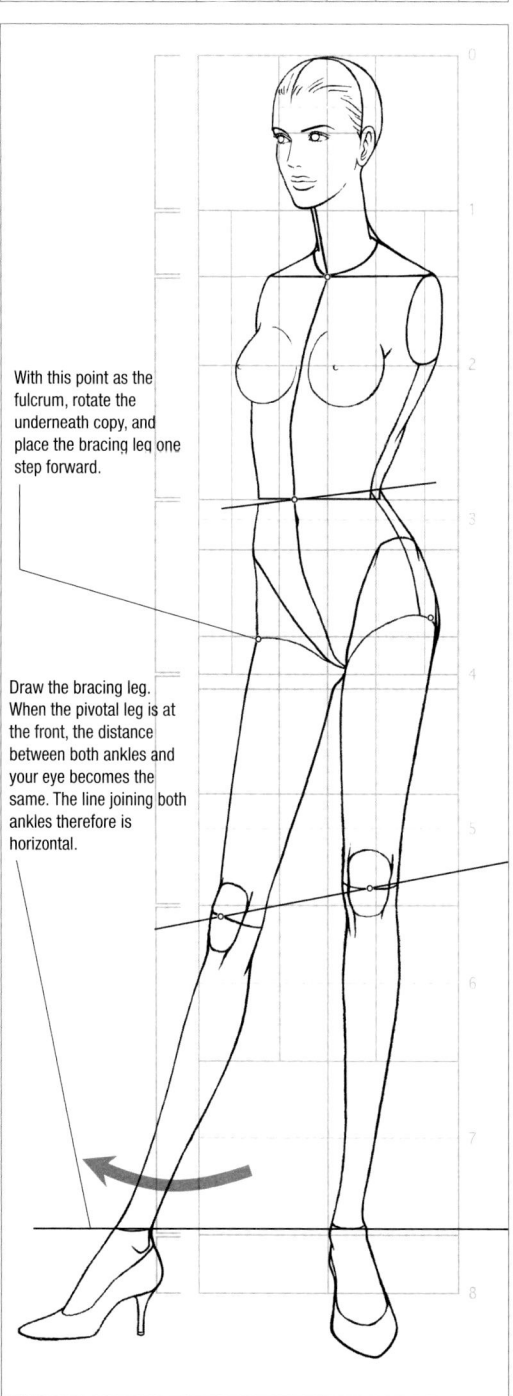

With this point as the fulcrum, rotate the underneath copy, and place the bracing leg one step forward.

Draw the bracing leg. When the pivotal leg is at the front, the distance between both ankles and your eye becomes the same. The line joining both ankles therefore is horizontal.

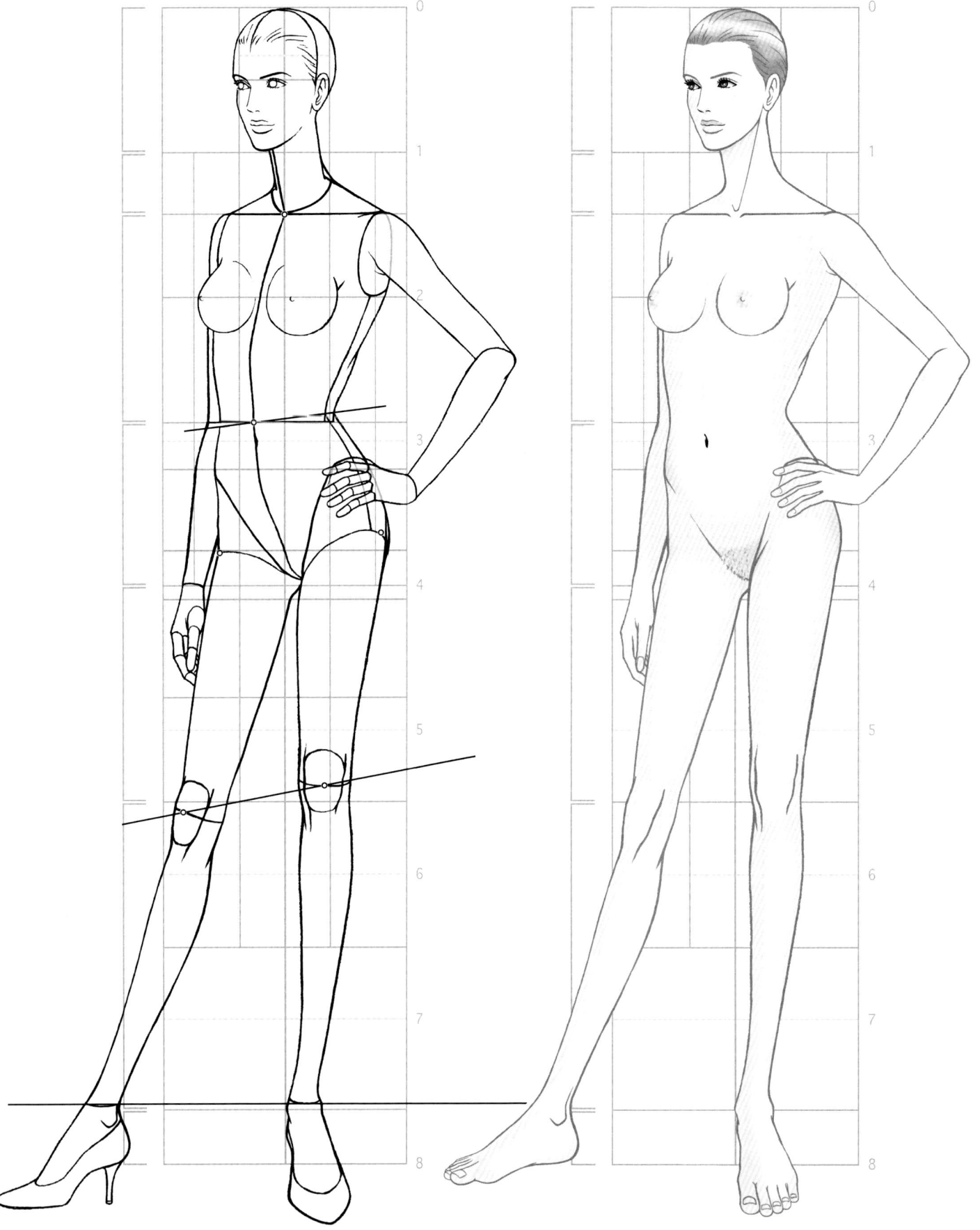

Draw the arms and hands to complete the pose.

Chapter 1 : The Body

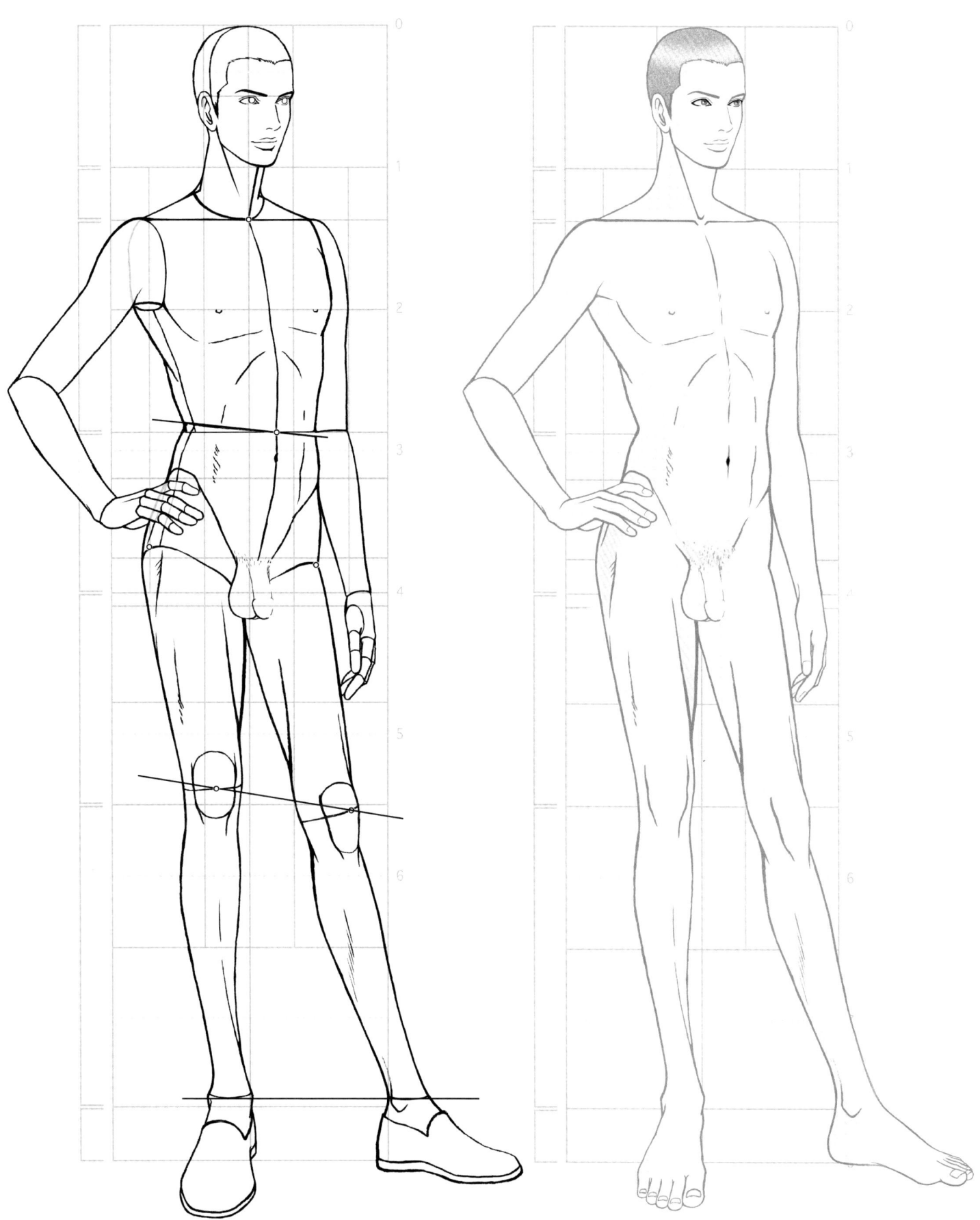

The same method can be applied to the male pose.

35

Basic parts for the diagonal pose with weight on one leg
Create variations of this pose, by adding movements to the face, hands and bracing leg.

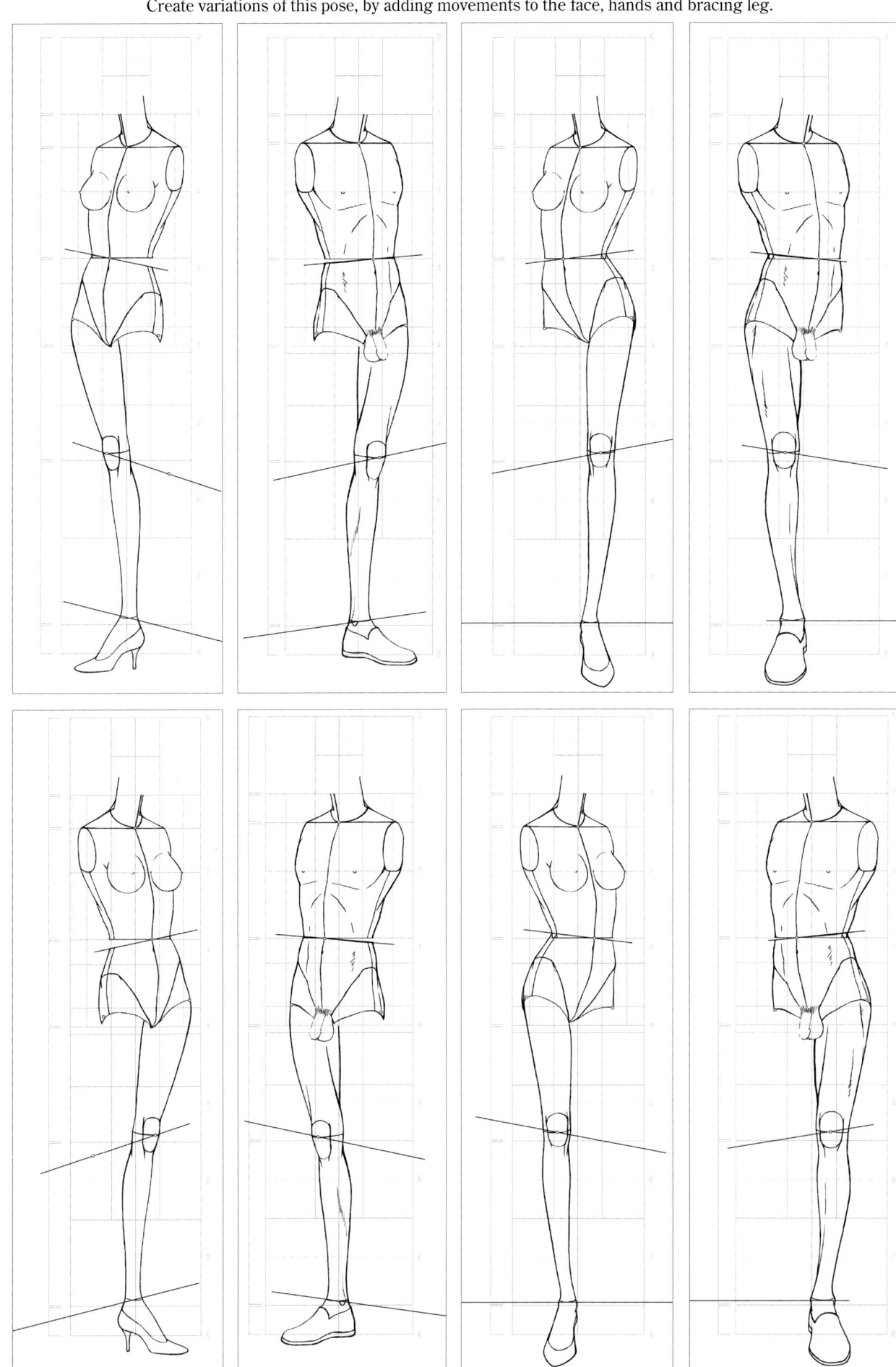

Chapter 1 : The Body

(4) Diagonal Pose with Weight on One Leg — Variations

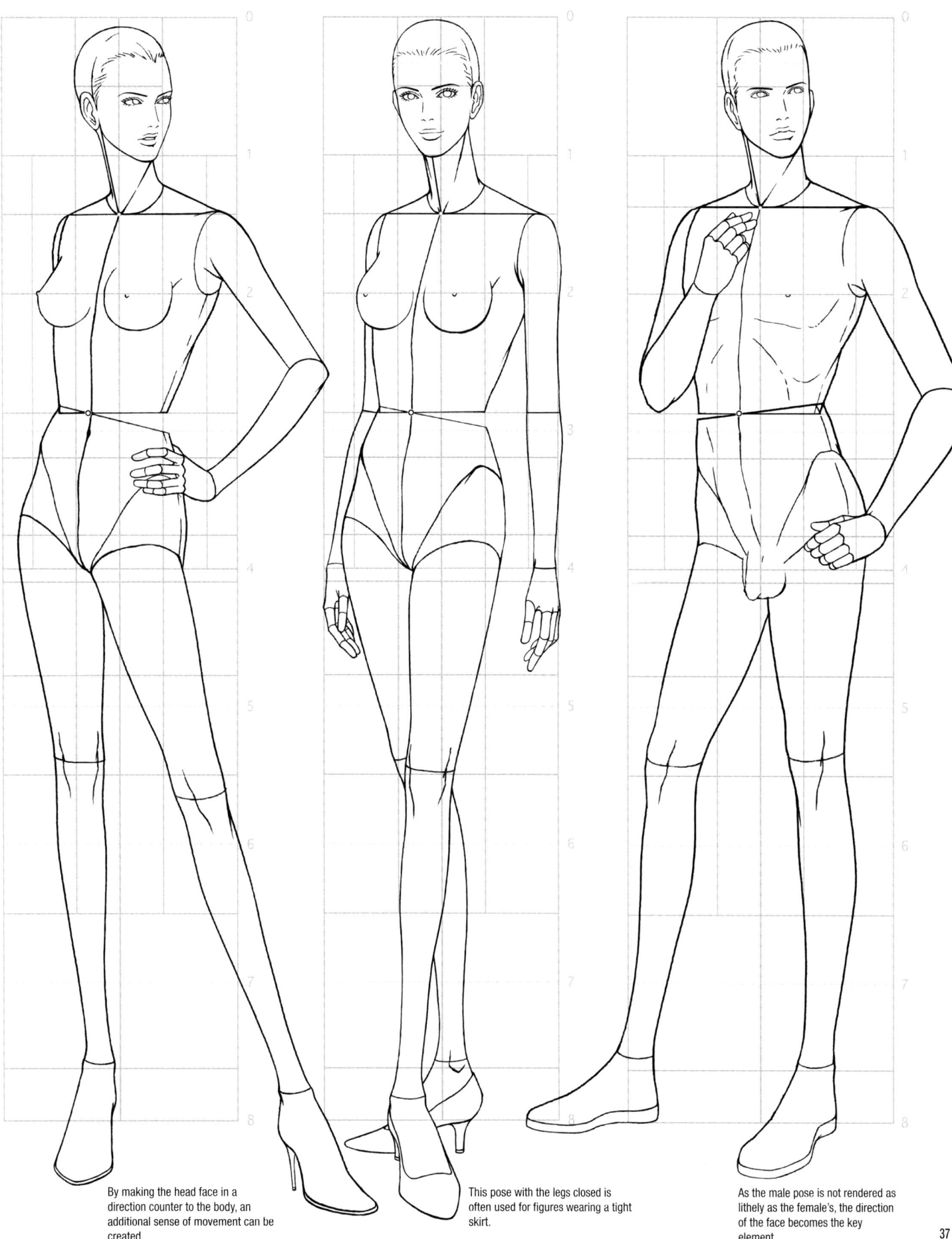

By making the head face in a direction counter to the body, an additional sense of movement can be created.

This pose with the legs closed is often used for figures wearing a tight skirt.

As the male pose is not rendered as lithely as the female's, the direction of the face becomes the key element.

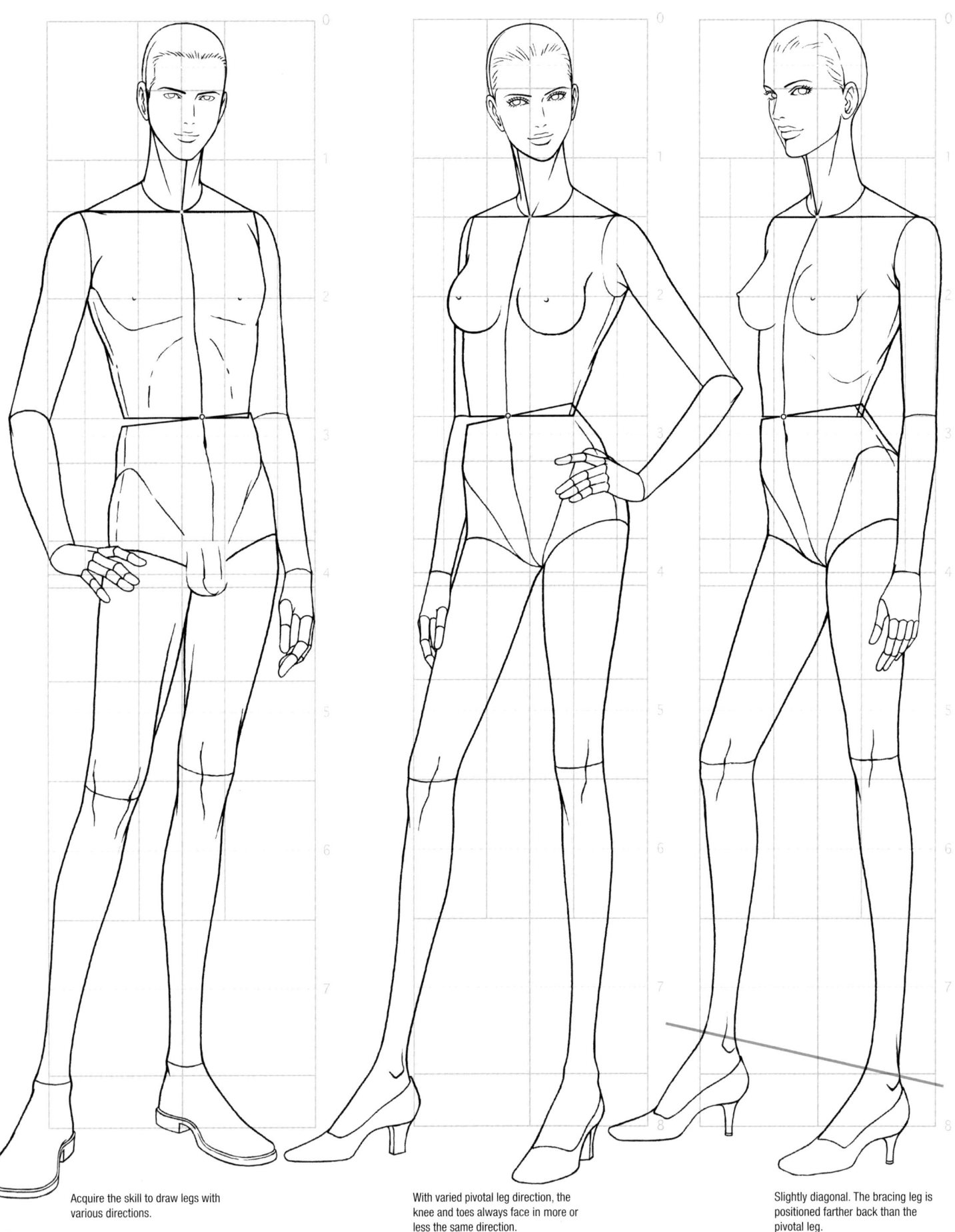

Acquire the skill to draw legs with various directions.

With varied pivotal leg direction, the knee and toes always face in more or less the same direction.

Slightly diagonal. The bracing leg is positioned farther back than the pivotal leg.

Chapter 1 : The Body

(5) Walking Pose
The walking pose can be drawn by applying the pose with weight on one leg.

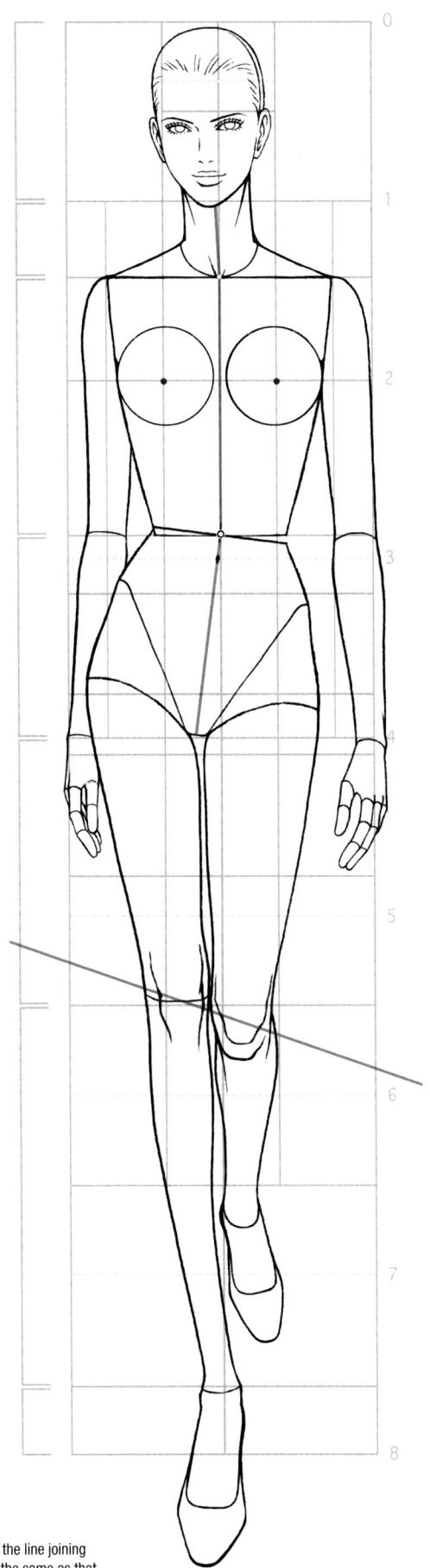

The angle of the line joining the knees is the same as that of the waistline.

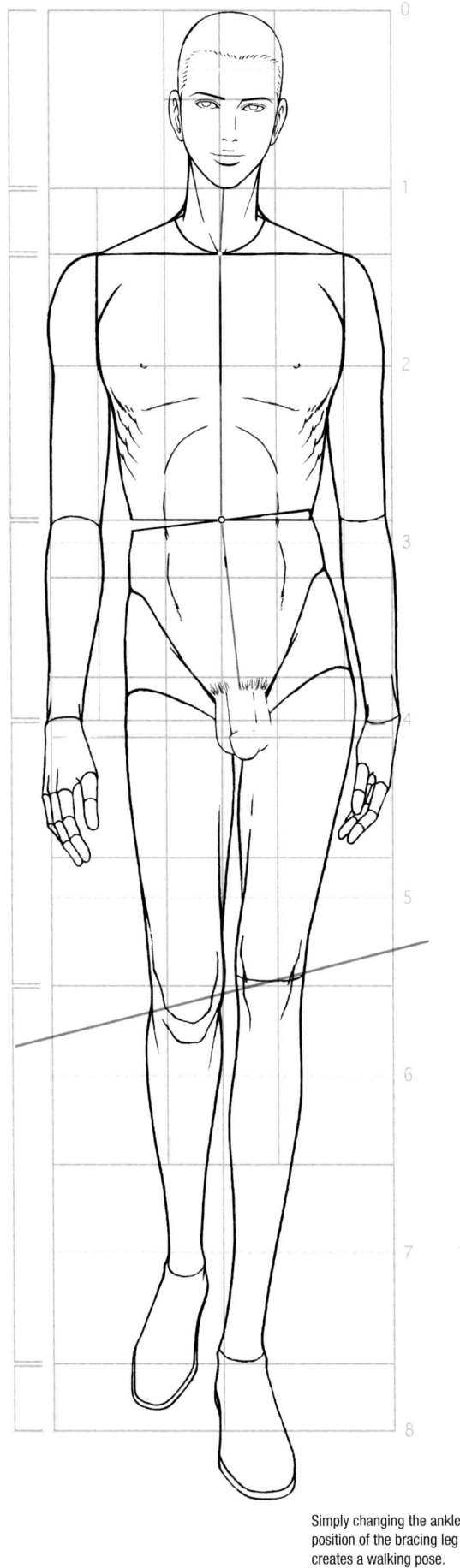

Simply changing the ankle position of the bracing leg creates a walking pose.

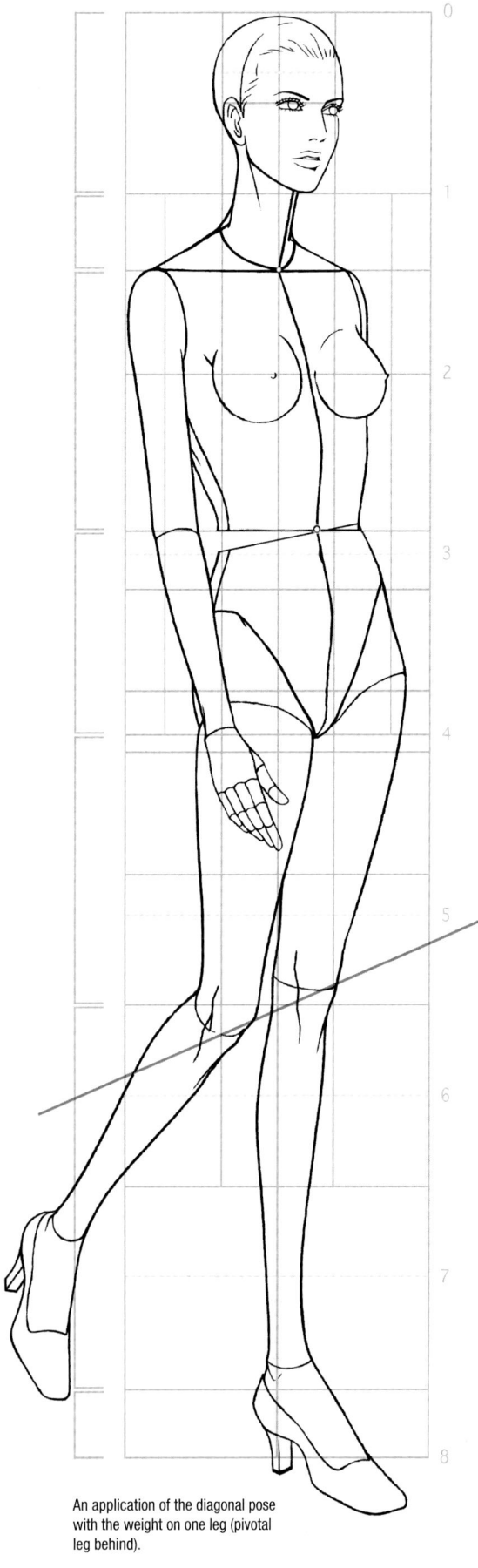

An application of the diagonal pose with the weight on one leg (pivotal leg behind).

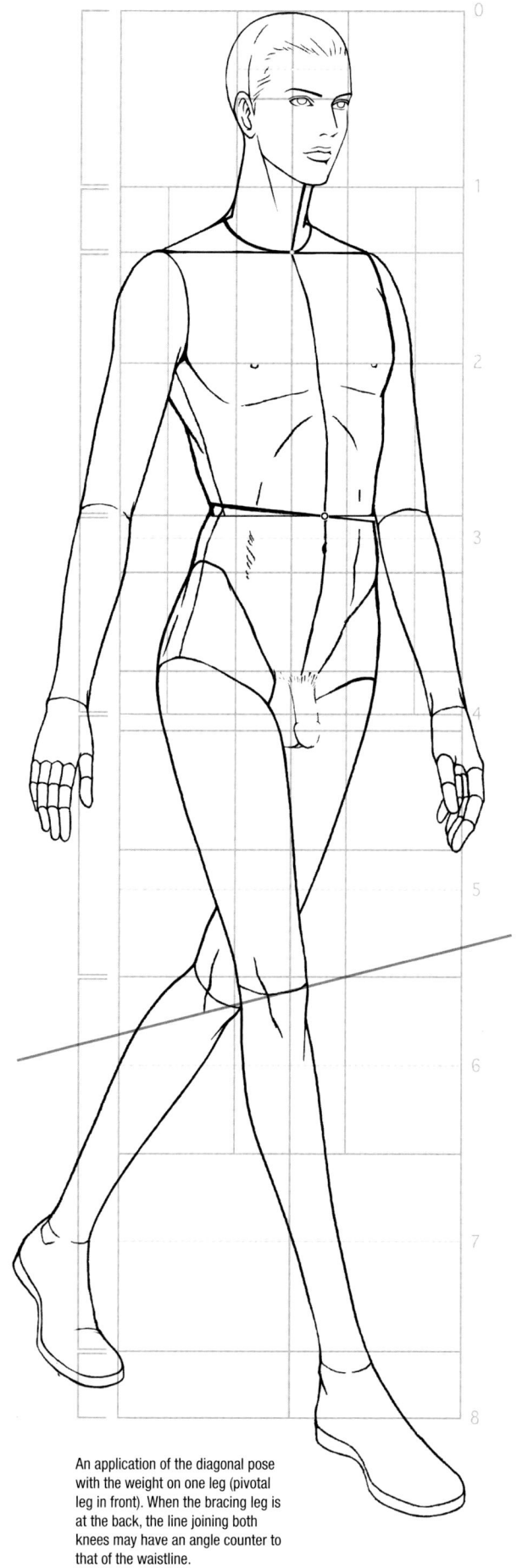

An application of the diagonal pose with the weight on one leg (pivotal leg in front). When the bracing leg is at the back, the line joining both knees may have an angle counter to that of the waistline.

Chapter 1 : The Body

(6) Movements of Each Part

As the movements you make increase, the more deviations tend to occur, pay due attention to the key points when moving the parts.

Head and Neck

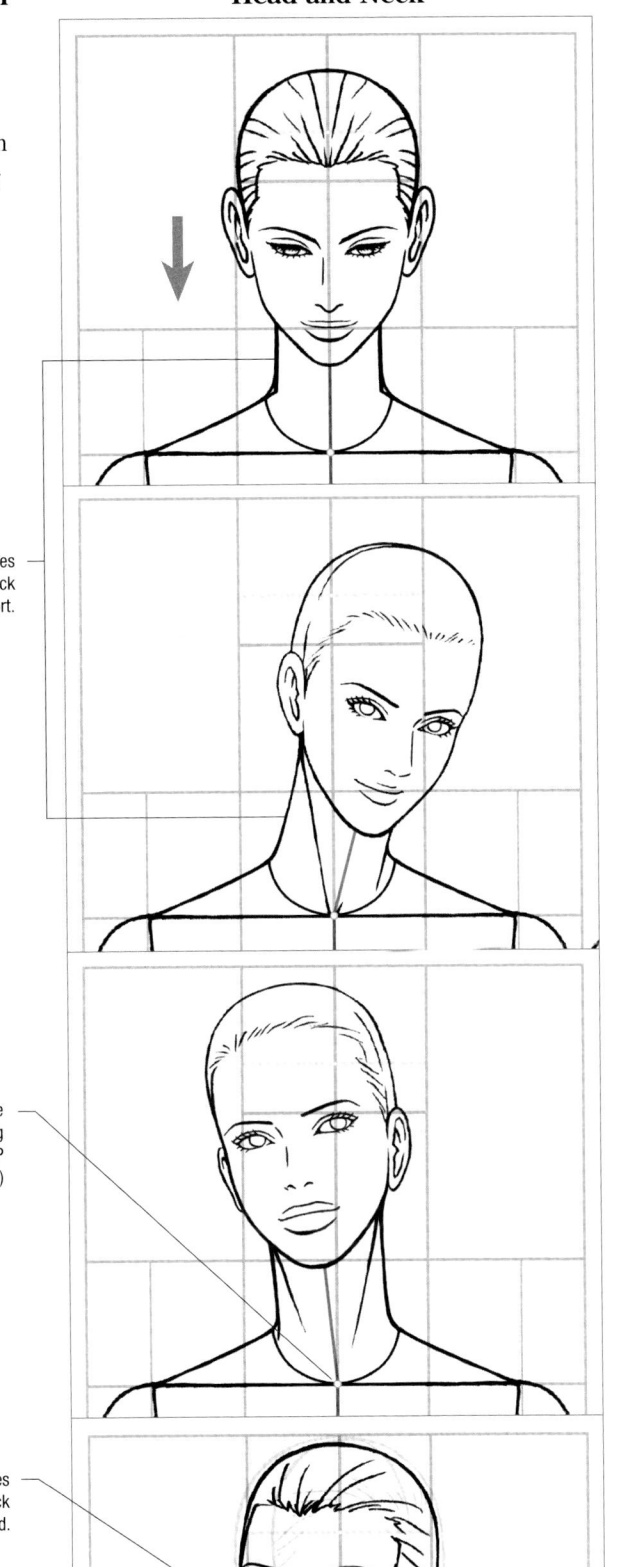

When the head faces downward, the neck appears short.

The neck should be moved by centering the FNP (front neck point)

When the head moves diagonally, the neck remains unchanged.

Shoulder

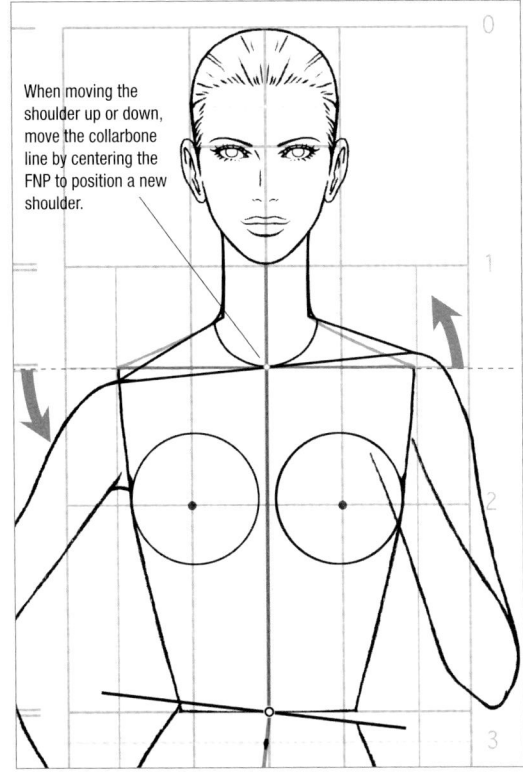

When moving the shoulder up or down, move the collarbone line by centering the FNP to position a new shoulder.

Upper Torso

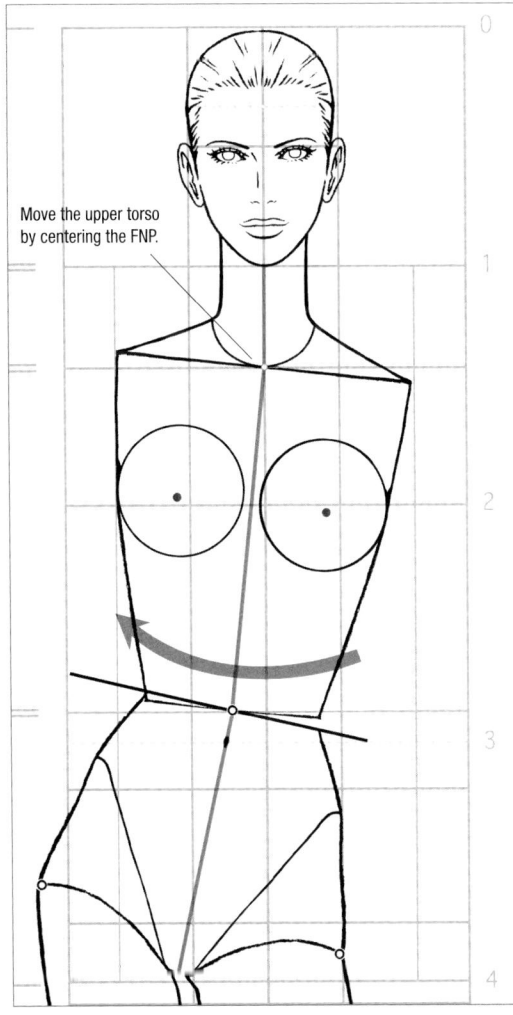

Move the upper torso by centering the FNP.

41

Arms

Diagonal with Weight on One Leg

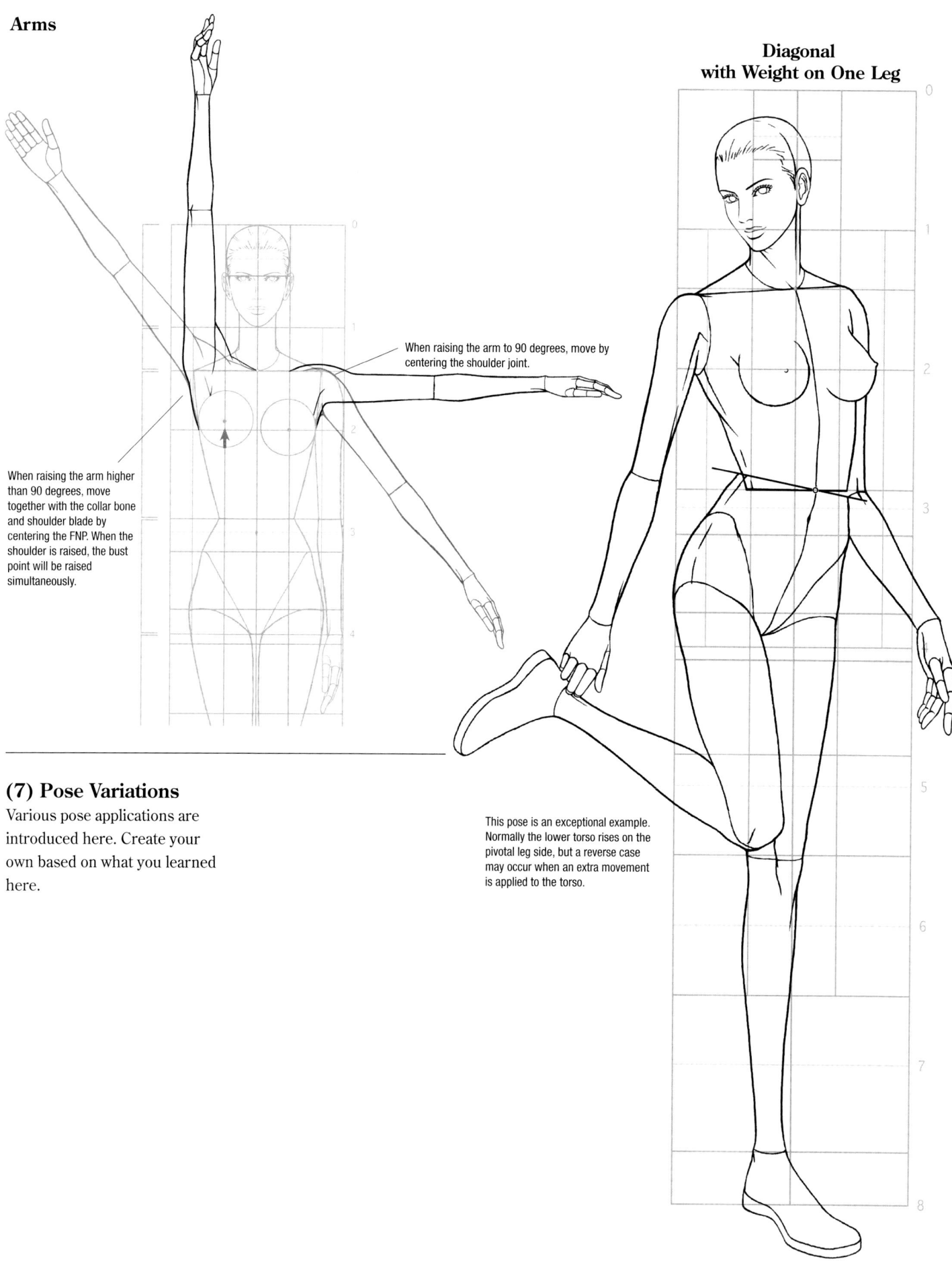

When raising the arm to 90 degrees, move by centering the shoulder joint.

When raising the arm higher than 90 degrees, move together with the collar bone and shoulder blade by centering the FNP. When the shoulder is raised, the bust point will be raised simultaneously.

(7) Pose Variations

Various pose applications are introduced here. Create your own based on what you learned here.

This pose is an exceptional example. Normally the lower torso rises on the pivotal leg side, but a reverse case may occur when an extra movement is applied to the torso.

Chapter 1 : The Body

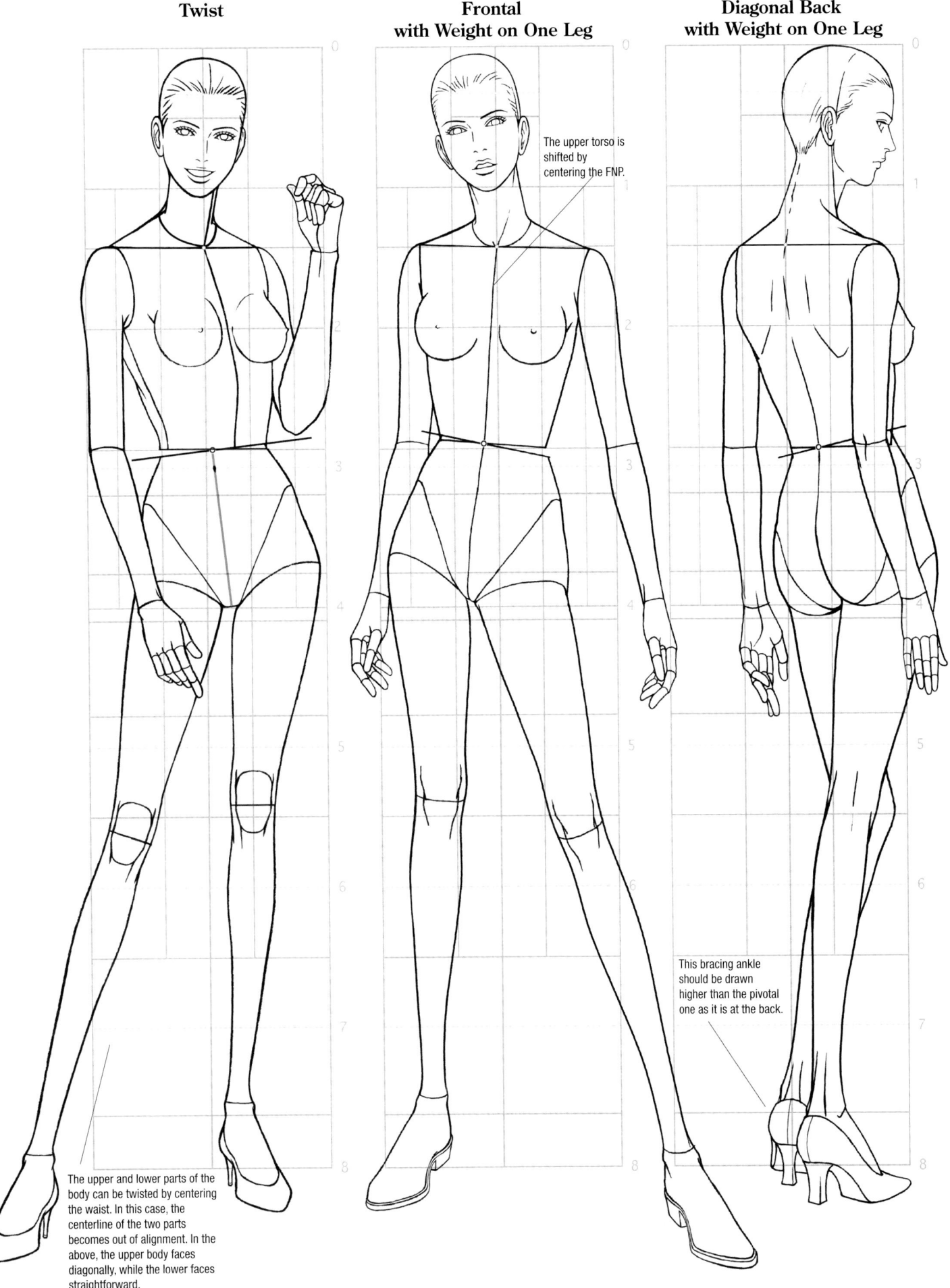

Twist

Frontal with Weight on One Leg

Diagonal Back with Weight on One Leg

The upper torso is shifted by centering the FNP.

This bracing ankle should be drawn higher than the pivotal one as it is at the back.

The upper and lower parts of the body can be twisted by centering the waist. In this case, the centerline of the two parts becomes out of alignment. In the above, the upper body faces diagonally, while the lower faces straightforward.

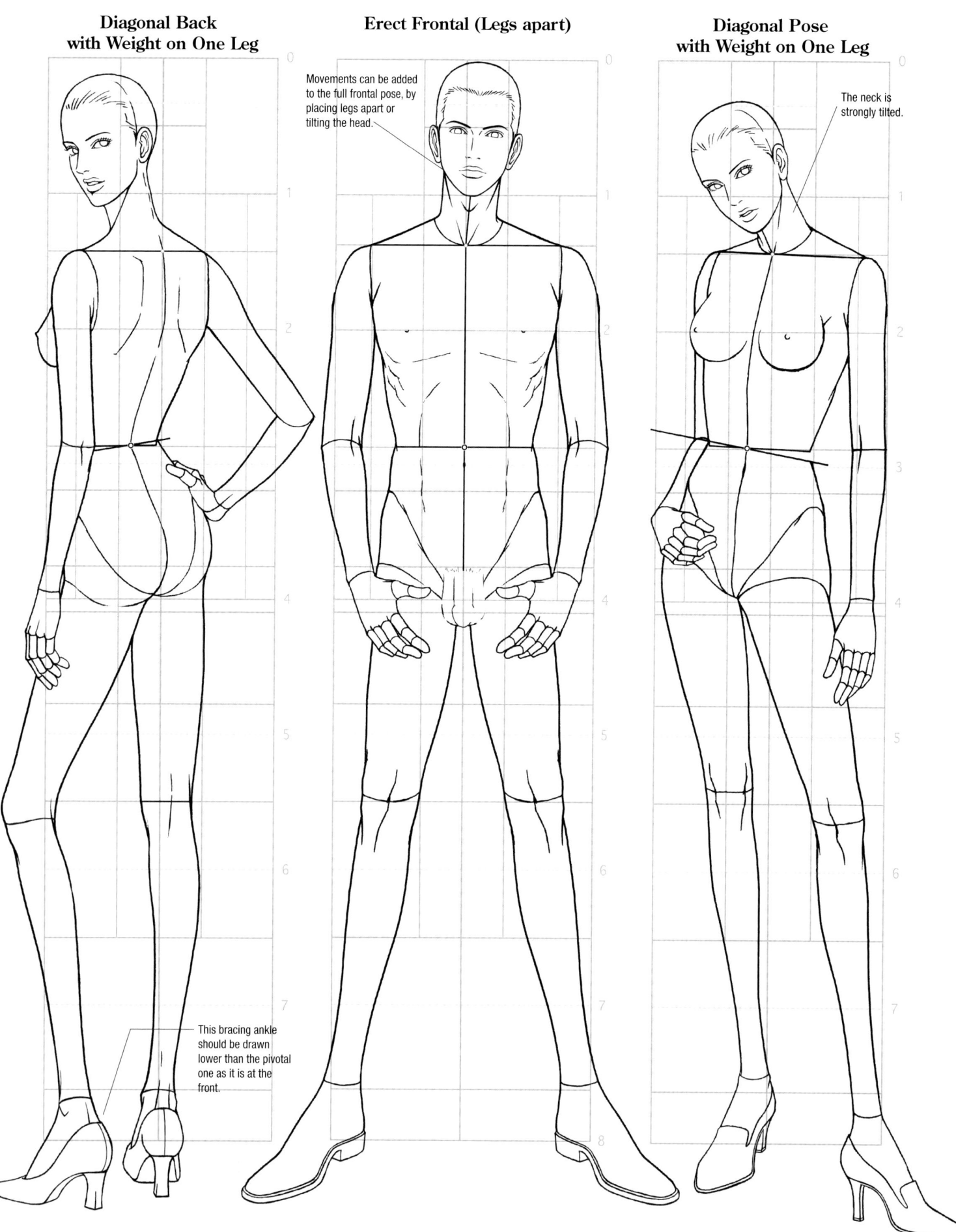

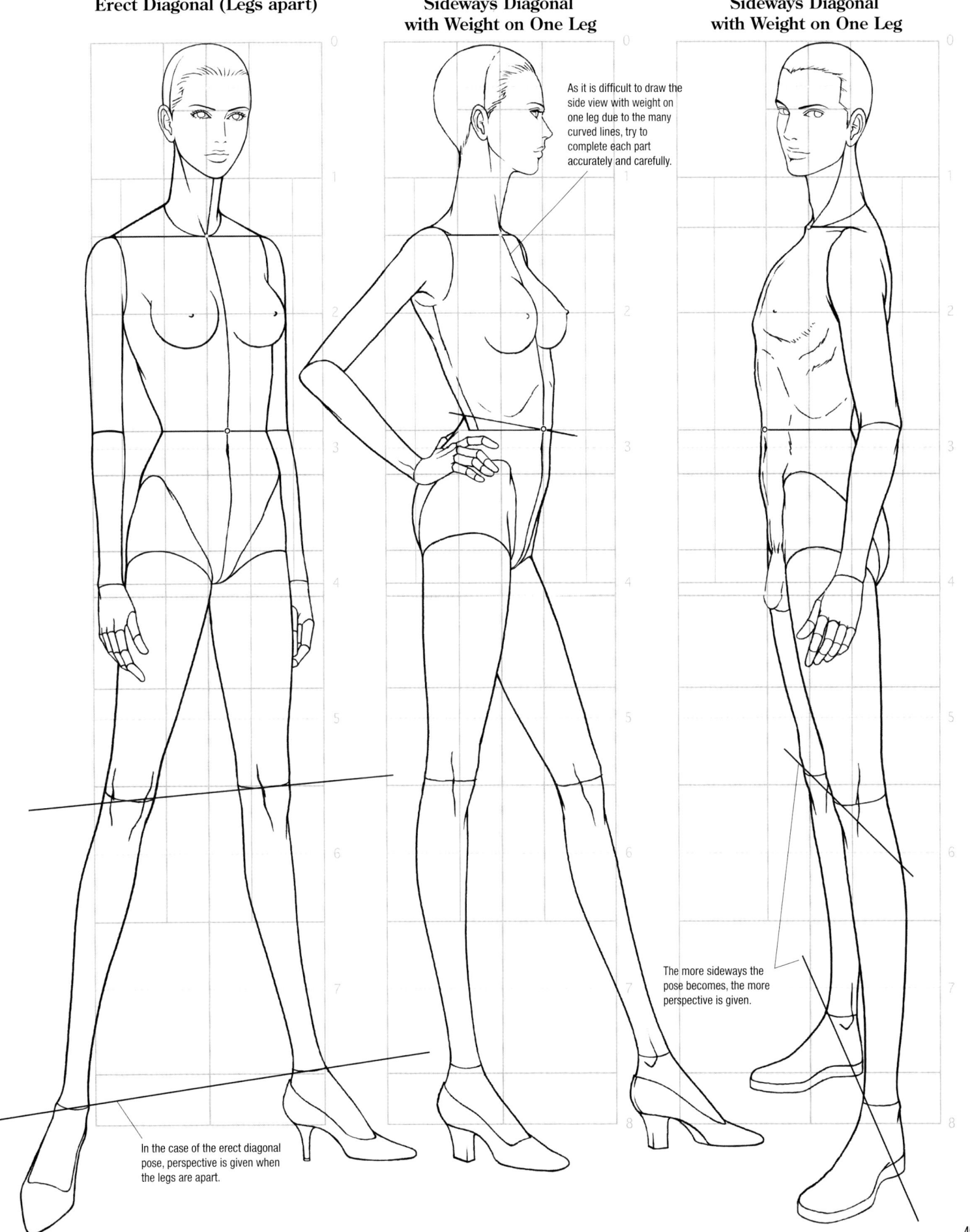

Erect Frontal (Legs apart) — **Sideways Diagonal with Weight on One Leg** — **Erect Diagonal (Legs apart)**

When the head and body face in opposite directions, movement is added to the overall pose.

The erect pose with legs apart is often used for the male pose.

Note perspective of the legs apart. (See p. 20)

[3] Method of Drawing Body Parts

Once you have acquired an understanding of the balance of the overall body, the next step is to master the balance of the head, hands and feet. These body parts are very important as they are often exposed even when the figure is dressed.

(1) How to Draw Hands

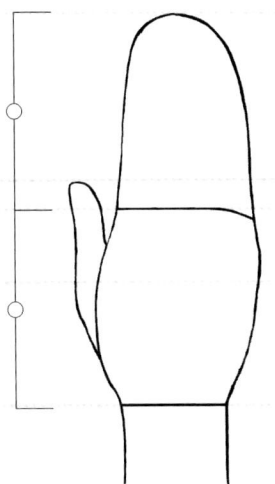

View hand by dividing it into the back, thumb and other four fingers. Note that the base of the thumb begins near the wrist for its holding function, and that the base of the little finger is lower than the other four.

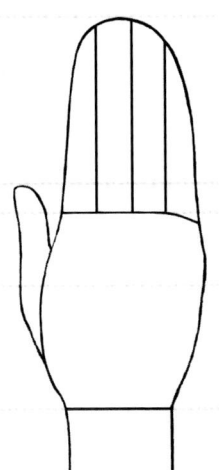

Make a division for the four fingers.

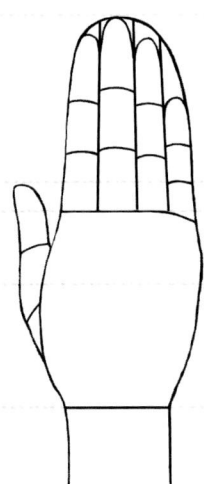

Draw each joint.

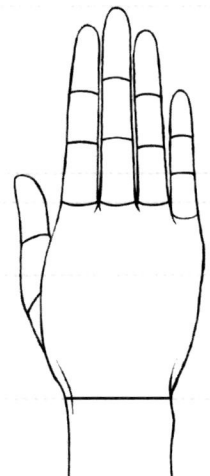

Complete by drawing each finger separately. With respect to the thickness of the hand in side view, the thumb and the back of the hand are about the same.

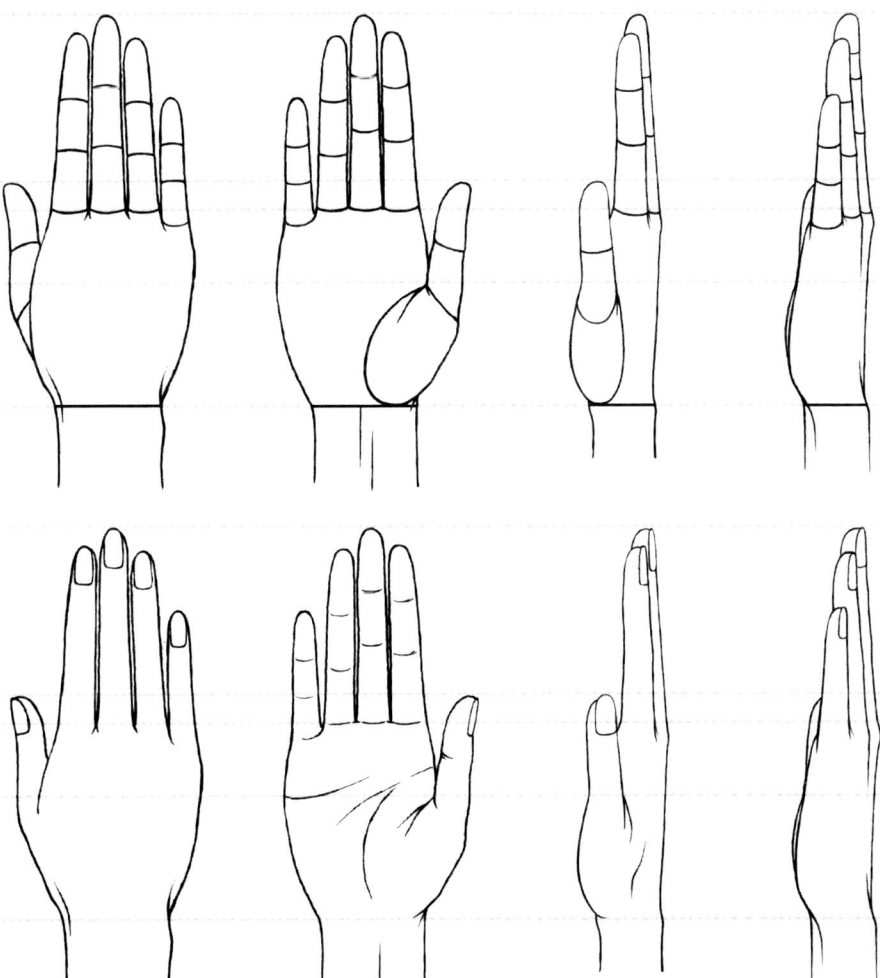

(2) Hand Pose Variations

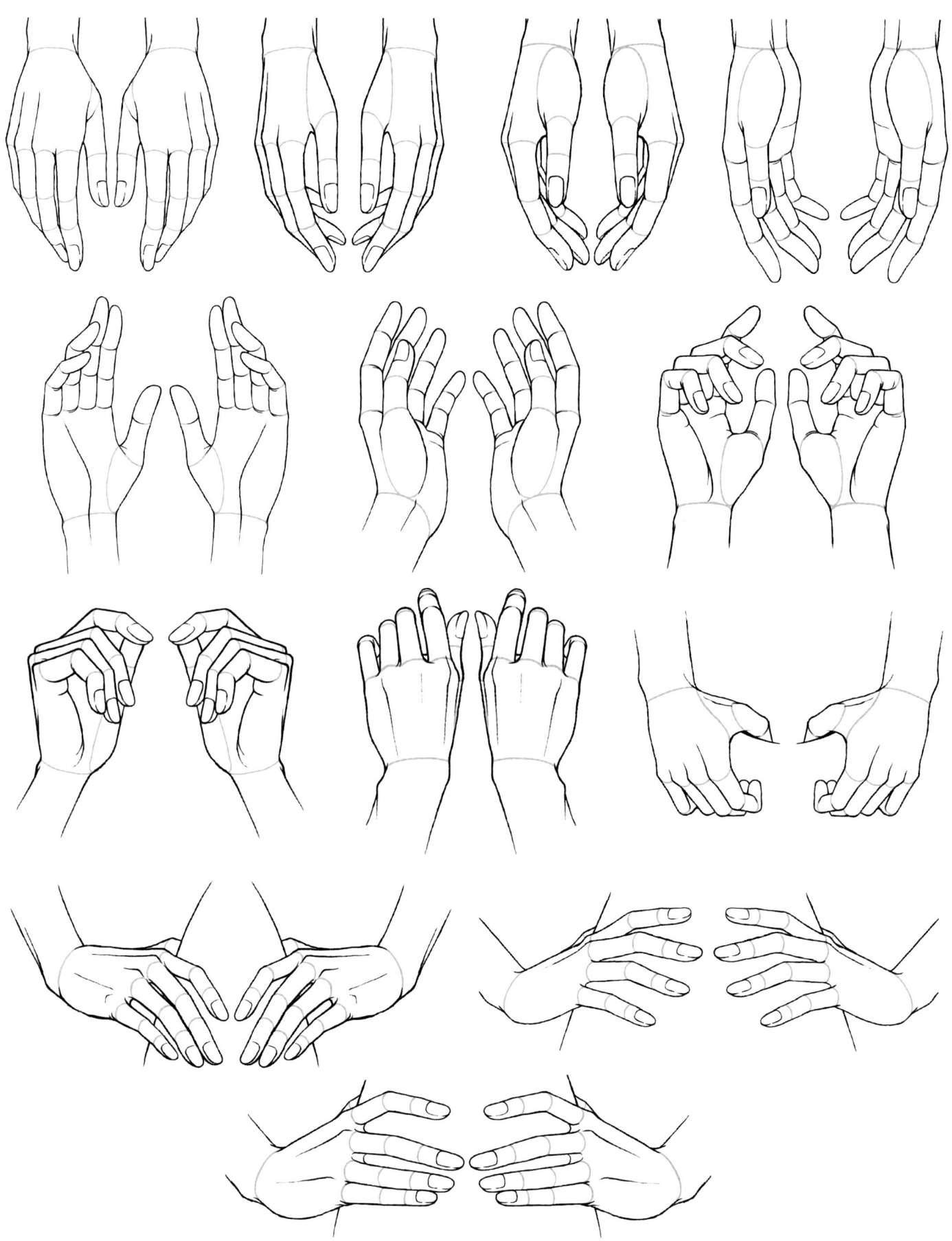

(3) How to Draw Feet

View the foot by dividing it into the heel, instep and toes. Note that the shape of the foot changes depending on the height of the shoe heels. Please refer to the guidelines, showing the outline of shoes, sandals, pumps and boots.

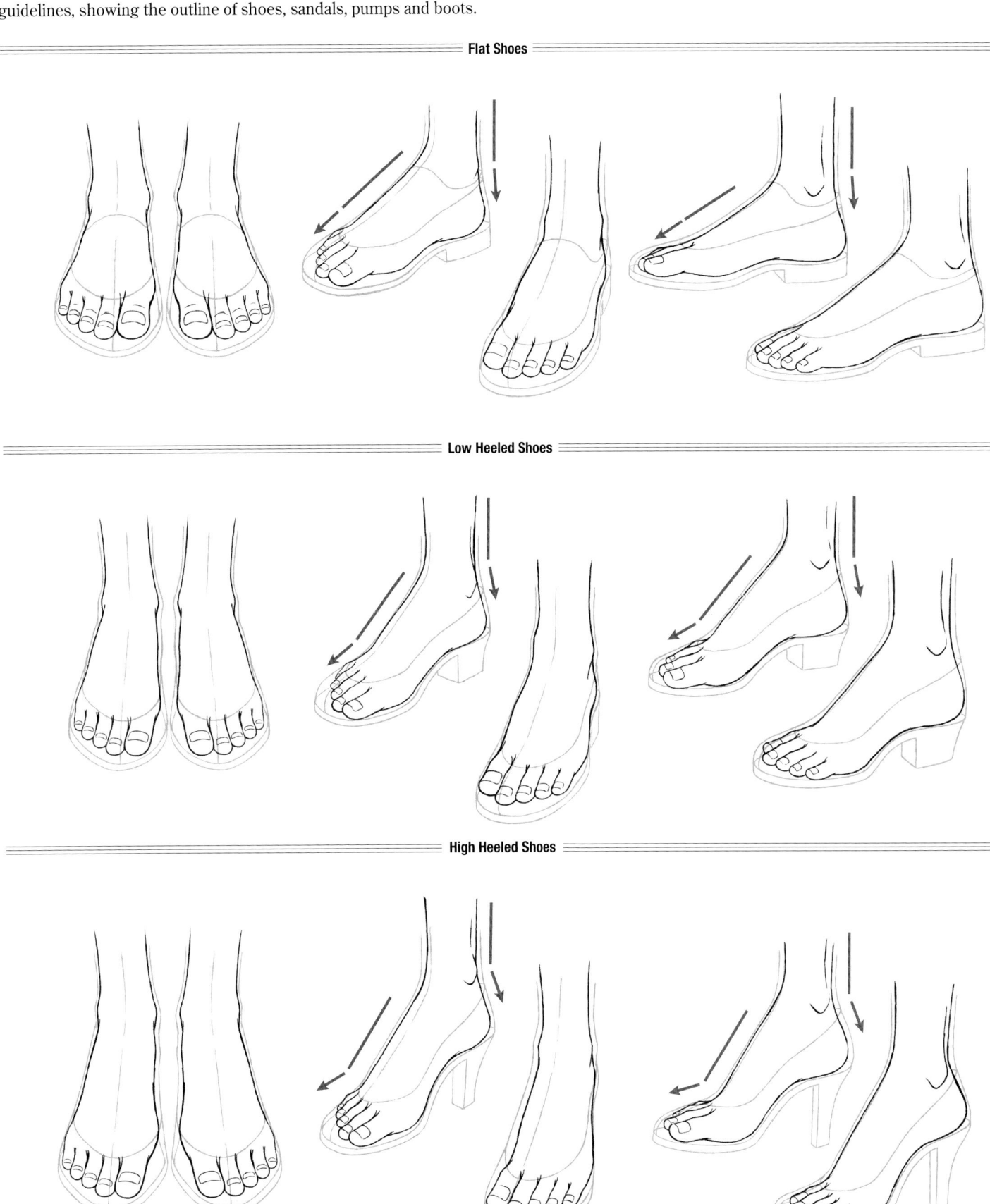

(4) How to Draw the Head

There are four important points to consider when drawing the head)
1. The outline should be drawn as an oval.
2. The size and position of the eyes, nose, mouth and ears.
3. The hairstyle
4. The make-up when coloring.

Balance of the Head

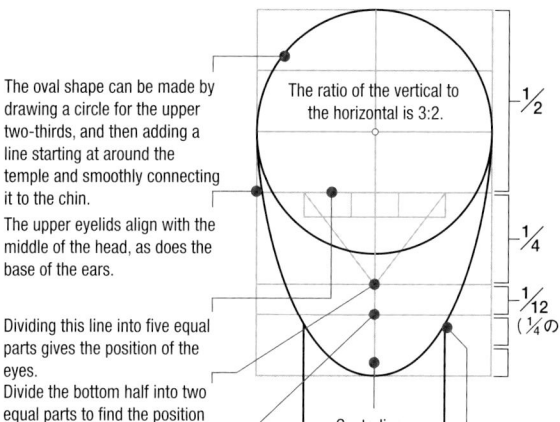

The oval shape can be made by drawing a circle for the upper two-thirds, and then adding a line starting at around the temple and smoothly connecting it to the chin.

The upper eyelids align with the middle of the head, as does the base of the ears.

Dividing this line into five equal parts gives the position of the eyes.

Divide the bottom half into two equal parts to find the position of the nostrils.

Divide the bottom quarter into three equal parts to find the position of the mouth.

The ratio of the vertical to the horizontal is 3:2.

When facing diagonally the neck is angled, but not as much as when facing sideways.

The side profile is 30% wider than the full frontal view.

How to Draw the Eyes, Nose and Mouth

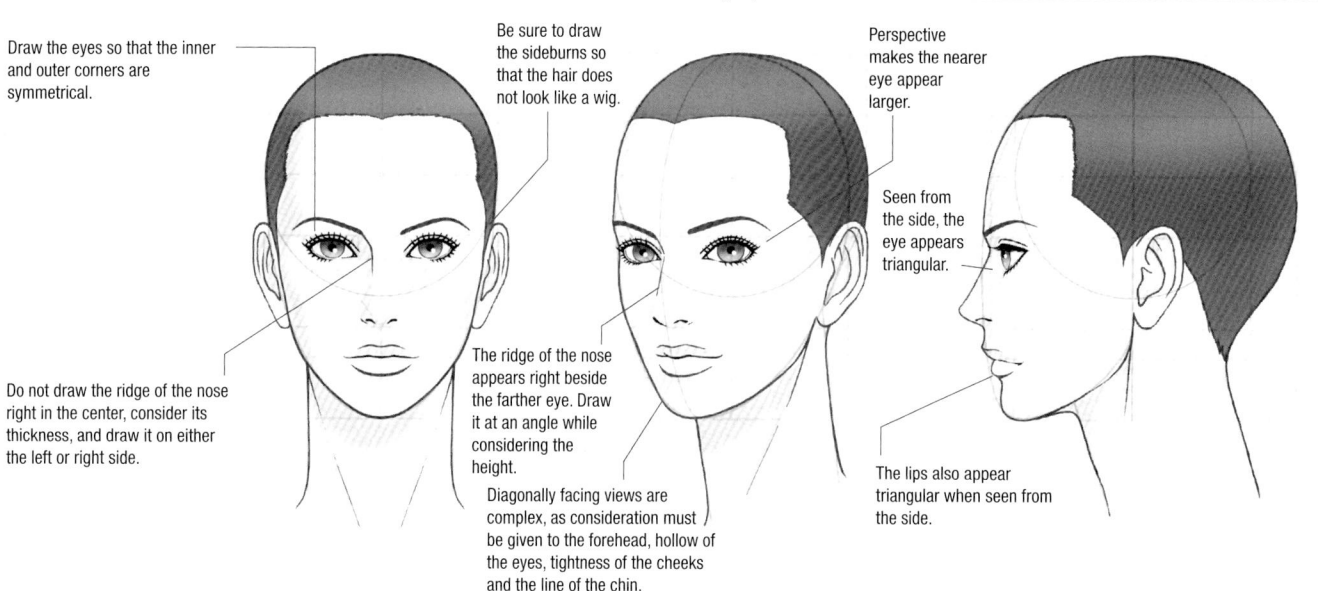

Draw the eyes so that the inner and outer corners are symmetrical.

Do not draw the ridge of the nose right in the center, consider its thickness, and draw it on either the left or right side.

Be sure to draw the sideburns so that the hair does not look like a wig.

The ridge of the nose appears right beside the farther eye. Draw it at an angle while considering the height.

Diagonally facing views are complex, as consideration must be given to the forehead, hollow of the eyes, tightness of the cheeks and the line of the chin.

Perspective makes the nearer eye appear larger.

Seen from the side, the eye appears triangular.

The lips also appear triangular when seen from the side.

How to Draw Faces in Perspective

Upward

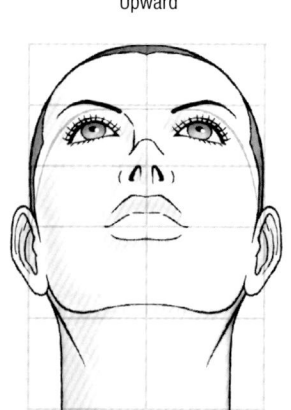

The ears appear lower, while the eyes appear higher.

Diagonal/upward

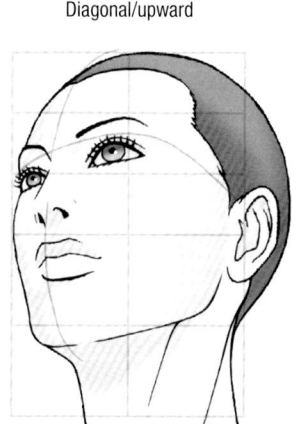

The eyes remain above the ears, and the chin line is more prominent.

Downward

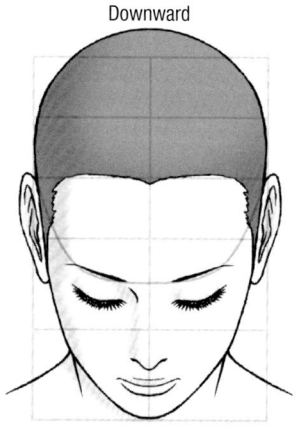

The ears appear higher, while the eyes appear lower.

Diagonal/downward

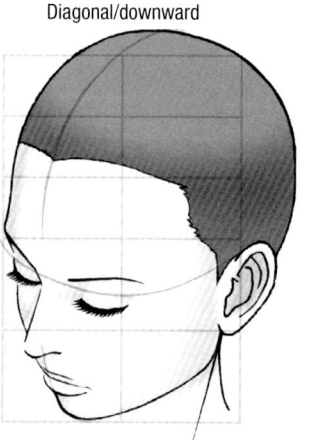

The eyes remain below the ears, and the chin is hardly visible.

(3) How to Draw Feet

View the foot by dividing it into the heel, instep and toes. Note that the shape of the foot changes depending on the height of the shoe heels. Please refer to the guidelines, showing the outline of shoes, sandals, pumps and boots.

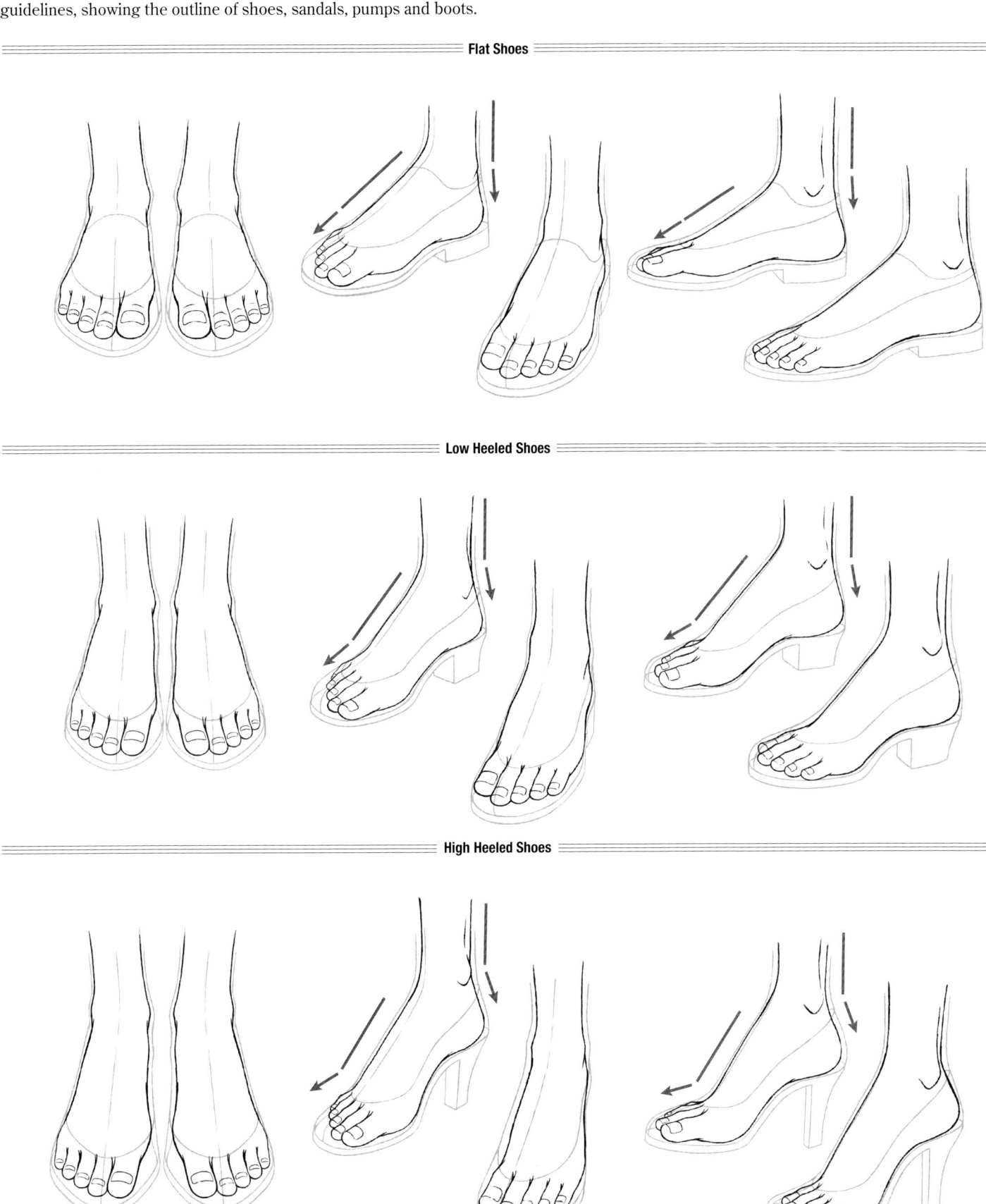

(4) How to Draw the Head

There are four important points to consider when drawing the head)
1. The outline should be drawn as an oval.
2. The size and position of the eyes, nose, mouth and ears.
3. The hairstyle
4. The make-up when coloring.

Balance of the Head

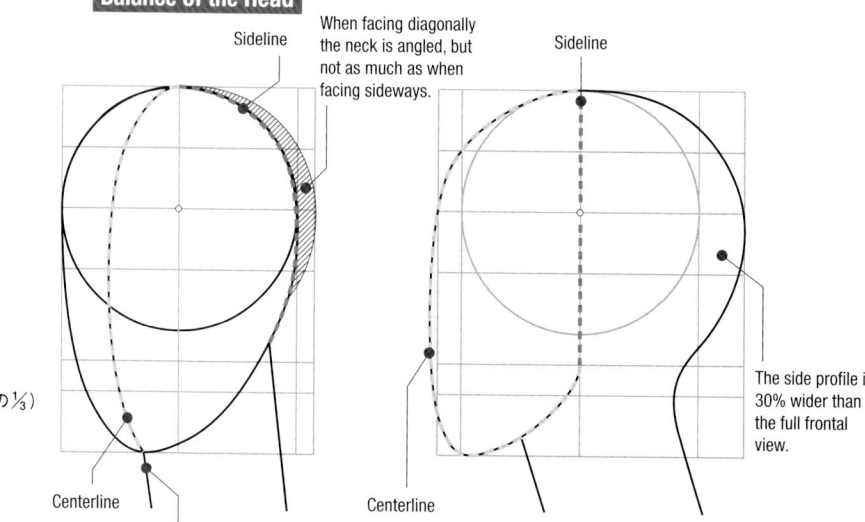

The oval shape can be made by drawing a circle for the upper two-thirds, and then adding a line starting at around the temple and smoothly connecting it to the chin.

The upper eyelids align with the middle of the head, as does the base of the ears.

Dividing this line into five equal parts gives the position of the eyes.

Divide the bottom half into two equal parts to find the position of the nostrils.

Divide the bottom quarter into three equal parts to find the position of the mouth.

The ratio of the vertical to the horizontal is 3:2.

When facing diagonally the neck is angled, but not as much as when facing sideways.

The side profile is 30% wider than the full frontal view.

How to Draw the Eyes, Nose and Mouth

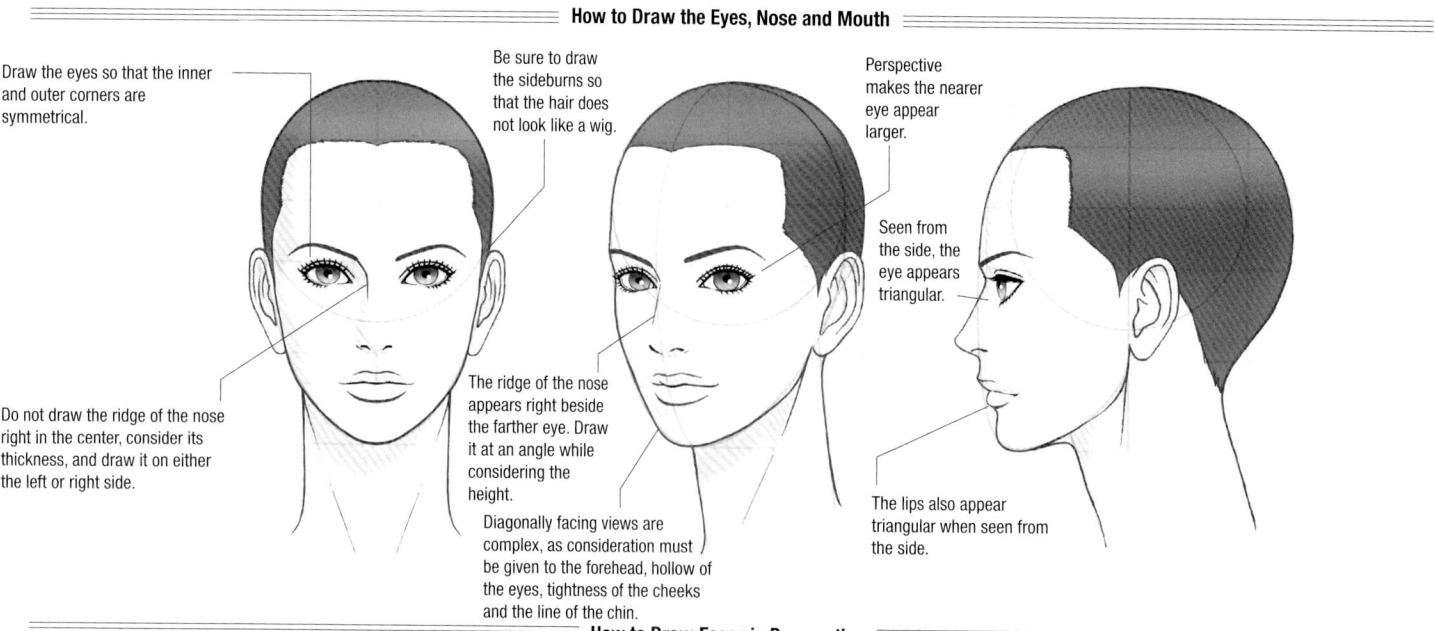

Draw the eyes so that the inner and outer corners are symmetrical.

Do not draw the ridge of the nose right in the center, consider its thickness, and draw it on either the left or right side.

Be sure to draw the sideburns so that the hair does not look like a wig.

The ridge of the nose appears right beside the farther eye. Draw it at an angle while considering the height.

Diagonally facing views are complex, as consideration must be given to the forehead, hollow of the eyes, tightness of the cheeks and the line of the chin.

Perspective makes the nearer eye appear larger.

Seen from the side, the eye appears triangular.

The lips also appear triangular when seen from the side.

How to Draw Faces in Perspective

Upward

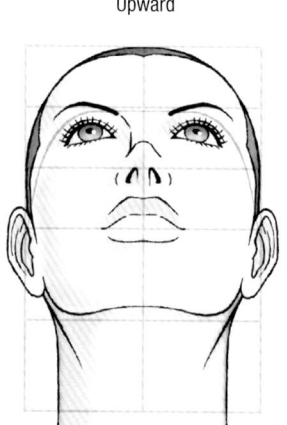

The ears appear lower, while the eyes appear higher.

Diagonal/upward

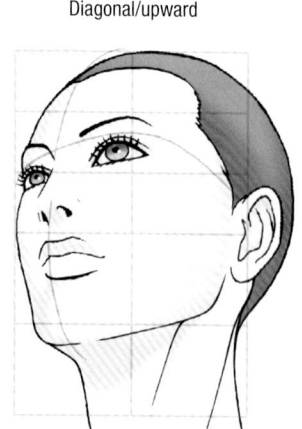

The eyes remain above the ears, and the chin line is more prominent.

Downward

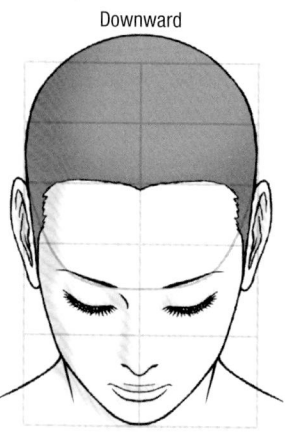

The ears appear higher, while the eyes appear lower.

Diagonal/downward

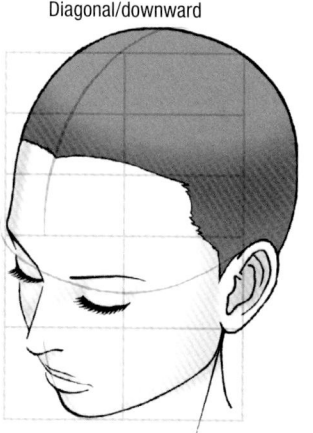

The eyes remain below the ears, and the chin is hardly visible.

(3) How to Draw Feet

View the foot by dividing it into the heel, instep and toes. Note that the shape of the foot changes depending on the height of the shoe heels. Please refer to the guidelines, showing the outline of shoes, sandals, pumps and boots.

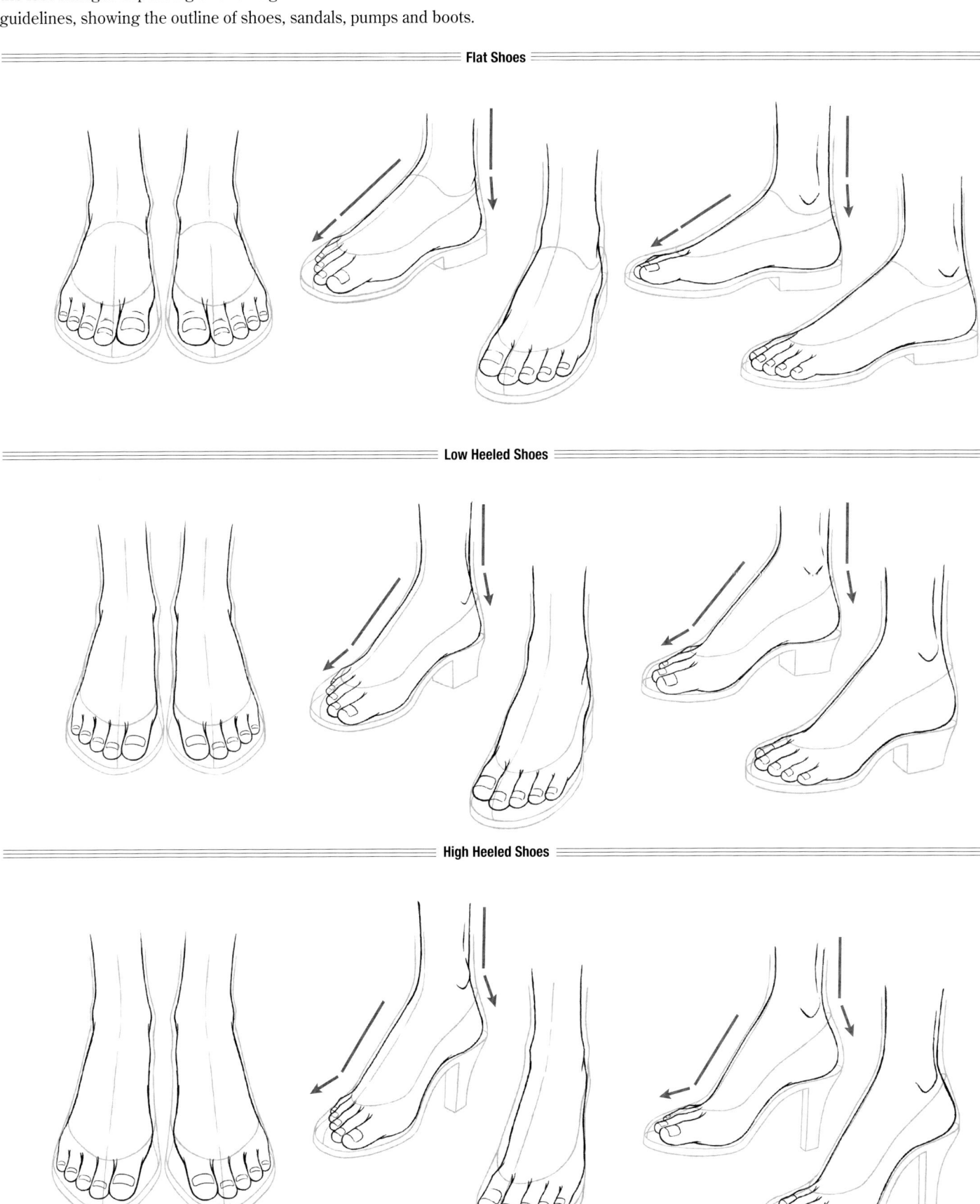

(4) How to Draw the Head

There are four important points to consider when drawing the head)

1. The outline should be drawn as an oval.
2. The size and position of the eyes, nose, mouth and ears.
3. The hairstyle
4. The make-up when coloring.

Balance of the Head

The oval shape can be made by drawing a circle for the upper two-thirds, and then adding a line starting at around the temple and smoothly connecting it to the chin.

The upper eyelids align with the middle of the head, as does the base of the ears.

Dividing this line into five equal parts gives the position of the eyes.

Divide the bottom half into two equal parts to find the position of the nostrils.

Divide the bottom quarter into three equal parts to find the position of the mouth.

The ratio of the vertical to the horizontal is 3:2.

1/2, 1/4, 1/12 (1/4 の 1/3)

Centerline

When facing diagonally the neck is angled, but not as much as when facing sideways.

Sideline

The side profile is 30% wider than the full frontal view.

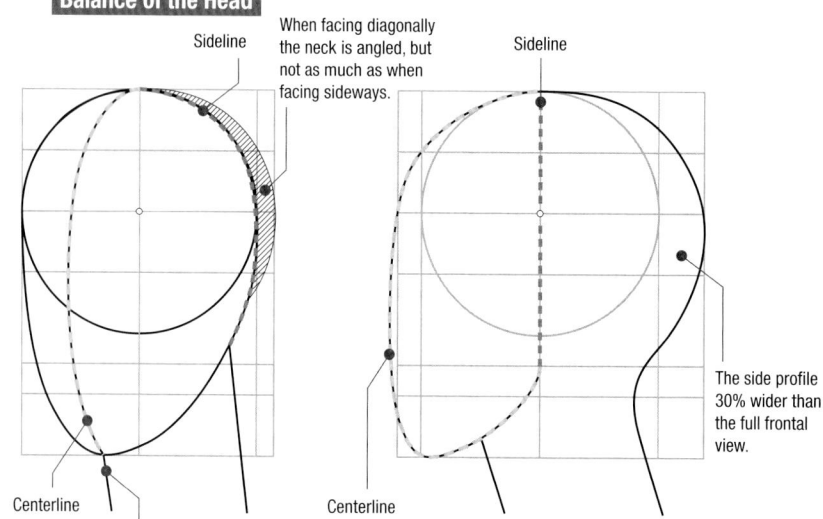

How to Draw the Eyes, Nose and Mouth

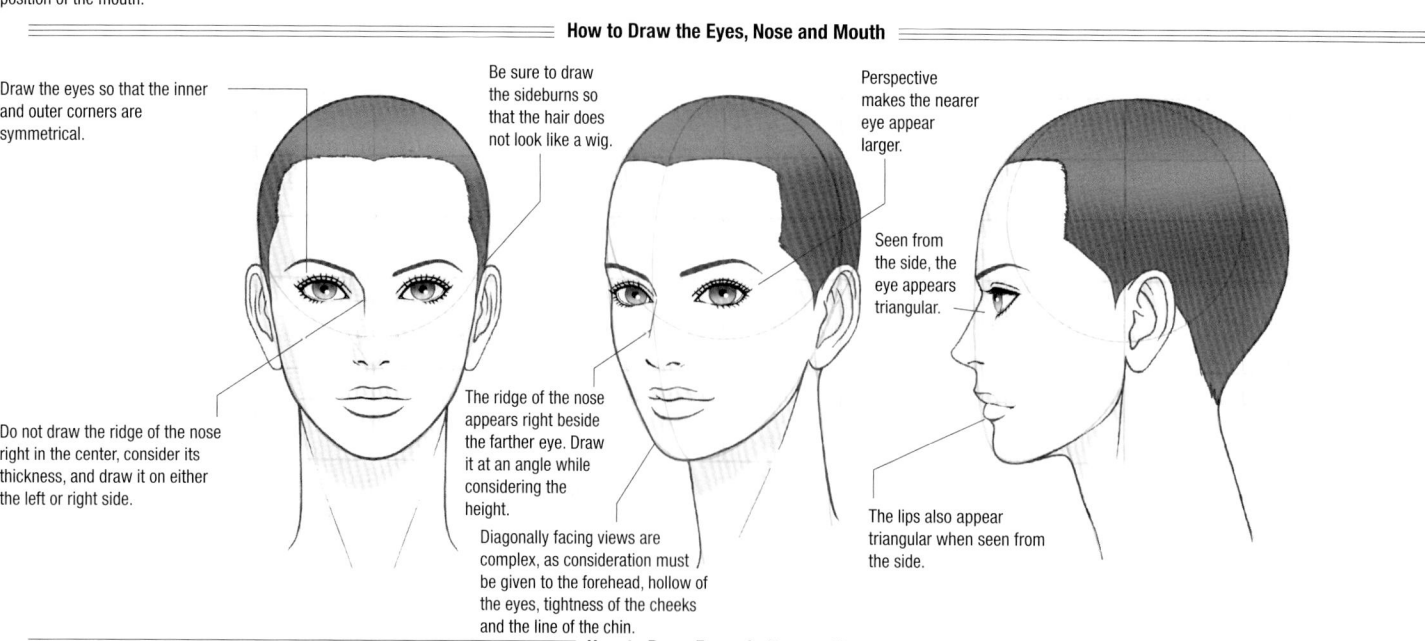

Draw the eyes so that the inner and outer corners are symmetrical.

Do not draw the ridge of the nose right in the center, consider its thickness, and draw it on either the left or right side.

Be sure to draw the sideburns so that the hair does not look like a wig.

The ridge of the nose appears right beside the farther eye. Draw it at an angle while considering the height.

Diagonally facing views are complex, as consideration must be given to the forehead, hollow of the eyes, tightness of the cheeks and the line of the chin.

Perspective makes the nearer eye appear larger.

Seen from the side, the eye appears triangular.

The lips also appear triangular when seen from the side.

How to Draw Faces in Perspective

| Upward | Diagonal/upward | Downward | Diagonal/downward |

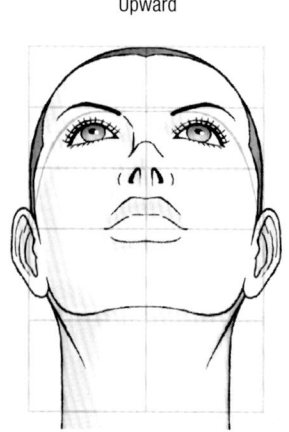 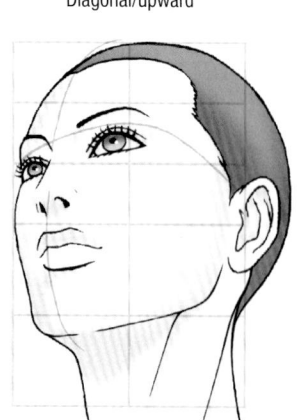 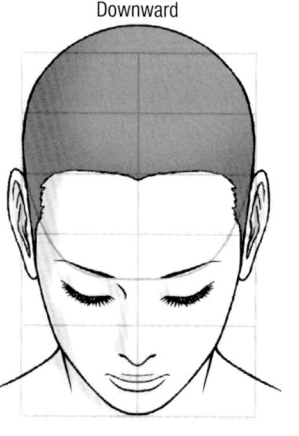 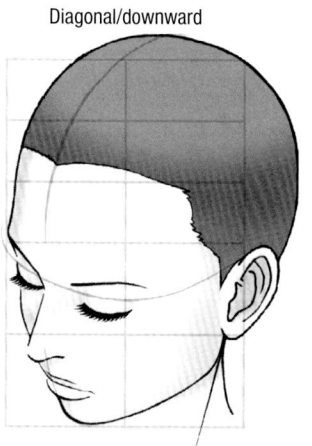

The ears appear lower, while the eyes appear higher.

The eyes remain above the ears, and the chin line is more prominent.

The ears appear higher, while the eyes appear lower.

The eyes remain below the ears, and the chin is hardly visible.

Chapter 1 : The Body

How to Draw Hair

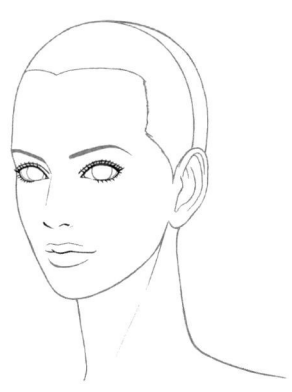

Regardless of the hairstyle, begin by drawing a skinhead, while paying attention not to spoil the balance of the top of the head.

Draw an outline of the hair. Allow extra room at the top of the head for the thickness of the hair.

Draw the flow of the hair clearly. While coloring think of a group of 100 hairs as a standard, rather than trying to color each hair individually.

How to Draw Hats

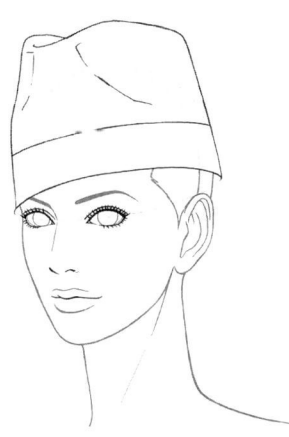

Draw a crown (mountain) on the skinhead. The rim of the hat should be drawn slightly larger to allow room for the hair.

Draw the brim of the hat.

Draw the hair.

How to Draw Glasses

Draw the lenses

Draw the frame and temples (the parts which extend to the ears).

A hat is combined here.

51

(5) Head Pose Variations

Try to draw heads facing in various directions and with different hairstyles using these examples as reference. When drawing from photographs, try to render in a simplified form using less lines, rather than simply replicating.

Chapter 2
Technical Drawing

Technical drawing is also referred to as "product drawing" or "planar drawing", meaning here the drawing of clothing only, without figures. Compared with fashion drawing, which renders an image of the total body wearing clothing, it is distinguished by flat, careful and articulate rendition of the configuration and forms of clothing. Although technical drawing does not have a glamorous image, it is widely used in the industry for sewing specifications, catalogs, product lists and other print material, as it provides detailed fashion design information very clearly in a user-friendly manner. It also plays an essential role as a tool in linking all professions involved in apparel manufacturing, such as designers, pattern makers, and sewing and pressing plants. There are mainly two types of technical drawing; one which depicts garments as if on a hanger, referred to here as "hanger illustration" and another which shows garments laid on a flat surface, known in Japanese as "hira-e" (flat drawing). The "hanger illustration" is the most common and is used in a broad range of information materials from sewing specifications to inserts for fashion drawings as additional visual information. The flat drawing is used when it is required to show parts of a garment laid out flat, for example, in order to highlight the design and details of sleeves without shoulder pads. In this chapter, I will introduce the common "hanger illustration". The flat drawing is mentioned on page 152.

Format of Technical Drawing

These bodies have been enlarged horizontally by 5% over those used in Chapter 1. When garments are laid out flat the horizontal width increases by the thickness of the body.

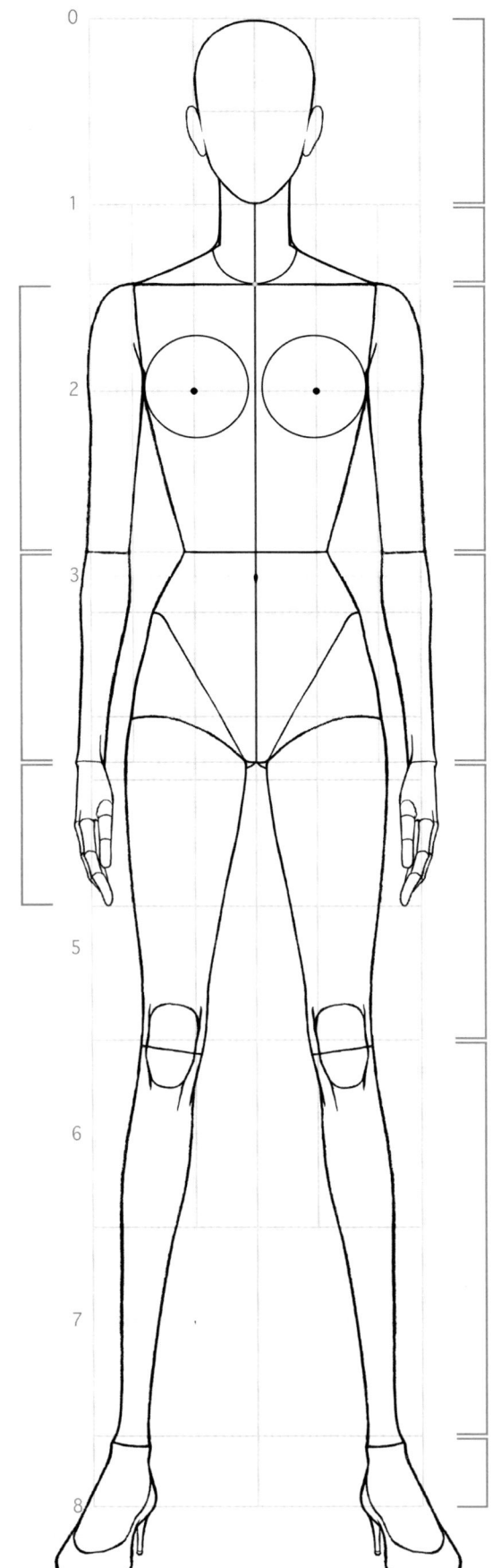
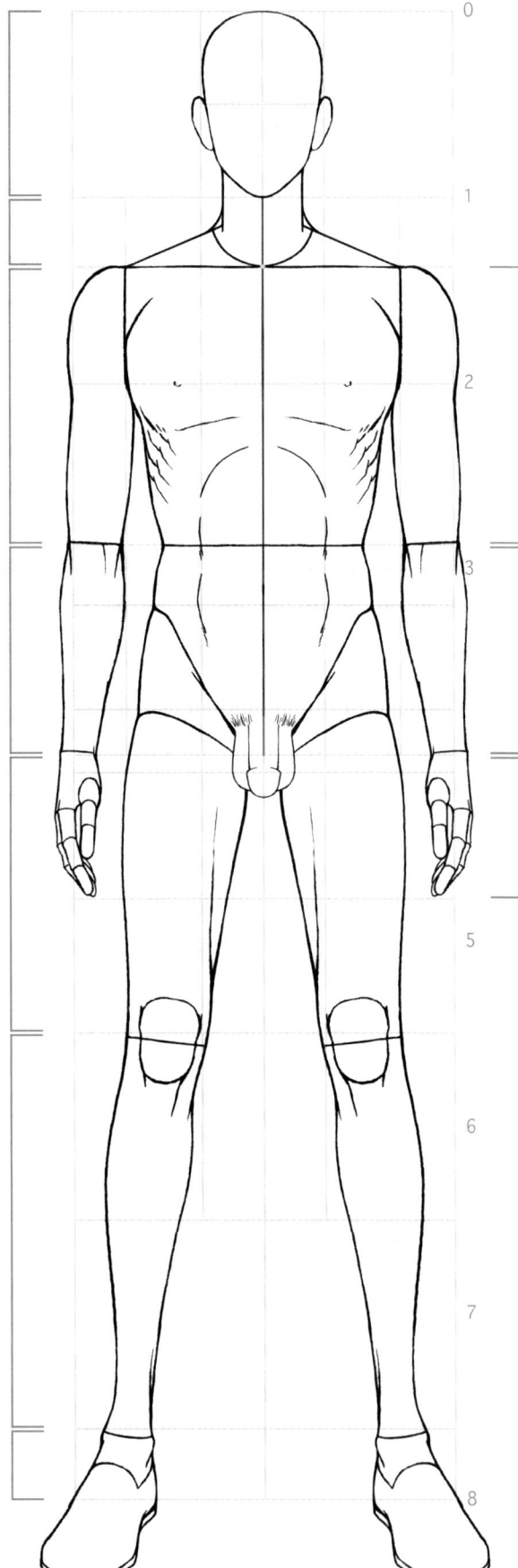

Chapter 2 : Technical Drawing

Drawing Method (Points in common)

Observe the following method in order to draw garments symmetrically.
1) Fold a piece of tracing paper in half (mountain-fold) and then open it out flat.
2) Align the fold line of the tracing paper with the centerline of the copy of the body drawing and secure it with masking tape.
3) First draw either the left or right half of the garment.
4) When you have finished drawing the half, mountain-fold the paper on the fold line and trace the other half. (When the draft has been made in a sketchpad, valley-fold and rub the back side of the paper. The pencil line will be transferred onto the other side.)
5) Finally, draw the details that appear in either the left or right side only, and complete the preliminary sketch.
6) Transfer the draft sketch to the Kent paper. Using a thick, soft leaded pencil such as a 6B, fill in the backside of the sketch. Place the tracing paper on top of the Kent paper and transfer the sketch by drawing over it with a hard leaded mechanical pencil.
7) Complete in ink by drawing over the transferred lines with drawing pens, ranging in thickness from 0.05 to 0.2 mm. Use a thick pen for outlines, and a thin one for details including stitches. Remove any dirt with an eraser.

Necessary materials:
- Make a copy of the format of technical drawings (bodies) on page 54.
- Tracing paper (or sketchpad)
- Ruler (approx. 20 cm)
- Kent paper
- Mechanical pencil
- Masking tape
- Pencil with soft lead such as 6B

[1] Shirts and Blouses

Shirts are tops and are basically innerwear however, depending on their thickness they could also be outerwear. Blouses were originally men's shirts that have been adapted for women.

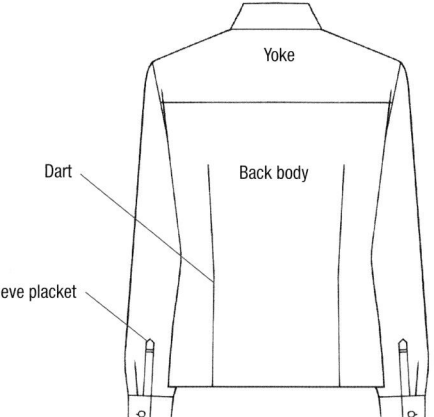

Drawing Method

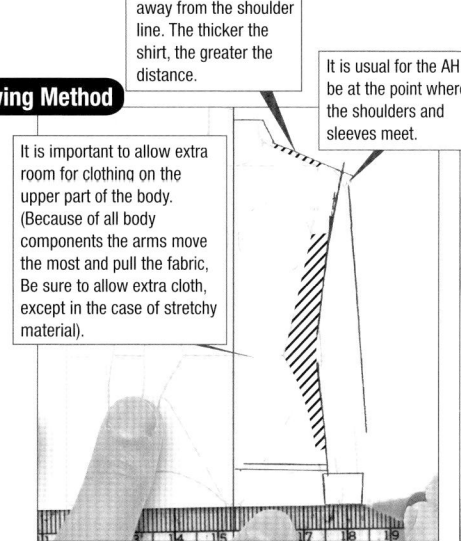

As shirts are innerwear, it is sufficient to allow a small distance away from the shoulder line. The thicker the shirt, the greater the distance.

It is important to allow extra room for clothing on the upper part of the body. (Because of all body components the arms move the most and pull the fabric, Be sure to allow extra cloth, except in the case of stretchy material).

It is usual for the AH to be at the point where the shoulders and sleeves meet.

1. Follow the steps based on the explanation under "How to Draw" above. Secure the tracing paper to the copy of the body and begin drawing with the silhouette. First draw the straight lines using a ruler.

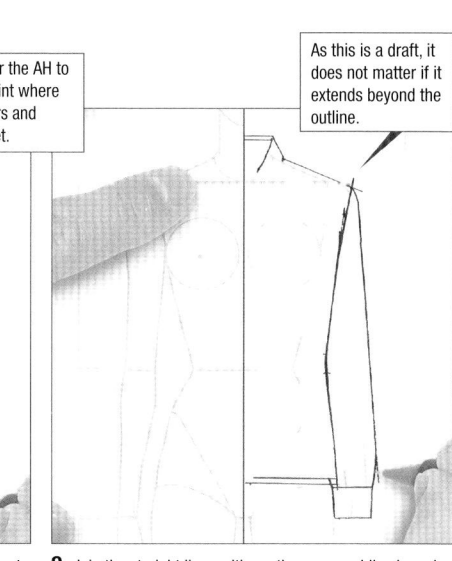

As this is a draft, it does not matter if it extends beyond the outline.

2. Join the straight lines with gentle curves, while observing an actual garment to see what it looks like.

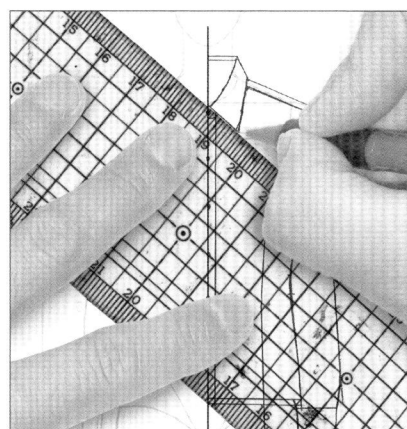

3. After completing the silhouette, draw details such as the collar and other structural lines. It may be better to begin with the side which has more detailed elements.

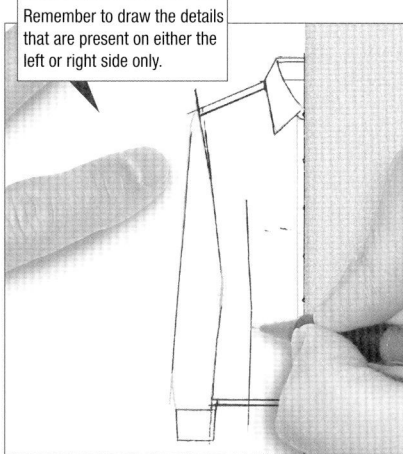

Remember to draw the details that are present on either the left or right side only.

4. Mountain-fold the paper and trace the other half. Once you have drawn both halves, use a thick, soft leaded pencil such as a 6B to fill in the backside of the sketch. Place the tracing paper on top of the Kent paper and transfer the sketch by drawing over it with a mechanical pencil. Then complete it in ink using a drawing pen.

Garment Variations

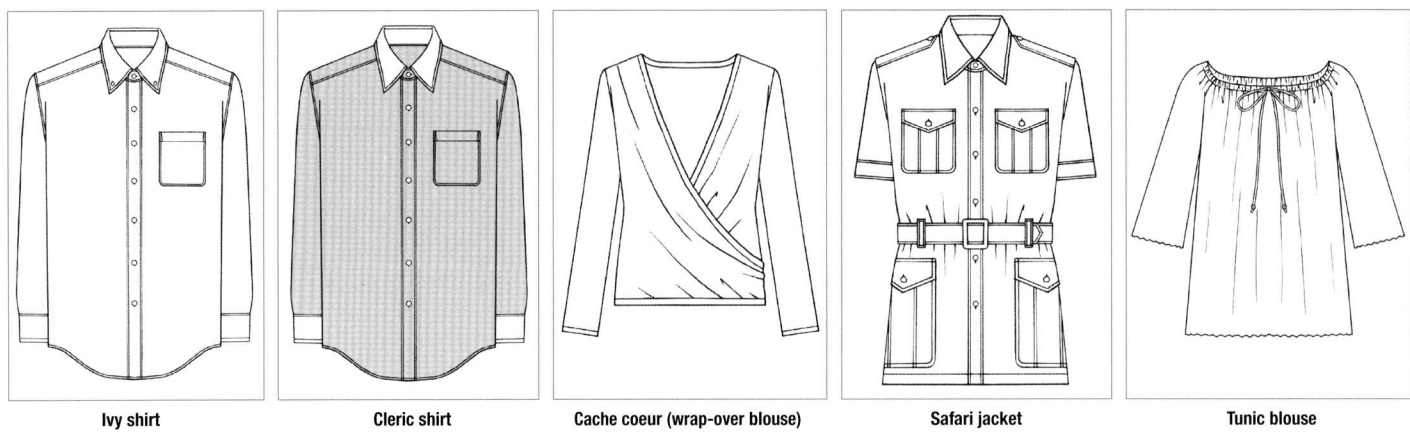

Collar Design Variations

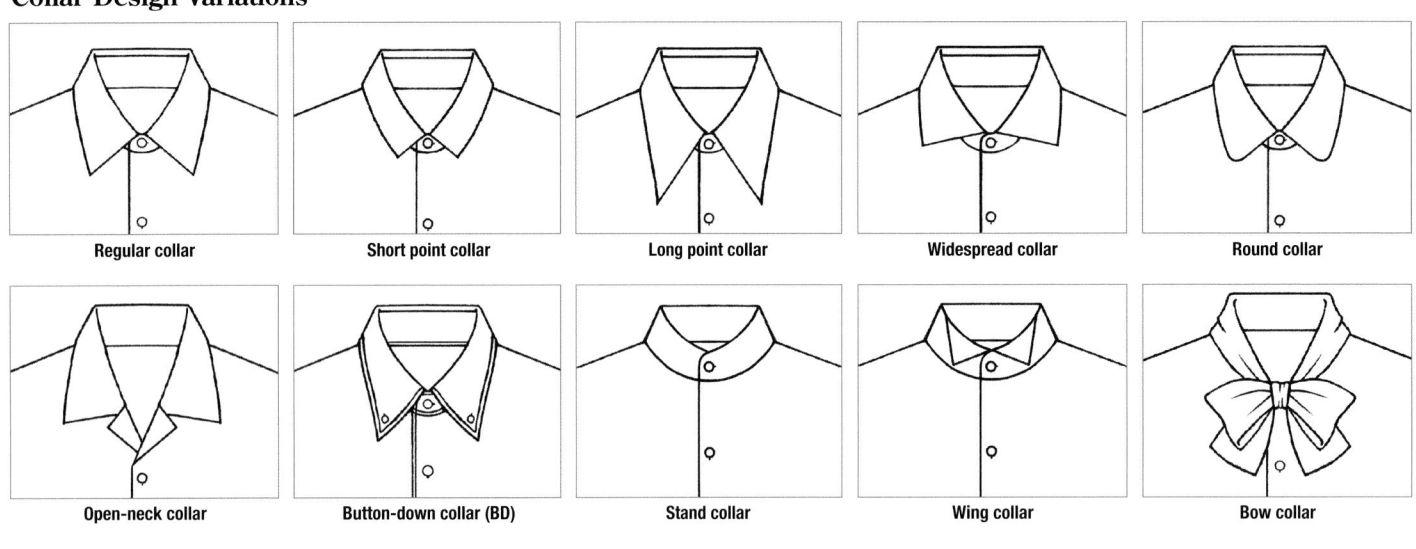

Neckline Design Variations

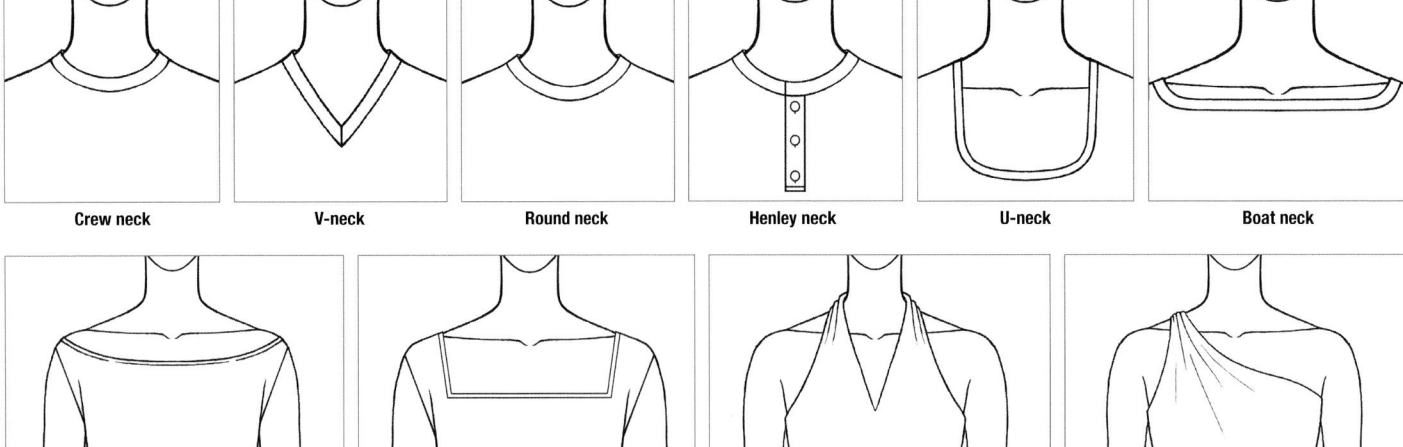

Cuff Design Variations

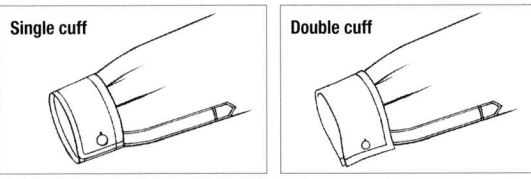

Pocket Design Variations

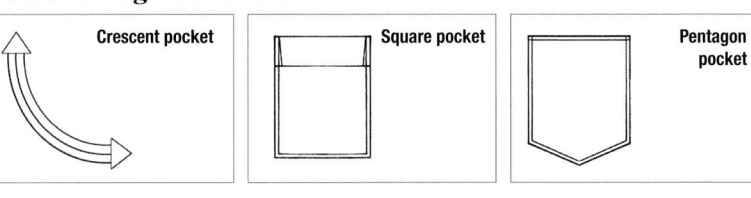

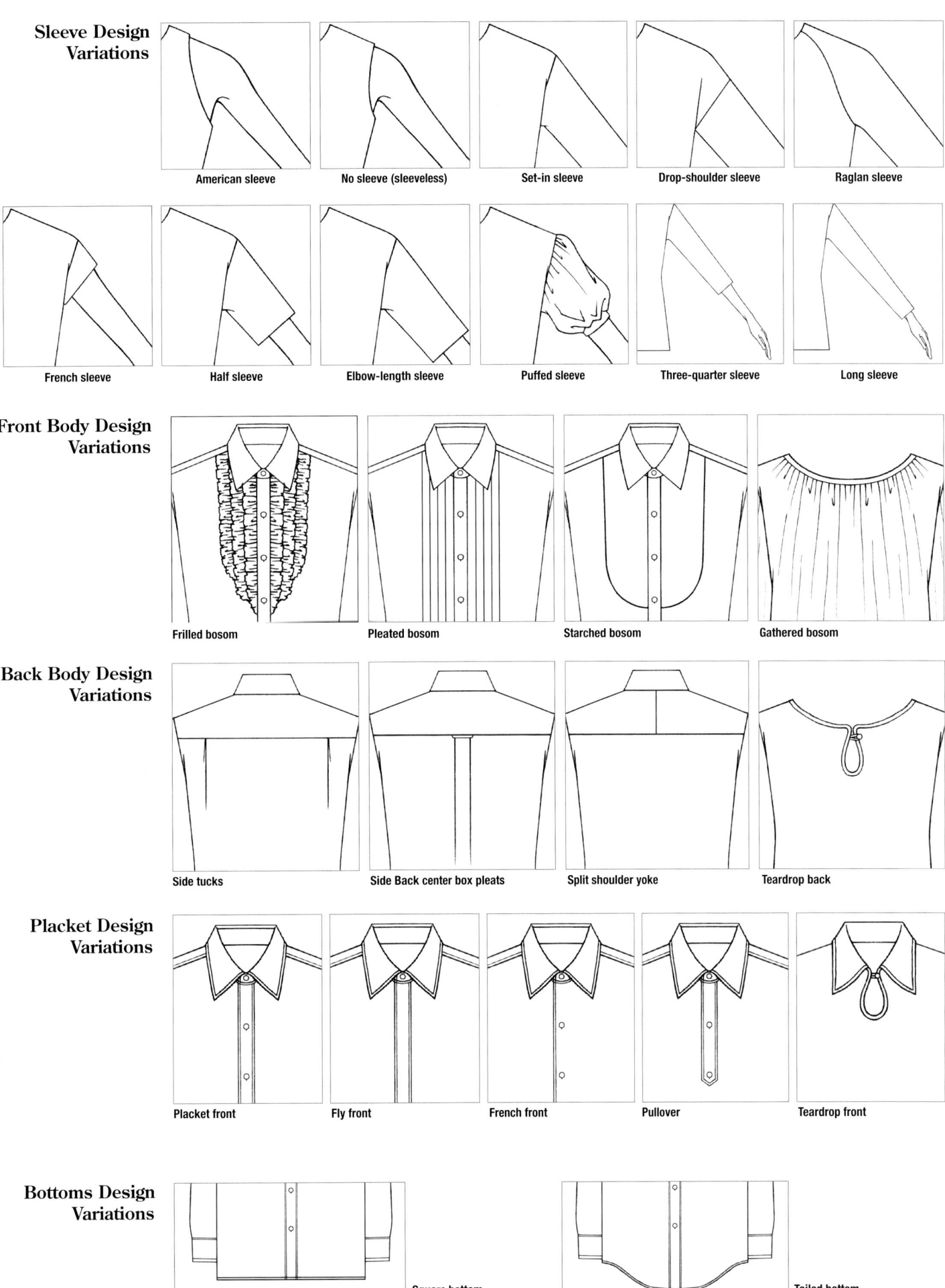

[2] Jackets and Blazers

Although in the broad sense, these include all upper garments including jumpers, the tailored jackets and blazers which are mainly worn by business persons are introduced here as examples.

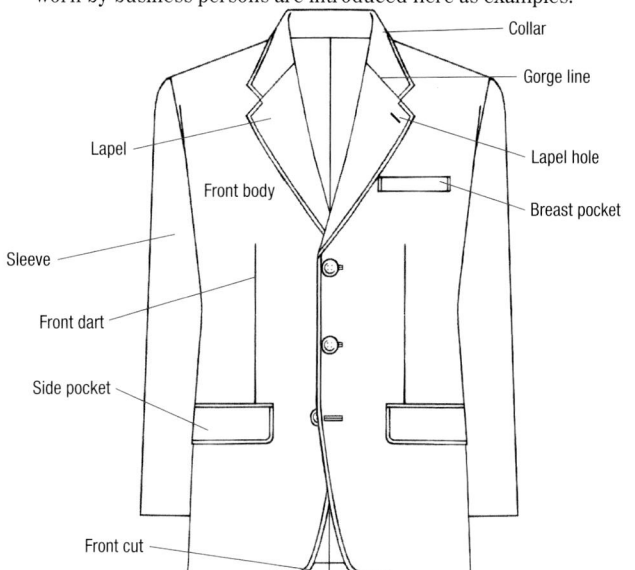

Tailored Jacket
(Three button single-breasted)

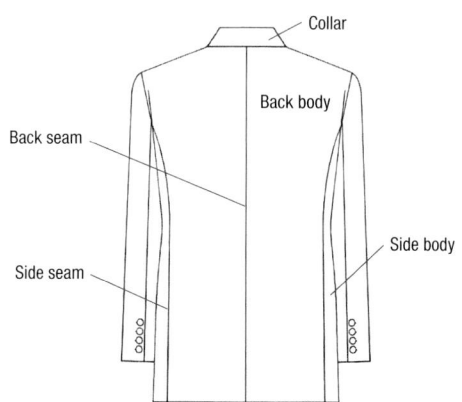

Drawing Method

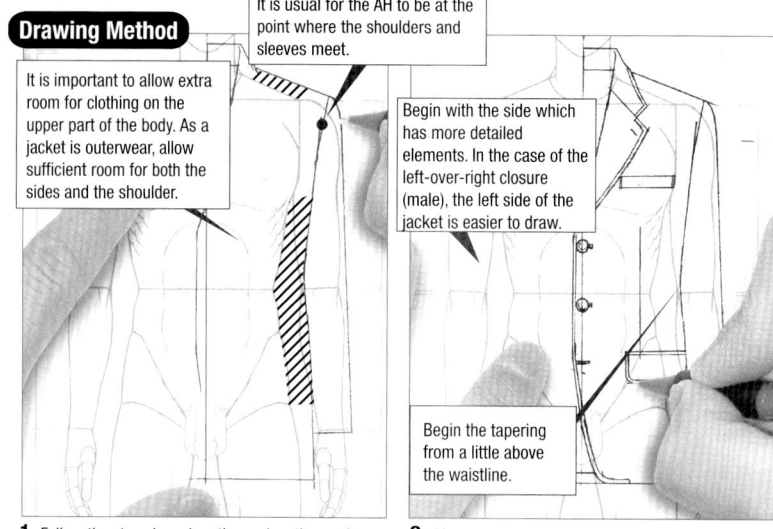

It is important to allow extra room for clothing on the upper part of the body. As a jacket is outerwear, allow sufficient room for both the sides and the shoulder.

It is usual for the AH to be at the point where the shoulders and sleeves meet.

Begin with the side which has more detailed elements. In the case of the left-over-right closure (male), the left side of the jacket is easier to draw.

Begin the tapering from a little above the waistline.

1. Follow the steps based on the explanation under "How to Draw" on page 55. Secure the tracing paper to the copy of the body and begin drawing with the silhouette. First draw the straight lines using a ruler.

2. After completing the silhouette, draw details such as the collar and other structural lines.

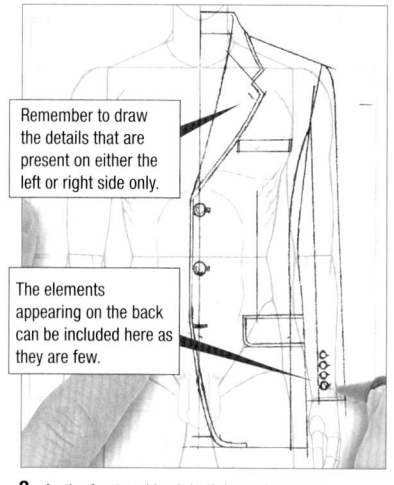

Remember to draw the details that are present on either the left or right side only.

The elements appearing on the back can be included here as they are few.

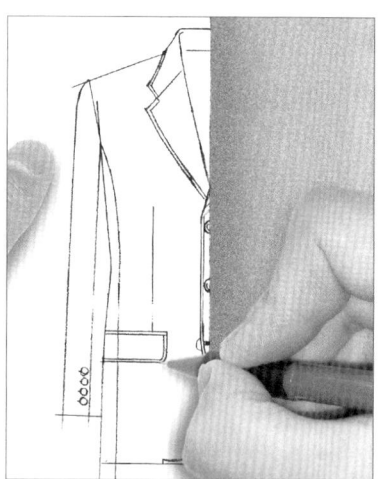

3. As the front and back both have the same silhouette, it is a good idea to combine them.

4. Mountain-fold the paper and trace the other half. Once you have drawn both halves, use a thick, soft leaded pencil such as a 6B to fill in the backside of the sketch. Place the tracing paper on top of the Kent paper and transfer the sketch by drawing over it with a mechanical pencil. Then complete it in ink using a drawing pen.

Garment Variations

Double-breasted jacket

Ivy blazer

Club Jacket

Collarless jacket

Short jacket

Chapter 2 : Technical Drawing

Lapel Design Variations

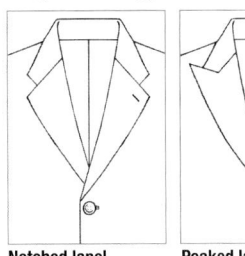 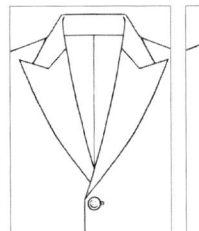 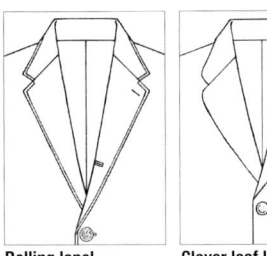 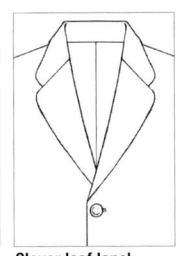

Notched lapel | Peaked lapel | Rolling lapel | Clover leaf lapel

Collar Design Variations

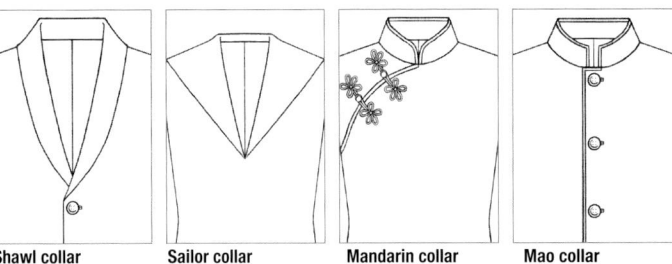

Shawl collar | Sailor collar | Mandarin collar | Mao collar

Front Closure Design Variations

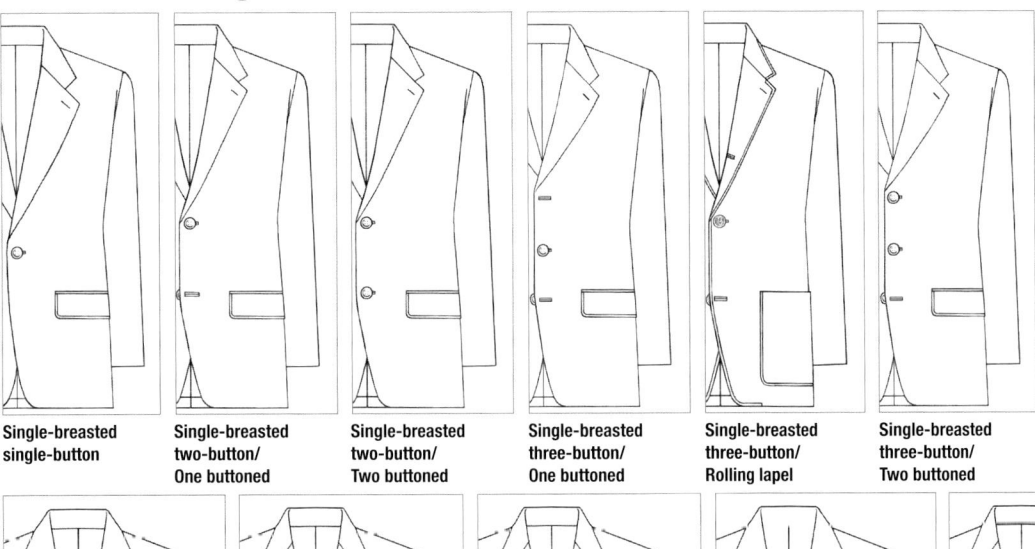

Single-breasted single-button | Single-breasted two-button/One buttoned | Single-breasted two-button/Two buttoned | Single-breasted three-button/One buttoned | Single-breasted three-button/Rolling lapel | Single-breasted three-button/Two buttoned

Double-breasted four-button Spread-out/One buttoned | Double-breasted four-button All-in-line/Top one buttoned | Double-breasted four-button All-in-line/Two buttoned | Double-breasted six-button Spread-out/One buttoned | Double-breasted six-button Spread-out/Two buttoned | Double-breasted six-button All-in-line/Three buttoned

Front Cut Design Variations

Regular cut | Square cut

Vent Design Variations

No vent | Center back vent | Side back vents

Pocket Design Variations

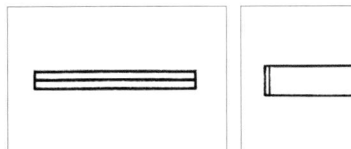 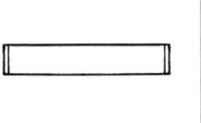 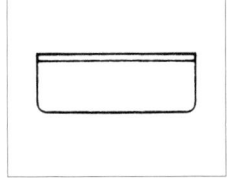 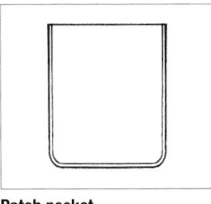 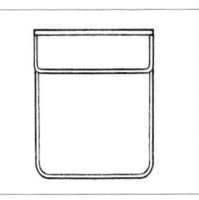 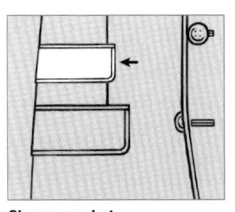

Double welt pocket | Broad welt pocket | Flap pocket | Patch pocket | Patch/flap pocket | Change pocket

[3] Jumpers (Short Jackets)

Upper garments called blouson in French.

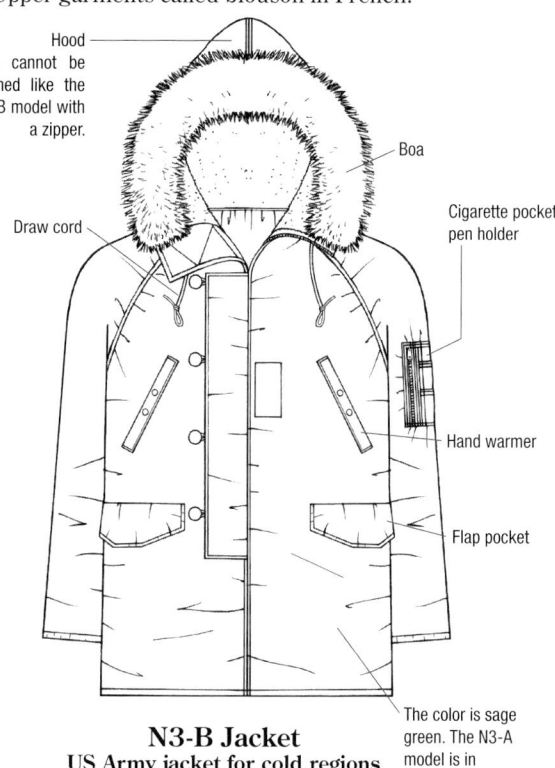

Hood — This cannot be opened like the N2-B model with a zipper.
Boa
Draw cord
Cigarette pocket/pen holder
Hand warmer
Flap pocket

N3-B Jacket
US Army jacket for cold regions

The color is sage green. The N3-A model is in air-force-blue.

Drawing Method

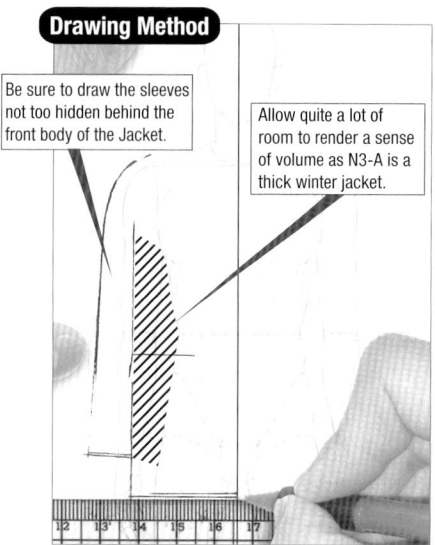

Be sure to draw the sleeves not too hidden behind the front body of the Jacket.

Allow quite a lot of room to render a sense of volume as N3-A is a thick winter jacket.

1. Follow the steps based on the explanation under "How to Draw" on page 55. Secure the tracing paper to the copy of the body and begin drawing with the silhouette. First draw the straight lines using a ruler.

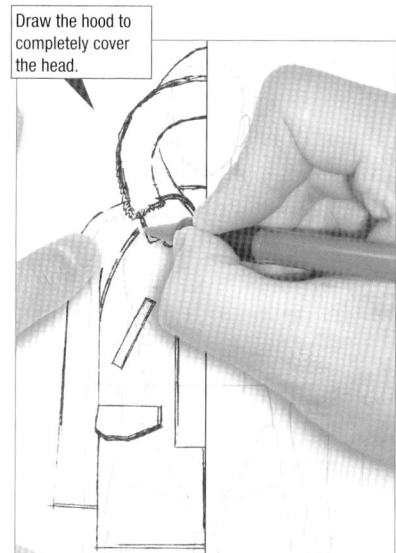

Draw the hood to completely cover the head.

2. Join the straight lines with gentle curves, and draw the garment structure.

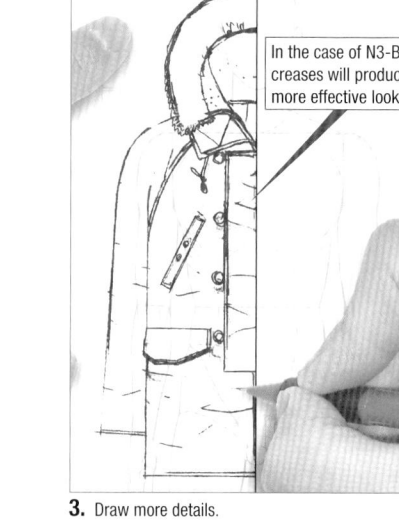

In the case of N3-B, adding creases will produce a more effective look.

3. Draw more details.

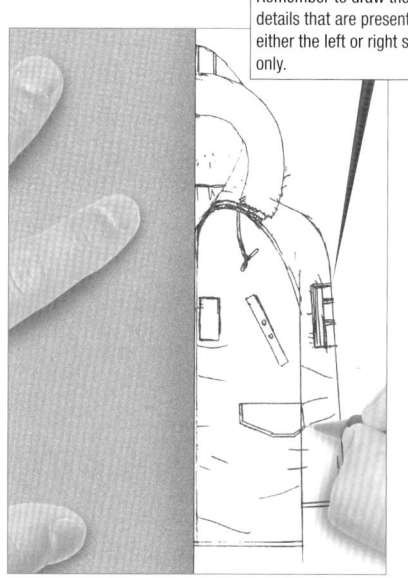

Remember to draw the details that are present on either the left or right side only.

4. Mountain-fold the paper and trace the other half. Once you have drawn both halves, use a thick, soft leaded pencil such as a 6B to fill in the backside of the sketch. Place the tracing paper on top of the Kent paper and transfer the sketch by drawing over it with a mechanical pencil. Then complete it in ink using a drawing pen.

Garment Variations

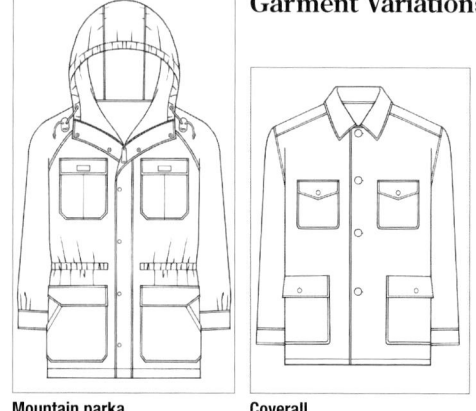

Mountain parka **Coverall**

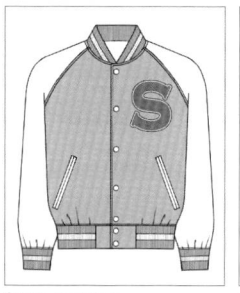
CWU-45P

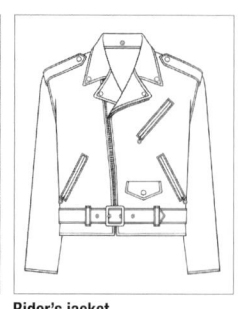
Stadium jumper

Rider's jacket

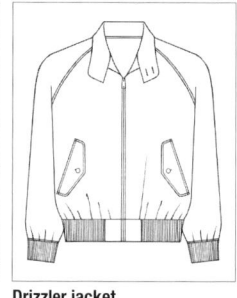
Denim jacket

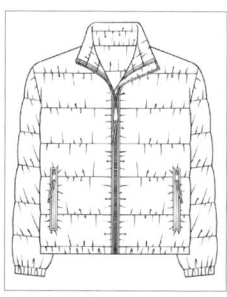
Drizzler jacket

Down jacket

Chapter 2 : Technical Drawing

[4] Knitwear

Garment produced by knitting. Those in jersey material with cutting and sewing processes are called 'cut-and-sewn' knitwear.

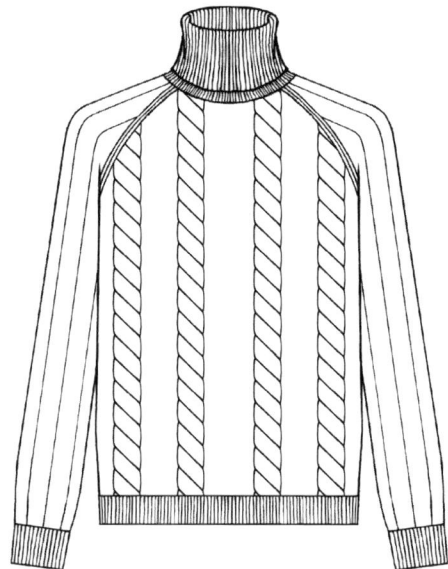

Turtleneck Sweater
A kind of high-necked sweater with the collar turned down.

Drawing Method

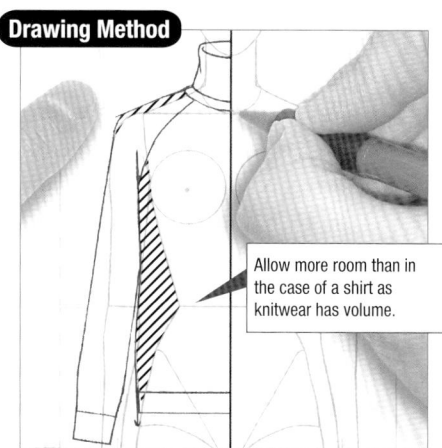

Allow more room than in the case of a shirt as knitwear has volume.

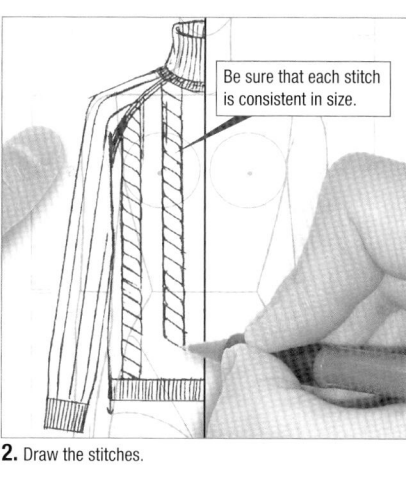

Be sure that each stitch is consistent in size.

1. Follow the steps based on the explanation under "How to Draw" on page 55. Secure the tracing paper to the copy of the body and begin drawing with the silhouette. First draw the straight lines using a ruler.

2. Draw the stitches.

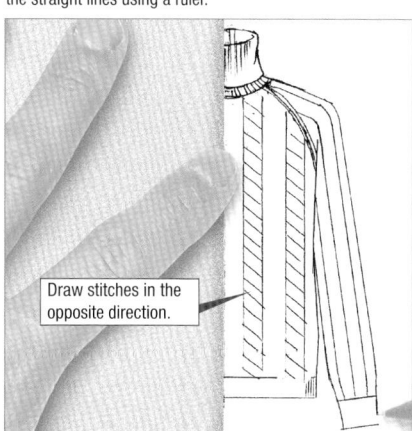

Draw stitches in the opposite direction.

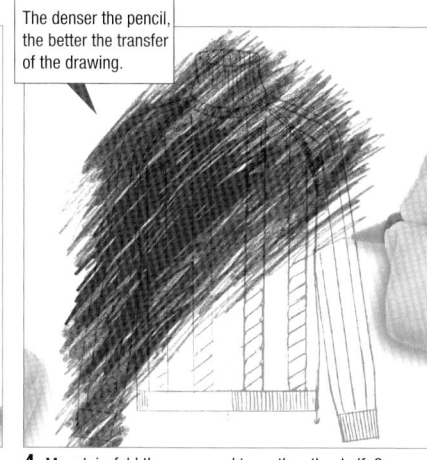

The denser the pencil, the better the transfer of the drawing.

3. When the first half is finished, mountain-fold the tracing paper, and draw the other half.

4. Mountain-fold the paper and trace the other half. Once you have drawn both halves, use a thick, soft leaded pencil such as a 6B to fill in the backside of the sketch. Place the tracing paper on top of the Kent paper and transfer the sketch by drawing over it with a mechanical pencil. Then complete it in ink using a drawing pen.

Garment Variations

Parka

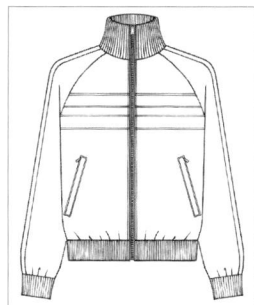
Jersey sportswear

Polo shirt

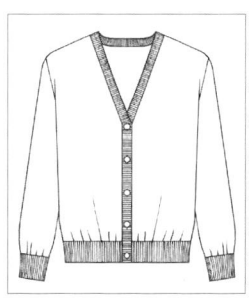
Cardigan

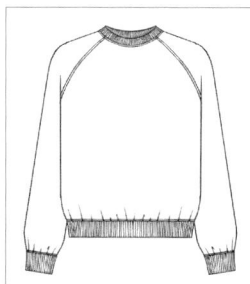
Sweat shirt

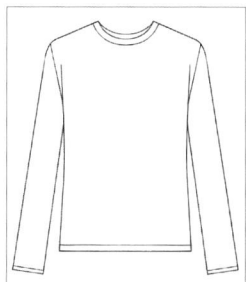
T-shirt

Baseball shirt

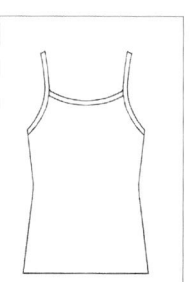
Camisole

Tank-top

[5] Vests (Waistcoats)

A sleeveless garment worn on the upper part of the body.

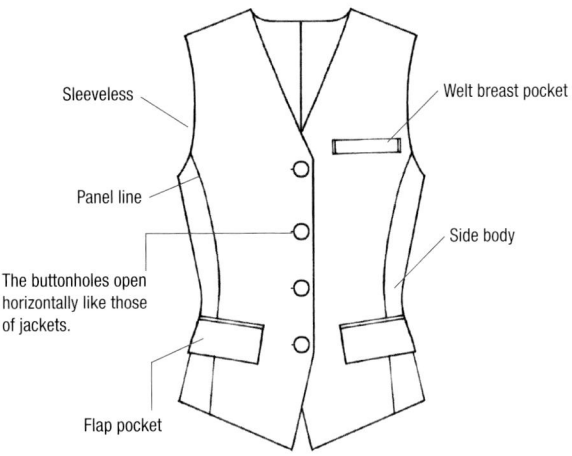

- Sleeveless
- Panel line
- The buttonholes open horizontally like those of jackets.
- Welt breast pocket
- Side body
- Flap pocket

Odd Vest
(Spare vest)

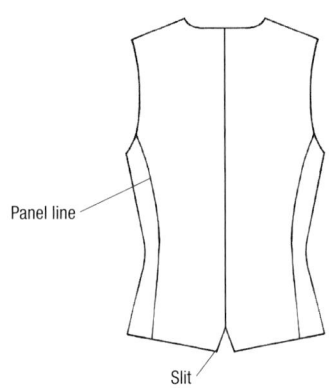

- Panel line
- Slit

Garment Variations

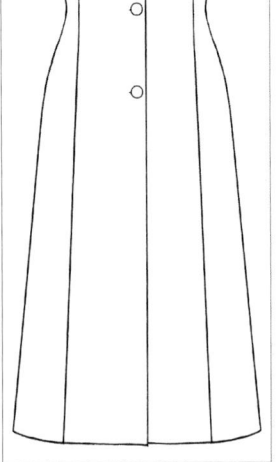
Long gilet

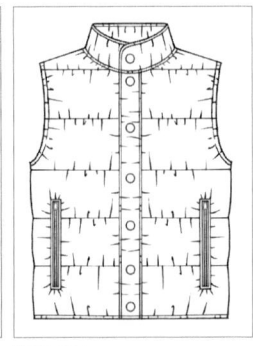
Casual vest

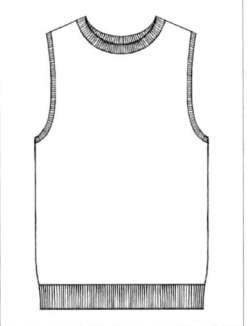
Down vest

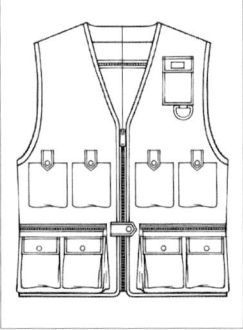
Knitted vest

Fishing vest

Drawing Method

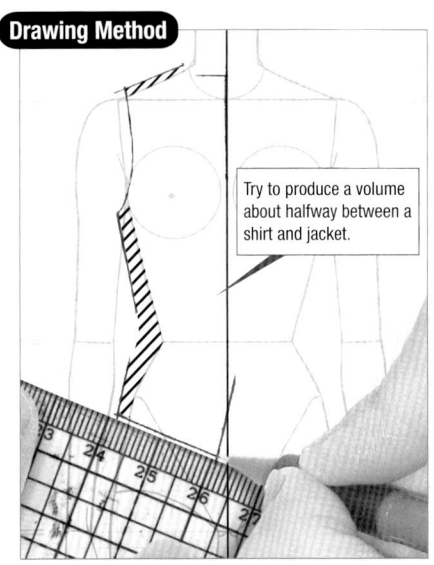

1. Follow the steps based on the explanation under "How to Draw" on page 55. Secure the tracing paper to the copy of the body and begin drawing with the silhouette. First draw the straight lines using a ruler.

Try to produce a volume about halfway between a shirt and jacket.

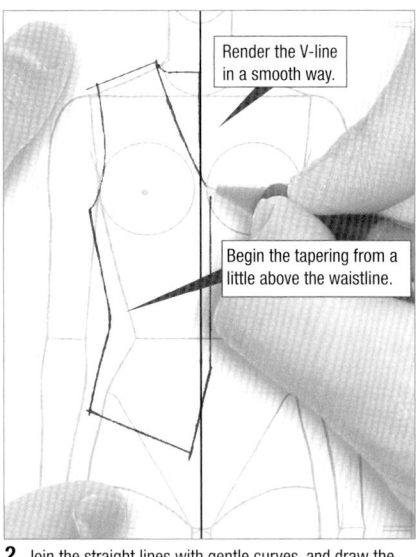

2. Join the straight lines with gentle curves, and draw the garment structure.

Render the V-line in a smooth way.
Begin the tapering from a little above the waistline.

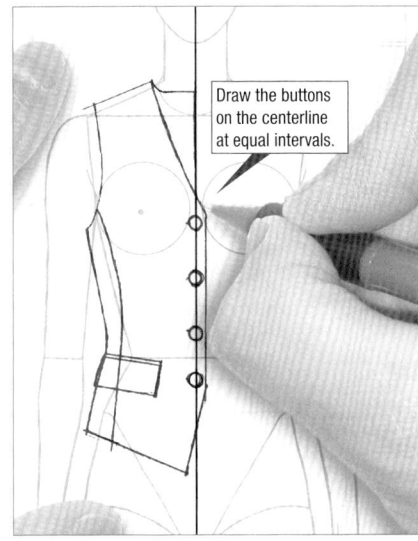

3. Draw more details.

Draw the buttons on the centerline at equal intervals.

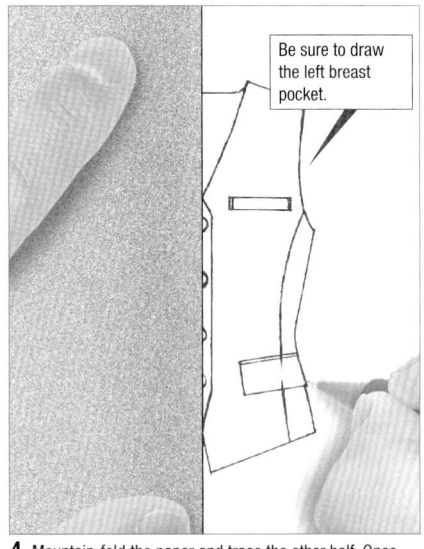

4. Mountain-fold the paper and trace the other half. Once you have drawn both halves, use a thick, soft leaded pencil such as a 6B to fill in the backside of the sketch. Place the tracing paper on top of the Kent paper and transfer the sketch by drawing over it with a mechanical pencil. Then complete it in ink using a drawing pen.

Be sure to draw the left breast pocket.

Chapter 2 : Technical Drawing

[6] Coats

Long outerwear, including short coats (above-knee length), half coats (knee length) and long coats (below-knee length).

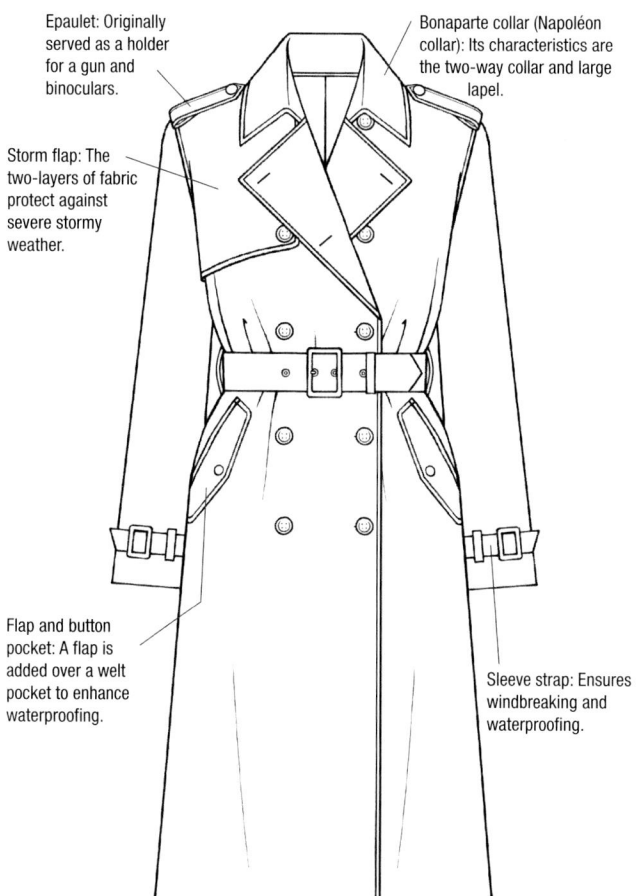

Epaulet: Originally served as a holder for a gun and binoculars.

Bonaparte collar (Napoléon collar): Its characteristics are the two-way collar and large lapel.

Storm flap: The two-layers of fabric protect against severe stormy weather.

Flap and button pocket: A flap is added over a welt pocket to enhance waterproofing.

Sleeve strap: Ensures windbreaking and waterproofing.

Trench Coat
During World War I, the British Army developed this design for trench warfare.

Drawing Method

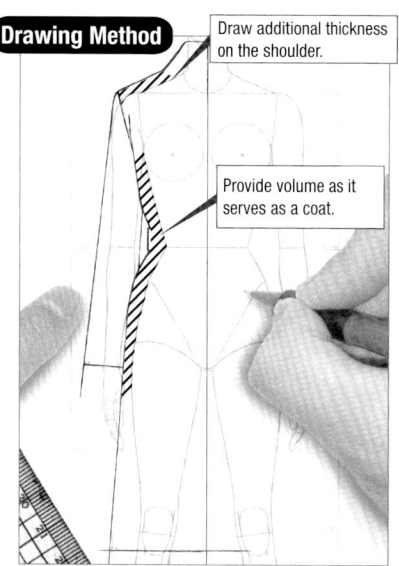

Draw additional thickness on the shoulder.

Provide volume as it serves as a coat.

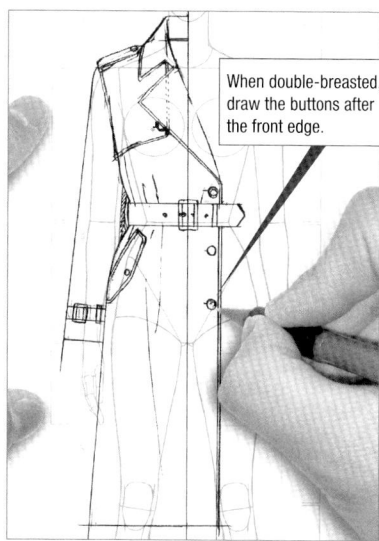

When double-breasted, draw the buttons after the front edge.

1. Follow the steps based on the explanation under "How to Draw" on page 55. Secure the tracing paper to the copy of the body and begin drawing with the silhouette. First draw the straight lines using a ruler.

2. Join the straight lines with gentle curves, and draw the garment structure.

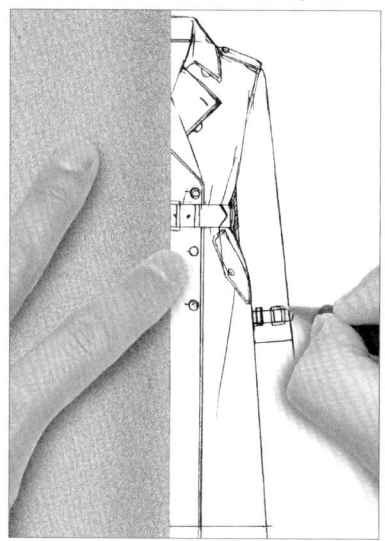

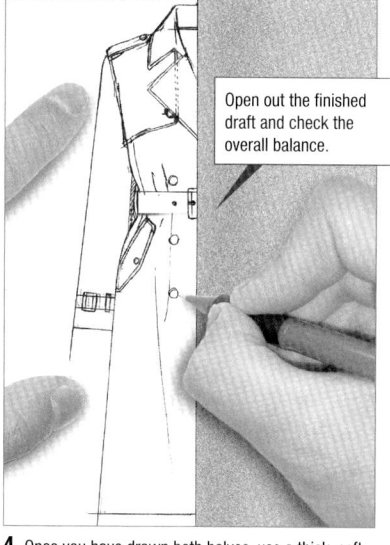

Open out the finished draft and check the overall balance.

3. Mountain-fold the paper and trace the other half.

4. Once you have drawn both halves, use a thick, soft leaded pencil such as a 6B to fill in the backside of the sketch. Place the tracing paper on top of the Kent paper and transfer the sketch by drawing over it with a mechanical pencil. Then complete it in ink using a drawing pen.

Garment Variations

Princess coat

Duffle coat

Pea coat

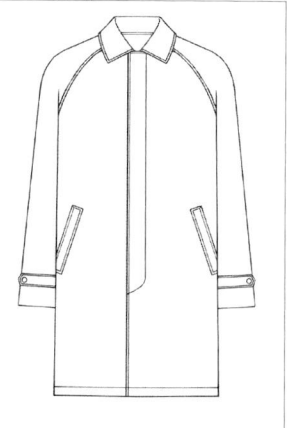

Soutien collar coat

63

[7] Pants/Trousers

A garment covering each leg separately.

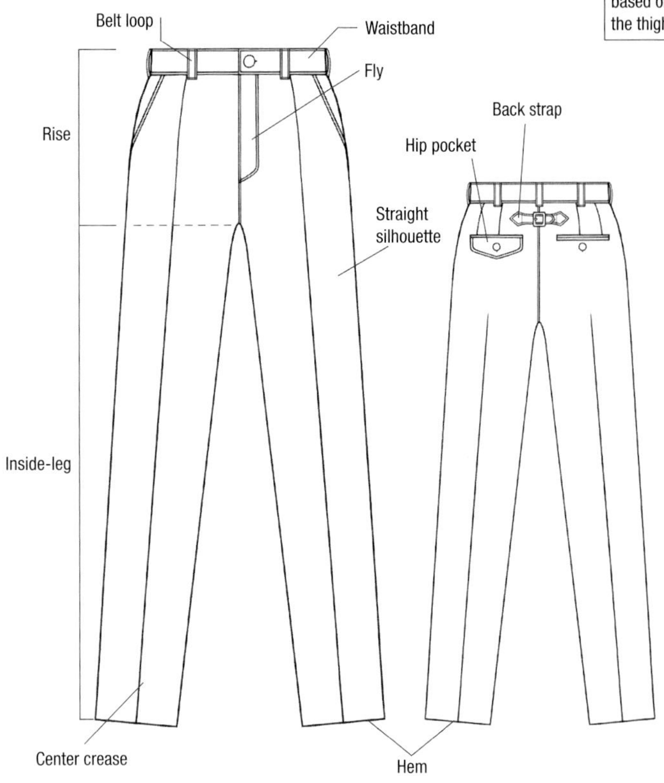

Straight Pants

Labels: Belt loop, Waistband, Fly, Back strap, Hip pocket, Straight silhouette, Rise, Inside-leg, Center crease, Hem

Drawing Method

The volume of the pant leg should be based on the size of the thigh.

The waistband is in principle at the height of the navel, but varies depending on the fashion.

For men's pants, allow room for the genitals.

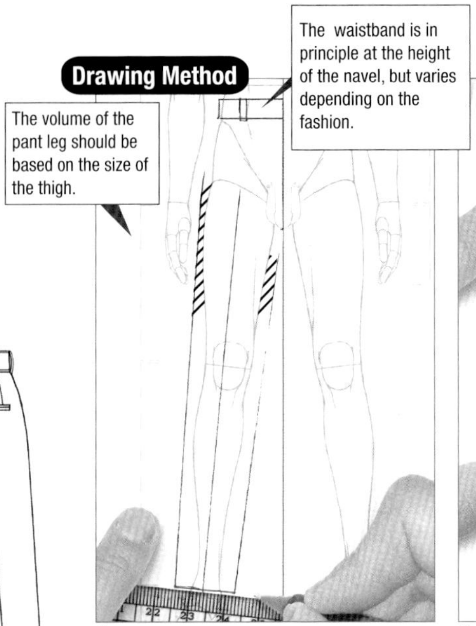

1. Follow the steps based on the explanation under "How to Draw" on page 55. Secure the tracing paper to the copy of the body and begin drawing with the silhouette. First draw the straight lines using a ruler.

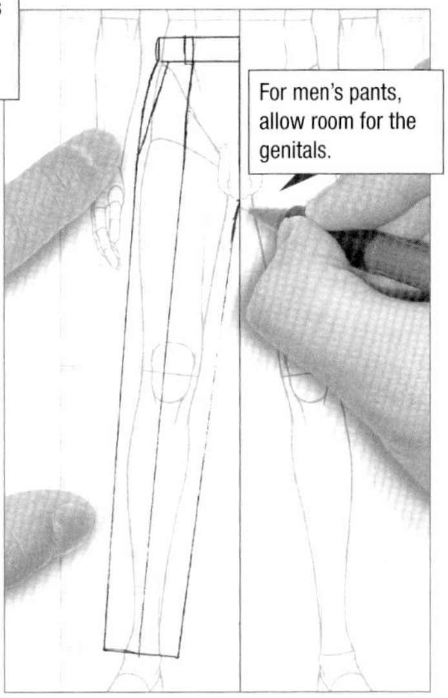

2. Join the straight lines with gentle curves, and draw the garment structure.

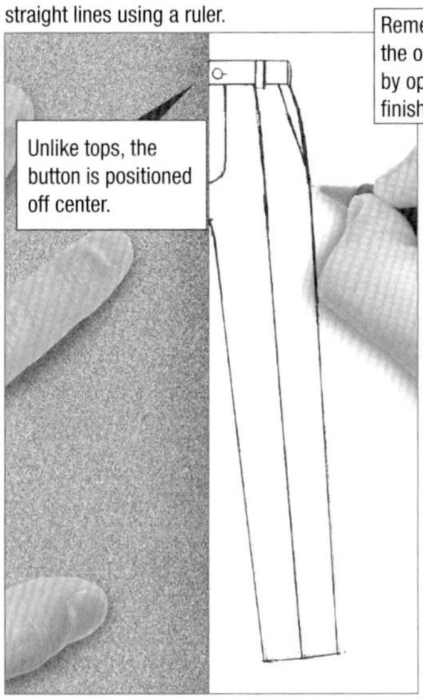

Unlike tops, the button is positioned off center.

Remember to check the overall balance, by opening out the finished draft.

3. Mountain-fold the paper and trace the other half.

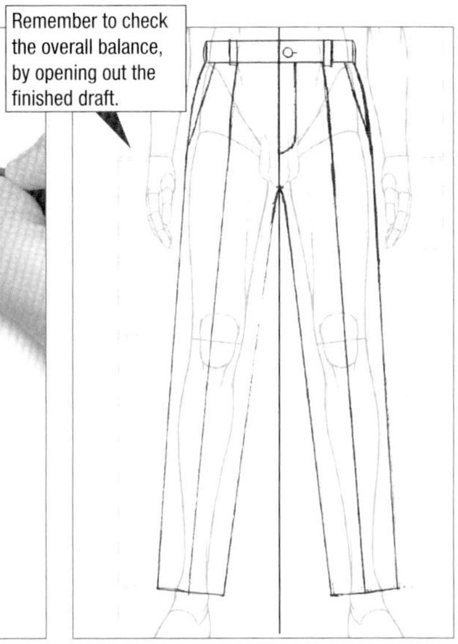

4. Once you have drawn both halves, use a thick, soft leaded pencil such as a 6B to fill in the backside of the sketch. Place the tracing paper on top of the Kent paper and transfer the sketch by drawing over it with a mechanical pencil. Then complete it in ink using a drawing pen.

Garment Variations (Silhouette)

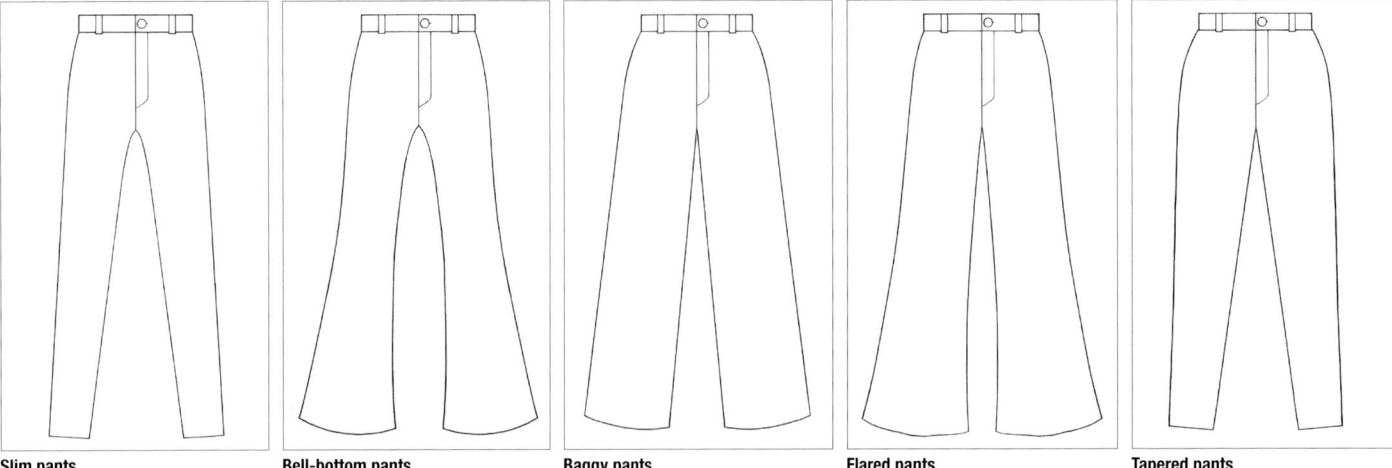

Slim pants | Bell-bottom pants | Baggy pants | Flared pants | Tapered pants

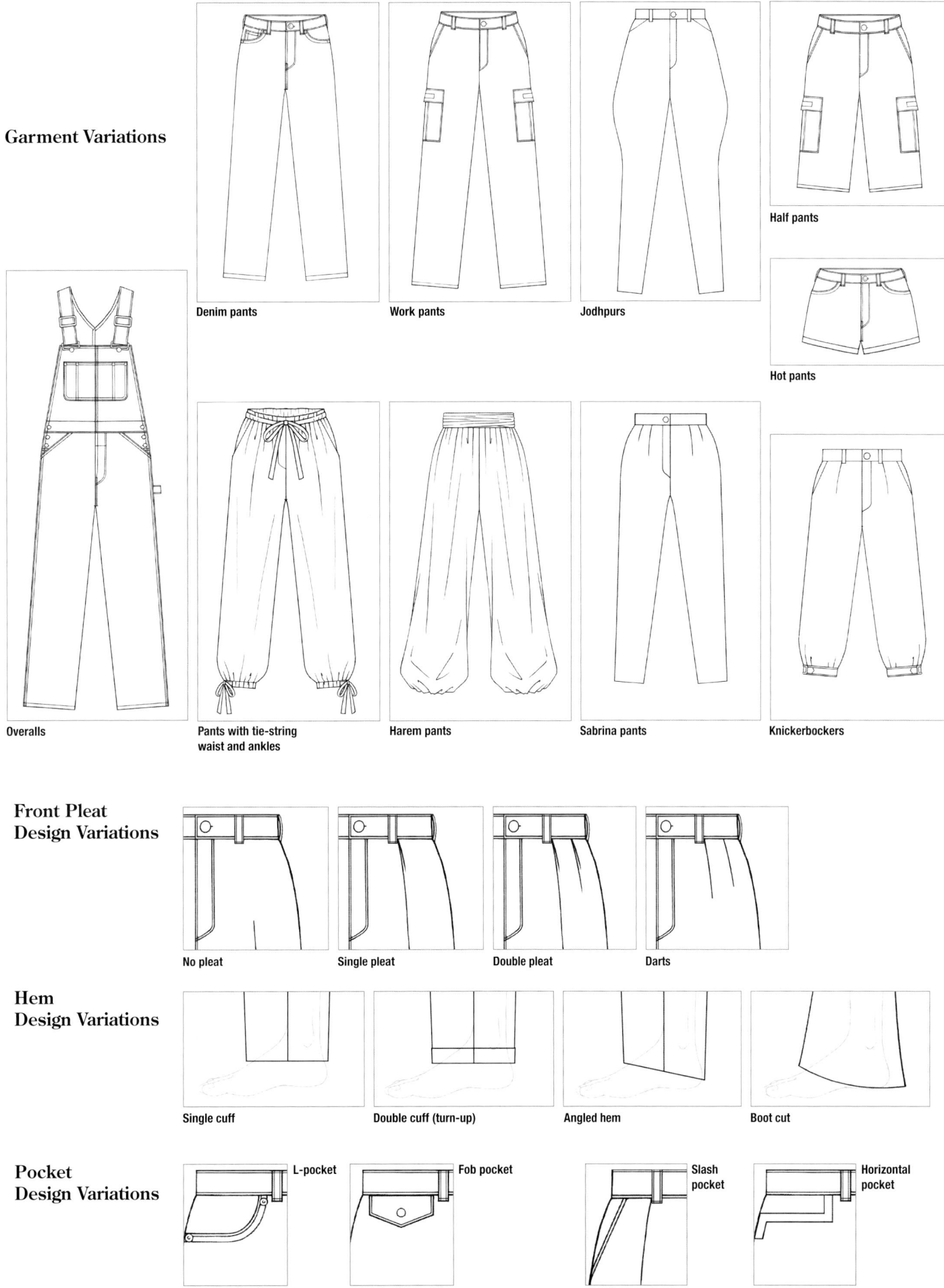

[8] Dresses

Clothing with top and bottom as one piece.

Drawing Method

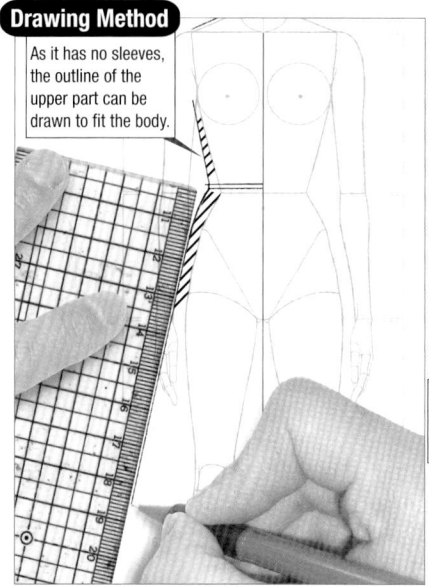

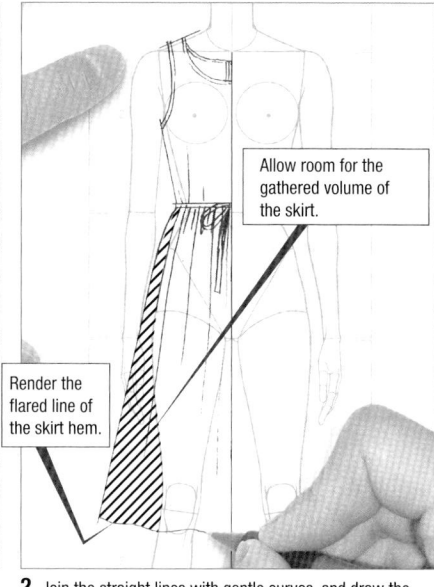

Allow room for the gathered volume of the skirt.

Render the flared line of the skirt hem.

As it has no sleeves, the outline of the upper part can be drawn to fit the body.

1. Follow the steps based on the explanation under "How to Draw" on page 55. Secure the tracing paper to the copy of the body and begin drawing with the silhouette. First draw the straight lines using a ruler.

2. Join the straight lines with gentle curves, and draw the garment structure.

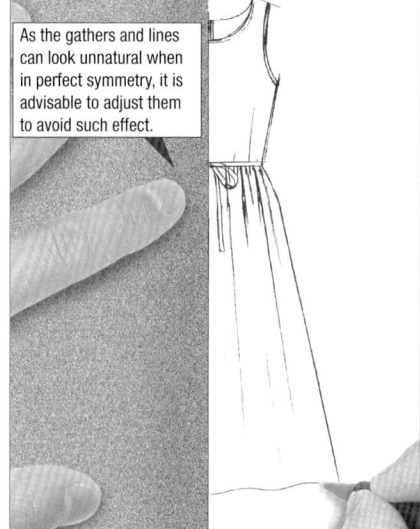

As the gathers and lines can look unnatural when in perfect symmetry, it is advisable to adjust them to avoid such effect.

When filled in well, the transfer of the drawing can be made successfully.

3. Mountain-fold the paper and trace the other half.

4. Once you have drawn both halves, use a thick, soft leaded pencil such as a 6B to fill in the backside of the sketch. Place the tracing paper on top of the Kent paper and transfer the sketch by drawing over it with a mechanical pencil. Then complete it in ink using a drawing pen.

Garment Variations (Silhouette)

Dress with shoulder bows

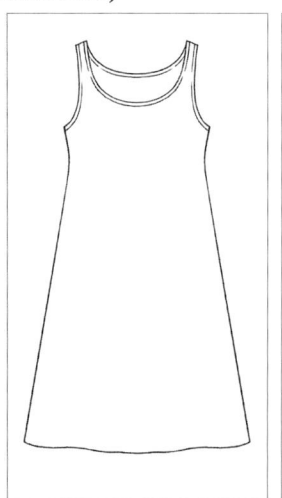
Camisole style dress

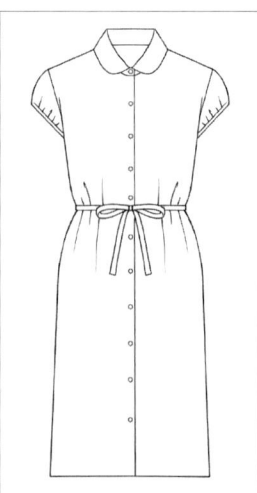
Dress with French sleeves

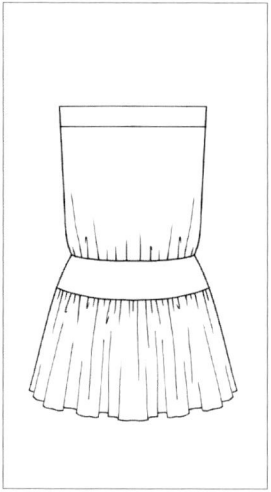
Strapless décolleté-type dress

[9] Skirts

Outer garments hanging from the waist with no leg separation. Originally meant the lower part of a dress.

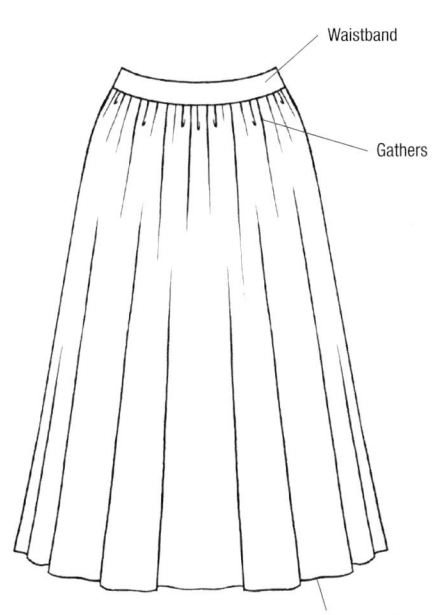

Gathered Skirt

- Waistband
- Gathers
- Draw the hem part three-dimensionally, as it has a full flare.

Drawing Method

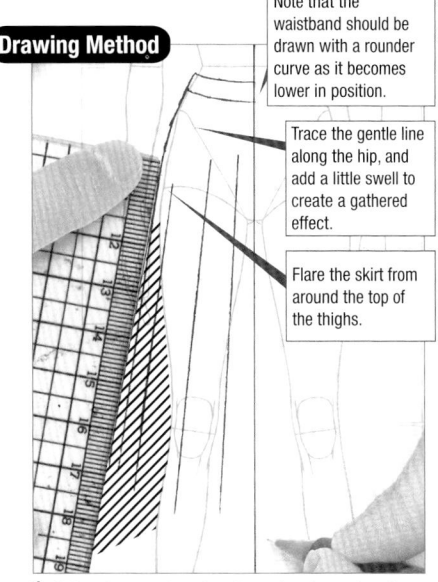

- Note that the waistband should be drawn with a rounder curve as it becomes lower in position.
- Trace the gentle line along the hip, and add a little swell to create a gathered effect.
- Flare the skirt from around the top of the thighs.

1. Follow the steps based on the explanation under "How to Draw" on page 55. Secure the tracing paper to the copy of the body and begin drawing with the silhouette. First draw the straight lines using a ruler.

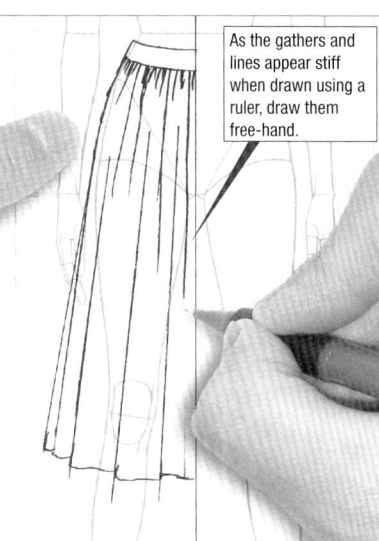

- As the gathers and lines appear stiff when drawn using a ruler, draw them free-hand.

2. Draw the garment structure.

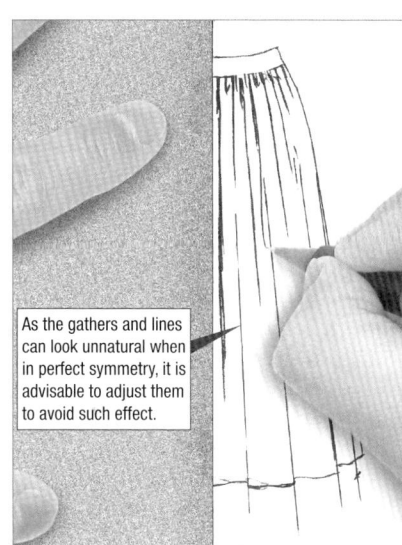

- As the gathers and lines can look unnatural when in perfect symmetry, it is advisable to adjust them to avoid such effect.

3. Mountain-fold the paper and trace the other half. Once you have drawn both halves, use a thick, soft leaded pencil such as a 6B to fill in the backside of the sketch. Place the tracing paper on top of the Kent paper and transfer the sketch by drawing over it with a mechanical pencil. Then complete it in ink using a drawing pen.

Design Variations Shown by Outlines

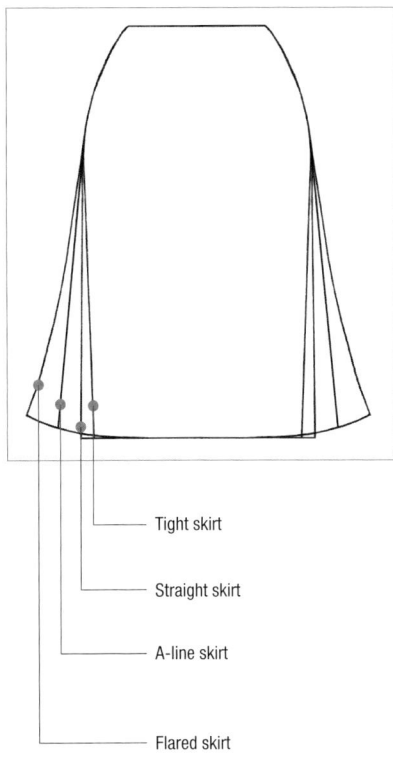

- Tight skirt
- Straight skirt
- A-line skirt
- Flared skirt

Design Variations Shown by Length

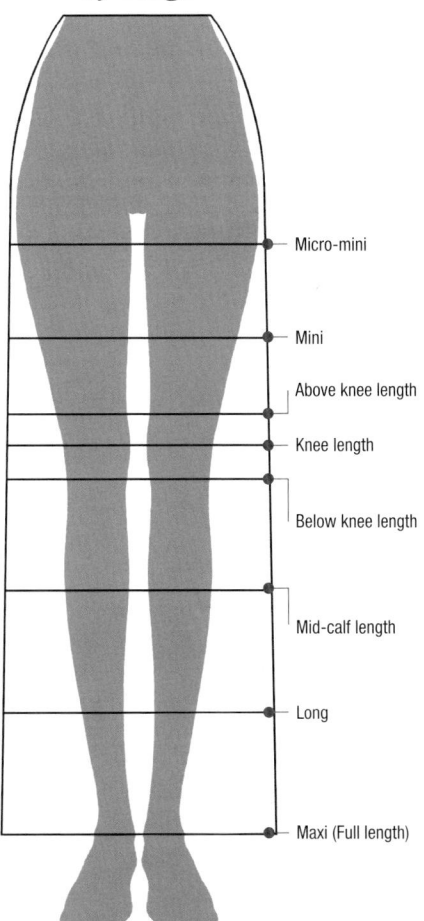

- Micro-mini
- Mini
- Above knee length
- Knee length
- Below knee length
- Mid-calf length
- Long
- Maxi (Full length)

Garment Variations

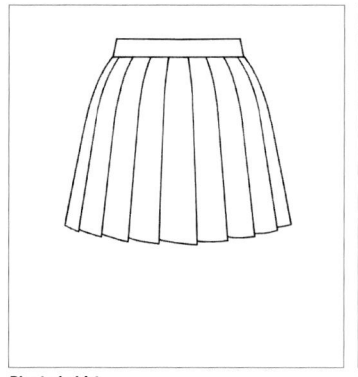
Pleated skirt

Wrapover skirt

Hip-hanger skirt

Irregular hemline skirt

Ruffled skirt

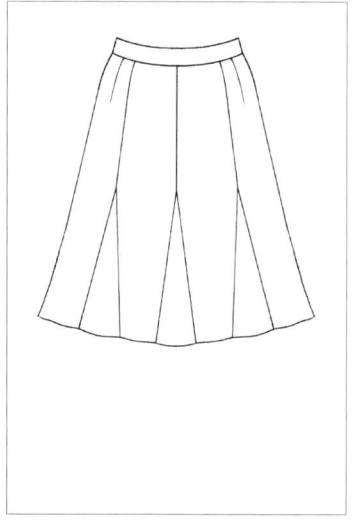
Gored skirt

Pleat Design Variation

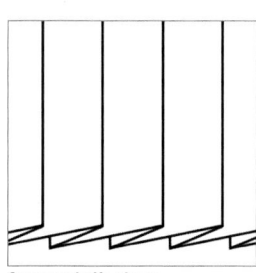
One-way knife pleats

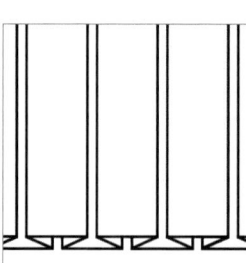
Box pleats

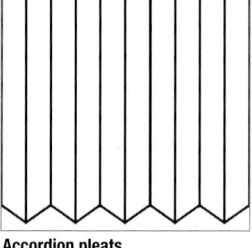
Accordion pleats

Sunburst pleats

Chapter 3
Fashion Drawing

Fashion drawing refers to the drawing of a dressed figure, which places emphasis on the total balance, including a combination of garments, the way of dressing, a sense of volume and other elements. Unlike technical drawing, which focuses on the clothes configuration, fashion drawing serves to present comprehensive images of styling, coordination, hair and make-up three-dimensionally. It is vital to have sufficient understanding of the three major elements of fashion design, in order to master fashion drawing.

The Three Major Elements of Fashion Design

(1) Silhouette
This refers to the outline of the overall garment, which is the most important element in fashion design. Draw the figure while allowing sufficient room (a sense of volume) for the clothes in relation to the body, as learned in Chapter 1.

(2) Details
This includes detailing of parts of the clothes, as well as the design of accompanying items such as belts, hats and shoes. Even with the same silhouette, if the details are different, innumerable variations are possible. Another important design point is the delicately varying length of clothing.

(3) Colors, materials and patterns
In the apparel industry, it is common to first decide on the fabric and then to design the garments. Even when the design is the same, simply changing the material or color can create an entirely different impression. Try to select fabrics that match the style.

When these three points are followed in this order, fashion drawings with clear design points will result. Use a pencil or pen for (1) and (2) as they are line drawings, and paints and other coloring tools for (3).

[1] Dressing

The most important points to consider when adding clothes to your drawing are the silhouette and a sense of volume. Even when the item of clothing is the same, by changing the sense of volume or the size, an entirely different design is achieved. The Mod-style of the sixties consisted of a suit that was so tight-fitting that the wearer could hardly sit down, while the style of the Backstreet Boys that was popular in the eighties consisted of extremely baggy, oversized clothing. In this way fashion changes from era to era. Also, if the length of clothing on the same silhouette is changed, the design changes. This is especially true in the case of skirts, for which length is such a vital design point that the name of the item changes depending upon its length.

Necessary materials:
- Copies of the five major basic body poses, shown in the following pages:
  (1) Erect frontal view (p.14 and 15)
  (2) Frontal pose with weight on one leg (p.26)
  (3) Erect diagonal view (p.17)
  (4) Diagonal pose with weight on one leg with the pivotal leg at the back (left in p.31 and p.32)
  (5) Diagonal pose with weight on one leg with the pivotal leg in front (left in p.34 and p.35)
  (In order to fully understand the positions of all the joints such as the waist, groin and knees, use mannequins instead of nude figures.)
- B4-size sketchpad
- B or softer pencil or mechanical pencil (Hard leads can damage the paper).

Drawing Method

Blouses

While paying attention to volume and length, clearly express the outline of the complete clothing. Ignore creases and other details, and try to draw the lines as simply as possible.

Adjust the shoulder line depending on the thickness of the clothing. If it is thin, position the line near to the body, if thick, position it farther away.

When drawing any top, pay extra attention to the arms. As they have the greatest movement, unless sufficient space is provided in the body of a shirt, their movement will be restricted. So allow extra space at the sides.

Draw the collar, pockets and buttons while paying attention to their position in relation to the total balance of the body, how big they are, and what shape they should be.

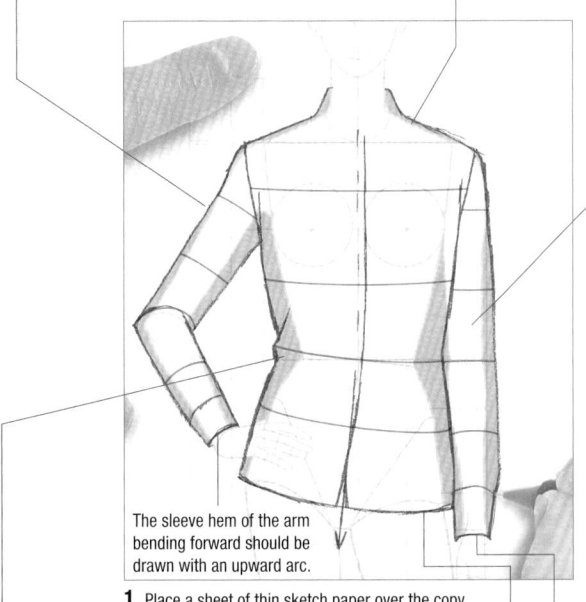

The sleeve hem of the arm bending forward should be drawn with an upward arc.

1. Place a sheet of thin sketch paper over the copy of the body and draw it.

2. Add details to the blouse.

Unless the figure is clad in full body tights, extra space should be allowed in various places. This influences the sense of volume in the clothing.

A hem with a downward arc. As explained on p.20, the eye level is in the area of the FNP (front neck point). This is why the hem should be drawn with a downward arc.

As the arm bends slightly forward, even when hanging straight down, the edge of the cuff should be drawn as a slight arc.

In areas around the joints where creases often occur, add "looseness" to produce a 3D effect.

Don't forget to include the structural lines such as those for the armholes, darts and yokes.

Chapter 3 : Fashion Drawing

Horizontal creases that are strongly influenced by human tensile strength.

Vertical creases that are strongly influenced by gravity

When the weight is placed on one leg, the hemline will angle in line with the waistline.

3. Add creases to complete the drawing.

Kinds of creases and their distribution — There are two kinds of crease.

1. Vertical creases that are created by gravity (indicated here by the dark arrows). They often arise in areas with volume.
2. Horizontal creases caused by the strength of humans pulling the cloth (indicated here by the light arrows). They often arise in areas where the cloth fits around the joints.
Allocating these two types of creases in a well-balanced way produces a 3D effect.

4. Apply the ink.
Using a soft lead pencil such as a 6B, fill in the backside of the sketch. Place the tracing paper on top of the Kent paper and transfer the sketch by drawing over it with a hard lead mechanical pencil. Then complete it in ink using a drawing pen. Another method is to use a light table to illuminate the drawing from behind and then to trace the image directly using a drawing pen. In this case, you can color with colored pencils.

Erect frontal view

The erect frontal pose is the style of drawing closest to "hanger illustration", which depicts garments as if on a hanger. However, adding creases is recommended for a 3D effect.

Small circles indicate tension points.

Vertical creases that are strongly influenced by gravity.

Diagonal view with the weight on one leg (pivotal leg behind)

Horizontal creases that are strongly influenced by human tensile strength.

Allow more room in the back than in the front.

Erect diagonal view

Because blouses are inner garments, show the swelling of the chest but be careful to allow enough room to avoid a too-tightly fitting look, which reveals the shape of the breasts too much.

Apart from joints such as the shoulders, elbows and waist, adding creases to the chest swelling also, creates a more 3D effect.

Diagonal view with the weight on one leg (pivotal leg in front)

When the weight is on one leg, the hemline will angle in line with the waistline.

71

T-Shirt (Regular size)

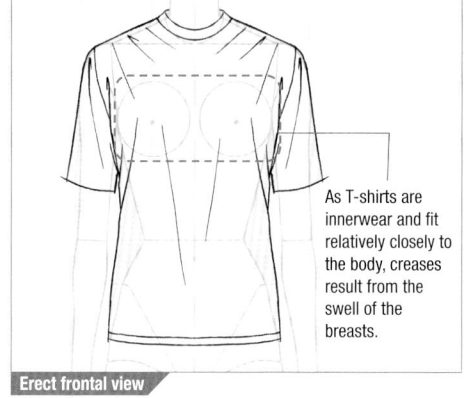

As T-shirts are innerwear and fit relatively closely to the body, creases result from the swell of the breasts.

Erect frontal view

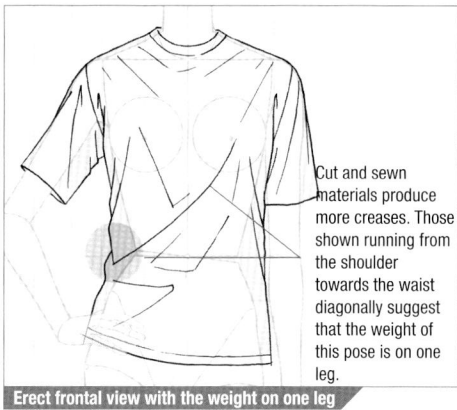

Cut and sewn materials produce more creases. Those shown running from the shoulder towards the waist diagonally suggest that the weight of this pose is on one leg.

Erect frontal view with the weight on one leg

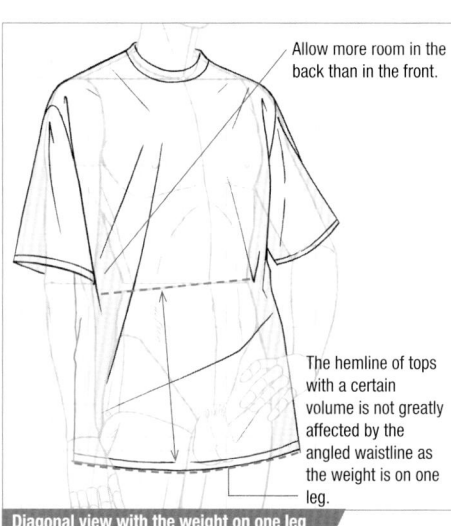

T-shirts are innerwear and are often worn next to the skin, but are roomy and breathable.

When the weight is on one leg, the hemline will angle in line with the waistline.

Diagonal view with the weight on one leg (pivotal leg behind)

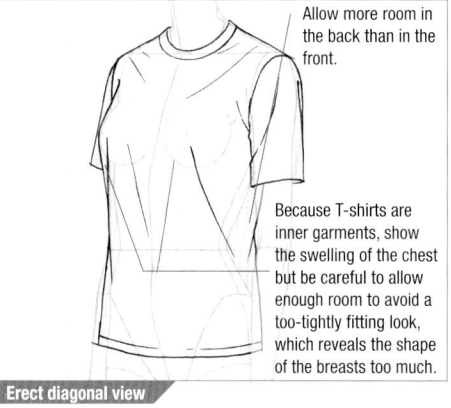

Allow more room in the back than in the front.

Because T-shirts are inner garments, show the swelling of the chest but be careful to allow enough room to avoid a too-tightly fitting look, which reveals the shape of the breasts too much.

Erect diagonal view

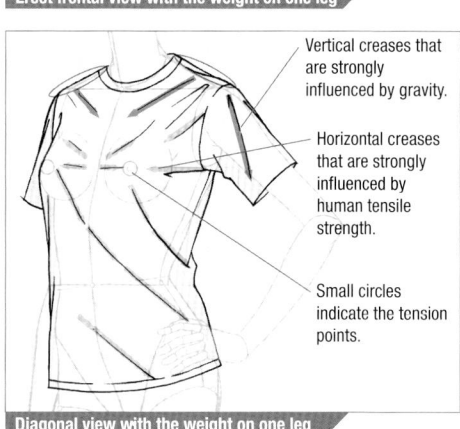

Vertical creases that are strongly influenced by gravity.

Horizontal creases that are strongly influenced by human tensile strength.

Small circles indicate the tension points.

Diagonal view with the weight on one leg

T-Shirt (Baggy fit)

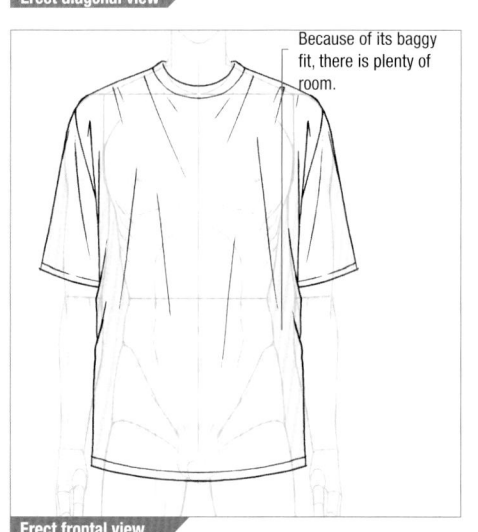

Because of its baggy fit, there is plenty of room.

Erect frontal view

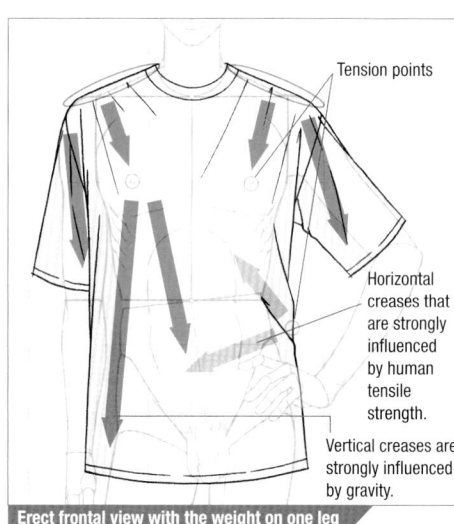

Tension points

Horizontal creases that are strongly influenced by human tensile strength.

Vertical creases are strongly influenced by gravity.

Erect frontal view with the weight on one leg

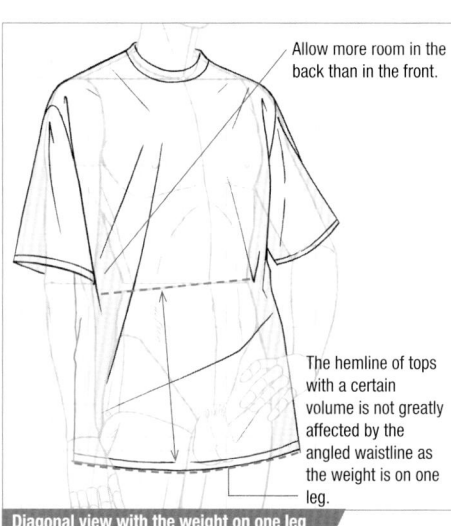

Allow more room in the back than in the front.

The hemline of tops with a certain volume is not greatly affected by the angled waistline as the weight is on one leg.

Diagonal view with the weight on one leg (pivotal leg behind)

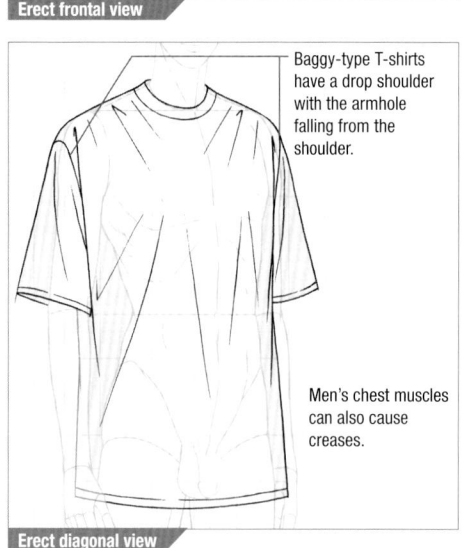

Baggy-type T-shirts have a drop shoulder with the armhole falling from the shoulder.

Men's chest muscles can also cause creases.

Erect diagonal view

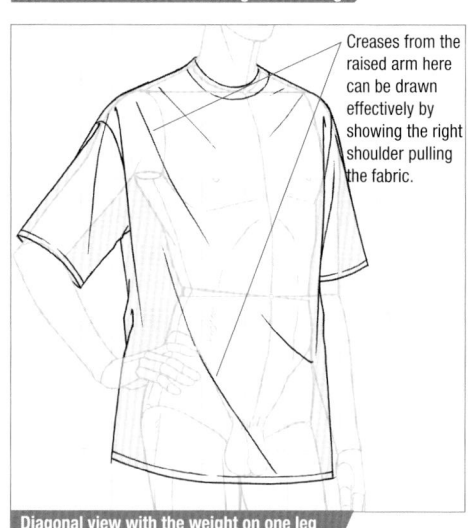

Creases from the raised arm here can be drawn effectively by showing the right shoulder pulling the fabric.

Diagonal view with the weight on one leg (pivotal leg in front)

Chapter 3 : Fashion Drawing

Tank top

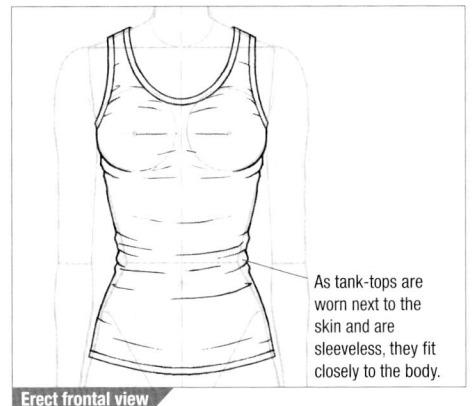
As tank-tops are worn next to the skin and are sleeveless, they fit closely to the body.
Erect frontal view

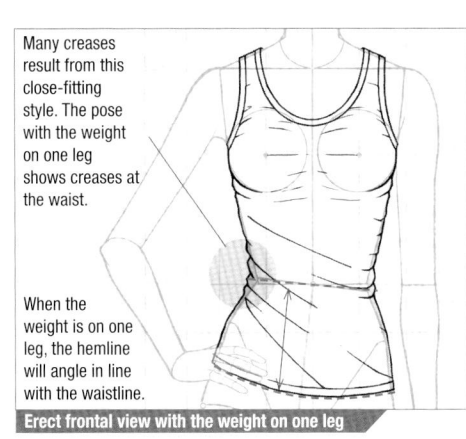
Many creases result from this close-fitting style. The pose with the weight on one leg shows creases at the waist.
When the weight is on one leg, the hemline will angle in line with the waistline.
Erect frontal view with the weight on one leg

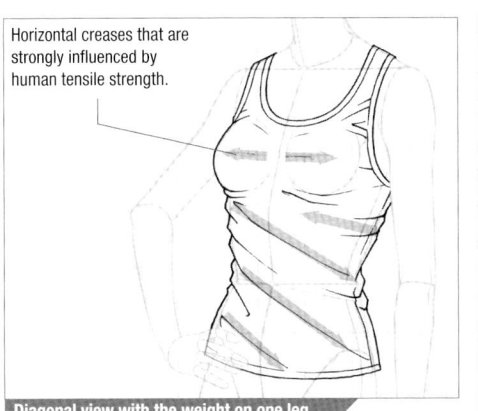
Horizontal creases that are strongly influenced by human tensile strength.
Diagonal view with the weight on one leg (pivotal leg behind)

There is also a little room at the back.
Erect diagonal view

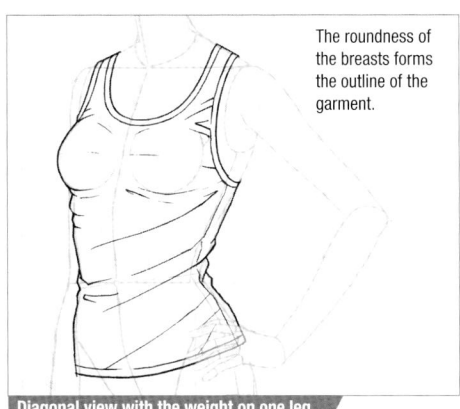
The roundness of the breasts forms the outline of the garment.
Diagonal view with the weight on one leg (pivotal leg in front)

Jacket

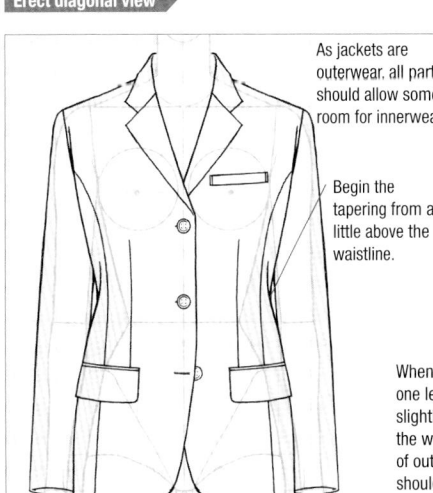
As jackets are outerwear, all parts should allow some room for innerwear.
Begin the tapering from a little above the waistline.
Erect frontal view

The shoulder pads create volume when the arm is raised.
When the weight is on one leg, the hemline will slightly angle in line with the waistline. In the case of outerwear, the angle should not be too obvious.
Erect frontal view with the weight on one leg

Vertical creases that are strongly influenced by gravity.

Horizontal creases that are strongly influenced by human tensile strength.

Tension points
Diagonal view with the weight on one leg (pivotal leg behind)

There is plenty of room also at the front and back.
Erect diagonal view

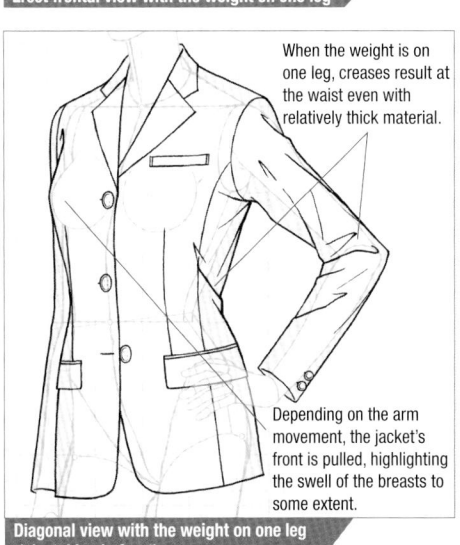
When the weight is on one leg, creases result at the waist even with relatively thick material.

Depending on the arm movement, the jacket's front is pulled, highlighting the swell of the breasts to some extent.
Diagonal view with the weight on one leg (pivotal leg in front)

73

Jumper

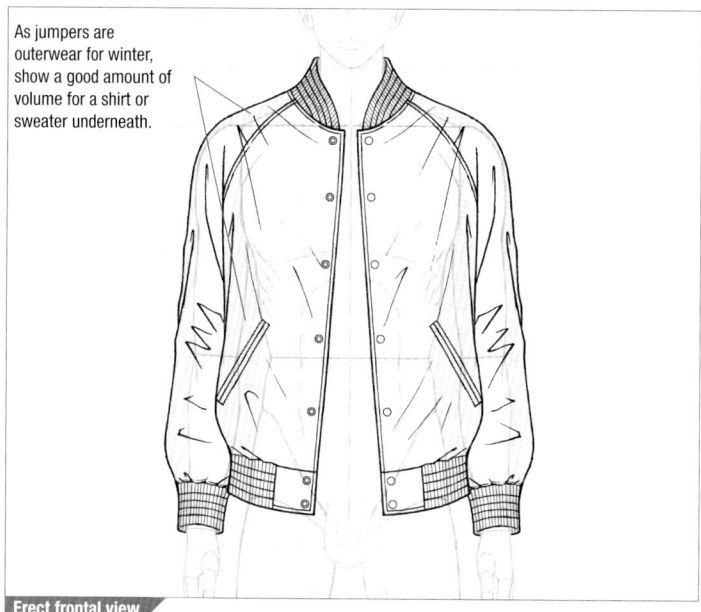

As jumpers are outerwear for winter, show a good amount of volume for a shirt or sweater underneath.

Erect frontal view

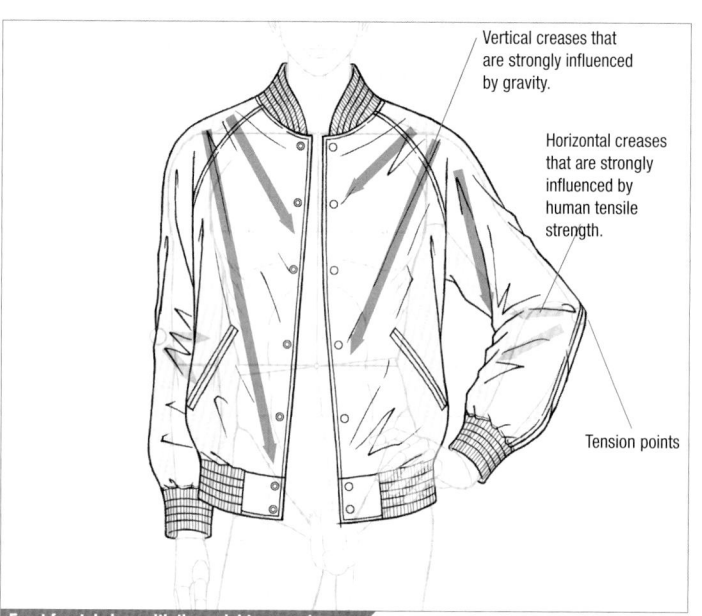

Vertical creases that are strongly influenced by gravity.

Horizontal creases that are strongly influenced by human tensile strength.

Tension points

Erect frontal view with the weight on one leg

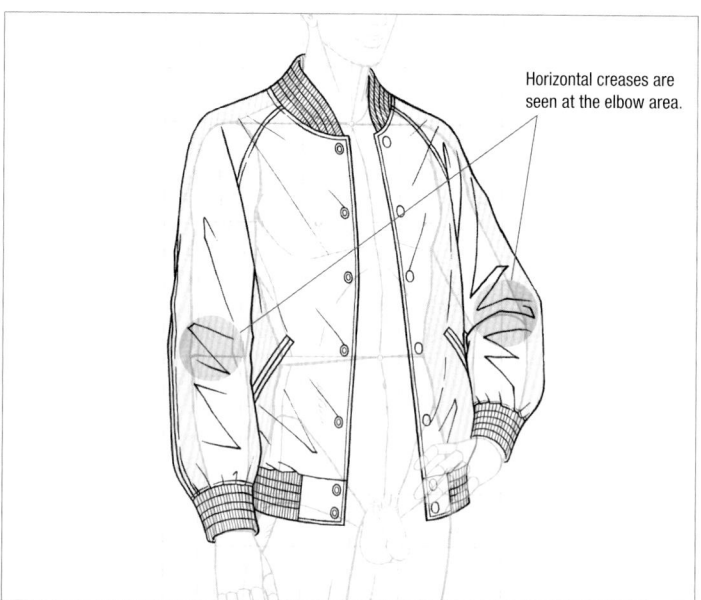

Horizontal creases are seen at the elbow area.

Diagonal view with the weight on one leg (pivotal leg behind)

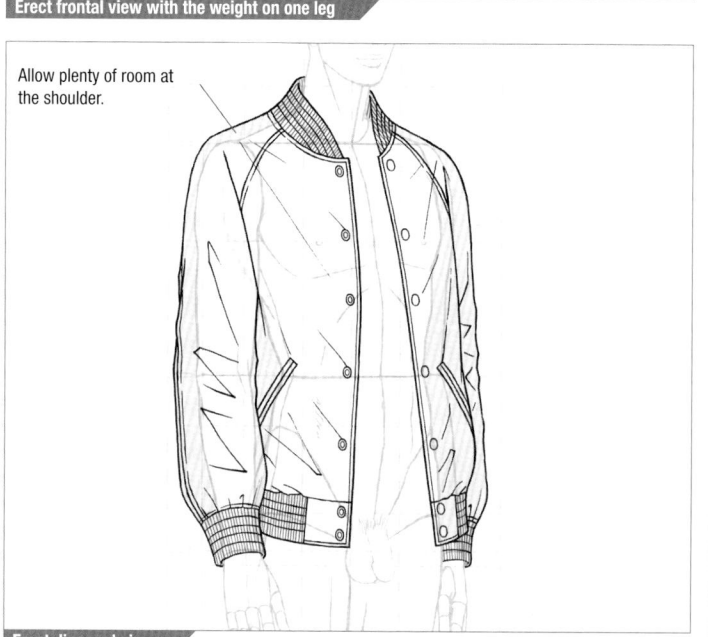

Allow plenty of room at the shoulder.

Erect diagonal view

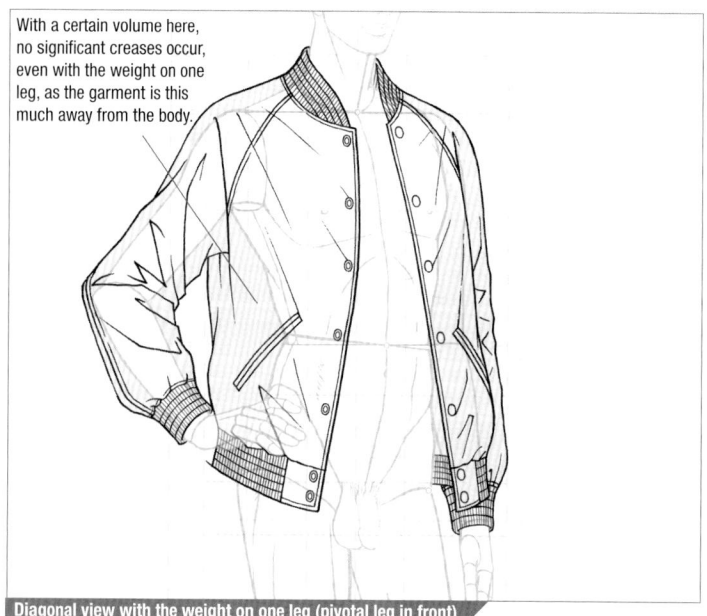

With a certain volume here, no significant creases occur, even with the weight on one leg, as the garment is this much away from the body.

Diagonal view with the weight on one leg (pivotal leg in front)

Chapter 3 : Fashion Drawing

Tank top

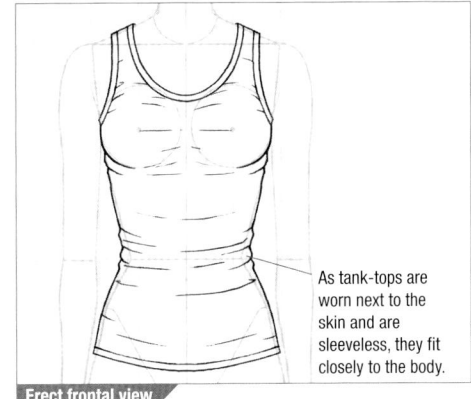
As tank-tops are worn next to the skin and are sleeveless, they fit closely to the body.
Erect frontal view

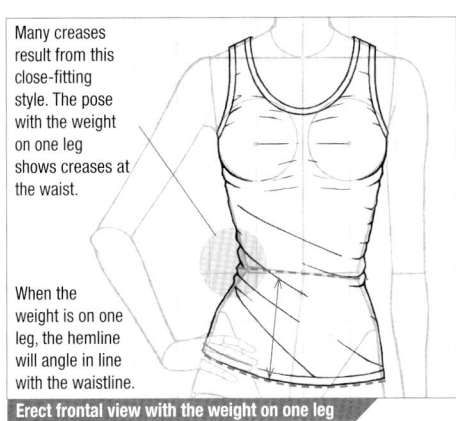
Many creases result from this close-fitting style. The pose with the weight on one leg shows creases at the waist.
When the weight is on one leg, the hemline will angle in line with the waistline.
Erect frontal view with the weight on one leg

Horizontal creases that are strongly influenced by human tensile strength.

Diagonal view with the weight on one leg (pivotal leg behind)

There is also a little room at the back.
Erect diagonal view

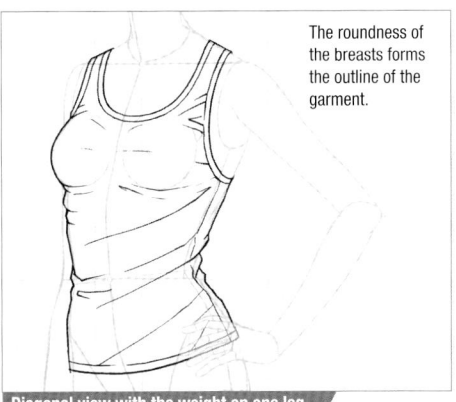
The roundness of the breasts forms the outline of the garment.
Diagonal view with the weight on one leg (pivotal leg in front)

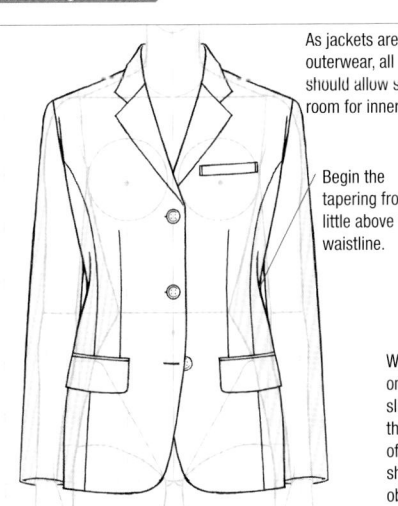
As jackets are outerwear, all parts should allow some room for innerwear.
Begin the tapering from a little above the waistline.
Erect frontal view

Jacket

The shoulder pads create volume when the arm is raised.
When the weight is on one leg, the hemline will slightly angle in line with the waistline. In the case of outerwear, the angle should not be too obvious.
Erect frontal view with the weight on one leg

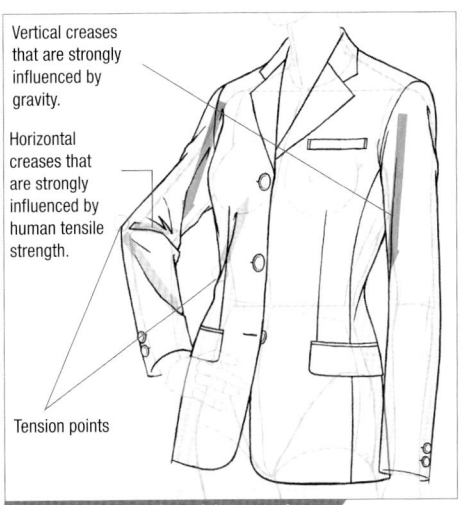
Vertical creases that are strongly influenced by gravity.

Horizontal creases that are strongly influenced by human tensile strength.

Tension points
Diagonal view with the weight on one leg (pivotal leg behind)

There is plenty of room also at the front and back.
Erect diagonal view

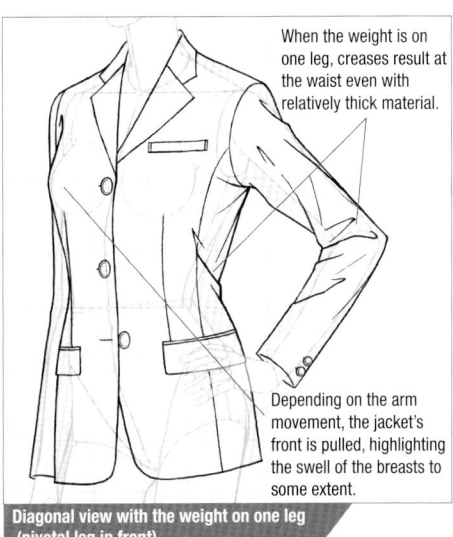
When the weight is on one leg, creases result at the waist even with relatively thick material.

Depending on the arm movement, the jacket's front is pulled, highlighting the swell of the breasts to some extent.
Diagonal view with the weight on one leg (pivotal leg in front)

73

Jumper

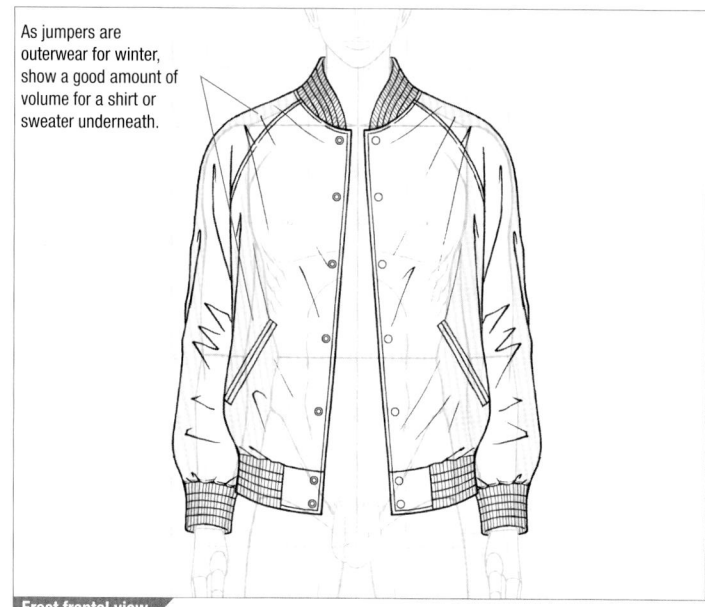

As jumpers are outerwear for winter, show a good amount of volume for a shirt or sweater underneath.

Erect frontal view

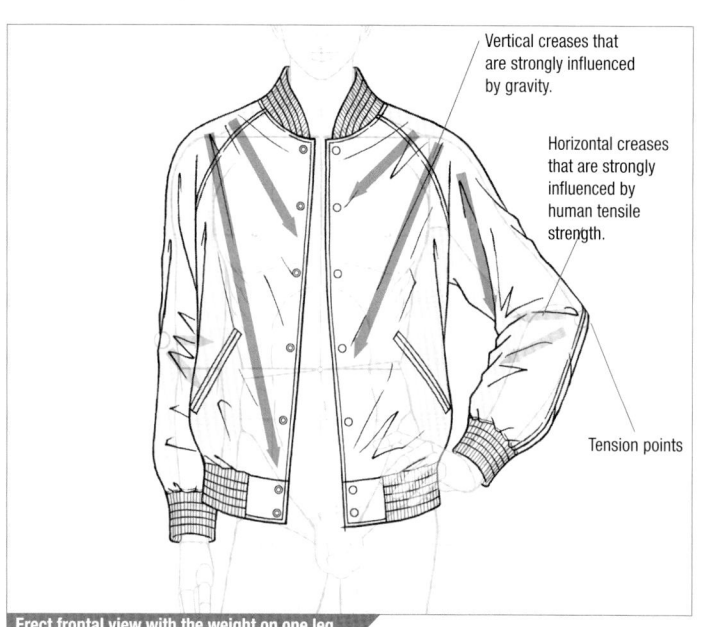

Vertical creases that are strongly influenced by gravity.

Horizontal creases that are strongly influenced by human tensile strength.

Tension points

Erect frontal view with the weight on one leg

Horizontal creases are seen at the elbow area.

Diagonal view with the weight on one leg (pivotal leg behind)

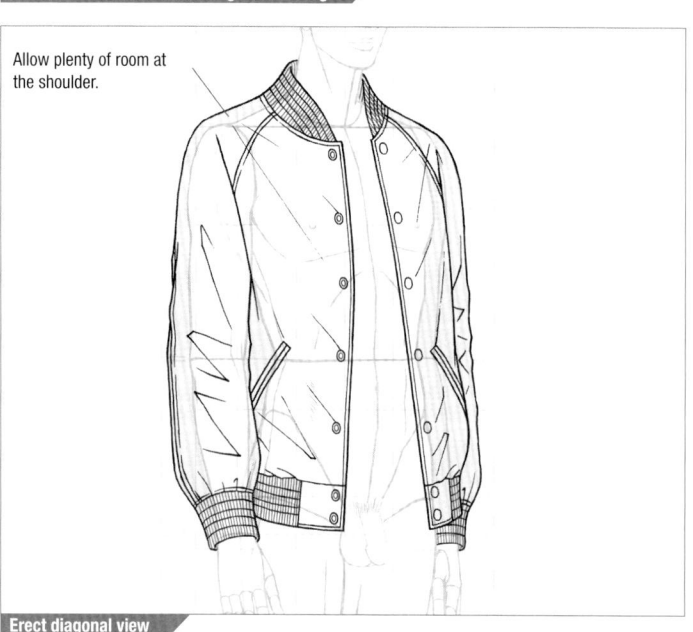

Allow plenty of room at the shoulder.

Erect diagonal view

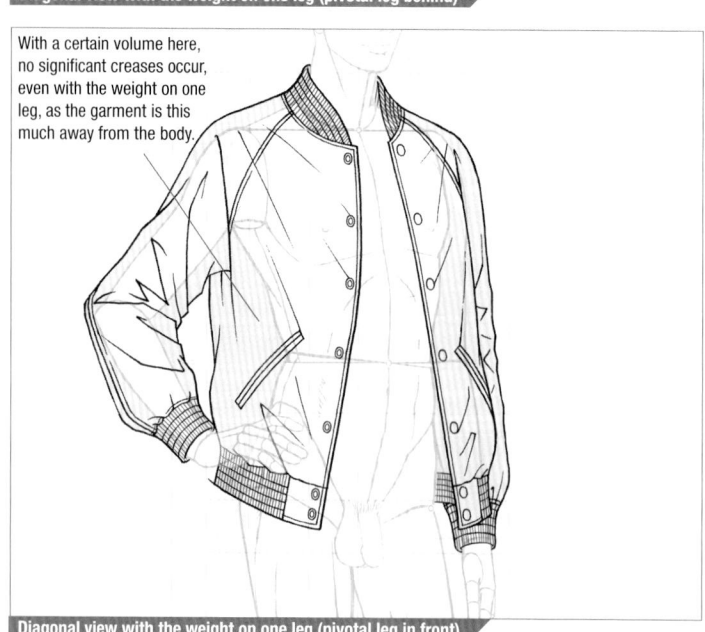

With a certain volume here, no significant creases occur, even with the weight on one leg, as the garment is this much away from the body.

Diagonal view with the weight on one leg (pivotal leg in front)

Chapter 3 : Fashion Drawing

Tank top

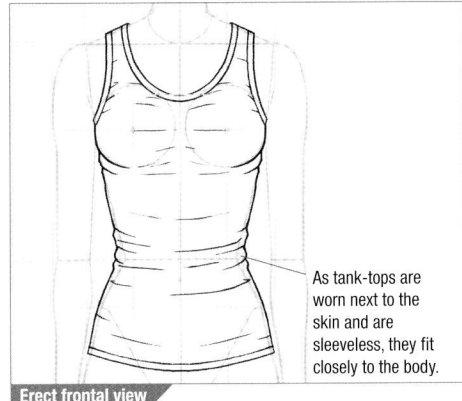
As tank-tops are worn next to the skin and are sleeveless, they fit closely to the body.
Erect frontal view

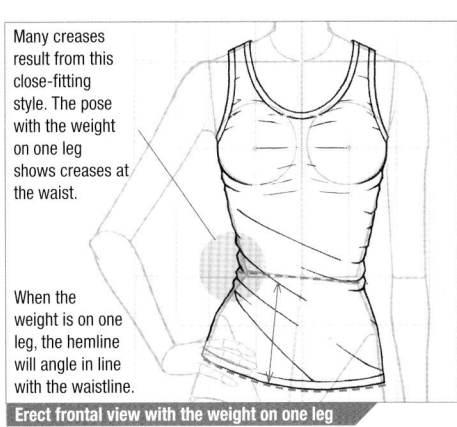
Many creases result from this close-fitting style. The pose with the weight on one leg shows creases at the waist.
When the weight is on one leg, the hemline will angle in line with the waistline.
Erect frontal view with the weight on one leg

Horizontal creases that are strongly influenced by human tensile strength.

There is also a little room at the back.
Erect diagonal view

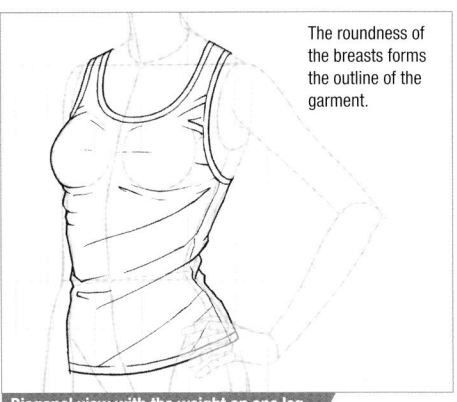
The roundness of the breasts forms the outline of the garment.
Diagonal view with the weight on one leg (pivotal leg in front)

Diagonal view with the weight on one leg (pivotal leg behind)

Jacket

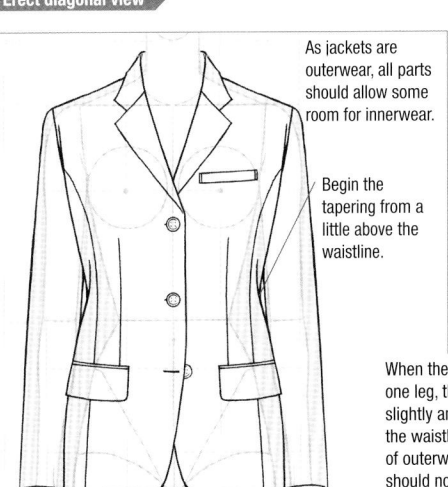
As jackets are outerwear, all parts should allow some room for innerwear.
Begin the tapering from a little above the waistline.
Erect frontal view

The shoulder pads create volume when the arm is raised.
When the weight is on one leg, the hemline will slightly angle in line with the waistline. In the case of outerwear, the angle should not be too obvious.
Erect frontal view with the weight on one leg

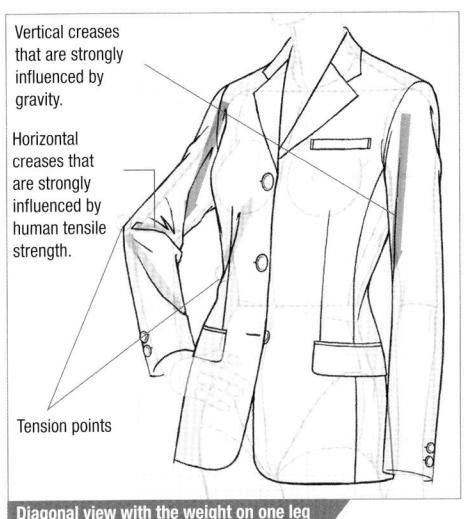
Vertical creases that are strongly influenced by gravity.

Horizontal creases that are strongly influenced by human tensile strength.

Tension points
Diagonal view with the weight on one leg (pivotal leg behind)

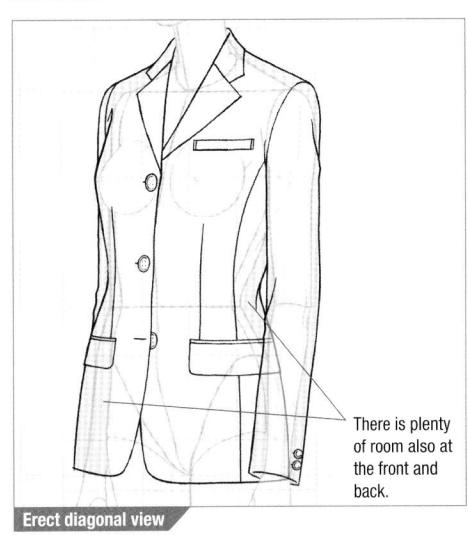
There is plenty of room also at the front and back.
Erect diagonal view

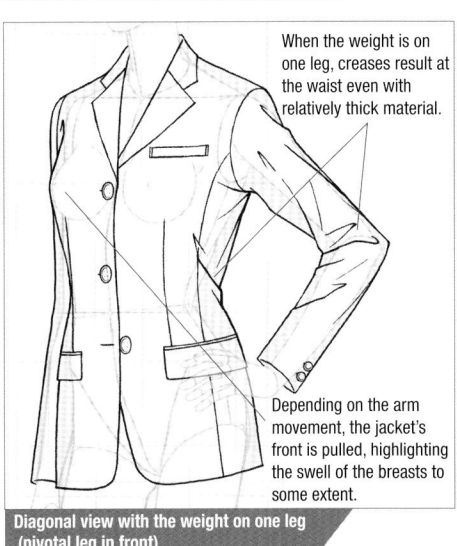
When the weight is on one leg, creases result at the waist even with relatively thick material.

Depending on the arm movement, the jacket's front is pulled, highlighting the swell of the breasts to some extent.
Diagonal view with the weight on one leg (pivotal leg in front)

73

Jumper

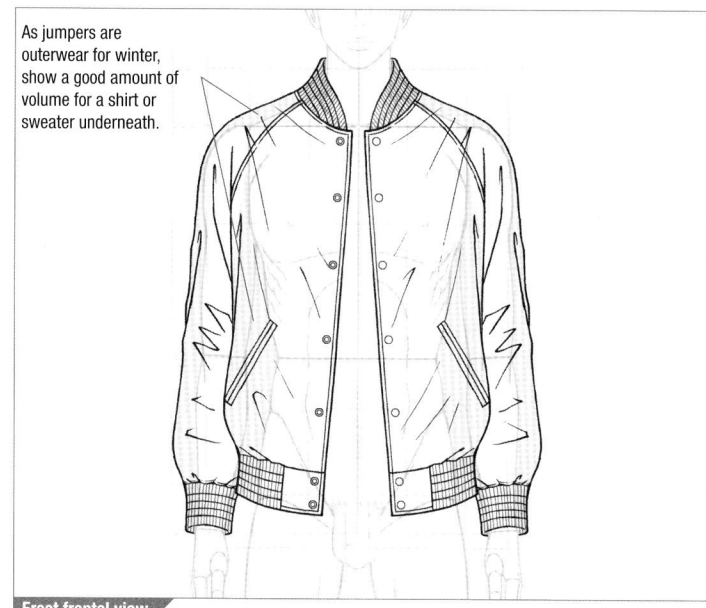

As jumpers are outerwear for winter, show a good amount of volume for a shirt or sweater underneath.

Erect frontal view

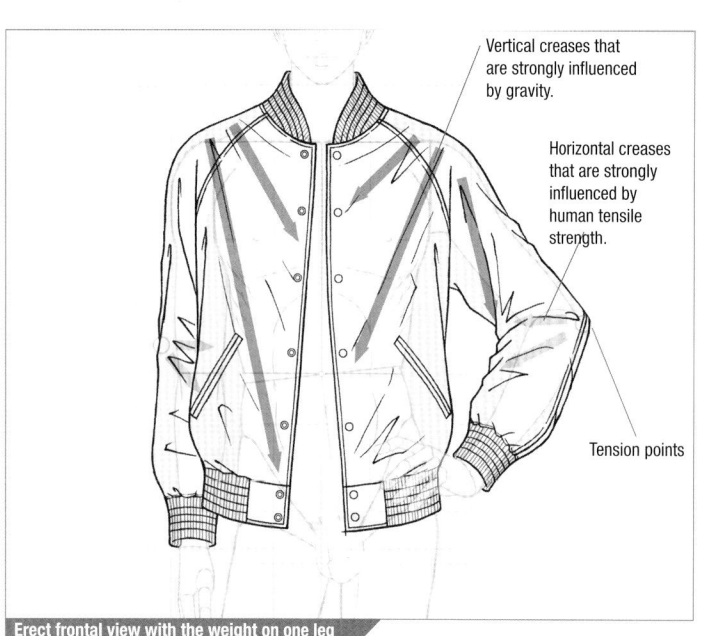

Vertical creases that are strongly influenced by gravity.

Horizontal creases that are strongly influenced by human tensile strength.

Tension points

Erect frontal view with the weight on one leg

Horizontal creases are seen at the elbow area.

Diagonal view with the weight on one leg (pivotal leg behind)

Allow plenty of room at the shoulder.

Erect diagonal view

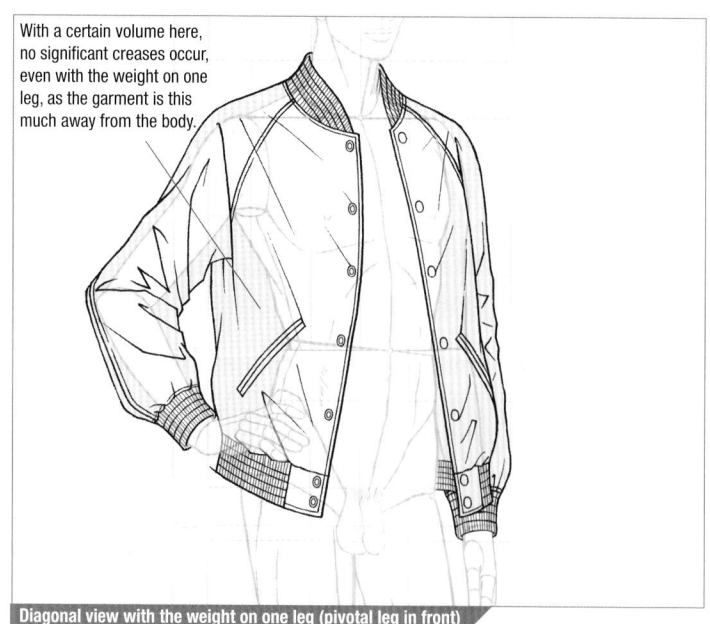

With a certain volume here, no significant creases occur, even with the weight on one leg, as the garment is this much away from the body.

Diagonal view with the weight on one leg (pivotal leg in front)

Chapter 3 : Fashion Drawing

Cardigan

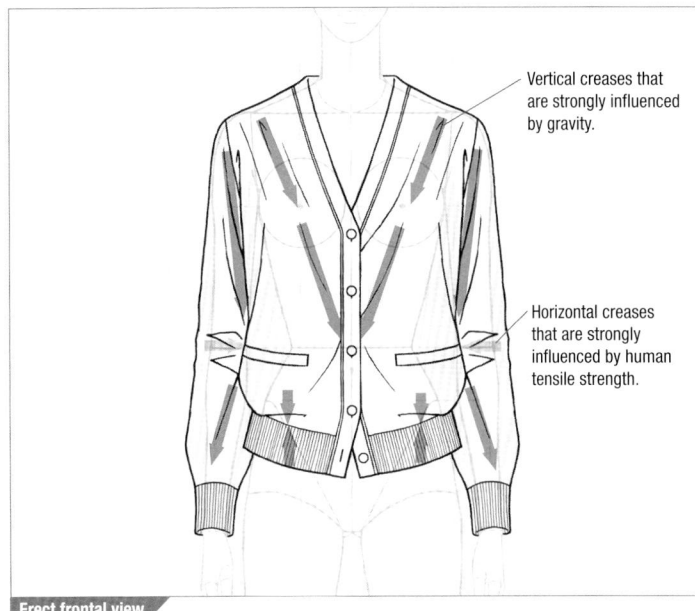
Vertical creases that are strongly influenced by gravity.

Horizontal creases that are strongly influenced by human tensile strength.

Erect frontal view

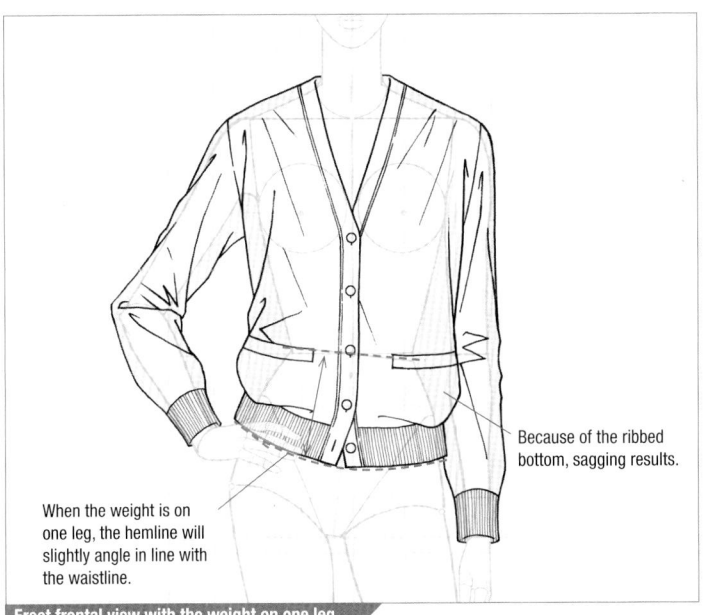
Because of the ribbed bottom, sagging results.

When the weight is on one leg, the hemline will slightly angle in line with the waistline.

Erect frontal view with the weight on one leg

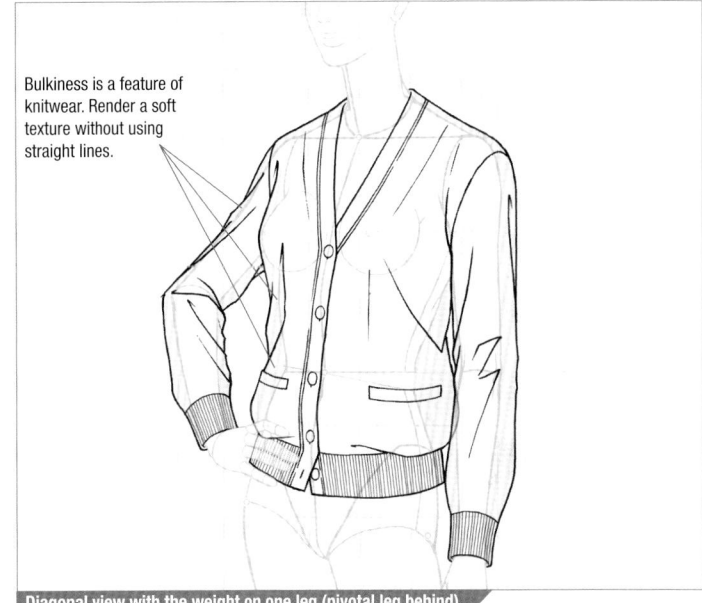
Bulkiness is a feature of knitwear. Render a soft texture without using straight lines.

Diagonal view with the weight on one leg (pivotal leg behind)

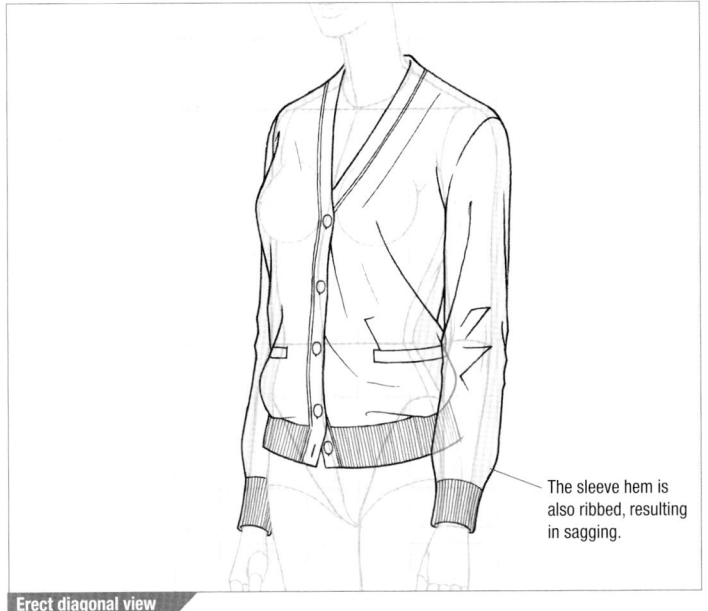
The sleeve hem is also ribbed, resulting in sagging.

Erect diagonal view

It is open in a V-shape here as the bottom button is not done-up, effectively suggesting the swell of the hip.

Diagonal view with the weight on one leg (pivotal leg in front)

Coat

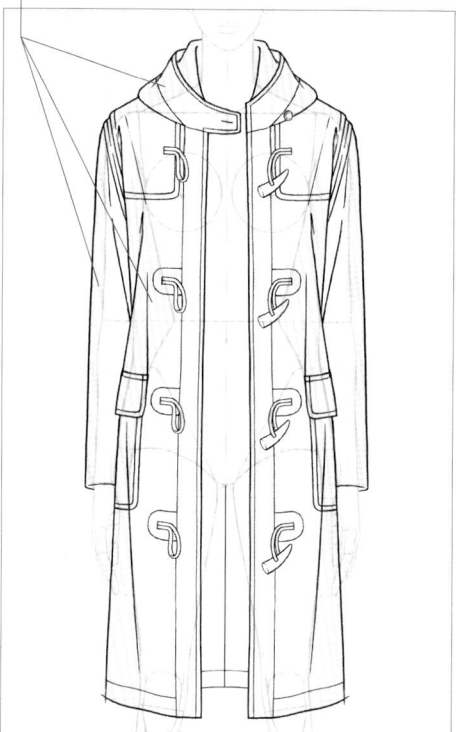

Coats are outerwear with the most volume. Be sure to allow sufficient room.

Erect frontal view

The placket is turned here. As it is difficult to draw a hood three-dimensionally, refer to and observe visual materials or the actual garment if available.

Erect frontal view with the weight on one leg

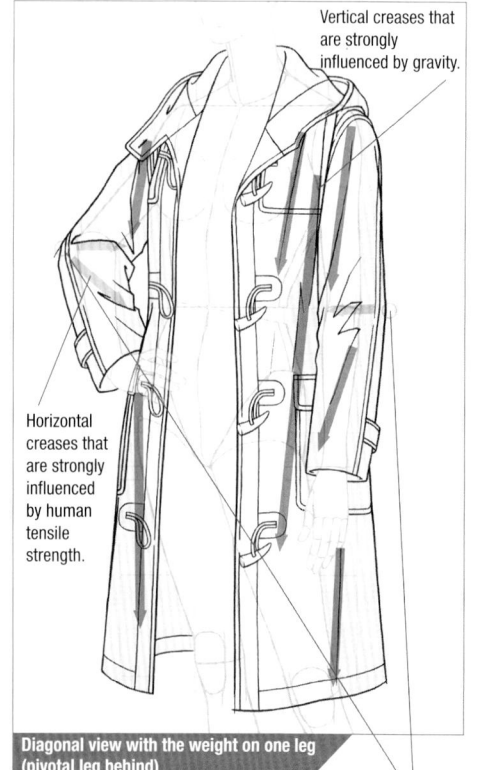

Vertical creases that are strongly influenced by gravity.

Horizontal creases that are strongly influenced by human tensile strength.

Diagonal view with the weight on one leg (pivotal leg behind)

Tension points

The large volume at the front is hiding the line from the armhole towards the sleeve.

Erect diagonal view

The large amount of room here makes the swell of the breasts less obvious.

Because of its large volume, the garment shows more vertical creases due to gravity.

Diagonal view with the weight on one leg (pivotal leg in front)

When the weight is on one leg, the hemline will slightly angle in line with the waistline. In the case of outerwear, the angle should not be too obvious, as the influence is little, especially with a large volume garment.

Chapter 3 : Fashion Drawing

Vest

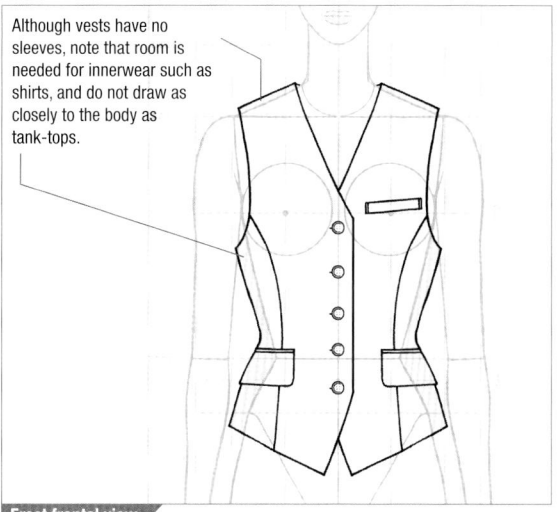

Although vests have no sleeves, note that room is needed for innerwear such as shirts, and do not draw as closely to the body as tank-tops.

Erect frontal view

Allow room at the back.

Erect diagonal view

Dress

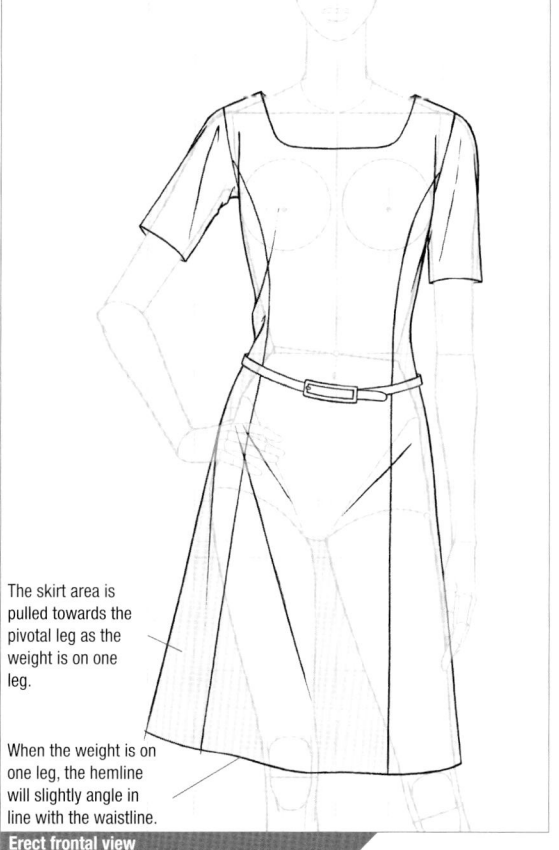

The skirt area is pulled towards the pivotal leg as the weight is on one leg.

When the weight is on one leg, the hemline will slightly angle in line with the waistline.

Erect frontal view

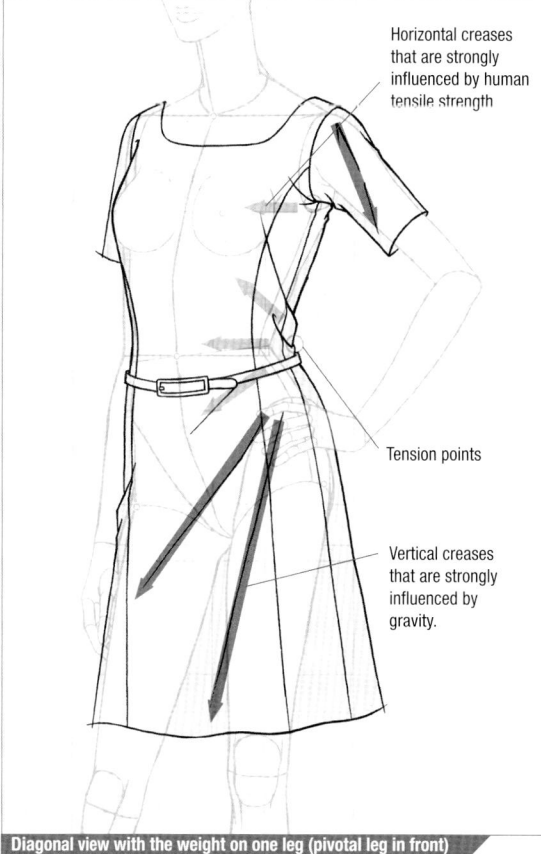

Horizontal creases that are strongly influenced by human tensile strength

Tension points

Vertical creases that are strongly influenced by gravity.

Diagonal view with the weight on one leg (pivotal leg in front)

77

Tight Skirt (Mini)

Draw skirts while being aware of the following two points, as they are often named after their length and volume.
· Volume: Tight skirt, A-line skirt, flared skirt, etc.
· Length: Mini skirt, knee-length skirt, long skirt, etc.

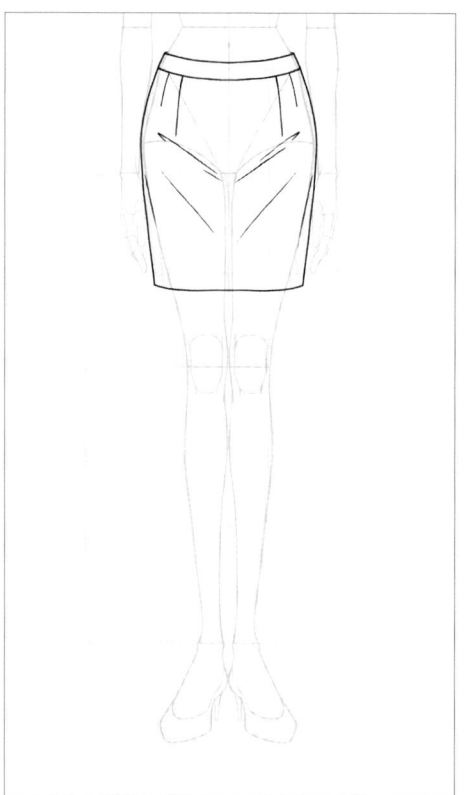

Erect frontal view

Draw creases from the hip of the pivotal leg towards the hem at the bracing leg, showing the fabric being pulled in such a direction.

Erect frontal view with the weight on one leg

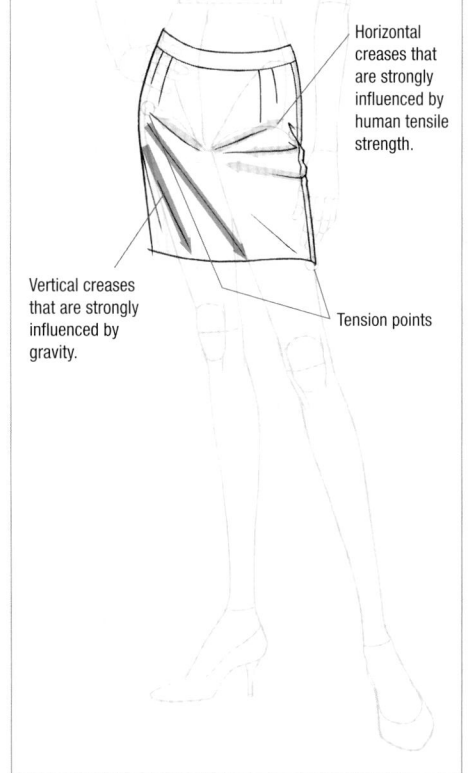

Horizontal creases that are strongly influenced by human tensile strength.

Vertical creases that are strongly influenced by gravity.

Tension points

Diagonal view with the weight on one leg (pivotal leg behind)

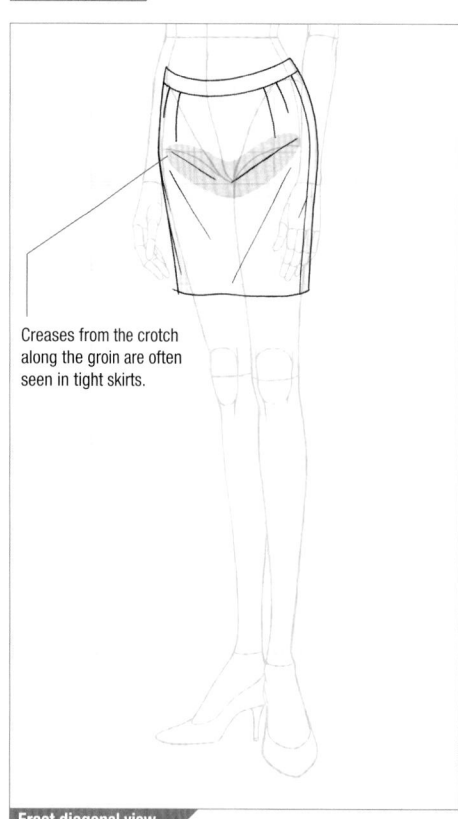

Creases from the crotch along the groin are often seen in tight skirts.

Erect diagonal view

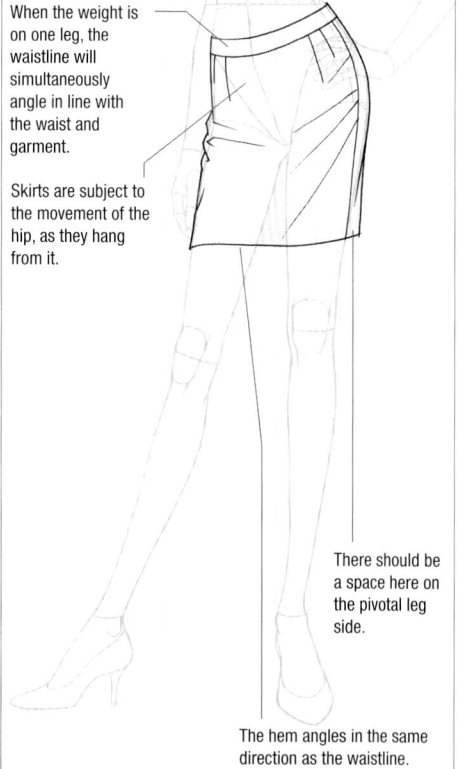

When the weight is on one leg, the waistline will simultaneously angle in line with the waist and garment.

Skirts are subject to the movement of the hip, as they hang from it.

There should be a space here on the pivotal leg side.

The hem angles in the same direction as the waistline.

Diagonal view with the weight on one leg (pivotal leg in front)

Chapter 3 : Fashion Drawing

Tight Skirt (Long)

Despite their name, tight skirts, when they are long, should have some room at the bottom to allow for walking. This however is not enough and a slit is usually made at the back or side to enable more comfortable walking.

When the weight is on one leg, the waistline will simultaneously angle in line with the waist and garment.

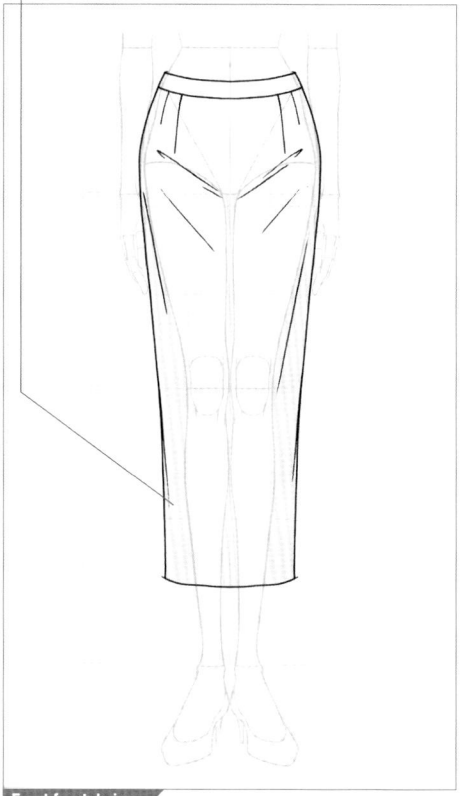

Erect frontal view

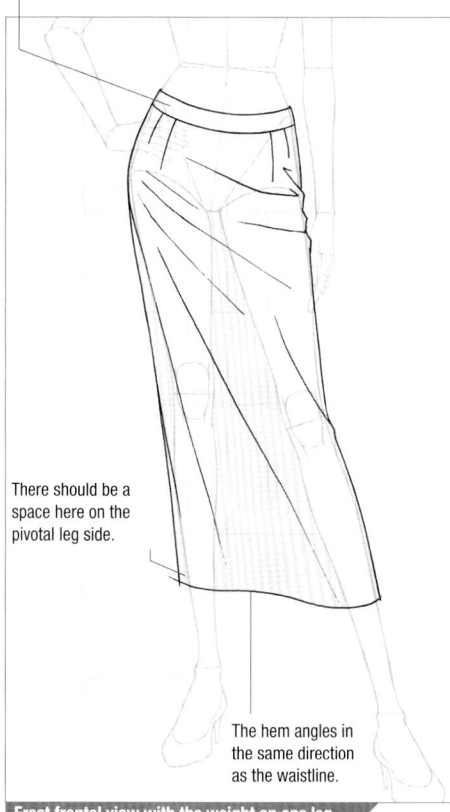

There should be a space here on the pivotal leg side.

The hem angles in the same direction as the waistline.

Erect frontal view with the weight on one leg

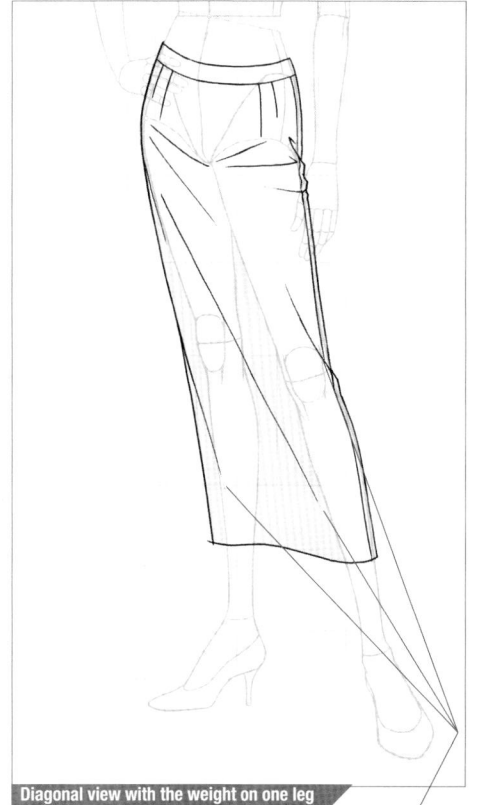

Diagonal view with the weight on one leg (pivotal leg behind)

As tight skirts are heavier when long, downward creases often result due to gravity.

Erect diagonal view

Unlike tops, bottoms have more space at the front. This results from the S-shape of the legs when viewed from the side (See p.16).

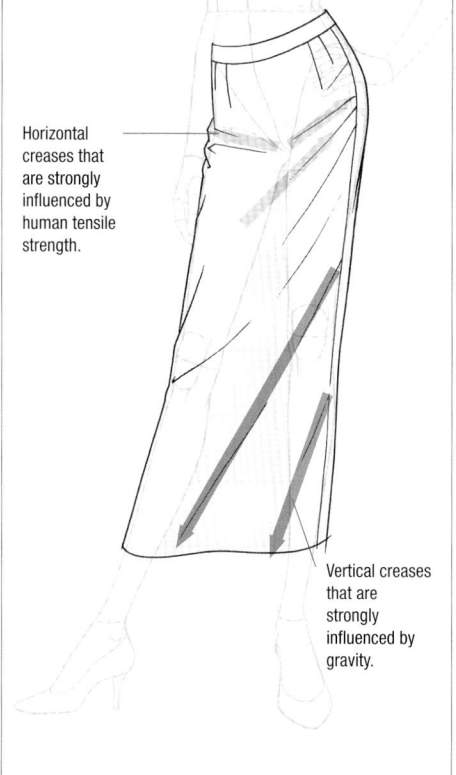

Horizontal creases that are strongly influenced by human tensile strength.

Vertical creases that are strongly influenced by gravity.

Diagonal view with the weight on one leg (pivotal leg in front)

79

Flared/Pleated Skirts (Mini) & Wrapover Skirt

Vertical creases that are strongly influenced by gravity.

As skirts are worn fixed at the waist, draw them as such while spreading from the hip area.

Erect frontal view

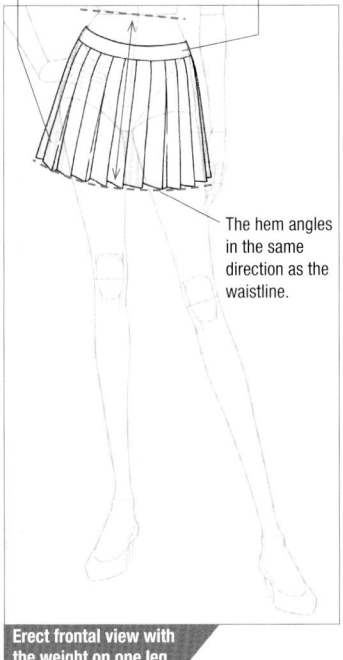

There should be a space here on the pivotal leg side.

When the weight is on one leg, the waistline will simultaneously angle in line with the waist and garment.

The hem angles in the same direction as the waistline.

Erect frontal view with the weight on one leg

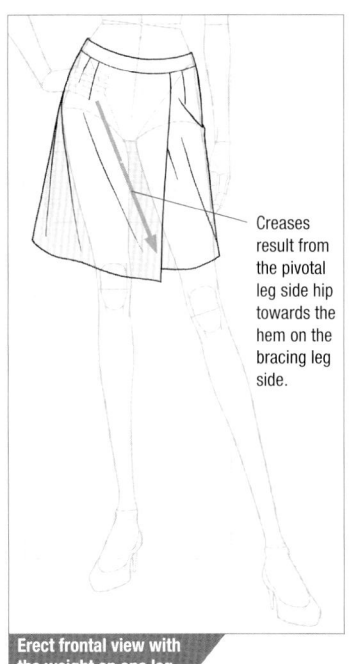

Creases result from the pivotal leg side hip towards the hem on the bracing leg side.

Erect frontal view with the weight on one leg

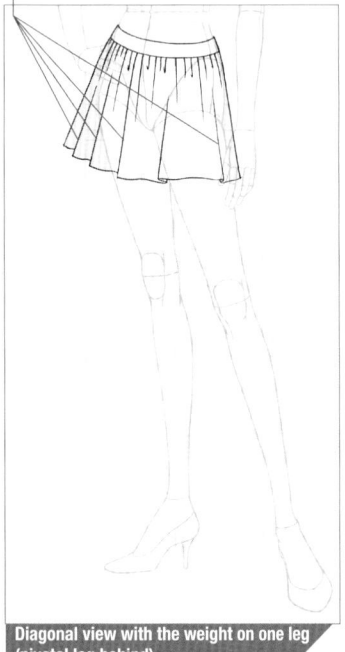

As flared skirts have a large volume of fabric which tends to fall, gathering around the hem, downward creases often result due to gravity.

Diagonal view with the weight on one leg (pivotal leg behind)

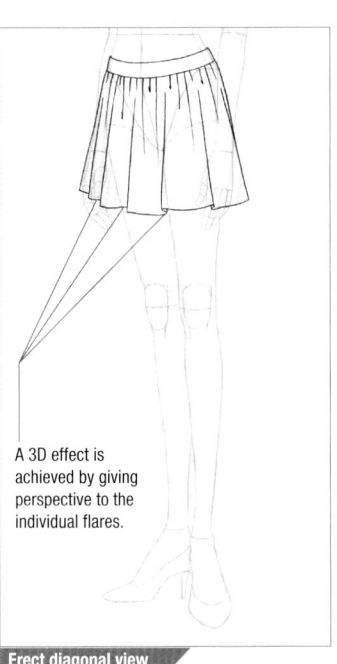

A 3D effect is achieved by giving perspective to the individual flares.

Erect diagonal view

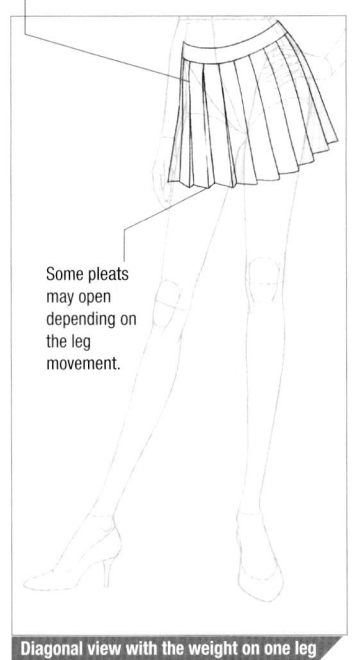

The pleats also use a lot of fabric like the flared skirt.

Some pleats may open depending on the leg movement.

Diagonal view with the weight on one leg (pivotal leg in front)

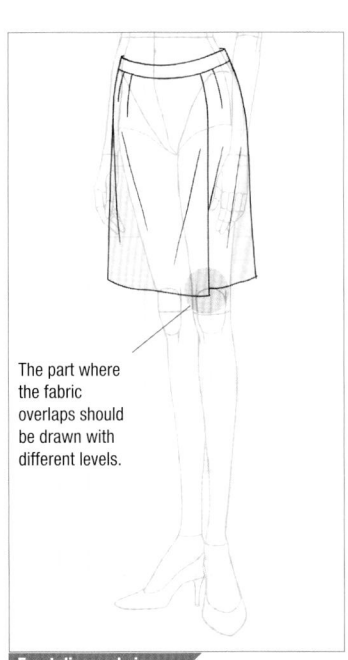

The part where the fabric overlaps should be drawn with different levels.

Erect diagonal view

Chapter 3 : Fashion Drawing

Flared/Pleated Skirts (Long)

As skirts are worn fixed at the waist, draw them as such while spreading from the hip area.

Be sure to draw the pleats with even width.

Draw the hem of a flared skirt with the bottom edge of each block curved.

Erect frontal view

Erect frontal view with the weight on one leg

Unlike tops, bottoms have more space at the front. This results from the S-shape of the legs when viewed from the side (See p.16).

Horizontal creases that are strongly influenced by human tensile strength.

Vertical creases that are strongly influenced by gravity.

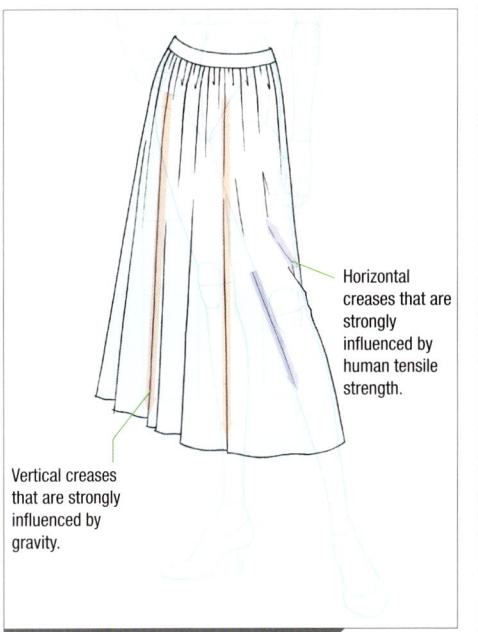

Diagonal view with the weight on one leg (pivotal leg behind)

Erect diagonal view

Pleats appear narrower the farther they are from the viewer.

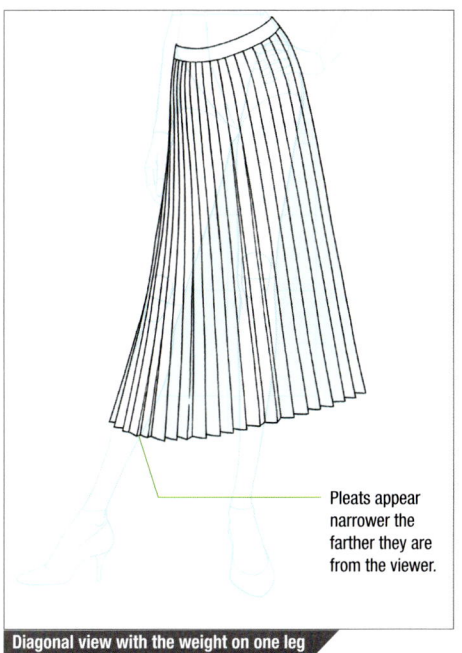

Diagonal view with the weight on one leg (pivotal leg in front)

81

Pants (Straight)

- As pants are worn fixed at the waist, draw them fitted around the waist.
- Creases are often seen at joints.
- Vertical creases that are strongly influenced by gravity.
- Horizontal creases that are strongly influenced by human tensile strength.
- Tension points

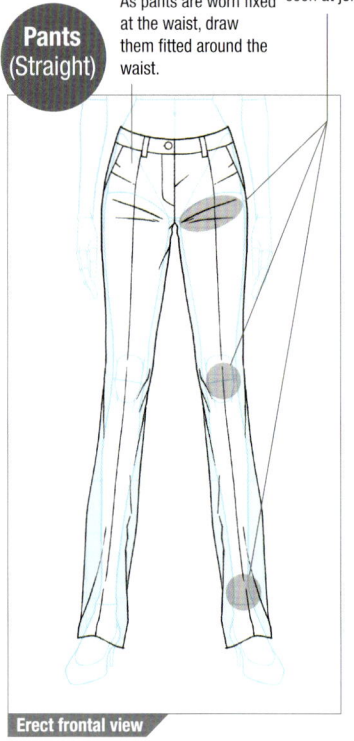
Erect frontal view

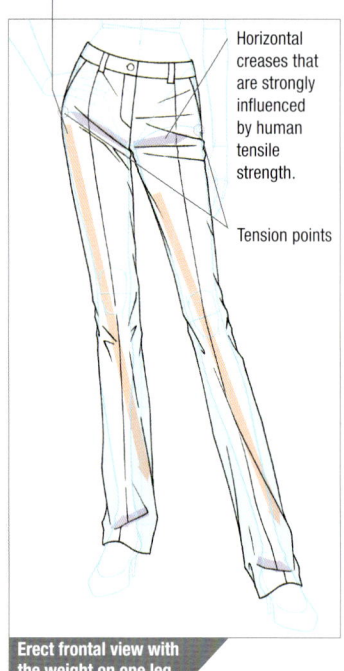
Erect frontal view with the weight on one leg

Pants (Slim)

- As they are closely fitting, horizontal creases result from human tensile strength.

- Bulge the bottom of pants to create a 3D effect.
- More creases occur as the legs are opened.
- When the legs are open, creases result originating at the groin of the bracing leg.
- When the legs are open, creases result originating at the groin of the bracing leg.

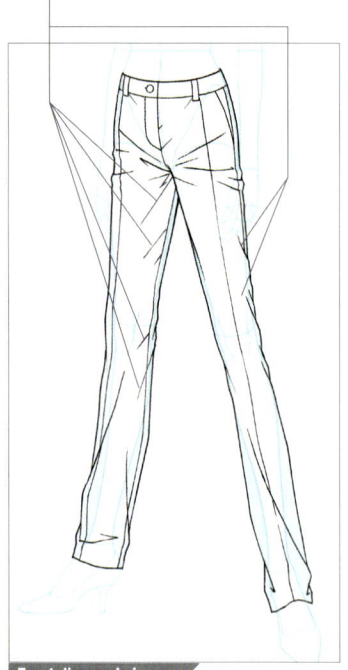
Diagonal view with the weight on one leg (pivotal leg behind) | **Erect diagonal view**

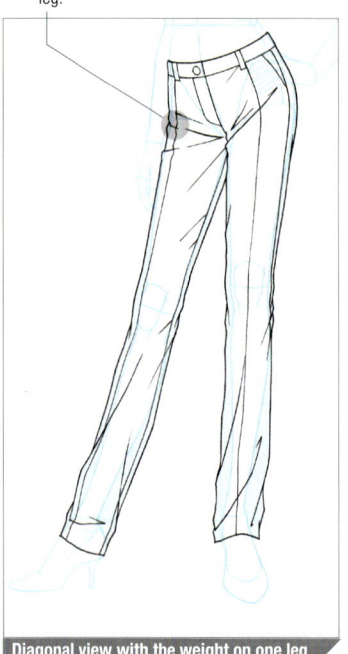
Diagonal view with the weight on one leg (pivotal leg in front)

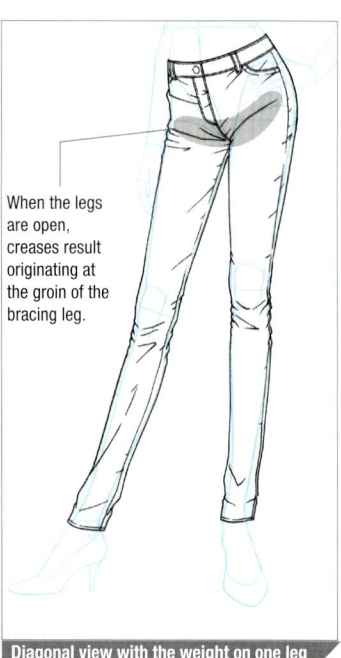
Diagonal view with the weight on one leg (pivotal leg in front)

Chapter 3 : Fashion Drawing

Pants (Bell-bottom)

When showing pants which sag near the ankles, be sure not to show them flared at the hem. Draw them as if tapered.

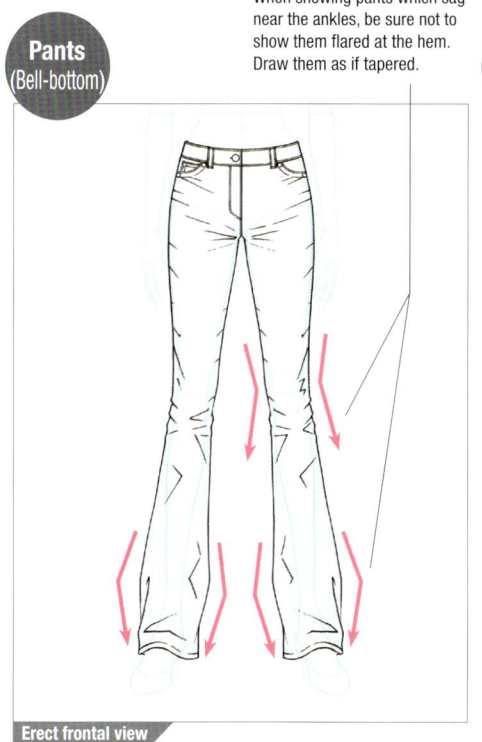

Erect frontal view

Pants (Wide)

As they are loose fitting, vertical creases result due to gravity.

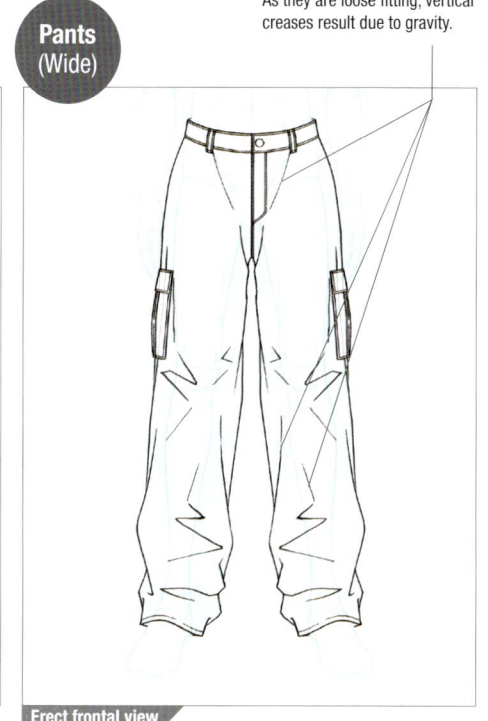

Erect frontal view

Pants (Inside-boot)

Men's pants are often loose around the crotch, to avoid too much tightness in this area.

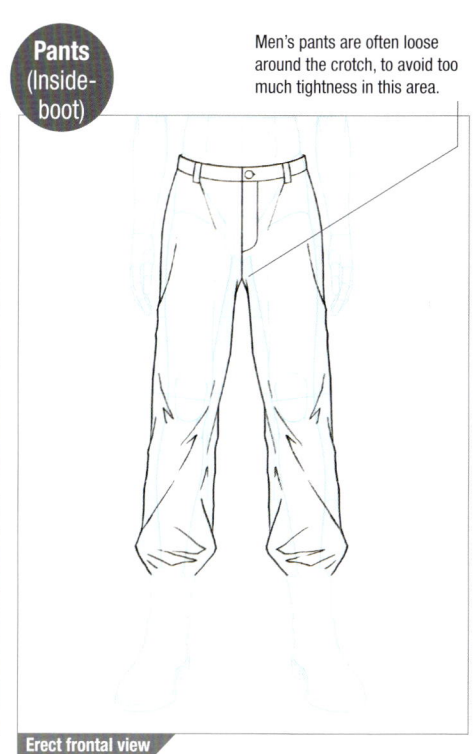

Erect frontal view

As they fit closely down to the knees, horizontal creases result from human tensile strength, while, as they are loose fitting below the knees, vertical creases result due to gravity.

Erect diagonal view

As men's pants have some room at the crotch area, the legs look shorter than those in the drawing at the left.

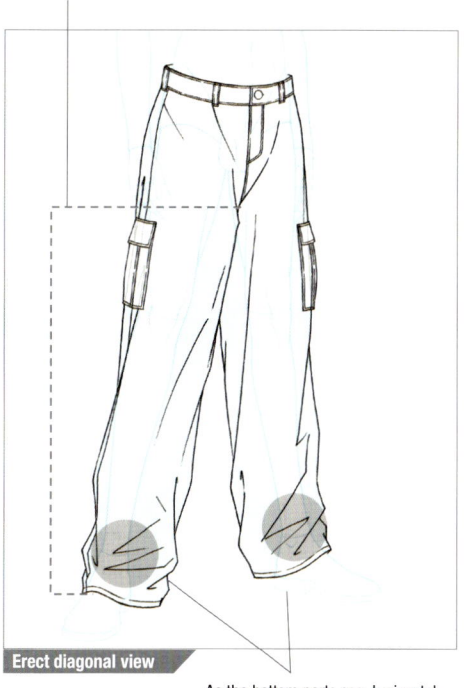

Erect diagonal view

As the bottom parts sag, horizontal creases result.

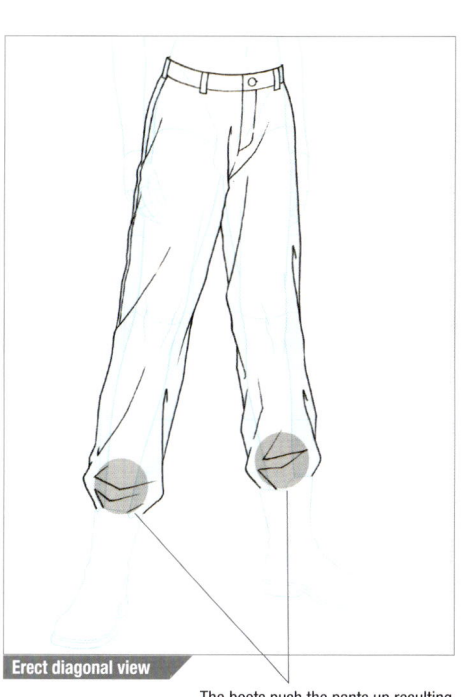

Erect diagonal view

The boots push the pants up resulting in bulges.

83

[2] Color Application
(1) Mechanisms of Color

CMYK

The number of colors that can be represented on paper using artist's materials is over 10 million, all of which are created through the combination of four colors: cyan (C), magenta (M), and yellow (Y), plus black (K). This corresponds to the combination of inks in a standard inkjet color printer.

● **Chromatic colors**

In the CMYK color system, cyan (C), magenta (M), and yellow (Y) are known as chromatic colors. This means that they have the three attributes of color: hue, brightness, and saturation. As the most basic of these, they are referred to as the primary colors of coloring agents. (Coloring agents here means the dyes and pigments mixed to perform color application).

● **Achromatic colors**

In the CMYK color system, black (K) is an achromatic color. This means that it has no color tone, only brightness. In other words it is a monotone.

Subtractive color mixing: when coloring agent is applied to pure white paper, reflected color is produced. When the three primary colors CMY are all mixed in equal proportions, the result is black. The more color is mixed into the coloring agent the darker (lacking light = black) it becomes. This is known as subtractive color mixing.

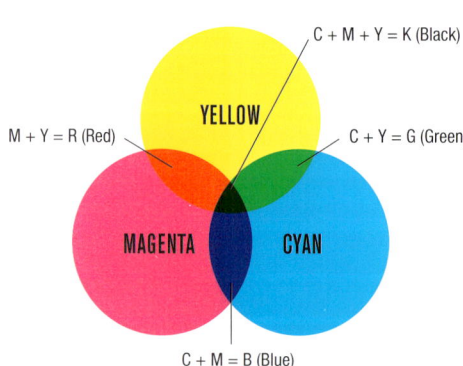

Subtractive Color Mixing

In contrast to coloring agents, the color of light is known as "colored light" and is created through the combination of red (R), green (G), and blue (B). The screens of computer monitors and televisions emit light, and as they do this they produce color by directly radiating the colors of the RGB system. When all three of the RGB are mixed, the product is white. Since colored light involves adding color from a state of complete darkness, its mechanism is known as additive color mixing. There is a difference in the range of color that can be represented using the RGB and the CMYK systems, the spectrum being much wider in the case of the former.

Hue

Hue circle: this is the name given to a circle which depicts the relationship between the five colors of the rainbow [red, yellow, green, blue, and purple (plus orange and indigo in Japan makes seven)]. Color preferences are said to be related to climate. The tendency is for primary colors to be preferred in warm regions and grayish colors with a low degree of saturation in cold regions. The reason why the number of colors used in the fashion industry in the last few decades has increased dramatically is probably because, unlike before, when designers came almost exclusively from Europe, fashion is now produced by designers brought up in a wide variety of countries and climates.

Brightness and Saturation

Tone Notation on the Color Solid Achromatic Cross-Section

Basic Colors for Garments

The basic colors for garments are the colors which most people like to wear regardless of age or gender. In color selection for fashion design, unlike in graphic design, the designer cannot use any color he chooses. Color selection must always be based on the tone set by the color of skin.

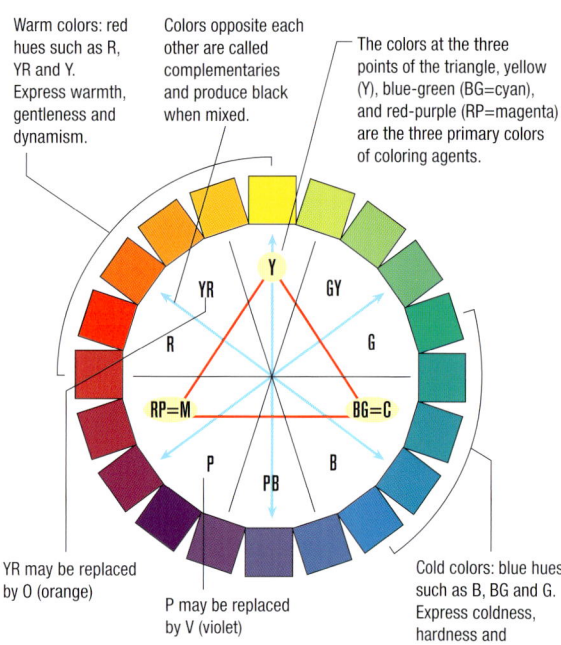

Hue Circle
Y: yellow, G: green, B: blue, P: purple, R: red

Relationship of the three attributes

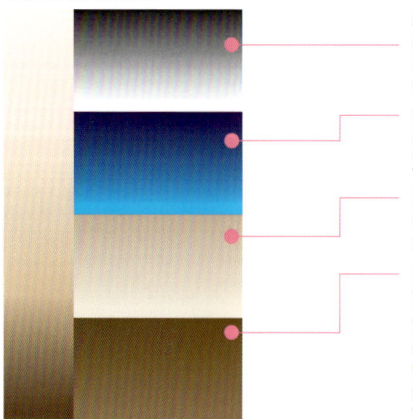

Achromatic color (monotone): Achromatic colors set off the freshness of skin and the healthy flush of blood, which are chromatic colors. These colors are used not just for ceremonial occasions but also on a wide range of occasions throughout the seasons.

Navy (blue): Being close to the complementary color for skin, using this color produces strong contrast. It is used widely in the west and east, for jeans and uniforms, as well as traditional Japanese cotton kimono (indigo).

Beige (ivory): As this color is similar to that of the skin, it produces an effect of harmony and integration. As it is a warm color, it produces a gentle atmosphere.

Brown: Being in the same color range as the skin, may produce a strong yet softer contrast, with a stylish and understated image.

The distinctive feature of the basic colors for garments is that they all contain white or black. When painting the color of clothing, instead of using the paint straight from the tube, it is recommended to mix it with a little white or black.
This extra work produces a color that matches the skin much better.

Chapter 3 : Fashion Drawing

(2) Artist's Materials for Coloring

Pencils
A simple and familiar drawing tool. Hardness of around B to 2B is recommended for smoothness. Light-colored pencils such as F and H have a hard lead that can damage the paper and are therefore not recommended. The letters B, H, and F indicate the darkness and hardness of the lead. B stands for black and H for hard. The higher the H number, the harder the lead and the lighter the color; the higher the B number, the softer the lead and the darker the color. F stands for firm and is intermediate between H and HB.

Color pencils:

Pastel color pencils
The lead is in powder form so is used mainly for rouge and eye make-up and to give a textured feel to winter fabrics.

Oil-based color pencils
The pigment contains wax or other substances to give waterproof properties. Producing distinctively vivid color, those with lower oil content can be applied on top of each other or mixed for versatile and simple use. Good for representing fabric texture and shade, make-up, and other detail.

Acrylic paints
Can be used not only on paper but also on stone, glass and metal and are waterproof once dry. Depending on the amount of water used to dissolve them, acrylic paints can be used either like transparent watercolor to express pale tones or like oil colors for a thickly applied effect. Acrylic gouache is opaque, but Liquitex is semi-transparent and Acryla transparent to semi-transparent. Different companies offer a variety of products.

Opaque watercolors (gouache)
As the base color does not show through, it allows layered use of paints and representation of checks and other patterns, and is suited to applying the dark colors (black or navy) that are prone to unevenness with transparent watercolors. Poster colors are one kind of opaque watercolor.

Transparent watercolors
As the base color shows through, suitable for representing soft and sheer fabrics, and translucency of skin. If a layer is applied and left to dry and another different color applied over it, the two blend to produce an attractive depth of color. The transparent drawing method is mainly used for shading, by application of layers of color, diluted with plenty of water without adding white. The opaque drawing method can also be applied, by using white with less water to produce lighter colors.

Mending tape
Becomes almost invisible after application and has a surface with a matt finish so produces almost no color even during printing or copying. Can also be conveniently drawn on.

Feather brush
Sweeps the paper clean of eraser residue and specks of dirt and dust.

Paint dish
It is useful to have around ten of these.

Brushes
Menso face brushes and shading brushes with long and fine bristles, as well as flat brushes should be used in combination. Before using for the first time, be sure to remove starch from brushes by repeatedly washing them in cold or lukewarm water.

Water holder
Comes in three convenient sections; for washing, rinsing, and holding water to be used as a 'colorless paint'.

Clips
Used to hold paper in place while drawing. Masking tape can also be used.

Design spray bond
Ensures even application and allows repeated mounting/dismounting. Useful when cutting/pasting fashion and technical drawings.

Fixative
Used to fix powder from pastels and pencils. Spray-type.

Art paper
Has a textured surface suitable for transparent watercolors and pastels. Especially suited for beginners because of its reasonable price. The different thickness grades (extra thick, thick, standard) are adapted to different tools and methods. Various products are available from Apollo, Muse, Maruman and other art suppliers, including those exclusively for watercolor.

Drawing pens
Often used for fashion and technical drawing. Available in various thickness grades, the most commonly used are from around 0.05 mm to 0.8 mm.

Color ball-point pens
Available in a rich variety of colors with some that can be applied on top of paints. Used for stripes, checks, detail of accessories, etc. White, gold and silver in particular are in frequent use.

Kent paper
Most commonly used for design drawing, and has a smooth surface adaptable to all types of tools. A wide range is available from different art suppliers.

Sketch pad
Suitable for pencil and therefore often used for draft sketching.

Alcohol-based markers
Produce good coloration and are fast-drying. Care is required as they can produce unevenness on a large surface area, but they offer a wide range of colors and are simple and easy to use. As they are highly transparent, the base color shows through. Can be used for drawing on photocopies, as they do not dissolve toner.

Water-based markers
Suitable only for intricate work (eyes and lips, accessories, checks, borders, stripes and other patterns), as they are very prone to unevenness.

85

Garment Variations

The following table shows the compatibility of artist's materials when their colors are layered (◯: Produce good color/△: Case-by-case/ ✕: Do not produce good color). It indicates that transparent/opaque watercolors, and markers are suitable for the base, while opaque watercolors, markers, pastels and pens are suitable for the detail drawing/coloring.

Base \ Detail Drawing/Coloring	Transparent watercolor	Opaque watercolor	Alcohol-based marker	Water-based marker	color pencil	Pastel	Color ball-point pen	Drawing pen
Transparent watercolor	△ Lighter than the base color: ✕	◯	△ Lighter than the base color: ✕	△ Lighter than the base color: ✕	◯	◯	◯	◯
Opaque watercolor	✕	◯	△ Lighter than the base color: ✕	△ Lighter than the base color: ✕	◯	◯	◯	◯
Alcohol-based marker	△ Lighter than the base color: ✕	◯	△ Lighter than the base color: ✕	△ Lighter than the base color: ✕	◯	◯	◯	◯
Water-based marker	✕ Dilutes base color	◯	△ Lighter than the base color: ✕	△ Lighter than the base color: ✕	◯	◯	◯	◯
Oil-based color pencil	△ Smears water-based color pencil	◯	✕ Rubs ink	△ Lighter than the base color: ✕	◯	◯	△ May reject ink	◯
Pastel Color pencil	✕ Dilutes pastel	✕ Dilutes pastel	✕ Dilutes pastel	✕ Dilutes pastel	◯	◯	△ May reject ink	◯
Color ball-point pen	✕ Dilutes ink	◯	◯	△ May smear ink	◯	◯	◯	◯
Drawing pen	◯	◯	◯	◯	◯	◯	◯	◯

(3) Coloring Method

Watercolors and markers are used for the basic coloring, with color pencils and other pens as supplements.

Coloring by watercolor

◆ Color matching

Practice in order to produce all colors by mixing four colors i.e. the three primaries; cyan (C), magenta (M) and yellow (Y), plus black (K), while adding white as needed.

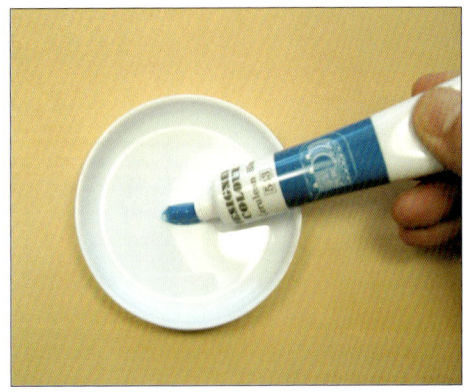

1. The Nicker Poster Color which is less apt to cause uneven finish is used here. Use about half an inch from the tube. A small addition of black or white will create a garment color suited to the skin. Note that garment coloration in primary colors only may look unnatural.

2. When producing pale colors, add three primaries little by little to the white base, to prevent the use of too much white. (Example) Saxe blue: Add blue, then red to white. In the case of transparent watercolors, use a good amount of water instead of white, and layer colors to produce shading.

3. Dilute with water to the consistency of milk lotion. Mix well using a thick brush until the colors thoroughly blend. As the more colors mixed, the duller the color becomes (subtractive color mixing, see p.84), add no more than three colors when a clear color is needed.

4. When desired color is obtained, test it on a separate paper. Be sure to confirm the color when dry, as in liquid form e.g. in the palette, it appears lighter.

5. Water holder consisting of three sections; for washing and rinsing brushes, and for solvent. Fill about two thirds to avoid spilling.

Chapter 3 : Fashion Drawing

◆ **Solid Coloring**
This is an exercise to acquire the basic skill of applying color evenly.

1. Before applying the paint, thoroughly strain out the water on the edge of the palette.

2. Apply the paint along the warp line of the fabric. Paint gently and carefully so that the moisture is properly absorbed into the paper. Divide the drawing into small areas and then color them, one at a time to ensure consistency. Be sure not to remove the brush from the surface before finishing each area. The more you retouch, the more uneven it becomes.

3. Lay the brush flat when painting large areas and hold it upright when painting small areas. Try holding it at different angles to find the one that is most comfortable.

4. Adjust the amount of water to ensure that the paper does not become soaked. The easiest way to do this is to soak up the extra water with a tissue paper.

5. Once the first coat is dry, start the second. (When using poster color, any unevenness will disappear after about three coats.)

6. If the paint runs over the edge like this, don't panic.

7. Using a brush that contains clean water only, float the color to the surface of the paper.

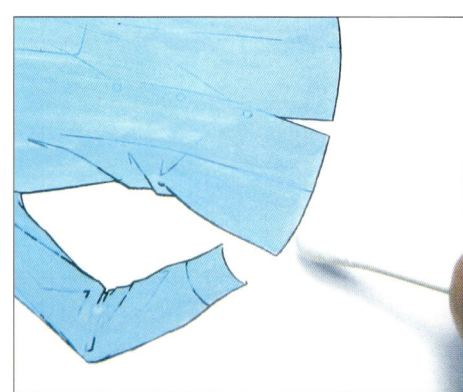

8. And wipe it off carefully with a cotton bud.

87

◆ **Shading**
Emphasize the three-dimensional appearance, by adding darker colors.

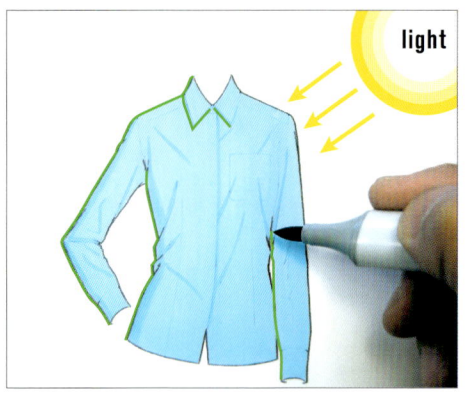

1. With the direction of light in mind, add shading to the opposite side of the shirt. (gray marker is used here). Be sure to use a color darker than the base color. It is sufficient to add shading by following the outline shown in green. Following this, work on the collar, the front and the sleeves, adding shading to each of them. Once you become comfortable with this, highlight the creases by applying shading to create a 3D effect.

2. Select a brown colored pencil for shading on red or yellow, and a dark blue one for shading on blue and green. For delicate colors that are difficult to judge, use a gray that is darker than the base color, or even select black. Shading should be applied gently using the side of the pencil lead.

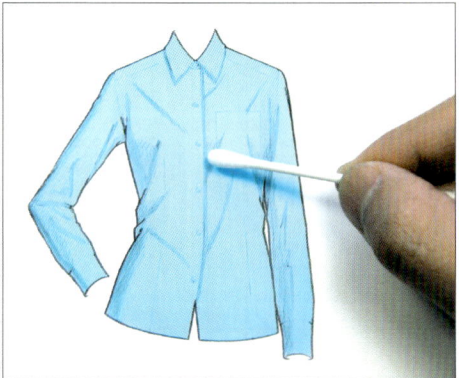

3. Blur the colored pencil lines using a cotton bud.

4. Redraw any lines that have disappeared. Note that lines drawn on top of paint become thicker.

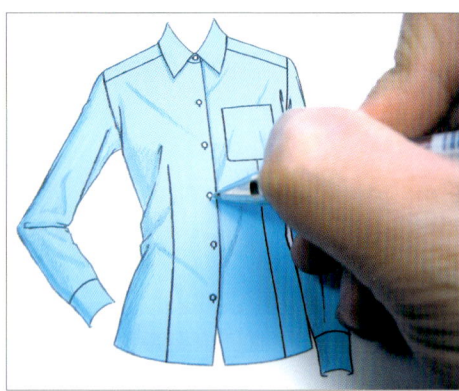

5. Use a white marker to color the buttons.

6. Vary the strength of the lines in order to emphasize the 3D effect. Use strong pressure on the brush to produce thick lines in the shaded areas, the lines of separation between parts (e.g. collar, front body, front closure), the deep creases (the elbow of the bent arm, the waist on the pivotal leg side), and the tension points (bent arms). In contrast, use less pressure to draw faint lines for the areas of light, shallow creases (extended arm and front body), and areas without tension.

7. As colors applied by colored pencil tend to rub off easily, they should be fixed using a spray fixative. This should be sprayed on lightly from a distance of about 20 cm.

8. Completed work

Chapter 3 : Fashion Drawing

◆ **Layered Painting**
This technique involves creating shadow by adding several coats of water-diluted paint. Transparent watercolor paints are best suited for this style of painting.

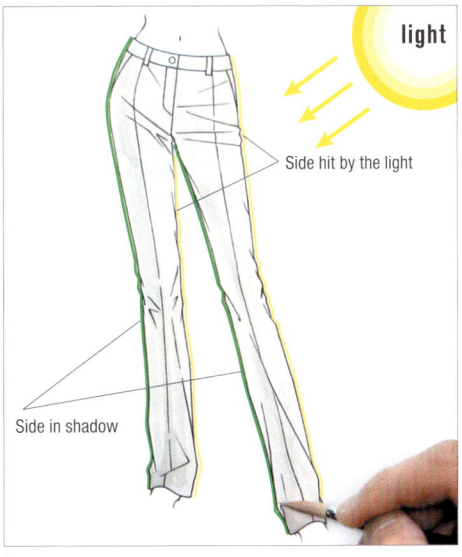

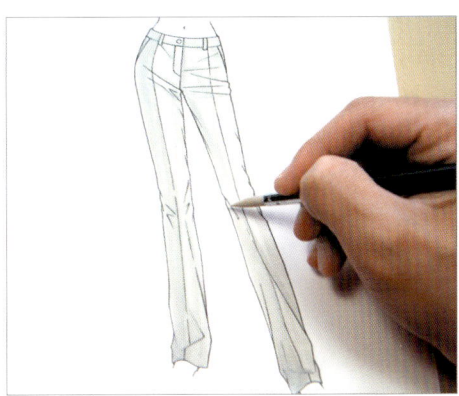

1. First set the light source from an angle above the right or left side of the figure. Dilute the paint with a lot of water, and apply coats on the shadow side. As the first coat will be quickly absorbed by the paper, resulting in unevenness, be sure to use well-diluted thin paint. Whitish, paler tones can be obtained without using white, by thinning the color with water.

2. Apply color in layers to the shadow area to create a sense of volume through graded effect. Add light and dark tones to the left and right legs.

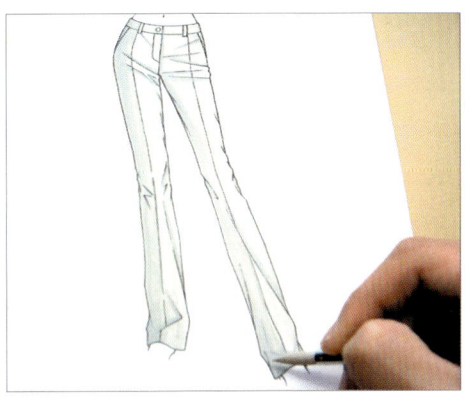

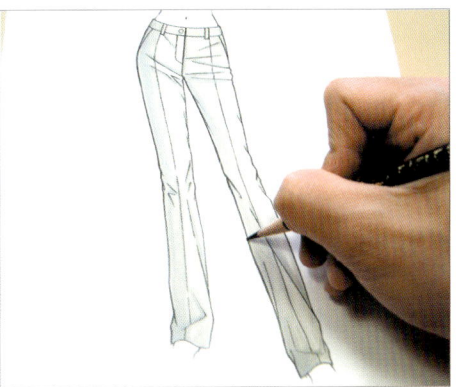

3. Add additional coats. When you are unable to create shading, darken the color itself by adding for example black. If you have applied too many coats, wet the surface with a brush soaked in clean water and carefully remove paint with a tissue or cotton bud. Wet the surface of the paper with a brush while it is still wet. Note that this technique can only be used for transparent watercolors. Acrylic paint cannot be removed once it is dry. If you want to strengthen the contrast you can finish by using colored pencils or markers to darken the shadows.

4. Retouch details that have become weak.

5. Vary the strength of the lines in order to emphasize the 3D effect. Use strong pressure on the brush to produce thick lines in the shaded areas, the lines of separation between parts (e.g. fly), the deep creases (the crotch area), and the areas where load is being applied (pivotal leg). In contrast, use less pressure to draw faint lines for the areas of light, shallow creases (ankles), and areas where strength is not being used (bracing leg).

6. Retain colors by spraying with fixative.

7. Completed work

◆ **Omitted Painting**

This is a technique which leaves areas on the lit side unpainted, instead of applying the solid painting method to the entire area. Opaque watercolors are best suited for this style of painting.

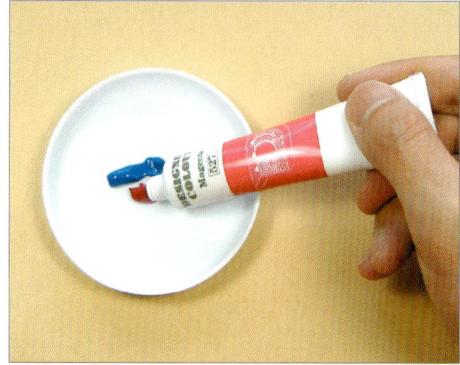

1. All colors are made from the three primaries; cyan (C), magenta (M) and yellow (Y), plus black. Let's practice in producing colors by using only these four.

2. Dark colors can be produced by adding black little by little to some combination of the primaries. In the case of dark blue, first create the bluish-purple base color by combining blue and red, plus black.

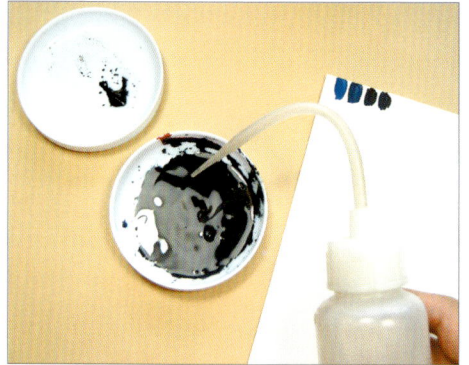

3. Add a good amount of water using a dropper, otherwise it becomes too thick, resembling oil paint.

4. Test colors first on a separate paper, as color containing water on a palette is different from the dried color on paper. This is a technique to improve your color coordination skill.

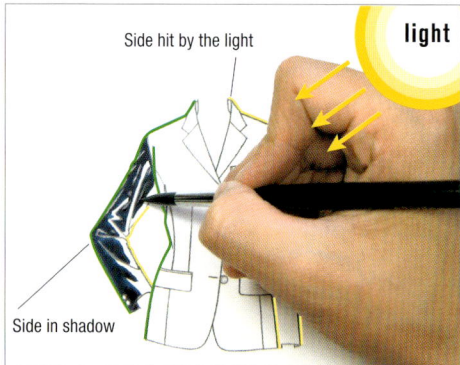

5. Decide on which side of light source (seen here on the right), and apply color to each part, such as the sleeve and front body while leaving the lit areas unpainted. If the color appears uneven, apply another layer. It will be good not to touch the detail lines.

6. Here, 20% of the far right of the front body is left unpainted. Even if the color becomes uneven, don't worry, you can apply another coat when it is dry.

7. Mix black in the paint to produce a color for shading.

8. Shadows appear on the opposite side to the light source.

9. Apply blurring by thinning colors at the edge of painted areas with a brush soaked in clean water.

10. Retouch lines that may have disappeared. When the garment is in a dark color, use a white pencil or ball-point pen.

11. Completed work.

Chapter 3 : Fashion Drawing

◆ **Layered Painting**
This technique involves creating shadow by adding several coats of water-diluted paint. Transparent watercolor paints are best suited for this style of painting.

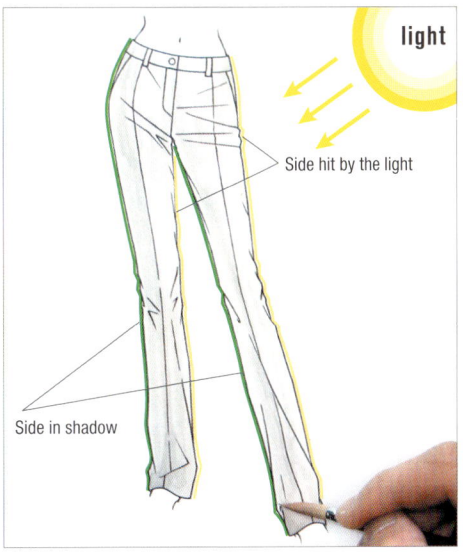

1. First set the light source from an angle above the right or left side of the figure. Dilute the paint with a lot of water, and apply coats on the shadow side. As the first coat will be quickly absorbed by the paper, resulting in unevenness, be sure to use well-diluted thin paint. Whitish, paler tones can be obtained without using white, by thinning the color with water.

2. Apply color in layers to the shadow area to create a sense of volume through graded effect. Add light and dark tones to the left and right legs.

3. Add additional coats. When you are unable to create shading, darken the color itself by adding for example black. If you have applied too many coats, wet the surface with a brush soaked in clean water and carefully remove paint with a tissue or cotton bud. Wet the surface of the paper with a brush while it is still wet. Note that this technique can only be used for transparent watercolors. Acrylic paint cannot be removed once it is dry. If you want to strengthen the contrast you can finish by using colored pencils or markers to darken the shadows.

4. Retouch details that have become weak.

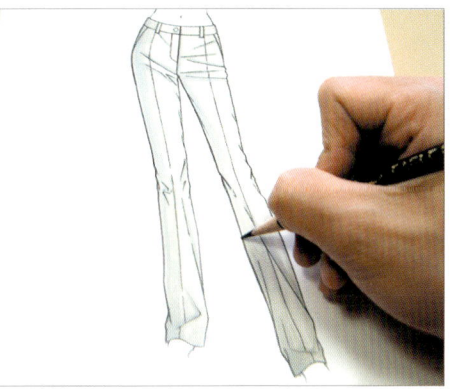

5. Vary the strength of the lines in order to emphasize the 3D effect. Use strong pressure on the brush to produce thick lines in the shaded areas, the lines of separation between parts (e.g. fly), the deep creases (the crotch area), and the areas where load is being applied (pivotal leg). In contrast, use less pressure to draw faint lines for the areas of light, shallow creases (ankles), and areas where strength is not being used (bracing leg).

6. Retain colors by spraying with fixative.

7. Completed work

◆ Omitted Painting

This is a technique which leaves areas on the lit side unpainted, instead of applying the solid painting method to the entire area. Opaque watercolors are best suited for this style of painting.

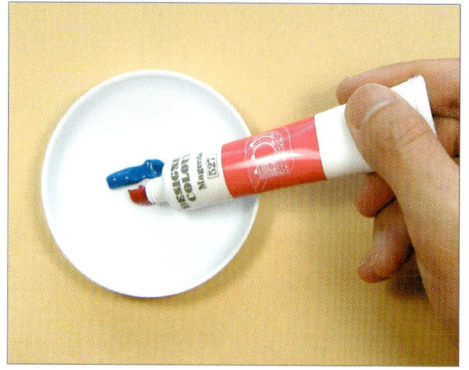

1. All colors are made from the three primaries; cyan (C), magenta (M) and yellow (Y), plus black. Let's practice in producing colors by using only these four.

2. Dark colors can be produced by adding black little by little to some combination of the primaries. In the case of dark blue, first create the bluish-purple base color by combining blue and red, plus black.

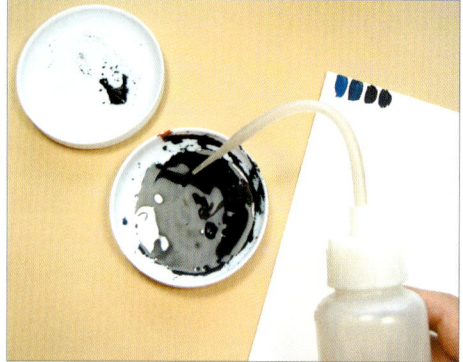

3. Add a good amount of water using a dropper, otherwise it becomes too thick, resembling oil paint.

4. Test colors first on a separate paper, as color containing water on a palette is different from the dried color on paper. This is a technique to improve your color coordination skill.

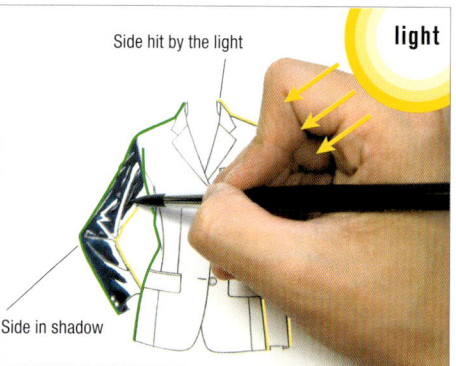

5. Decide on which side of light source (seen here on the right), and apply color to each part, such as the sleeve and front body while leaving the lit areas unpainted. If the color appears uneven, apply another layer. It will be good not to touch the detail lines.

6. Here, 20% of the far right of the front body is left unpainted. Even if the color becomes uneven, don't worry, you can apply another coat when it is dry.

7. Mix black in the paint to produce a color for shading.

8. Shadows appear on the opposite side to the light source.

9. Apply blurring by thinning colors at the edge of painted areas with a brush soaked in clean water.

10. Retouch lines that may have disappeared. When the garment is in a dark color, use a white pencil or ball-point pen.

11. Completed work.

Coloration with a marker

Markers are known as a very useful painting tool for their rich color variations, color quality and fast-drying property. Nevertheless, you have to have a good assortment to make full use of them, and 300 yen per marker easily adds up and becomes expensive. It would be efficient and economical to first purchase the colors you often use such as a skin color and gray, and then later gradation colors of the three primaries.

◆ **Recommended assortment of Copic Sketch markers**

1st Stage: Skin Color tones
Skin tones: E00 and YR00
Shading: E13
Warm grays: W1/W3/W5/W7

2nd Stage: Gray tones
Neutral grays: N1/N3/N5/N7
Black: 110
Blender: 0

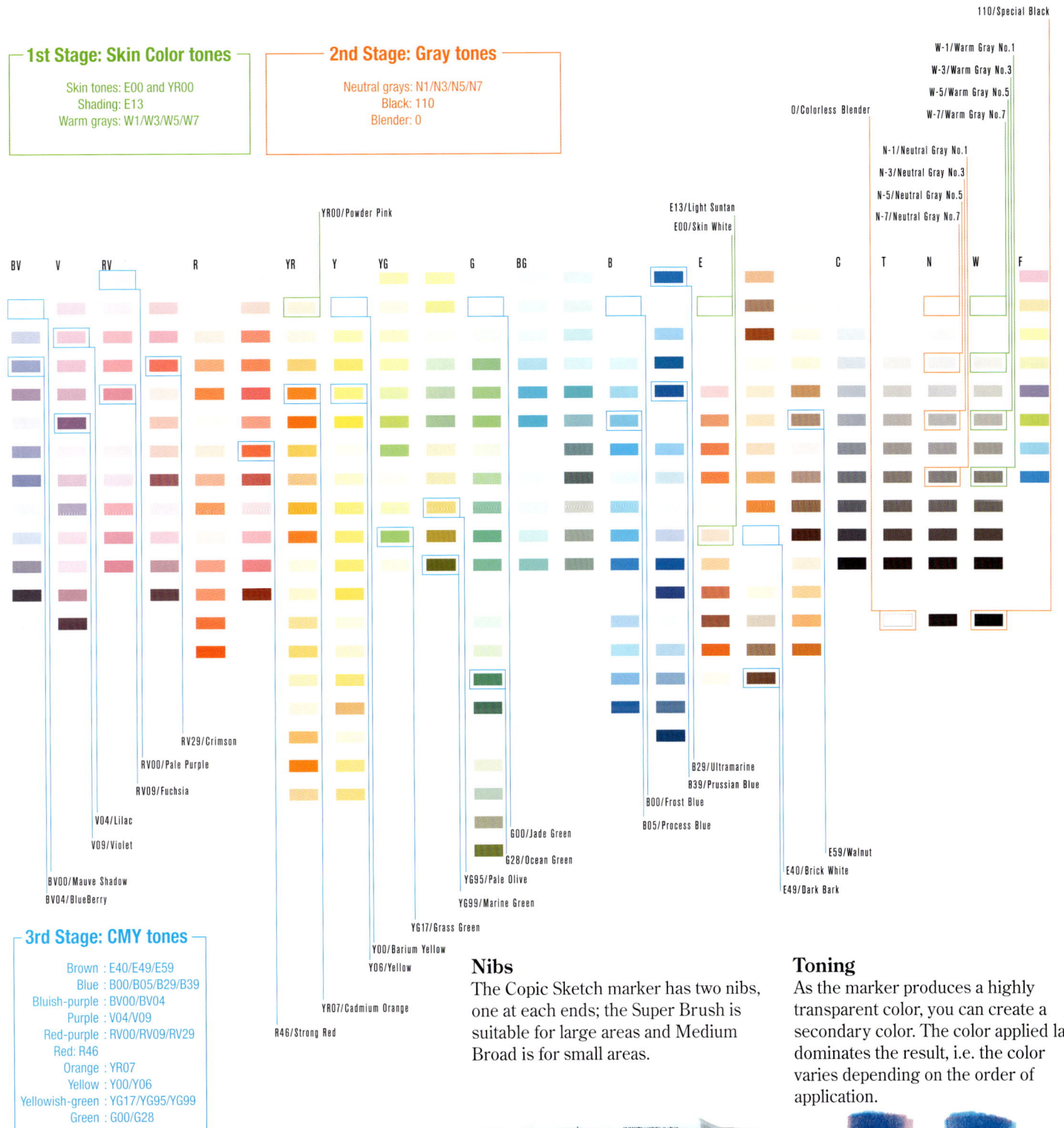

3rd Stage: CMY tones
Brown : E40/E49/E59
Blue : B00/B05/B29/B39
Bluish-purple : BV00/BV04
Purple : V04/V09
Red-purple : RV00/RV09/RV29
Red : R46
Orange : YR07
Yellow : Y00/Y06
Yellowish-green : YG17/YG95/YG99
Green : G00/G28

Nibs
The Copic Sketch marker has two nibs, one at each ends; the Super Brush is suitable for large areas and Medium Broad is for small areas.

Toning
As the marker produces a highly transparent color, you can create a secondary color. The color applied later dominates the result, i.e. the color varies depending on the order of application.

Red + Blue = Bluish-purple

Blue + Red = Reddish-purple

◆ Solid Coloring

This is an exercise to acquire the basic skill of applying color evenly.

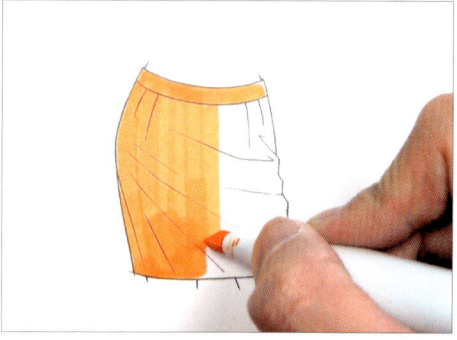

1. Apply the ink slowly and gently along the fabric's warp line. Lay the brush flat for large areas and hold it upright for small areas. Divide the drawing into small areas and then color them, one at a time. Be sure not to remove the brush from the surface before finishing each area. The photograph shows the waistband and body of the skirt colored separately.

2. When unevenness becomes too visible, first reapply two or three layers to the area, when the unevenness has more or less disappeared, add the shading. Select a marker one shade darker than the one used earlier for the base color and add the shading (volume). If you do not have a marker one shade darker, you can still produce a shadow effect by applying several coats of the same color.

3. Create additional shading effects by using a gray marker. Select the one that matches the base color from the four available gray series of the Copic Sketch marker.

4. Once again, apply the original base color over the sketch.

5. Completed work

- N : Neutral gray (The most general gray tones. This series is basically sufficient.)
- W : Warm gray (Reddish-gray tones. Use for shading on skin, beige and ivory colors.)
- C : Cool gray (Bluish-gray tones. Use for shading on blue and green colors.)
- T : Toner gray (Brownish-gray. Use for shading on brown colors.)

◆ Layered/Omitted Coloring

- A method of coloring that combines elements of the "layered coloring" and "omitted coloring", learned in the painting using watercolors.
- Express the form of a garment three-dimensionally through rendition of light and shadow.
- Use gradations produced by layering colors towards the shadow.

1. Test the color. Try producing gradations by applying several layers of color. Light and dark differ according to the garment fabric. The greater the reflected light in a material, the larger the difference between light and dark. In metal the light parts are white and the dark are black.

2. First apply the omitted coloring. Decide on which side of the light source, and apply color to each part, such as the sleeve and front body while leaving the lit areas unpainted. It will be good if you can manage not to touch the detail lines. If the color appears uneven, apply another layer.

3. Secondly, apply layered coloring by adding shadow using a color darker than the base color.

4. Use a lighter color than the base to color the entire surface and allow it to blend in.

5. Redraw any lines that have disappeared. Because the base color is dark, a white pencil is used here.

6. Create contrasts by adding thick lines in dark areas, tension points (elbows), and areas with deep creases.

7. The completed work. If more contrast is desired, finish by adding more shadow with a colored pencil.

Chapter 3 : Fashion Drawing

◆ **Coloring Faces**
Since you will color the skin, hair, eyes and lips every time you make a drawing, markers are the most useful tools. In the case of Copic Sketch markers, E00 and YR00 for the base skin tone, and E13 for the shading of the skin are appropriate. If you have particular colors that you prefer for the eyes and hair, it is a good idea to have them ready.

1. First decide on the direction of the light, and color the skin while leaving some areas unpainted. The forehead, cheek and side of the nose closer to the light are left partially white. Use a color one shade darker to add the shadows. The areas below the hair; between the eyes and eyebrows; under the nose, lower lip and chin all tend to be in shadow.

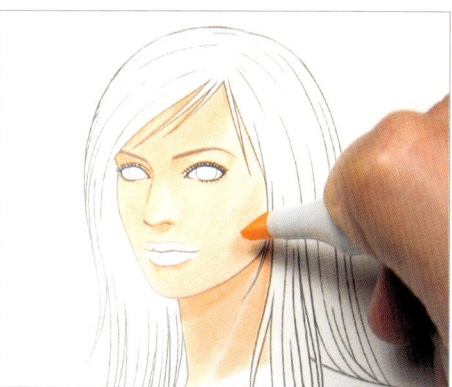

2. Apply tone to the entire surface, using a color one shade lighter than the skin color.

3. Color the hair in line with its flow and, to make the head appear three-dimensional, add several highlights, indicated here by the blue bands. Leave them white.

4. Make the highlights stronger by adding shading.

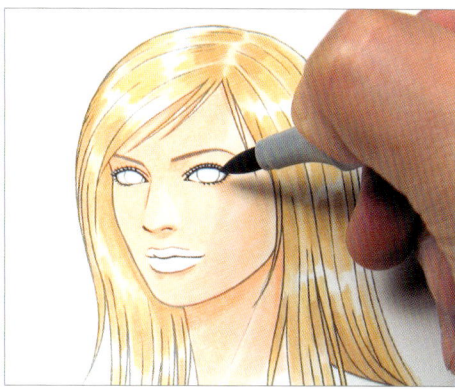

5. Add the shadow of the eyelids to the eyeballs.

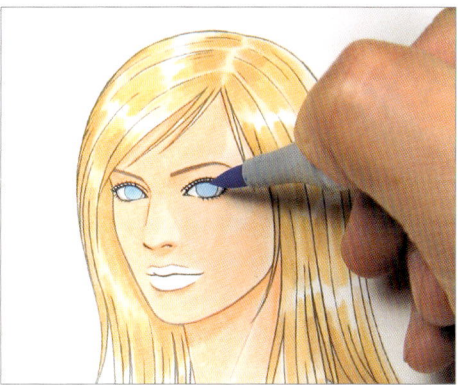

6. Apply color to the iris. The upper one-third to one-half of the iris is hidden by the eyelid. Note that if the entire iris is visible it will give the appearance of surprise.

7. Add color to the lips. The upper lip is in shadow so the color should be darker. The sheen of the lower lip can be made with a colored pencil or pastel.

8. Draw the pupils. If they are large the eyes will appear "forceful".

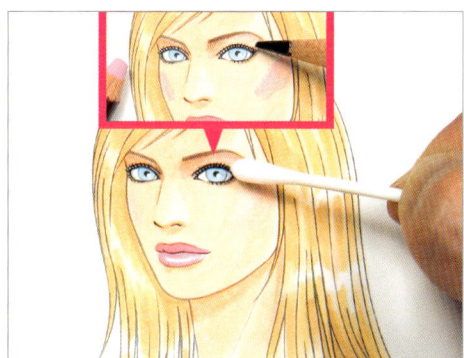

9. Apply eyeliner and mascara, using colored pencils. Using pastels, add eye shadow and blusher. Spread and blend in using a cotton bud.

Face Coloring Variations

Completed work of the coloring on page 93.

In the case of a wavy hairstyle, the color should be omitted at the parts closest to the viewer.

As styles such as dreadlocks, curly-hair and sauvage-hair produce an irregular reflection, omitted coloring should be finely applied.

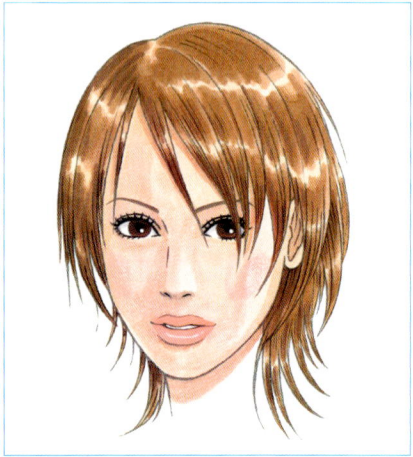
About two bands of highlights are suitable for short hairstyles.

Create a 3D effect on erect hair by finely omitting the color.

The color of the part where the light hits can be boldly omitted and left white.

[3] Textile Rendition

The most important thing for coloring fabrics is to thoroughly understand the characteristics of materials and patterns, and to make good use of various painting tools. Retail stores have a wide range of colors and patterns for one garment of the same design, in order to meet consumer needs. The same design can give different impressions when its material or pattern is changed. These are key elements which also expand the design potentials.

Key points

(1) Downsizing
It is necessary to reduce the actual size of a pattern to 20% in order to render it as a design drawing based on B4 size. (When coloring by looking at the actual fabric, render its texture as seen from two meters away.)
(2) Coloring order
First color the base, and then the patterns and texture.
(3) Coloring materials
No special attention is needed concerning choice of tools when coloring dark colored patterns on a light base color, but when the other way around (e.g. white dots on black), take care how you use the tools. Combine opaque watercolors which do not show the base color through them, with markers perfect for fine coloring and color ball-point pens. In some cases, a make-up kit may work as a perfect coloring tool. Refer to the Color Compatibility Table on page 86 for compatibility of artist's materials for the base and detail drawing/coloring.

Chapter 3 : Fashion Drawing

How to Draw Nubby Tweed

Fabric sample (reduced to 45%):
Nubs should be rendered as fine layered colored dots, so opaque watercolors are more suitable than transparent ones. Here poster colors were used for both the base color and the nubs.

1. Prepare the base color; pink-beige by making pale gray and adding red.

2. Paint vertically along the fabric's warp line.

3. Put some paint on the brush and push it down on the palette to separate the bristles.

4. This is how the bristle ends should open.

5. Tap the bristle ends gently on the paper. Be sure not to tap them too strongly, or the dots will be too big. The key points are; 1. to hold the brush straight up, 2. to hold the brush near its base, 3. to squeeze the bristle to remove excess water.

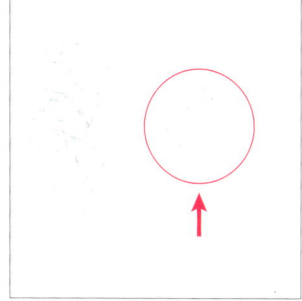

6. Single dots can be very small (Approx. 0.1 mm)

7. Repeat tapping until the base color cannot be seen, to produce the thickness of the tweed.

8. When the entire surface has been covered, change the color to a lighter and darker one for further tapping.

9. Paint the 'spice' colors finely scattered. Here they are salmon pink, maroon, mustard, light blue and purple.

10. Add some white dots to adjust the color tone.

Wool Variations (Harris tweed)

11. Render the rough texture using a brown color pencil.

12. Completed.

This Harris tweed sample has a check pattern. Use color pencils to render the check as those in tweed appear 'splashed'.

Student Works

By Arisa Hara: Painting of another tweed. The nub texture is well rendered. Student's comment; "I applied color many times."

By Naoko Takahashi: Depth is achieved by the thoroughly and finely rendered nubs. Student's comment; "I applied colors while crushing the bristles and trying many times. Color preparation was most difficult and I added lacking colors after finishing the process as instructed".

How to Draw Flannel

Fabric sample (45%): This method can be applied to all napped fabrics, including velvet (warp-pile woven fabric in silk), velveteen (or cotton velvet, weft-pile woven fabric in cotton), suede (leather, especially kidskin, with the flesh side filed to create a velvety nap).

1. First paint the base color, and then render the rough texture using the side of the leads of color pencils or pastels.

2. Completed.

How to Draw Denim

Fabric sample (45%)

1. The base coloration. Any tools such as markers and various watercolors can be used. When preparing the color, note that the denim blue contains a small amount of red. If using Copic Sketch markers, B39 is suitable. Creating intentional unevenness produces a well-worn denim quality.

2. The twill weave of denim can be rendered with color pencils or pastels. Color diagonally using white first.

3. Then using black or dark blue, add the final touch.

4. Completed.

Fabric sample (45%): For lighter color denim, B23 or B45 are suitable if using Copic Sketch markers.

The twill weave on the denim surface is the key feature here also. Keeping this in mind, apply colors using color pencils and pastels. To create the vintage denim look, it is important to render a sense of vertical wearing. Apply vertical strokes with pastels.

Chapter 3 : Fashion Drawing

How to Draw Fur

Fabric sample (45%): The short fine soft hair of certain animals. The length differs depending on the animal.

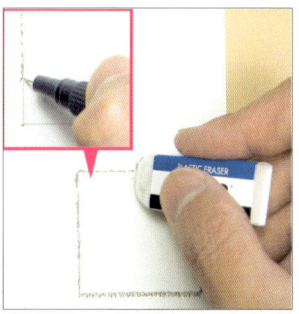

1. The outline is an important element for fur drawing. Try to draw with a fur-like touch. After the penwork, go over carefully with an eraser.

2. After painting the base color with a marker or watercolor, draw the fur.

3. As fur has a 3D appearance, add shading gently using the side of the lead of color pencils, while considering the direction of light.

4. Add pastel with a cotton-tipped swab, by first making it into powder form by rubbing onto a separate paper.

5. Finally, adjust the overall balance by drawing fine hairs using pencils in colors lighter and darker than the base color.

6. Completed. Note that color pencils and pastels are essential for the rendition of wool fabrics.

Student Works

Fabric sample: Leopard-print pattern. Irregular patterns are delightfully laid out.

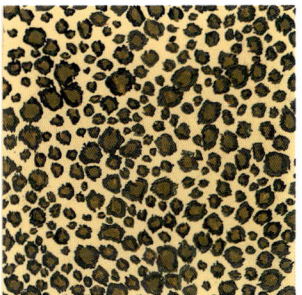

By Reimi Muranaga: Color the base and then render unique leopard skin patterns on top. Markers are recommended for both brown and black. Student's comment; "As all the hairs were in different directions, I tried to render them by turning the paper."

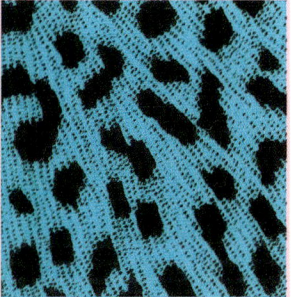

Fabric sample: Animal patterns vary widely. The important thing to remember is to try to reduce the size of patterns to 20% of the actual fabric patterns.

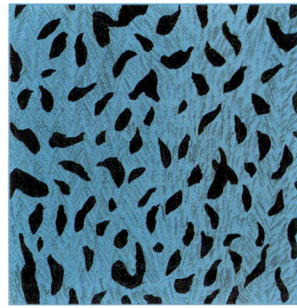

By Miki Minagawa: She first rendered the base fur and the animal skin patterns. Student's comment; "As the base color had a fluorescent quality, it was difficult to reproduce."

How to Draw Corduroy

Fabric sample (45%): Vertical ribs are the distinctive feature.

1. The ribs can be rendered by scribing the paper using a mechanical pencil without lead.

2. Grooves are created on the paper, representing the corduroy's unique ribs. Scribe with even 1 mm intervals.

3. Completed.

How to Draw Polka-Dots

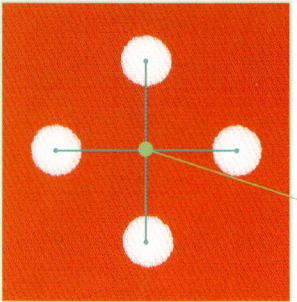

Dots of 1 to 2 mm in diameter are called pin-dots, dots of 5 to 10 mm are polka-dots and dots of 2 to 3 cm are coin-dots.

To render dots, use a semispherical cross-section surface, for example, the end of a pencil, toothpick or brush, from left to right here. Put paint on the end and stamp the color on a paper. All of these produce good circles.

Crossing point of gridlines for dots.

Dots are placed on every second crossing point of the gridlines. This means that each gridline interval is half of the dot interval.

1. Color the base with a marker or opaque watercolor, and draw the gridlines. Draw the intervals at 20% of those in the actual fabric. When working by observing a fabric, measure the actual dimension and divide it by five. Here when calculated based on the actual interval of 12.5 mm, it became 2.5 mm, I then rounded it to 3 mm for use as the gridline intervals, which should be lightly drawn as they will be erased later.

2. Color dots on every other crossing point of the gridlines. Try to make them all the same size. As the actual dot is 7 mm in diameter, apply them in 1.4 mm.

3. Colored ball-point pen can be used to render dots. Erase the gridlines and correct any missing parts.

4. Completed.

Student Work

Fabric sample: The gridline intervals are 1 mm, 20% of the actual value. The diameter of dots was reduced to 0.6 mm, which was rounded up to 1 mm.

By Eriko Yamanaka: Minute dots so closely placed reflect the student's strong power of concentration. Student's comment; "In order to maintain the same gridline intervals, I took the utmost care, by wiping the paint off from the toothpick after every stamping and constantly telling myself to make it the same interval".

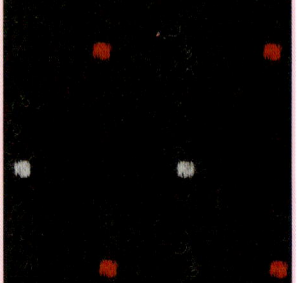

Fabric sample (65%): The gridline intervals are 7 mm, 20% of the actual value. The diameter of dots was reduced to 0.6 mm, which was rounded up to 1 mm.

By Aya Izumida: Alternated red and white dots form a beautiful work. Student's comment; "To represent a piece of 'fabric' in a mere four centimeter square space required enormous patience and effort".

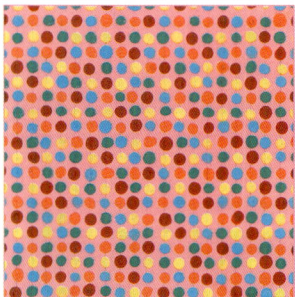

By Mariko Arimatsu: Bright multi-color dots produced a vivid piece of work. Student's comment; "Knowing that the proper gridlines are the key to success, I worked carefully at drawing them".

By Kumiko Yamaguchi: Every dot is very carefully rendered. Student's comment; "It was very difficult to produce circles or dots all in the same size".

Chapter 3 : Fashion Drawing

How to Draw Linear Patterns/Student Works

Fabric sample (65%): Stripes (including all stripes, but meaning vertical stripes in the narrow sense). This is a sample of a multi-colored stripe.

By Manami Miyoshi: It is important to grasp the rule of repeating pattern to master multi-stripes. Student's comment; "I accepted this task as a challenge as I like straight line drawing using the grooved ruler, but they became very uneven due to the pale colors. It was also very difficult as all the lines became nearly the same width when drawn to 20%".

Fabric sample: Lateral stripes. Red bands on a white base.

By Tomomi Kobayashi: Red bands are placed at even intervals. It is not necessary to paint the white background. Use the glass rod and grooved ruler to draw straight lines (see p.102). Draw gridlines outside of the frame in pencil to achieve even intervals. Student's comment; "It was enjoyable and satisfying as I could smoothly draw bold and long stripes".

   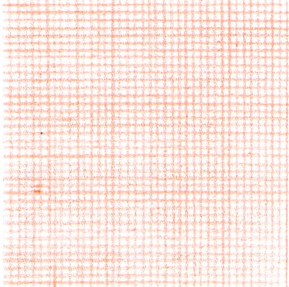

Fabric sample: Knitted stripes.

By Saori Osawa: It is fine to focus on the pattern rendition, without expressing the texture of gauges. Student's comment; "It was difficult to draw the gray and navy lines in the same width. I am satisfied with the red and white lines as I could draw them straight, but the difficult thing was to draw them thinly right on the center of the gray and navy lines respectively.

Fabric sample (45%): Gingham Check, plain-weave fabric made from dyed cotton yarn and woven into checked pattern. The sample here consists of a 6 mm by 6 mm check pattern.

By Toshie Nagai: The line intervals are reduced to 1 mm i.e. 20% that of the sample. The unique splashed woven appearance of the Gingham is rendered with a color pencil. Student's comment; "It was a hard exercise drawing the lines with one millimeter intervals. Despite some unevenness, I am content with what I did".

How to Draw Knit Fabric

Fabric sample: The key point for knitted fabrics is the way to render gauges and the fuzzy surface texture.

1. Apply the base color using markers or watercolors.

2. Finely draw gauges in a darker color than the base at even intervals in the same way as the ribs of corduroy.

3. Render the fuzzy surface texture using the side of the leads of color pencils. This is the same method used for flannel.

4. Completed.

99

How to Draw Yoryu Crepe

A distinctive feature of this fabric is the fine vertical crepings resembling flowing willow branches.

1. Apply the base color using paints or markers. Use color pencils for the creping lines. Finish each line with a fast sweeping stroke, without stopping on the paper.

2. Completed.

How to Draw Hound's Tooth Check

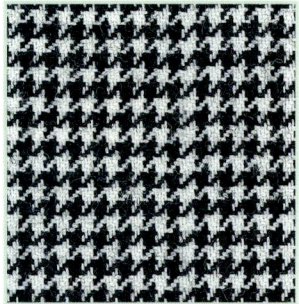

As the name suggests, the pattern looks like a dog's fang, while the black and white parts have exactly the same form. Render in a simplified form to save time.

By reducing the pattern to a ninja-star like design, draw each one centered on the crossing point of the gridlines, using a drawing pen with a 0.05 nib.

Practice first with 4 mm gridline intervals.

Continue practicing with 2 mm gridline intervals.

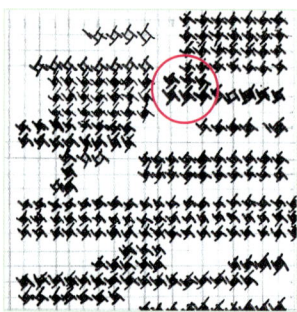

Note that if the patterns are too large, the white area becomes too small.

1. After mastering the drawing of one row of the patterns in the same form and size, you can begin the actual exercise. To create the grid, first mark the intervals with a mechanical pencil. As a small size is aimed for here, intervals of 2 mm were selected.

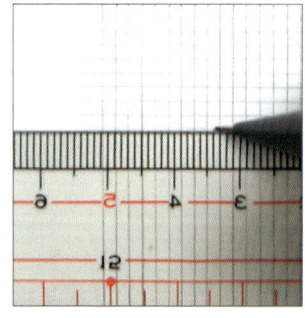

2. Be sure to make the intervals accurately, as a little deviation will influence all the rest.

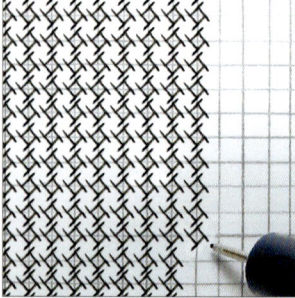

3. Draw the outline of each pattern centered on the crossing point of the gridlines.

4. Complete it by filling in the center.

Chapter 3 : Fashion Drawing

Student Works

By Saori Osawa: Drawn with the greatest care and concentration. Student's comment; "I strained my eyes badly and had a stiff shoulder. The tension due to the mental pressure that making a single mistake would spoil everything, kept me going and I could finish in no time".

By Naoko Takahashi: She worked very carefully. Student's comment; "I drew while paying attention to the proportion of black and white areas. It was difficult to draw the pattern of a hound's tooth well, even after redrawing a number of times. I almost gave up, but tried to render them to look like a hound's tooth at least from a distance".

How to Draw Glen Check

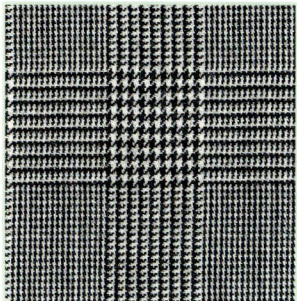

This is a pattern combining the hound's tooth check with hairline stripes.

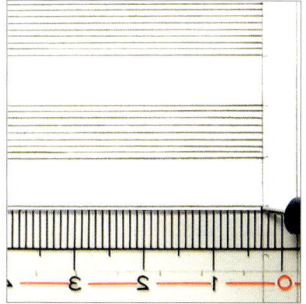

1. Draw checks. Based on the actual sizes; vertical intervals at 30 mm and horizontal intervals at 35 mm, the sizes are reduced to 20%; 6 mm and 7 mm respectively. One pattern consists of nine lines each for both the vertical and horizontal blocks.

2. The hound's tooth check pattern should be further simplified for such a small rendition. As shown here, the check marks resemble a hound's tooth.

3. Enter the pattern at each crossing point of the check lines.

4. Draw details in the checks.

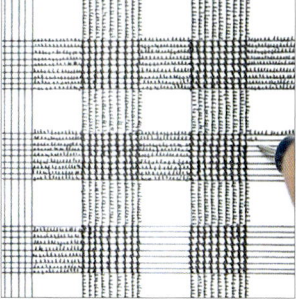

5. Continue the detailing.

6. Draw in hairlines to finish.

7. Completed.

How to Draw Tartan Check

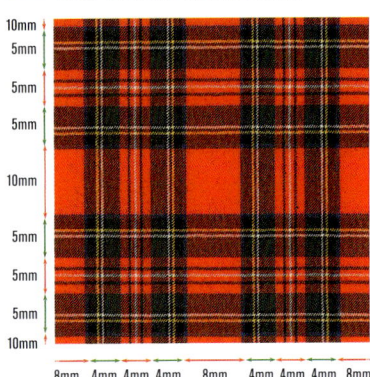

Fabric sample (20%): When drawing complex check patterns such as a tartan, first designate a "key color pattern" as a guide, and draw in the other patterns based on the sequence of such key color pattern. Here, the red/green bold stripe was selected for this (as indicated by the green arrows at each end), as it represents the boldest line of the tartan and is placed regularly. The photograph shown here is already reduced to 20% of the original sample, as are the interval sizes shown.

To draw a straight line with a brush, the grooved ruler is recommended. Hold the brush and glass rod together, while inserting the middle finger in between to keep them parallel.

Any rod which fits in the groove of the ruler can be used.

1. Place the ruler a little lower than the position of the line you wish to draw. Draw a line sliding the tip of the rod along the groove of the ruler. It is advisable to draw moving the elbow rather than the wrist, which should be fixed. Master this, as it will enable you to draw various sizes of lines by changing the drawing pressure and brush. Apply wax or oil to the groove for smooth sliding.

2. Paint the base color with a marker or opaque watercolor, and mark the gridlines outside the frame.

3. Outline the bands of the key color pattern using the grooved ruler and rod. To prevent the drawing becoming soiled, keep the ruler clean by wiping dirt off or place a sheet of paper underneath.

4. Color the inside of the key color pattern. Free-hand is OK, but avoid running off the edge.

5. In the same way, outline and color the inside of the vertical bands of the key color pattern.

6. Add dark green to the part where the two bands meet. Opaque watercolor is recommended for a good finish as it covers the base color. Free-hand is OK, but avoid running off the edge.

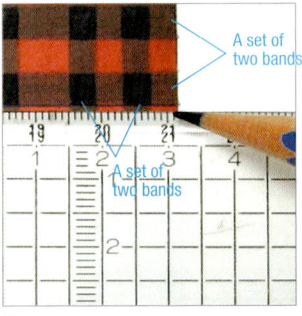

7. The key color pattern consists of two bands both vertically and horizontally. Draw dark blue lines on the outer edges of the outer bands. Paint can be used, but a color pencil is better for such a fine line.

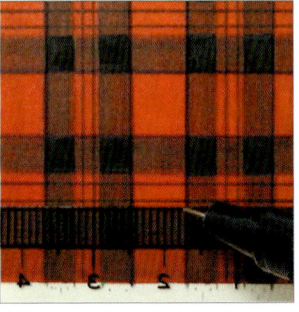

8. Add two black lines in between the two bands using a drawing pen with a nib of 0.05 mm.

9. Add yellow lines using the grooved ruler and rod, slightly toward the edges of the two bands.

10. Add white lines using the grooved ruler and rod, in the center of the two bands and in between the two black lines.

11. Add the rough surface texture of wool with a color pencil. Render the twill texture with diagonal strokes.

12. Completed.

Chapter 3 : Fashion Drawing

Student Works

By Aya Izumida: Each process is carefully implemented, resulting in an excellent work. Student's comment; "I enjoyed to find that the more I tried the better the lines became. I also learned that each drawing technique has a knack and that one will always be rewarded for hard work."

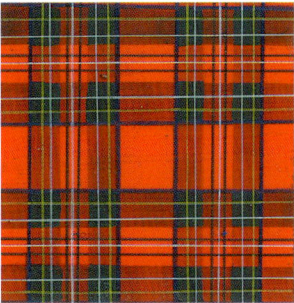

By Tomomi Kobayashi: The yellow and white lines are beautifully drawn. Student's comment; "I had to prepare many different colors and use various brushes, it was a lot of work. The idea of redrawing from the beginning i.e. coloring the green parts made me tense, but I was happy when I could successfully draw a fine line. I learned that the amount of water is a key point.

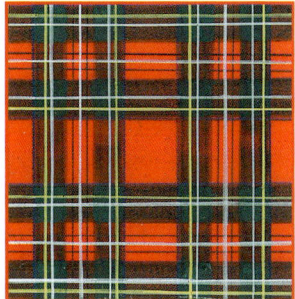

By Toshie Nagai: A very sincere approach can be seen in this work. Student's comment; "I tried my best, putting spirit into this. The fine lines were difficult to draw, but I am quite happy with the results".

Check Variations   I introduce various checks through the works of students.

Fabric sample: Checkers or Ichimatsu pattern. A kind of block check. In Japan, this became popular since an actor called Ichimatsu used it for his stage costume.

By Kumiko Yamaguchi: Diagonally designed check patterns. Student's comment; "There were so many corners and it was exhausting to paint them all".

Fabric sample: A variation of shepherd's check, featuring prominent diagonal twill patterns in blocks of darker color.

By Asami Tajima: Student's comment; "I used a toothpick for the red stitches, and color pencil and drawing pen for the twill blocks".

Fabric sample (65%): Tone-on-tone check, two or more different colors are woven over the base color.

By Tomomi Chikai: Student's comment; "I used six colors here. The splash look was rendered by coloring with color pencils on top of paint. When using color pencils, I placed two rulers on the edges of the area to be colored, to avoid going over the edge".

Fabric sample: A variation of tartan check.

By Chizuru Suzuki: Student's comment; "Having practiced several times to draw fine lines beforehand, I am quite happy with the results, although I feel that the watercolored white parts are a little too thin in appearance".

Fabric sample: Argyle check.

By Naoko Takahashi: Student's comment; "I colored this following the drawing method for tartan check. The change of color on the finer lines was tricky. I first applied one color for the lines and added another on top of these where necessary".

Collaboration: Saitama Prefectural Niiza Sougou Technical High School

How to Draw Shiny Materials

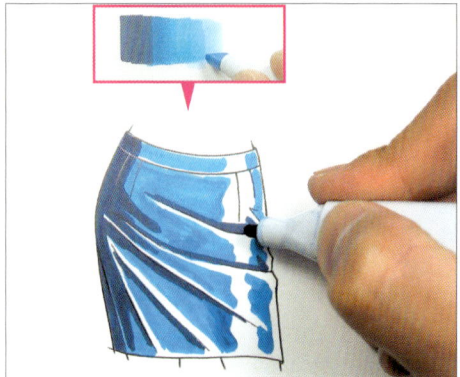

1. The color of shiny materials e.g. satin, velvet and enamel, differs greatly depending on whether it is in light or shadow. After first deciding the direction of the light, color the subject while leaving the lit areas white. Highlighting the creases by doing so will be effective. Markers are used here, in which case you should prepare a gradation sample first as shown above.

2. Color the edge of the white areas one shade lighter than the base color. The shinier the material is, the greater the difference of the color gradation. As the light source is supposed to be at the top right of the drawing, the area above and on the right side of the crease line is lit, and the area underneath and on the left side of the line is in shadow.

3. Color to make the entire surface blend in, using another shade lighter than that used in 2.

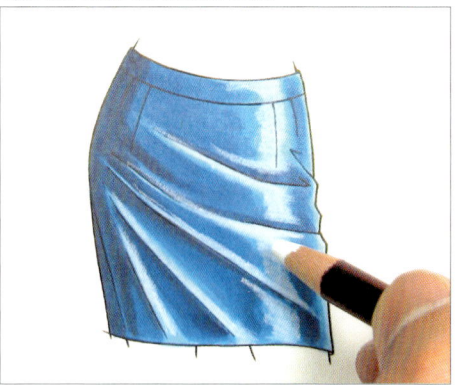

4. Apply white pastel to the lightest areas.

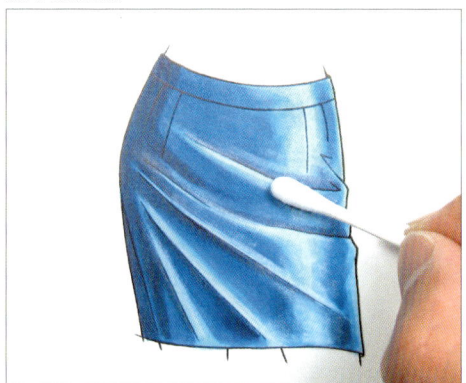

5. Spread the pastel with a cotton bud.

6. Completed.

How to Draw Leather

1. In the case of leather and enamel, the shiny areas can be boldly omitted and left white. This drawing is colored with opaque watercolors using shading brushes. Color with the light direction in mind, leaving the creases and details white.

2. A shading brush can be used in various ways; when held upright, it can color small areas, when held horizontally, it can color large areas. Leave significant areas in white to create a shiny look.

3. Thin the color at the edge of colored areas with a brush soaked in water.

4. Continue patiently, thinning little by little.

Chapter 3 : Fashion Drawing

5. A good amount of area is left white.

6. To further accentuate the white areas, apply pastel.

7. Apply pastel as if rubbing in onto the paper.

8. Go over the pastel to make it blend in.

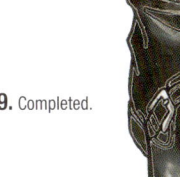

9. Completed.

How to Draw Sheer Fabrics

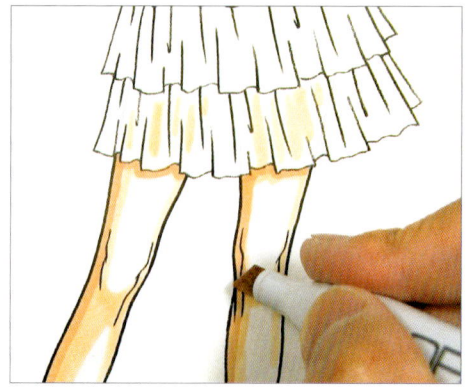

1. When drawing chiffon, organdy, georgette, voile and other sheer materials, begin by coloring the part which is underneath and seen through the fabric.

2. Color the part of the legs which are seen through the fabric, a little lighter than the part that is exposed.

3. Transparent watercolors are perfect for sheer fabrics. Dilute the watercolor as much as possible by taking up a brush full of water.

4. Be sure to use thin watercolor especially for the first and second coatings, as water is absorbed rapidly by the paper, which causes uneven color.

5. Decide the direction of the light, and layer the same color on the areas in shadow. Make sure the previous coat is completely dry. Drying time varies depending on the season, but 2 to 3 mins for watercolors and 1 to 2 mins for acrylic colors are usual.

6. Apply more coats. Two to three coats produces a good contrast, yet the color underneath is still well visible as it is a transparent watercolor.

7. Add more contrasts by shading with pastel.

8. Blend the pastel in with a cotton bud.

9. Completed.

Chapter 3 : Fashion Drawing

How to Draw Stockings and Fishnet Tights

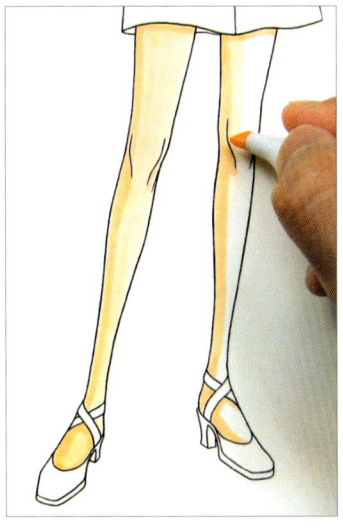
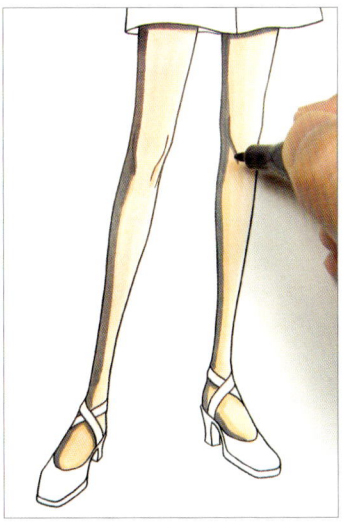

1. This is an application of the method for sheer fabrics. Use markers as they are also transparent.

2. Color the legs keeping the direction of light in mind.

3. Begin coloring the stocking with the part in shadow.

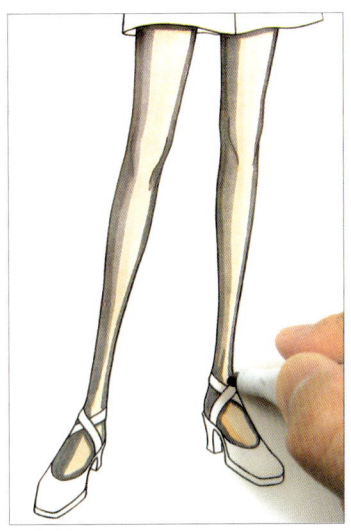
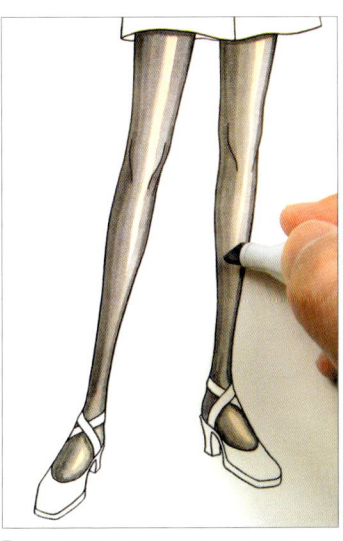
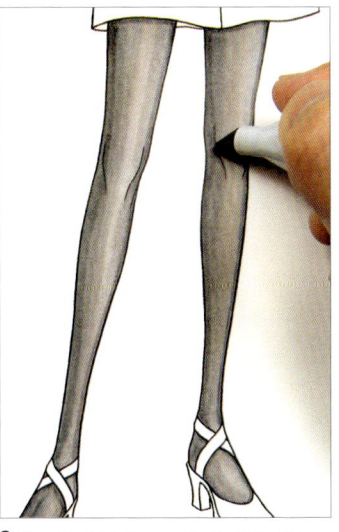
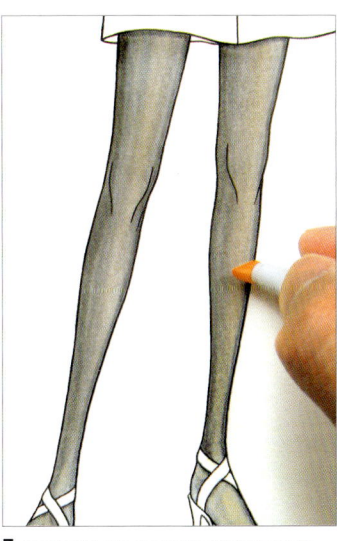

4. Apply a color one shade lighter than 3. to the area that should be one degree lighter.

5. Repeat 4. by applying a color one shade lighter.

6. Color the lightest area and adjust the entire area by blending.

7. Lightly add skin color in the lightest area to produce a more transparent look.

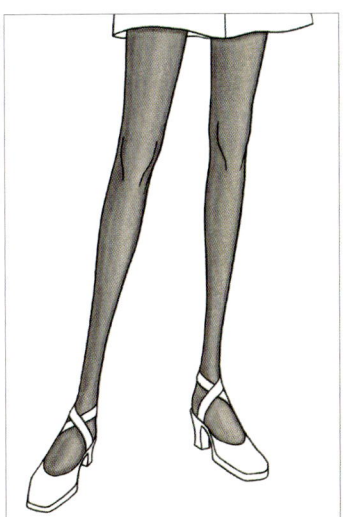
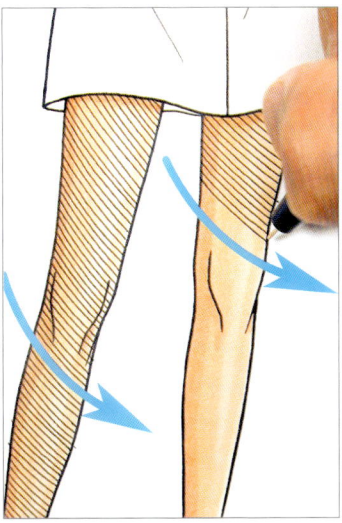
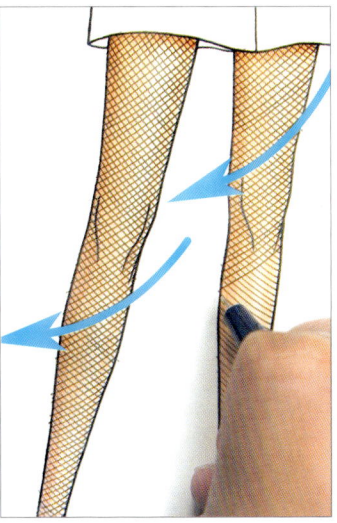
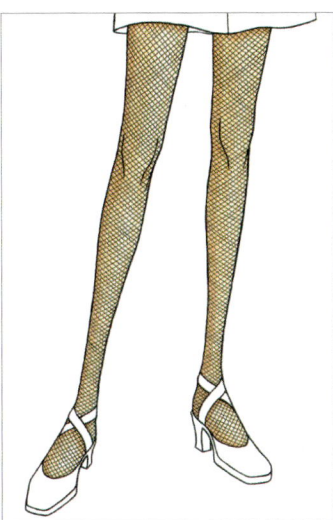

8. Completed. The lightest area effectively shows the skin seen through the most.

1. Draw the mesh lines of the tights. Try to produce the appearance that they are wrapped around the legs.

2. Draw the lines in opposite directions. Keep in mind the column-like leg form.

3. Completed.

107

How to Draw Lace

1. Lace is a fine open fabric woven in patterns. Shading should be applied first as it cannot be added later.

2. Render the fine mesh with white opaque watercolor. In the case of colored lace, use drawing pens, color pencils or color ball-point pens.

3. Draw patterns.

4. Highlight the patterns with color pencils.

5. Completed.

[4] Warp Lines of A Garment

It is essential to be aware of the warp lines of a garment, when you draw patterns on it. The warp lines of garments, which otherwise form straight lines, change in various ways when dressed on a figure in relation to the size and movement of the body. In such a case, draw one or two gauge lines for each part as a guide to follow the warp line three-dimensionally (as shown in orange lines here). Draw the warp line based on these gauge lines, and you will not fail. Here we observe the garment warp lines while drawing stripe and check patterns.

Blouse

The warp lines of the front body and sleeves are vertical, while those of reinforcing parts such as the yoke and cuffs are horizontal.

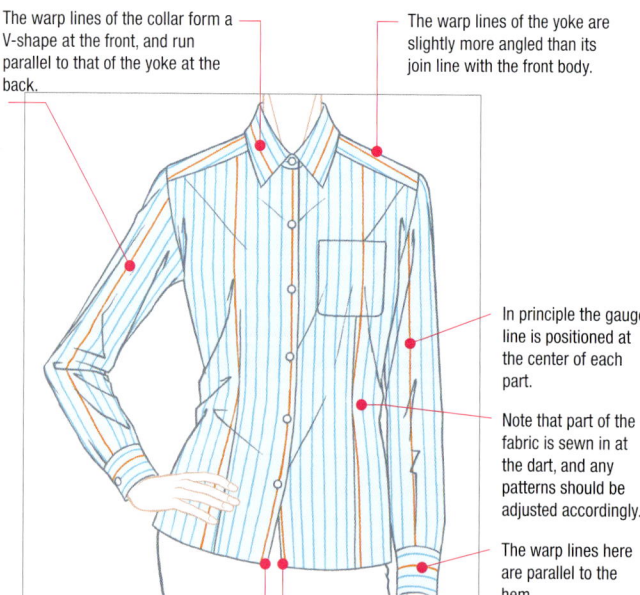

- The warp lines of the collar form a V-shape at the front, and run parallel to that of the yoke at the back.
- Enter the gauge line first in the center of the sleeve.
- The warp lines of the yoke are slightly more angled than its join line with the front body.
- In principle the gauge line is positioned at the center of each part.
- Note that part of the fabric is sewn in at the dart, and any patterns should be adjusted accordingly.
- The warp lines here are parallel to the hem.
- The warp lines of the front body should be in line with the front center. Note that the front hem is open, reflecting the volume of the body.

Chapter 3 : Fashion Drawing

T-shirt

The border patterns are drawn in line with the weft line here. The lines in the front body and the sleeves are parallel to their hems respectively.

The weft lines of the front body vary depending on the volume of the body. In principle, they should be parallel to the hem, except for the area around the bust. The curve caused by its swell should be taken into consideration.

The lines of the sleeve should be parallel to its hem.

Tank-Top

As tank-tops have no sleeves, drawing their warp lines is simple.

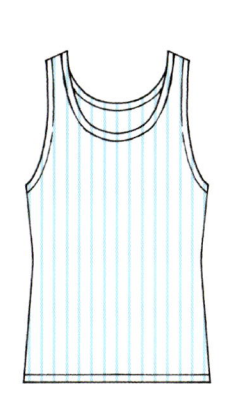

Set the gauge line on the front centerline, then enter lines on both sides, keeping the swell of the breast in mind.

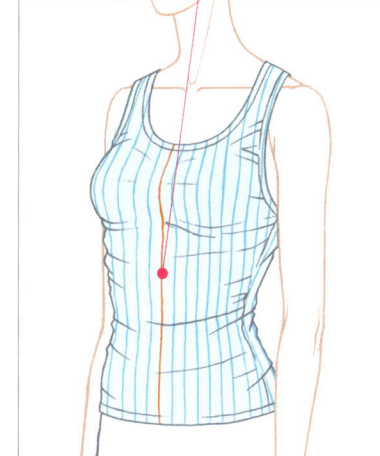

Jacket

As jackets have many parts, the warp lines may become complex. Especially to the collar and lapel; the collar run at a right angle to the outer edge, while the lapel run parallel to the outer edge.

The warp lines of the lapel may vary depending on its size, but in principle they run parallel to the outer edge.

The warp lines of the collar are at a right angle to its outer edge, and have perspective.

Enter the gauge line at the center of the sleeve. When the arm is bent, the gauge line also is bent.

The direction of warp lines is changed slightly at the border of the side body panel and front body.

As fabric is sewn in at the dart, the lines run inward.

The warp lines run vertically here.

The warp lines run parallel to the front centerline.

Cardigan

The warp lines of the sleeves and the front body are slightly tapered toward the ribbed bottom.

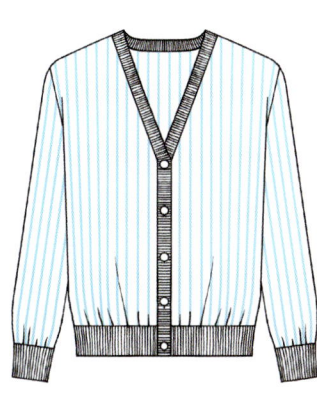

As knitted material is heavier than woven fabric, the warp lines run closely along the bodyline.

Ribs may be drawn both horizontally as shown in the technical drawing on the left, and vertically as shown here.

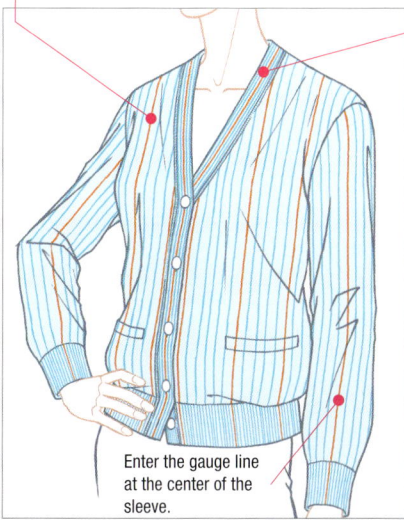

Enter the gauge line at the center of the sleeve.

Jumper

The key point is the warp lines of the raglan sleeves. Draw the curve bent at the shoulder. When straight lines are preferred, spread the sleeves more horizontally.

The warp lines are tapered toward the ribbed bottom.

The warp lines of the raglan run almost parallel with the outline from the shoulder to the arm.

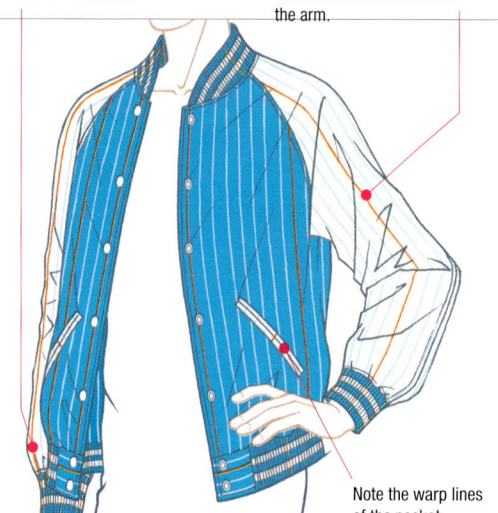

Note the warp lines of the pocket welting.

Dress

As the fabric is gathered at the waist, the warp lines also follow.

Tight Skirt

Serving as a reinforced cloth, the waistband's warp lines run nearly at a right angle to the skirt front.

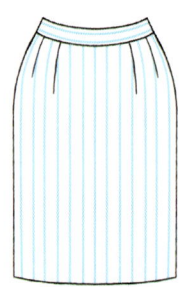

Pleated Skirt

As check patterns are common for the pleated skirt, both the warp (blue) and weft (green) lines are shown here.

Wrapover Skirt

Note the warp lines at the darts.

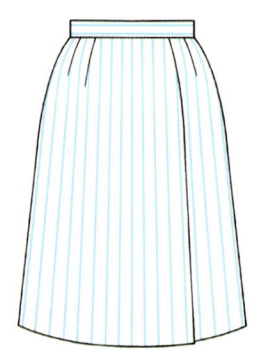

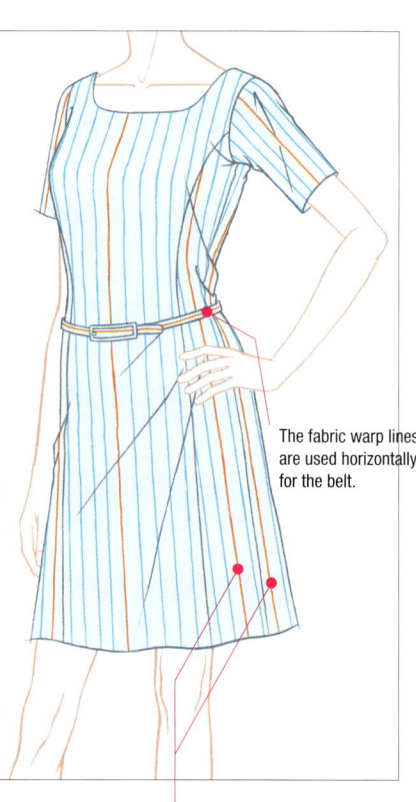

The fabric warp lines are used horizontally for the belt.

Note that the warp lines are curved, as the fabric, having side bodies, is sewn in at the side seams.

Mistakes are often made at the darts. Enter the warp lines with a curve appropriate to how the fabric is sewn in here.

Serving as a reinforced cloth, the waistband's warp lines run nearly at a right angle to the skirt front.

Serving as a reinforced cloth, the waistband's warp lines run nearly at a right angle to the skirt front.

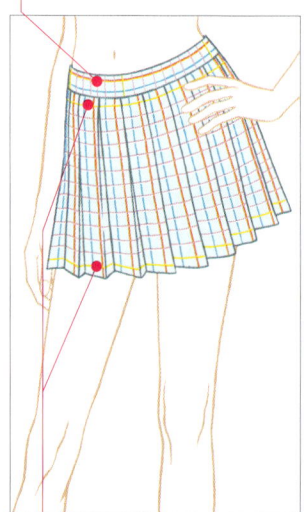

As the fabric is sewn in at the dart, the warp lines form a curve.

More fabric is sewn in toward the center in the case of double darts.

The key is the weft lines, which are ragged at the hem and gently curved at the waist. Draw these from both ends one by one, and then adjust them to meet naturally at the center.

As the legs open, the overlapping part opens also.

Chapter 3 : Fashion Drawing

≡ Gathered Skirt

The warp lines are tapered toward the gathered waist part.

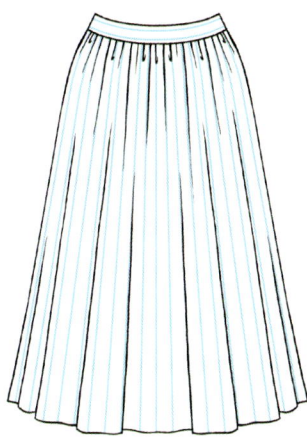

≡ Pants/Trousers (Straight)

The warp lines of pants run at a right angle to the hem of both legs, with the most central ones forming an upside-down V-shape at the center of the waist.

≡ Pants/Trousers (Wide)

The warp lines of wide pants also run at a right angle to the hem of both legs. Although the pants shown here have no center crease, the gauge line should be at the center.

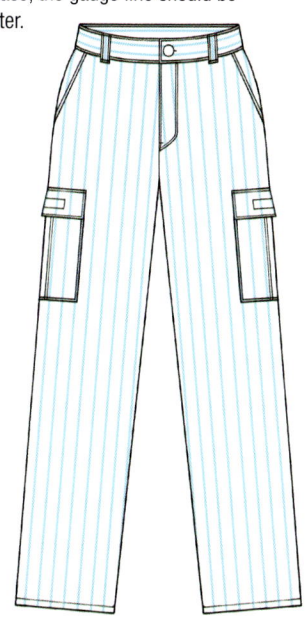

Serving as a reinforced cloth, the waistband's warp lines run nearly at a right angle to the skirt front.

Without being misguided by the twists of the fabric, make the warp lines wider apart little by little toward the bottom, to compensate for the amount tapered for the gather.

Serving as a reinforced cloth, the waistband's warp lines run nearly at a right angle to the skirt front.

The belt loop's warp lines are vertical.

The warp lines change direction near the groin. The gauge line should be on the center crease.

Serving as a reinforced cloth, the waistband's warp lines run nearly at a right angle to the skirt front.

The gauge line should follow the way the fabric sags at the hem.

[5] Fashion Drawing Step-by-Step

Let's now try to make a fashion drawing, based on what you have learned here. When you cannot draw as expected, identify at which point you have failed, and go back to the relevant chapter to review the exercise.
The process of fashion drawing is as follows;

1. Draft sketch
Body: Based on the eight head-length proportion, make drawings of various poses suitable for the design of a garment.
Dressed figure: Allowing some room for a garment, draw the silhouette, details and creases of each garment thoroughly.

2. Final drawing
Transfer the draft to another paper for coloring; either by using a light from underneath, or filling in the backside of the draft with black pencil and drawing over it from the topside. Once you have mastered processes 1. and 2., do it on one piece of paper.

3. Coloring
The coloring order is; the skin, garment, smaller items, hair and make-up. It is important to select a color for the skin color. Layered painting with a good amount of water is recommended for areas of pale colors and thin materials, solid painting and omitted painting with less water are for areas of dark and thick materials.

4. Finishing
Color hair and apply make-up, and redraw any lines that have disappeared. Finally, highlight lines to give contrast, while adjusting the overall balance.

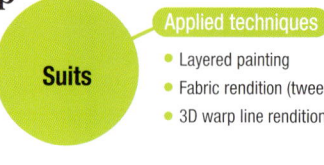

Suits

Applied techniques
- Layered painting
- Fabric rendition (tweed)
- 3D warp line rendition

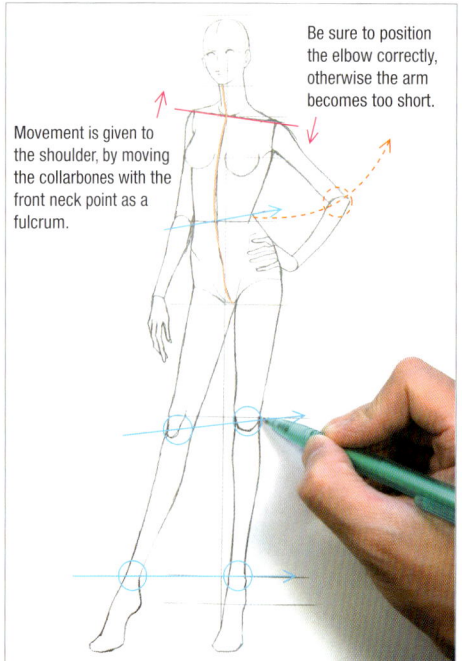

1. Draft sketching. Diagonal pose with weight on one leg (pivotal leg in front)

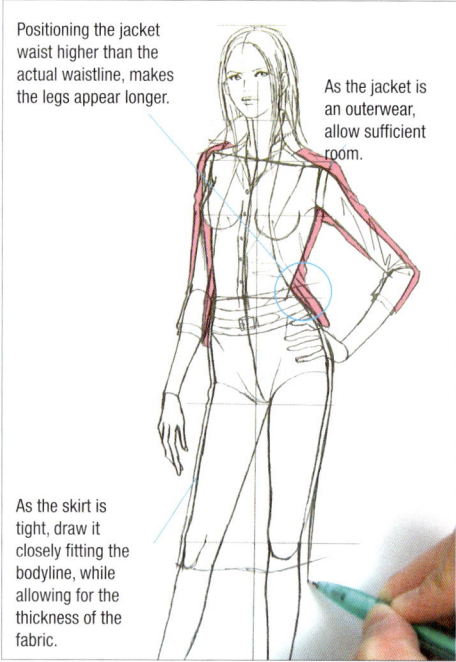

2. Balance by first drawing the silhouette, and then the details. The rendition of creases is not required so much at this point.

3. As lines become rather busy at this point, complete the draft by placing a sheet of paper on top. Too many crease lines may be mistaken for lines of details. Keep them simple by concentrating on areas mainly around joints.

5. Set the light source on either side of the figure (set on the right facing the drawing here). Make the lines in shadow bolder to accentuate them.

For the final drawing, drawing pens are often used. In this case, use the following information as a guide.

0.05: Eyes, nose and mouth
0.1: Outline of face, hairs and small elements including stitches, buttons etc.
0.3: Outline of hair/head, borderlines of each garment and part.
0.5: Outline of thin garments
0.8: Outline of thick garments
10 or thicker: Strengthening of outlines

4. Final drawing. Using a light table, transfer the draft to a Kent paper. "Schwan STABILO Original 87/750" was used to render the lines here. When a light table is not available, see Chapter 2, "Drawing Method (Points in common)" on page 55.

6. When the final drawing was done with color pencils, use fixative to fix lines by spraying with a horizontal movement, parallel to the paper, 30 cm away. Application for one second should be enough, as too much of it may hinder coloring of the following step.

Chapter 3 : Fashion Drawing

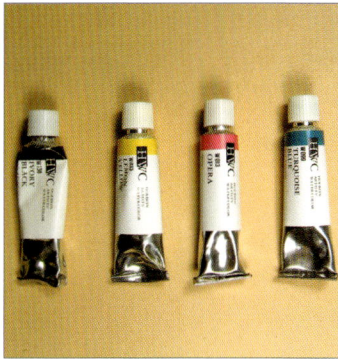

7. Now, apply color by mainly layered painting here, for which transparent watercolors are suitable. Transparent watercolor sets offer the full range of colors, but try creating all colors by mixing the base colors of CMYK, and you will see a big improvement in your color coordination skill. As the colors in the set may not necessarily match skin tone without adjustment, adopt the regular practice of producing colors by mixing, to acquire the habit of controlling subtle color coordination. In the Holbein Artist's Watercolors, C is represented by 'Turquoise Blue', M 'Opera', Y 'Lemon Yellow', and K 'Ivory-Black'.

8. Start coloring with the skin tone. To represent a fresh skin appearance, layered painting using extra water is suitable. Opaque watercolors can also be used to create the same effect, if the amount of water used is increased further. Create skin tone by mixing a reddish-orange and thinning with water. White is not used in layered painting. Prepare the color by adding yellow (melanin pigment) little by little, to the base color magenta (blood).

9. First lightly apply a single coat. Be sure not to use too much yellow, as this will produce an unhealthy complexion. In the case of layered painting with heavy use of water, the greatest cause of mistakes is the amount of water used. While applying color, use a tissue to wipe off excess water from the tip of the brush so that the paper does not become soaked.

10. Do not panic if you have applied too much color. Trace over the part to thin out with a brush dipped in water only, to bring the color back out.

Draw in white blouses using shading only. Dilute black with water to produce gray. White is not used. The amount of water added is the key to adjusting the shading.

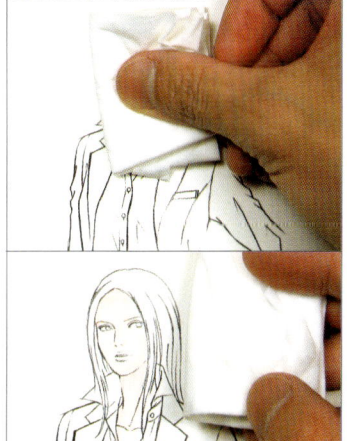

11. Press firmly with a tissue, and the color will be absorbed onto the tissue together with the water and thin out. If color remains around the edges repeat the process.

12. Apply color successively following the lines on the shadow side.

13. Continue to apply layers of color on shaded areas of the hair and blouse to achieve a 3D effect.

14. Use a brush dipped in water only, to brush over the whole surface. This creates a smoother effect by eliminating color gradations.

15. Next draw the base color of the suit. This is done by layered painting also, and a relatively large amount of water is used.

16. Following the lines of the shadow side, apply color successively. As the tweed pattern will be drawn after this, the light-dark contrast should be emphasized. Crease lines are where the shade contrast is greatest, so color should be applied in layers here too. As a basic rule, color is applied below the lines.

17. Now the tweed effect will be drawn. Opaque watercolors that do not allow the base color to show through are best suited for this. Apply about three colors until the base color becomes almost unnoticeable.

18. Continue applying the colors carefully and evenly.

19. Apply the rough texture using the side of the leads of color pencils.

20. Draw checks. When checks are not clearly seen due to napped fabric, use a color pencil to render such appearance.

21. For a drawing finished with color pencils, use also color pencils to apply shading.

22. A gold ball-point pen is suitable for coloring a belt buckle.

23. Layered painting is suitable for light and smooth looking hair. Apply layers with the highlighted places in mind.

24. Use a drawing pen with a 0.05 nib for the eyeline.

25. Use color pencils for eyeshadow and lipstick. For cheek rouge, rub pastel onto a separate paper, and take the loose powder with a cotton bud and lightly apply on the cheek.

26. Accentuate lines where necessary in proportion with the entire figure. Be sure to redraw any lines that have disappeared.

27. Complete by fixing the lines with a fixative spray.

Chapter 3 : Fashion Drawing

Street Style (male)

Applied techniques
- Layered painting
- Omitted painting
- Solid painting
- Fabric/material rendition (velvet, denim, leather)
- Emphasizing outlines

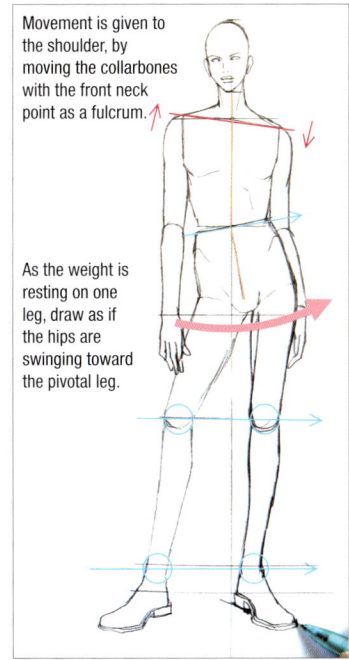

Movement is given to the shoulder, by moving the collarbones with the front neck point as a fulcrum.

As the weight is resting on one leg, draw as if the hips are swinging toward the pivotal leg.

1. Draft sketching. Frontal pose with weight on one leg.

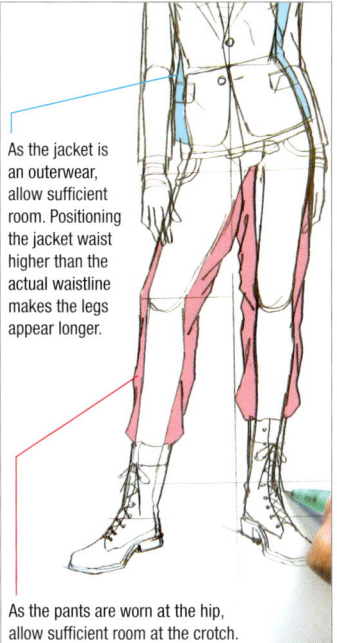

As the jacket is an outerwear, allow sufficient room. Positioning the jacket waist higher than the actual waistline makes the legs appear longer.

As the pants are worn at the hip, allow sufficient room at the crotch.

2. When dressing, balance by first drawing the silhouette, and then the details. Rendition of creases is not required so much at this point.

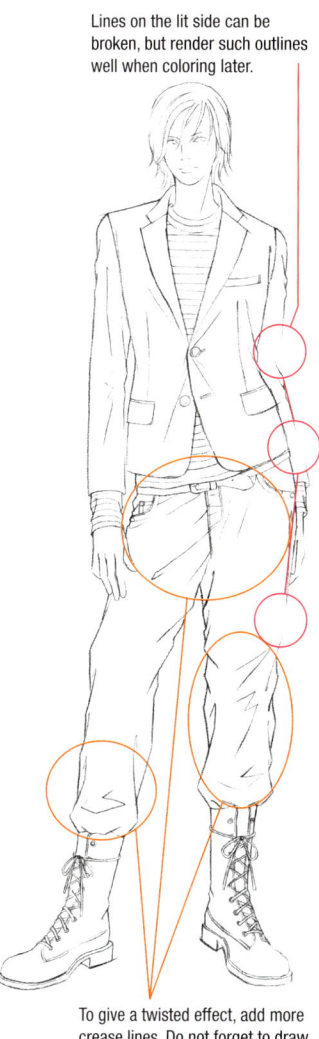

Lines on the lit side can be broken, but render such outlines well when coloring later.

To give a twisted effect, add more crease lines. Do not forget to draw them around the joints. This helps to clarify the real proportion even when the pants are worn loosely.

3. Final drawing. When the final drawing was done with color pencils, use fixative to fix lines by spraying with a horizontal movement, parallel to the paper, 30 cm away. Application of one second should be enough, as too much of it may hinder coloring of the following step.

4. Solid and omitted painting is tried here. Opaque watercolors are suitable as they have a good covering effect. Try to prepare all colors by mixing the base colors of CMYK, as with transparent watercolors. The photograph shows Nicker Poster Colors. C is represented by 'Cerulean Blue', M 'Magenta', Y 'Lemon Yellow', and K 'Black', plus white.

5. Skin is always drawn by layered painting. As a bright and strong color is used for borders, apply the omitted painting method. The side facing the light is left white.

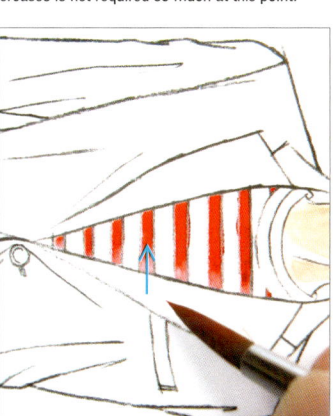

6. Blur by using a brush dipped in clean water to brush over the surface from the white areas toward the colored areas. Repeating two to three times should create a good effect.

7. Black is handled in the same way. As the gray of innerwear is plain-colored, apply the solid painting method.

8. The jacket is in velvet, featuring a fine nap look with dark shine. As the color is dark, the base color should first be applied by omitted painting. The basic rule is to leave areas along and above the crease lines on the lit side white.

9. Blur by using a brush dipped in clean water to brush over the surface from the white areas toward the colored areas. Repeating two to three times should create a good effect.

10. Represent the napped effect of velvet with pastel-type color pencils.

11. Layered painting was applied to denim to produce a nicely worn look.

12. Carefully draw in fine twills using black and white sharpened pencils. Be sure to cover all areas.

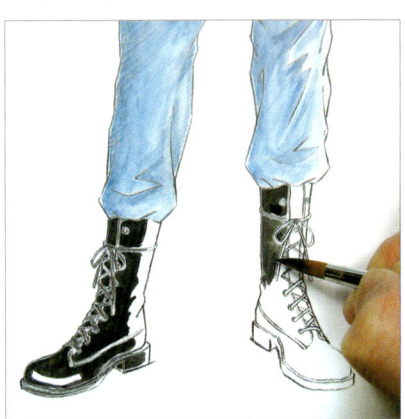

13. Color mainly around crease lines with white pastel-type color pencils to produce an additional faded look.

14. Paint the belt, stitches and rivets. Gold color pencil is best for rivets.

15. Apply omitted painting to the shoes. Make the toe ends appear shiny for a 3D effect.

16. As leather is a shiny material, blur only the edges while leaving the white areas unpainted.

17. Lightly paint the hair. It is fine to leave the areas white as shown here.

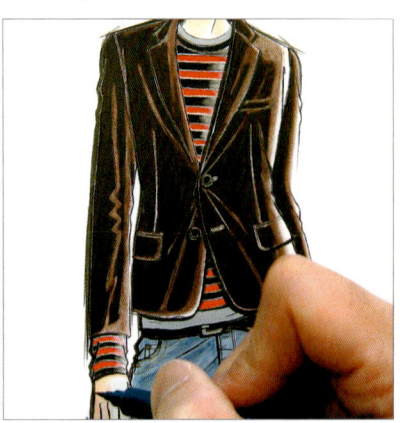

18. Accentuate lines where necessary in proportion with the entire figure. Be sure to redraw any lines that have disappeared.

The outline is drawn with a Nouvel Pigma Graphic brush-type marker. The bold lines contribute to producing impact.

19. Completed.

Chapter 3 : Fashion Drawing

Street Style (female)

Applied techniques
- Coloration with markers
- Fabric/material rendition (fur, leopard-skin/floral patterns, lacy knit, mesh, metallic look)

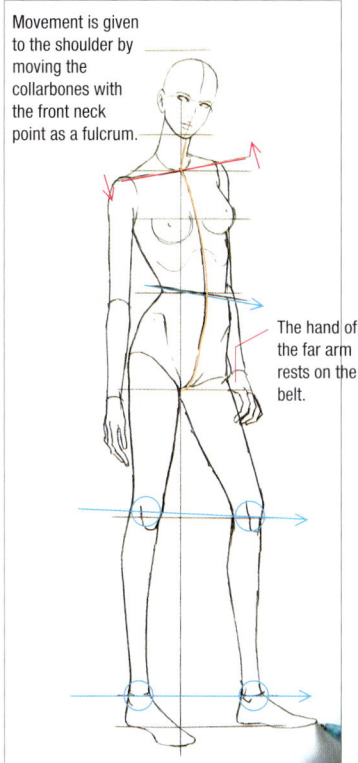

Movement is given to the shoulder by moving the collarbones with the front neck point as a fulcrum.

The hand of the far arm rests on the belt.

1. Draft sketching. Diagonal pose with weight on one leg (pivotal leg in front).

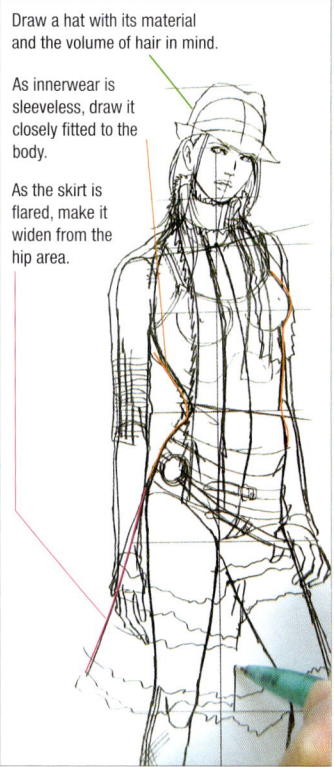

Draw a hat with its material and the volume of hair in mind.

As innerwear is sleeveless, draw it closely fitted to the body.

As the skirt is flared, make it widen from the hip area.

2. When dressing, balance by first drawing the silhouette, and then the details. Rendition of creases is not required so much at this point.

As innerwear is made of soft fabric, crease lines running downward from the bust are added.

Gather and flare lines should be represented with vigorous strokes. First drawing the hem line, think how far such lines can be extended. Draw quickly in a single stroke.

3. Final drawing. Using a light table, transfer the draft to a Kent paper. Drawing with a brown color pencil creates a soft effect. When the final drawing was done with color pencils, use fixative to fix lines.

4. Apply color using markers here. The technique used is a mixture of layered and omitted painting. Markers produce good colors and can be mixed to produce secondary colors. It is recommended to build up a good collection using the information on p.91. First apply omitted painting to the skin using E00.

5. Use YR00 to draw shadows. As shown in the arm here, the basic rule is to apply shade along the lines on the shadow side. Apply it also to any border area where elements create shadow against the body, and along crease lines.

6. Go over with E00 again to blend in the entire area. This completes three gradations.

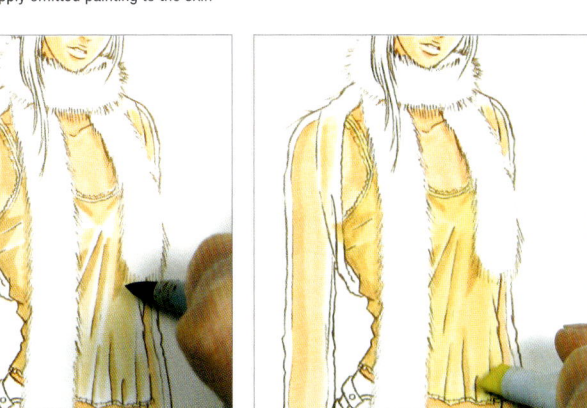

7. Paint the camisole in the same way as the skin, starting with "omitted painting of the base color", followed by "shading" and "blending in using the base color". Apply shading strongly as pattern coloring follows.

8. When your collection of markers has grown, use a different color from the base color for the blending in work. This will add further contrast.

9. If the base color is pale, markers can be used to draw in on top of it. If dark, use opaque watercolors.

10. Addition of leaves completes the floral pattern. As the base shading is strong, effective contrast remains with the pattern.

11. Apply the base color of the fur.

12. Apply shading as if drawing the hairs, little by little along the edges on the shadow side.

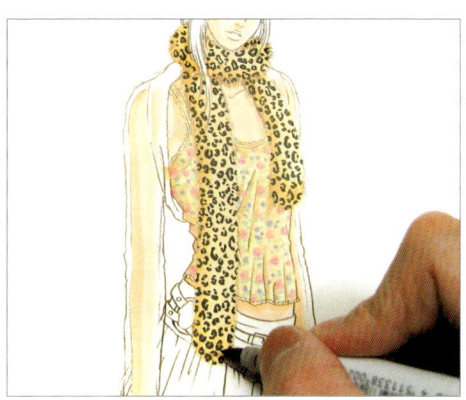
13. Draw a leopard-skin pattern.

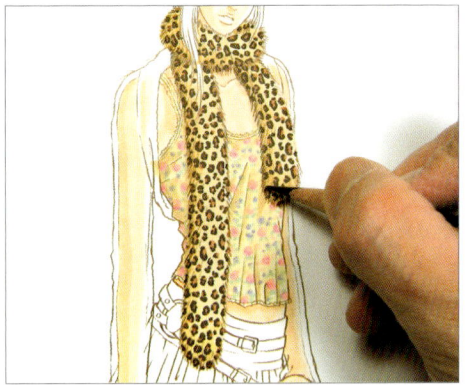
14. Create a 3D effect by adding hairs using brown and black color pencils for areas in shadow, while using white for the lit areas.

15. Color the hat also by omitted painting. After this step, go over with a paler color to blend in the entire area.

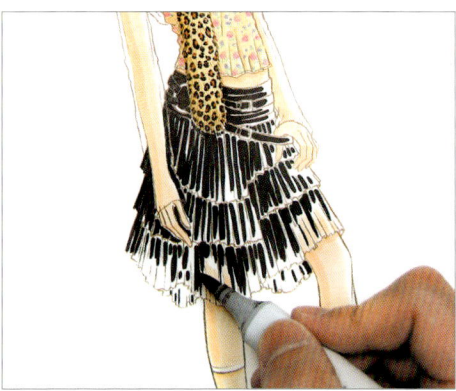
16. As tiered skirts have many flares, use omitted painting to produce a 3D effect.

17. When the base color is black, blend in the entire area with 70% gray first to make it somewhat less black, and then apply shading with black.

18. Draw the meshes of the lacy knit. These are effective if drawn in a wavy manner. Color ball-point pens with which you can draw on black paper are recommended. They are useful also for drawing stripes.

19. Finish with pastel-type color pencils in white or the same color tone to produce a napped knit fabric look.

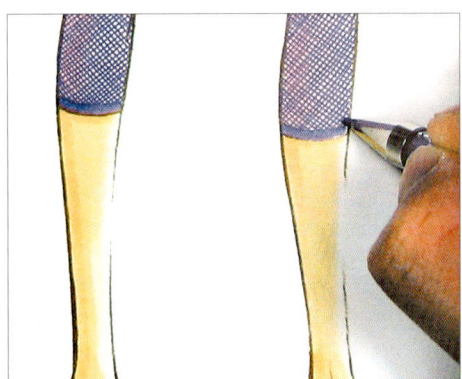
20. Color pencils can be used for mesh type tights. Color ball-point pens are also good when brilliant colors are desired.

21. Use a silver ball-point pen to draw metal parts e.g. rivets and buckles.

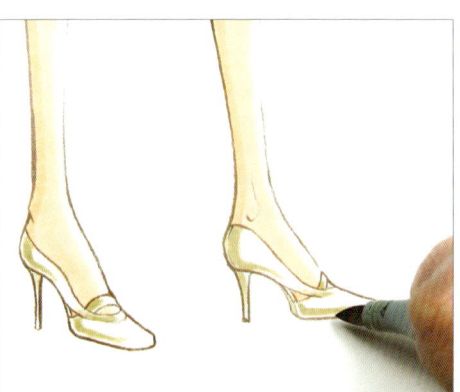
22. Let's paint shoes in light gold.

Chapter 3 : Fashion Drawing

23. For metallic colors, apply strong contrast concerning light and dark tones, in extreme cases, use white for the light area and black for the dark.

24. Color the hair and eyes with markers.

25. Use a drawing pen with a 0.05 nib for eyeline, and color pencils for eyeshadow and lipstick. For cheek rouge, use pastel.

26. Redraw any lines that have disappeared. White color pencil is suitable for details of the dark color area.

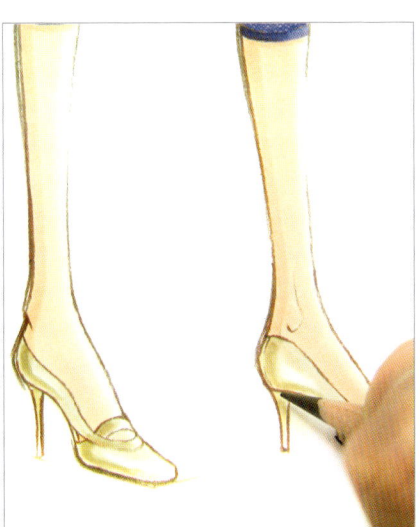

27. Accentuate lines using a brown color pencil, in proportion with the entire figure.

28. Complete by fixing with a fixative spray.

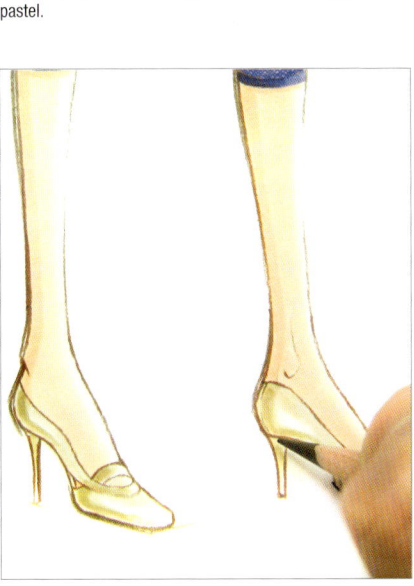

[6] Stylized Fashion Drawing

Once you acquire the skill for basic fashion drawings, attempt the stylized drawing in which you express your image directly without draft sketching.

1. When your image takes shape, dash off the drawing. If you are not sufficiently confident, pre-draw a bone structure or the like in light yellow or other pale color pencil. However, make it simple, otherwise it will hinder fresh and vigorous drawing.

2. The lower half of the body is particularly important. Represent the legs in single brush strokes while accentuating the strength by holding the brush upright or horizontally.

3. Paint the hair and shirt lightly with markers. You do not have to color the skin.

4. Apply stripes with a color pencil. Be sure not to over draw.

5. Highlight the silhouette, and draw minimum crease lines and details with color pencils. Be sure not to over draw.

6. Completed. More colors can be used for this type of drawing, and multi-colors can be layered by using opaque watercolors. The illustration on the cover for example was made by this method, to which the floral pattern is added after processing by Photoshop. (See p.125)

Chapter 3 : Fashion Drawing

More colors are used for a female drawing to add femininity.

A hand drawn fashion drawing was scanned in and digitized. First, the flower pattern image produced by Illustrator (p.156) was opened in Photoshop. Next, it was made into a pattern (p.136), given a clip mask (p.144), and pasted onto the dress. The make-up was also applied using Photoshop (p.132). For further instructions, see page 125 onwards.

[7] Proportion by Age

Our heads are large in proportion to the body when born. This changes as we grow older. The limbs grow rapidly along with development of the motor ability. At the same time our chins grow larger as teeth develop, resulting in our eye-level becoming higher in relation to the head-length.
Let us look at the difference in proportions according to gender and age. Although there is no difference between the male and female body proportions at a young age, it shows a dramatic change once they reach and pass the secondary sex character stage (age 10 to 15). Girls develop breasts and their waist becomes relatively small as the hips develop, while boys develop muscles. The female is known to mature earlier than the male, but the male normally becomes taller than the female by half a head (We use the measurement of 185 cm here i.e. "23 cm head-length multiplied by eight").

Age 1
Head-length: Approx. 17 cm
Height: Approx. 70 cm
Head-height ratio: 1 to 4

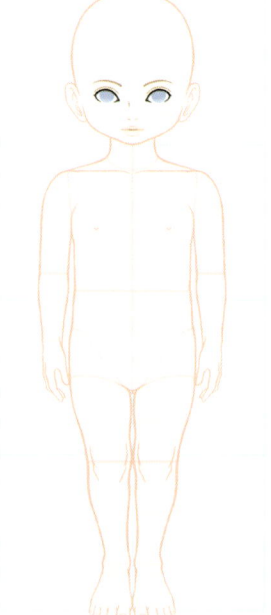

In the first year, the height increases 50%.

Age 3
Head-length: Approx. 17.5 cm
Height: Approx. 90 cm
Head-height ratio: 1 to 5

They still have a rounded body form with big stomach.

Age 5
Head-length: Approx. 18 cm
Height: Approx. 105 cm
Head-height ratio: 1 to 6

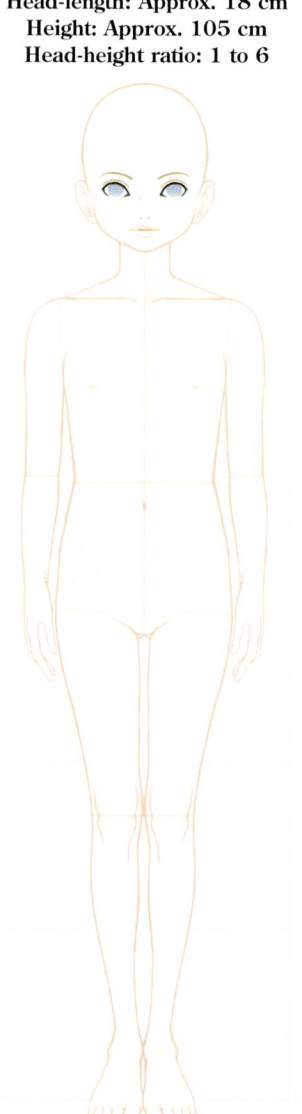

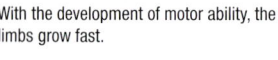

With the development of motor ability, the limbs grow fast.

Age 7
Head-length: Approx. 18.5 cm
Height: Approx. 120 cm
Head-height ratio: 1 to 6.5

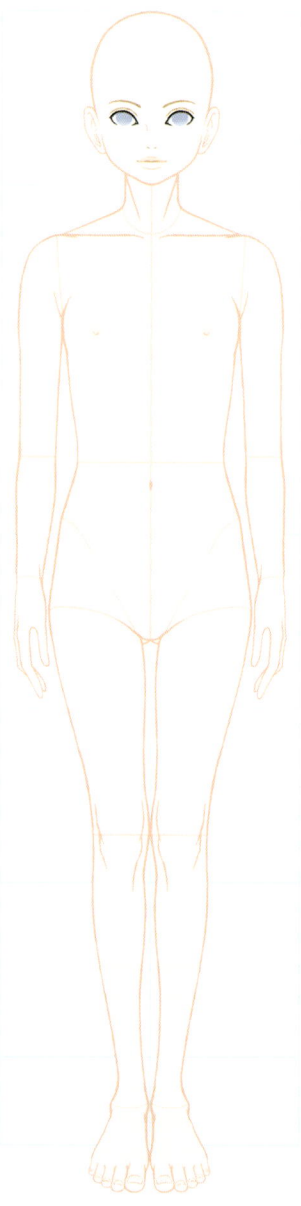

Having new teeth and a developed chin, the body has a sharper line. The eye-level is relatively higher in the face.

Chapter 3 : Fashion Drawing

Age 10
Head-length: Approx. 20 cm
Height: Approx. 140 cm
Head-height ratio: 1 to 7

Age 15
Head-length: Approx. 22 cm
Height: Approx. 165 cm
Head-height ratio: 1 to 7.5

Age 18 - 21
Head-length: Approx. 22 cm
Height: Approx. 175 cm
Head-height ratio: 1 to 8

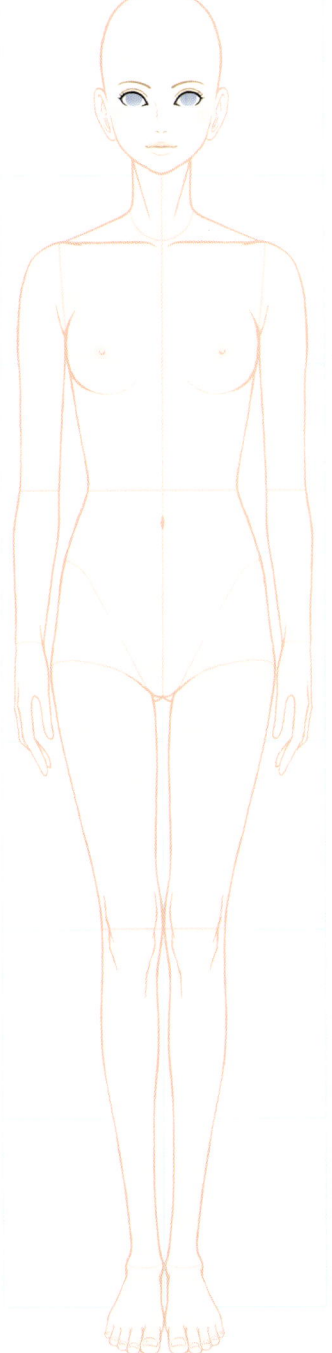
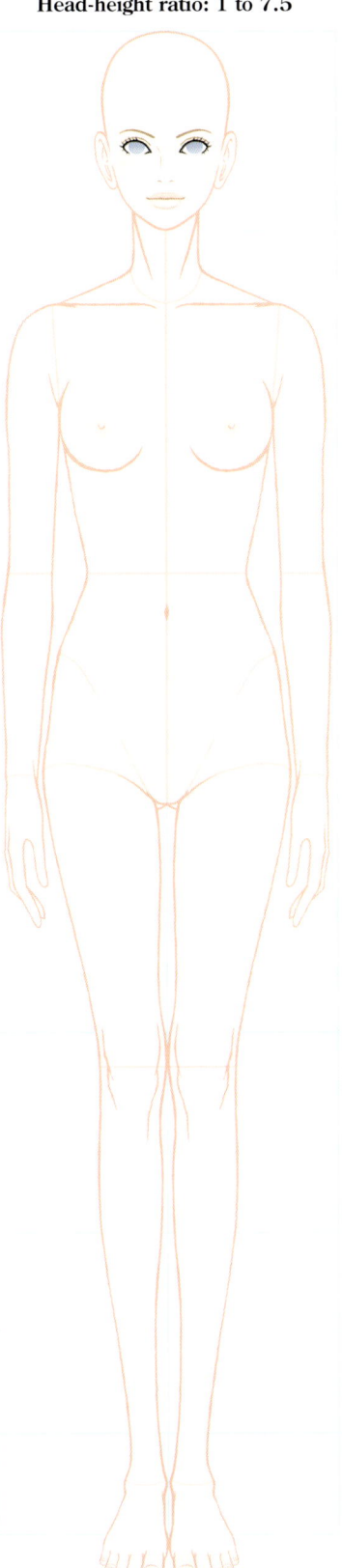
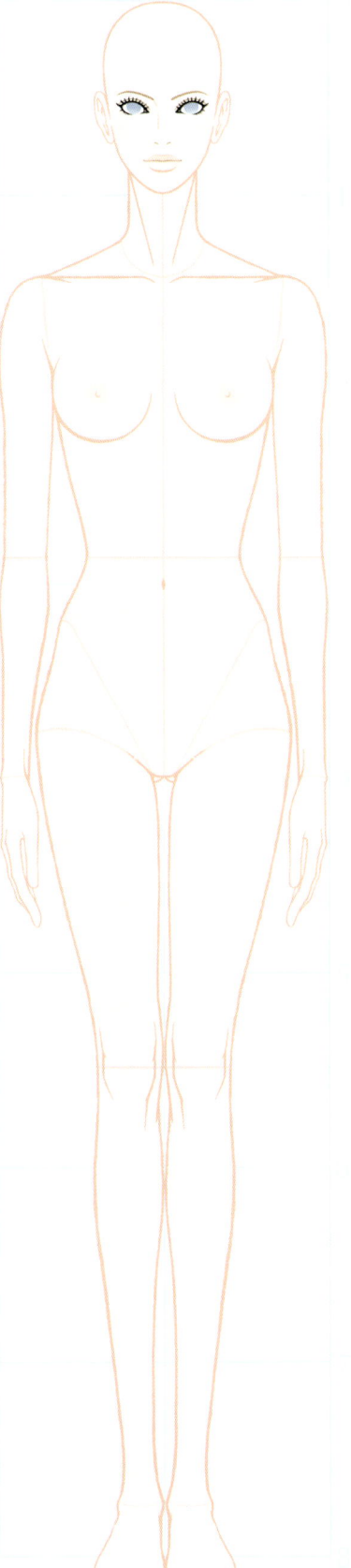

Showing the secondary sex character, the body begins to develop a feminine form, growth of the breasts and a thin waist especially become prominent.

Although the head has already reached maturity, the rest of the body, including the face is a little round.

An ideal and well-proportioned slim body form. Following this stage, the overall body will loose firmness as aging causes sagging including cheeks, breasts and abdomen area. The posture will also tend to bend forward

Drawing of Children

Pay attention when drawing children, as the proportion of their body parts varies depending on age.

- With the head being large and chin under developed, the eye-level is relatively low.
- The body in general is round.
- There is little gender difference.

Age 5 Age 3 Age 1

Chapter 4
Computer Graphic Techniques

In the past, although computer graphic design was limited to the fashion world, we now see it used in the education sector as well. This means that it is now possible for amateurs to effectively and efficiently create their own designs using a computer. For example, you may not be very apt at expressing your subject matter or image using traditional techniques, but using computer graphic design software, it is possible to set colors with a single click of a mouse, to perform color variation, and so on using very simple processes on your screen.

There are two main computer operating systems (OS). Windows OS, which is used on most of the worlds PCs, is a reasonable price and is the most compatible, and thus enjoys the largest market share. The Macintosh OS, designed specifically for Macintosh hardware, (which is slightly more expensive than PCs), is generally better designed than Windows, and is thus very popular in the design world. In recent times Macintoshes have become popular in educational institutions as well.

In this chapter, we are going to learn about graphic design techniques using basic computer knowledge.

Required Hardware

- A Macintosh or Windows based computer
- Display: 15 Inch or greater is recommended
- Memory: Since systems with low amounts of memory will suffer from performance degradation, it is recommended that you upgrade to as much memory as your system can handle. Please check with your computer manufacturer or inquire at your local computer shop.
- Scanner: It is highly recommended you use a scanner that can handle sizes greater than B4, although A4 is sufficient. If scanning at sizes greater than A4, you can always scan the paper in two parts.
- Printer: A printer that can handle A3 output is recommended.
- Drawing tablet: This is a computer that uses a pen in place of a mouse. There are times where you may get better results using a tablet, instead of the traditional mouse.

Software

The most popular graphic design software is Adobe's Photoshop and Illustrator. Adobe, headquartered in the US, is one of the largest software companies in the world, specializing in digital imaging and design software, etc. Illustrator is graphic design software, and in the fashion industry, it is used for the development of resumes, individual visual image parts, and textiles. This author uses the CS version. Photoshop is perfect for the management of digital images, and in the fashion industry, the software is used for the manipulation of design images, the development of individual image parts, and textiles, for example. This author also uses the CS version of Photoshop.

With respect to the keyboard layout, this book is based on Macintosh. Please refer to the illustration on the right, for the corresponding Windows key layout.

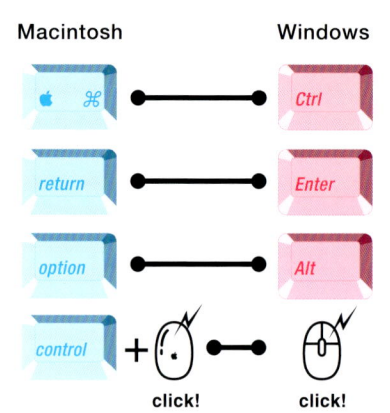

[1] Using Photoshop

The Photoshop Graphical User Interface (GUI)

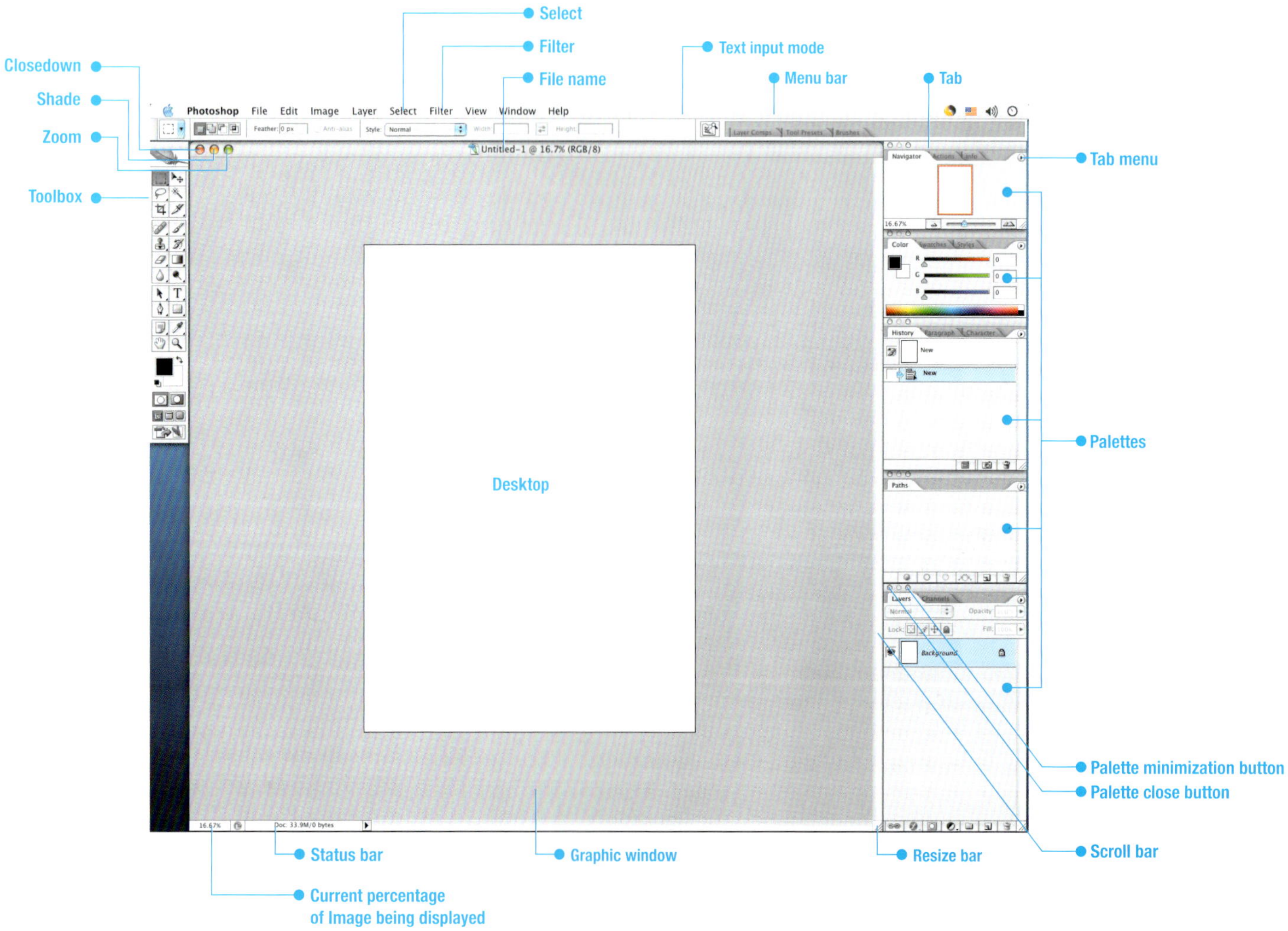

Chapter 4 : Computer Graphic Techniques

Toolbox

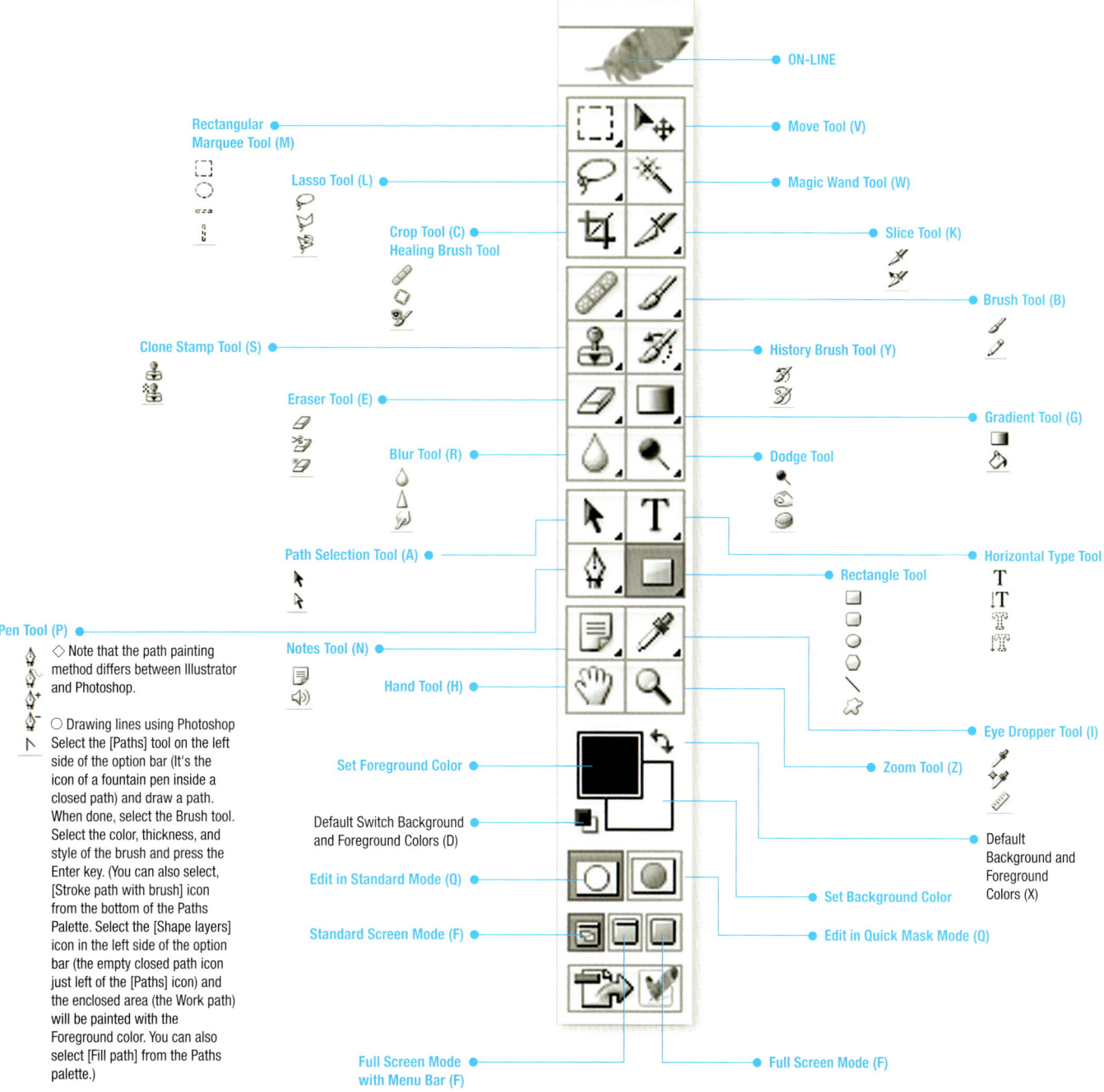

- ON-LINE
- Rectangular Marquee Tool (M)
- Move Tool (V)
- Lasso Tool (L)
- Magic Wand Tool (W)
- Crop Tool (C) / Healing Brush Tool
- Slice Tool (K)
- Brush Tool (B)
- Clone Stamp Tool (S)
- History Brush Tool (Y)
- Eraser Tool (E)
- Gradient Tool (G)
- Blur Tool (R)
- Dodge Tool
- Path Selection Tool (A)
- Horizontal Type Tool
- Pen Tool (P)
- Rectangle Tool
- Notes Tool (N)
- Eye Dropper Tool (I)
- Hand Tool (H)
- Zoom Tool (Z)
- Set Foreground Color
- Default Switch Background and Foreground Colors (D)
- Default Background and Foreground Colors (X)
- Edit in Standard Mode (Q)
- Set Background Color
- Standard Screen Mode (F)
- Edit in Quick Mask Mode (Q)
- Full Screen Mode with Menu Bar (F)
- Full Screen Mode (F)

◇ Note that the path painting method differs between Illustrator and Photoshop.

○ Drawing lines using Photoshop
Select the [Paths] tool on the left side of the option bar (It's the icon of a fountain pen inside a closed path) and draw a path. When done, select the Brush tool. Select the color, thickness, and style of the brush and press the Enter key. (You can also select, [Stroke path with brush] icon from the bottom of the Paths Palette. Select the [Shape layers] icon in the left side of the option bar (the empty closed path icon just left of the [Paths] icon) and the enclosed area (the Work path) will be painted with the Foreground color. You can also select [Fill path] from the Paths palette.)

127

Palette

Layer Palette (F7)

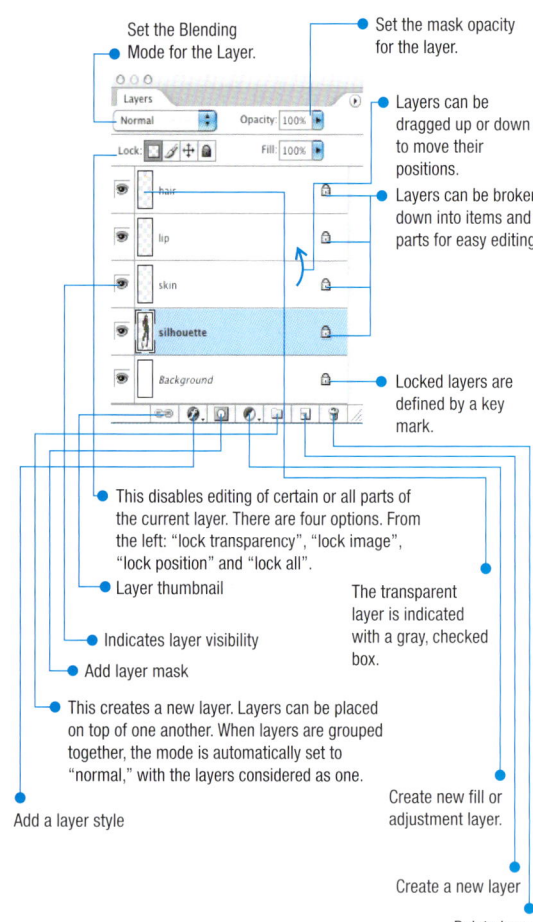

- Set the Blending Mode for the Layer.
- Set the mask opacity for the layer.
- Layers can be dragged up or down to move their positions.
- Layers can be broken down into items and parts for easy editing.
- Locked layers are defined by a key mark.
- This disables editing of certain or all parts of the current layer. There are four options. From the left: "lock transparency", "lock image", "lock position" and "lock all".
- Layer thumbnail
- Indicates layer visibility
- Add layer mask
- This creates a new layer. Layers can be placed on top of one another. When layers are grouped together, the mode is automatically set to "normal," with the layers considered as one.
- Add a layer style
- The transparent layer is indicated with a gray, checked box.
- Create new fill or adjustment layer.
- Create a new layer
- Delete layer

History palette   Layer Comps

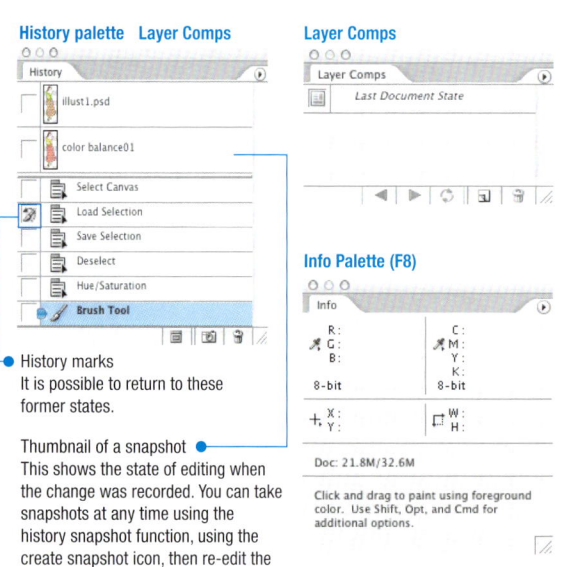

- History marks
  It is possible to return to these former states.
- Thumbnail of a snapshot
  This shows the state of editing when the change was recorded. You can take snapshots at any time using the history snapshot function, using the create snapshot icon, then re-edit the snapshot in its former state at anytime.

Layer Comps

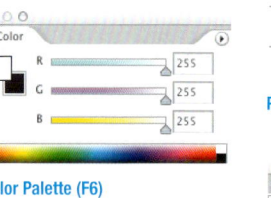

Info Palette (F8)

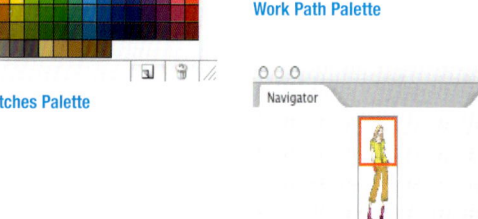

Channels

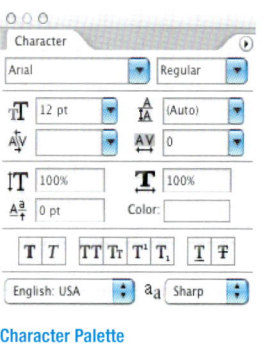

Choose an area, and from the menu, choose [Save selection as channel] which allows you to create a new channel. This is called an Alpha channel. Alpha channels can be loaded from the menu using the [Load channel as selection] at anytime.

Color Palette (F6)

Swatches Palette

Character Palette

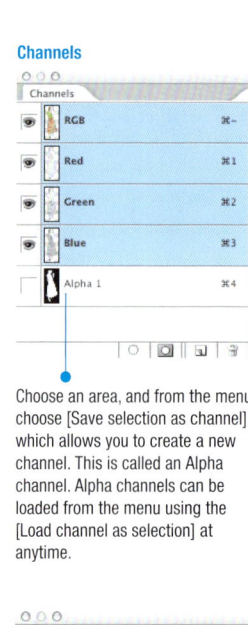

Paragraph Palette

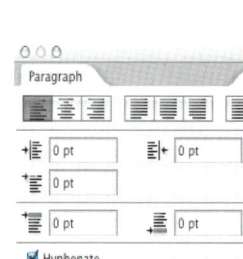

Work Path Palette

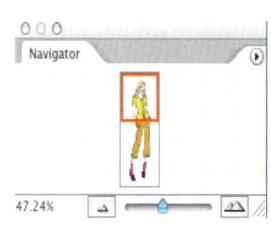

Navigator Palette

Style Palette

Histogram Palette

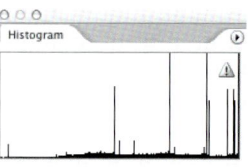

Tool Presets Palette

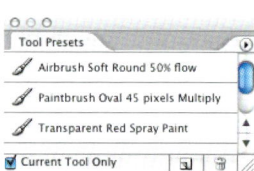

Brush Palette

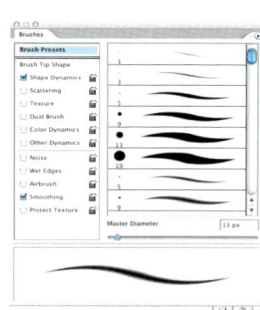

Action Palette

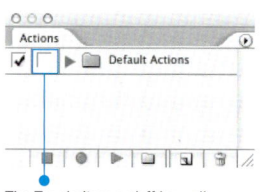

The Toggle item on/off box, allows you to change modal control, which pauses an action so that you can specify values in a dialog box.

Chapter 4 : Computer Graphic Techniques

(1) How to Create A Fashion Drawing

We are now going to use Photoshop to create a fashion drawing. The outline should be hand drawn. By saving the data using Photoshop it will be simple to change the colors and patterns of the clothes, etc.

Digitizing Draft Sketch

How to transfer images to your computer

1. Switch your scanner on.
2. Prepare your handwritten image. When scanning your image, be sure not to leave any open lines in your images. This is important as Photoshop places colors within the selected area of the photo.
3. Turn your computer on, and start Photoshop. Select your file from, "File" and then "Import", "Select Scanner", and point to the area you wish to scan. Next, choose, "Preview", with a resolution of 350 dpi, and in gray scale.
4. If your picture is B4 and your scanner is unable to handle it in one go, you should scan it in two parts.

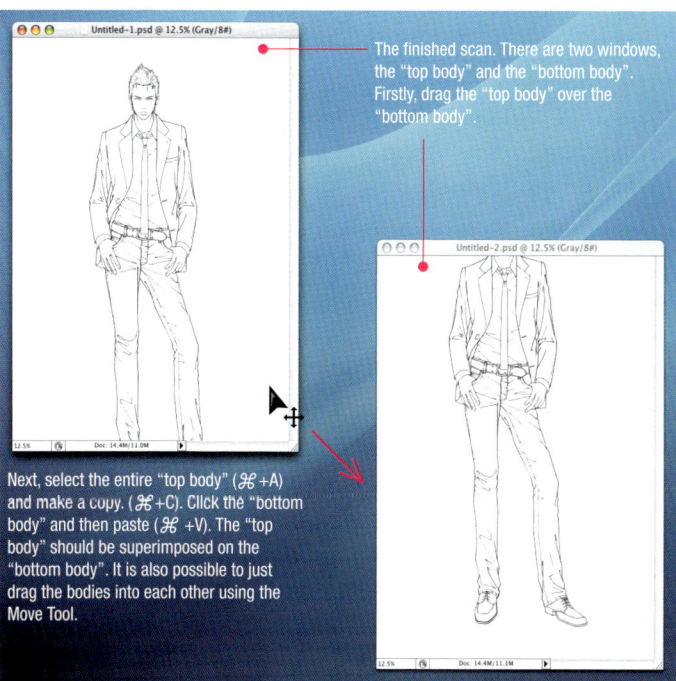

The finished scan. There are two windows, the "top body" and the "bottom body". Firstly, drag the "top body" over the "bottom body".

Next, select the entire "top body" (⌘+A) and make a copy. (⌘+C). Click the "bottom body" and then paste (⌘+V). The "top body" should be superimposed on the "bottom body". It is also possible to just drag the bodies into each other using the Move Tool.

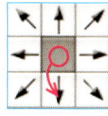

5. The size of our picture is a little small, so select from the menu, [Image/Canvas Size], and move the anchor to the bottom position. Next, set the width at 100% and the height at 120%. Size can be adjusted in various increments, but percentage is easier to work with.

Here, the "top body" and "bottom body" have been placed side by side.

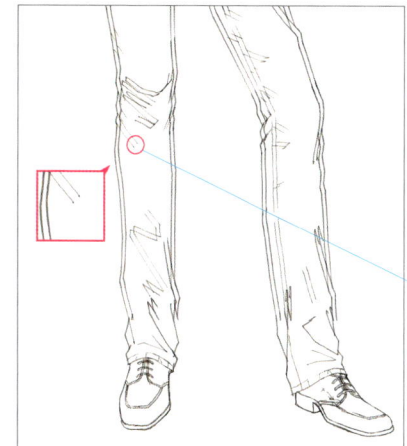

6. The two parts are out of sync and we want to fuse them together. Do this by changing the top half of the body layer to "multiply" using the "Set the blending mode for the layer". Next, use the Move tool (V) to match up the layers. When scanning, be sure to scan the images in straight and not on an angle, otherwise they may not match up.

Using the Zoom function also helps to better match them up. The Zoom short cut key is: ⌘+spacebar+drag and click, or ⌘ and "+").

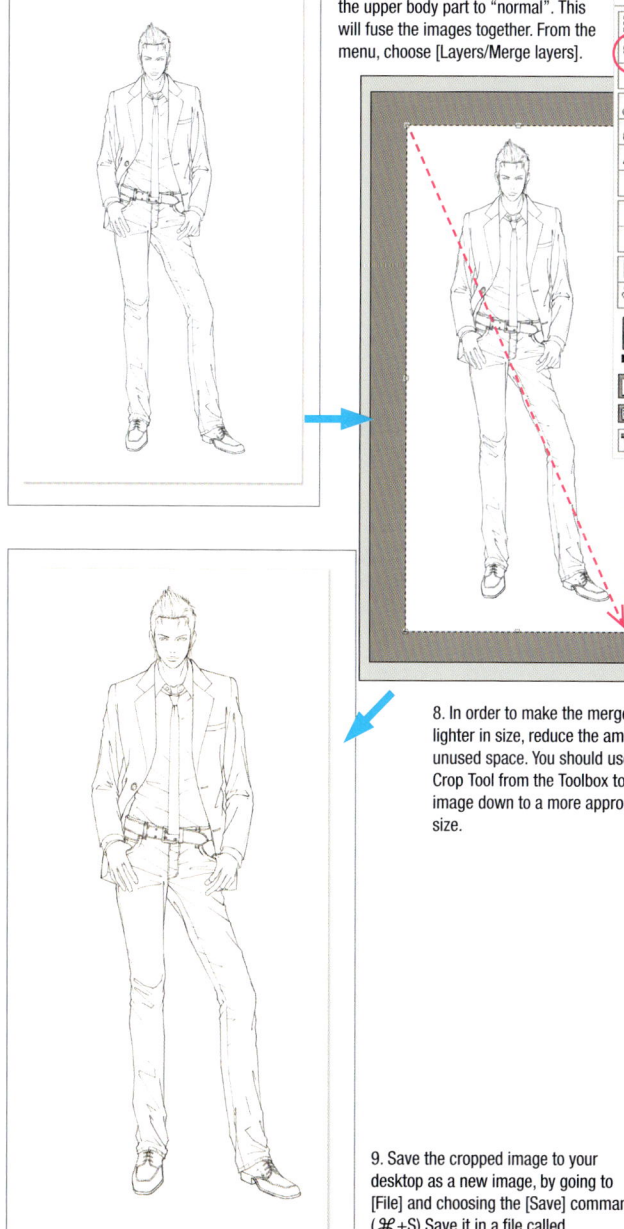

7. After the two layers are perfectly placed, use the "Set the blending mode for layer option", and set the mode for the upper body part to "normal". This will fuse the images together. From the menu, choose [Layers/Merge layers].

8. In order to make the merged data lighter in size, reduce the amount of unused space. You should use the Crop Tool from the Toolbox to cut the image down to a more appropriate size.

9. Save the cropped image to your desktop as a new image, by going to [File] and choosing the [Save] command. (⌘+S) Save it in a file called "Drawing01", in Photoshop format.

129

Modifying Lines

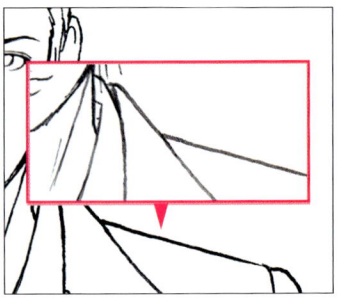

10. In order to align all lines, make a color adjustment revision. From the menu, select [Image/Adjustments/Levels]. Move the slider to about 100/1.00/225. Concentrate on making the lines black. Don't worry about small unnecessary areas.

11. Use the Brush Tool (B) and the Eraser Tool (E) to amend the lines and erase the unnecessary pixels. Brush size: 5 to 20 pixels

When one enlarges the image, some faults will always be visible; however it is enough to correct the work so that any faults will not be apparent when the image is viewed at 100%.

Paint-type tools are easier to use if you know the size of the brush, so adjust the settings accordingly. From the menu, choose [Edit/Preferences/Display and Cursors] to select "Paint Cursors" and "Brush Size" in order to adjust the setting.

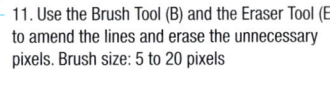

As the background is white, do not use the Eraser Tool; instead edit by using the Brush Tool using white. Here, you can use the shortcut key X to reverse the foreground and background colors.

Change the brush color (image color) to black and the eraser color (background color) to white.

12. Once the line drawing is complete, select only the lines to make a channel. This way you can freely change the color of the lines. (From the arrow at the upper right of the channel palette, choose "Duplicate Channel". Name your new image "Drawing". Be sure to click "Invert". After you have created the new channel, return to the "Gray" channel).

13. In order to use the full range of colors, change the image from "gray scale" to "RBG". From the menu, select [Image/Mode/RGB]. Compared with CMYK and Lab, RBG has more common applications. If you need to use CMYK for printing purposes, you can change the mode once the work is completed.

Applying Color

After setting the drawing as a "Background Layer", it will be possible to place other layers of drawings on top.

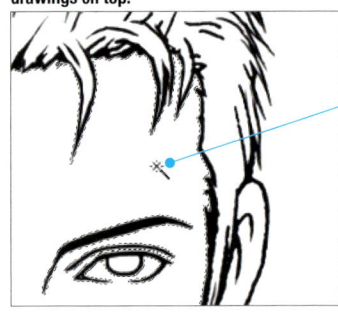

14. First, choose the area you want to paint. Use the Magic Wand Tool to choose the surrounding area. "Tolerance" is set at 32 by default.

Click on the area you wish to select. If it does not select in one go, you can hold down the Shift key and select additional areas

When using the Magic Wand on automatic setting it will select all areas until it finds a solid line, i.e. areas outside the part you want may also be selected. To avoid this problem, you should join all broken lines using the brush tool beforehand.

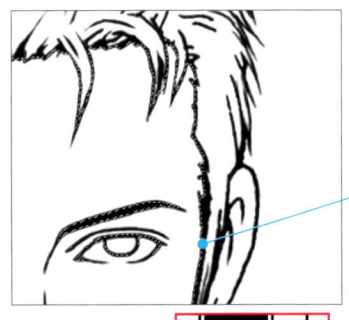

15. Enlarge the selected area so that the colors can penetrate deep into the lines. From the menu, choose [Select/Modify/Expand/Expand by]. Set it at 2 pixels.

You can see here that the selected area has been enlarged.

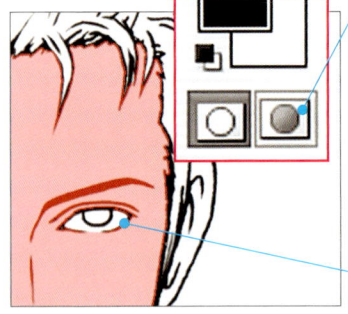

16. Amend the selected area with the quick mask mode. Click on "Edit in the Quick Mask Mode" under the Toolbox.

When making a quick mask, only the area you select will be displayed in the mask's color. (The default color is 50% transparency in opaque red). If you use the Brush Tool, it will color only the selected area. Using the Eraser Tool will delete parts of the selected area only.

In this case, we deleted the eyeball using the Eraser Tool. Finally, the selection was erased.

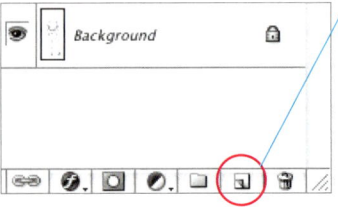

17. As you are not applying color to the background, create a new layer. Click here under the layer palette. If you want to change the name, double click the layer name. By default, the layers are called "layer1", "layer2" and so on. The Create a New Layer shortcut key is ⌘+Shift- N.

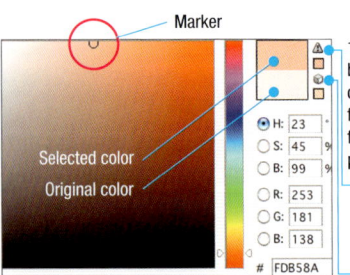

18. Return to "Edit in Standard Mode" (At the bottom of the toolbar on the left) to decide on your colors. Click on the "Foreground Color" to choose from the color picker. (You can also select this from both the color palette and the switch palette).

If the "Warning: Not a web safe color" appears this means that the color is not suitable for the web.

To choose a safe color, click the colored box.

19. Fill in the selected area. In the menu, choose [Edit/Fill/Contents: Foreground Color]. Blending should be set to "normal", and opacity to 100%. The shortcut key for the Fill command is Shift+F5.

20. When you have finished painting, deselect the selected area. In the menu, choose [Select] and then [Deselect]. (⌘+D)

As the lines are partially covered, change the blending mode in the layer palette from [Normal] to [Multiply].

Chapter 4 : Computer Graphic Techniques

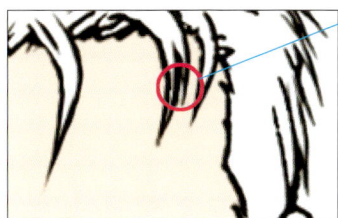

21. If you missed a few areas, you can correct them with the Brush Tool. Pay attention in particular to the hair, where the lines are complex.

Repeat the above steps, adding color to the face, hands, hair, jacket, shirt, belt etc. Create a new layer for each.

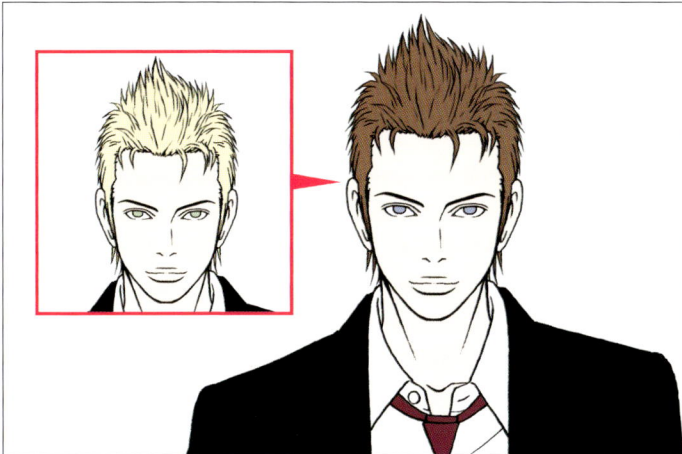

22. To make delicate adjustments to the color, from the menu, select [Image/ Adjustments/Hue/Saturation] (⌘+U). Here we have adjusted the color of the hair and eyes.

Shading

There are two methods of shading: 1) layering the dark colors using the Brush Tool, and 2) Drag with the Dodge Tool to adjust the degree of brightness and saturation. We will first learn the method of adding shading using the Brush Tool, which allows for detailed adjustments.

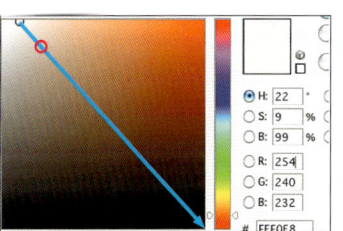

23. In the lock section at the upper left part of the layer palette, click on "Lock Transparent Pixels". This protects the transparent pixels, and color cannot be added to areas other than those already colored. Select your shading color and paint it using the Brush Tool. Select the shading by moving the cursor in the direction of the arrow, in the Color Picker.

24. Here is the shadow created with the Brush Tool. If the difference between the light and dark parts is too distinct it will be necessary to blur them. From the menu, choose [Filter/Blur/Gaussian Blur]. Set the radius at about 3-6 pixels. The edges of the colors should be slightly blurred.

25. If you over-emphasize the three-dimensional element, the result can be overwhelming, so do not overdo it. It is enough to simply add shadow to the parts that you want to emphasize when adding make-up (a clear forehead, large eyes, sexy lips and high nose).

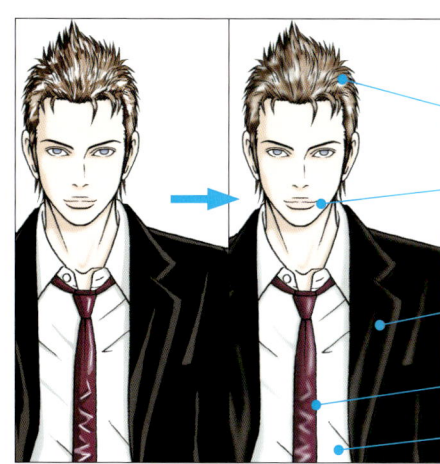

26. Add shading and "blurring" to each individual part.

Because the hair is quite glazed, use white to add highlights as well as shading.

Create a separate layer for the lips, in addition to the one for the skin, and fill it in. Setting the mode to "multiply" will allow it to blend with the skin.

As it is not possible to add shading to black clothes, use gray shading for the brighter parts.

Here, gloss was added to the necktie.

Use gray to add shading to the white shirt.

27. For items of clothing with deep creases, a stronger contrast is made between the light and dark parts.

Giving a Line Drawing Transparent Background

In order to give the line color, it is necessary to create an individual line layer and make the background transparent.

28. From the menu choose [Select/Load Selection] and choose "Drawing" in the Channel. This is how it appears when only the lines have been selected. In this state, create a new layer by clicking on the new layer box. Name it: "Lines"

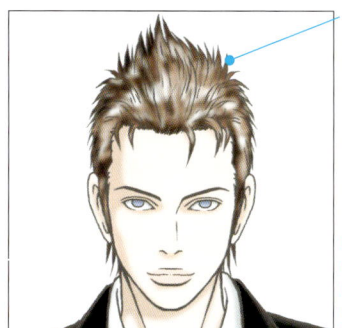

29. Fill the picture using brown. From the Menu choose "Edit", and "Fill". "Use" should be set at Foreground color, with the mode at "normal," and opacity to 100%.

You now have a layer of your picture, "Lines". Set the "Lock transparent pixels" in the layer palette, and drag "lines" to the top layer. Keep the blending mode at "normal". As this is only a line drawing, you will be able to see other layers below.

By creating a "Drawing" channel of the line drawing in this way, it is possible to add color to the lines. Also, if you copy and process this channel, it is possible to change the colors of the lines in different areas.

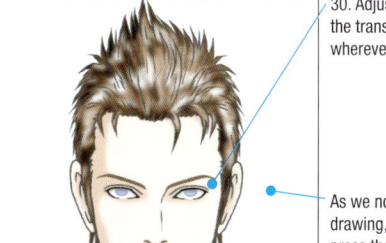

30. Adjust the eyebrows and eye colors. Because the transparent areas are protected, you can paint wherever you like and they will not be disturbed.

As we no longer need the "background" line drawing, you can delete it. Select all (⌘+A) and press the delete key. Note that if the "background color" is not set to white, it will be filled in.

131

31. Completed work.
Save the file by selecting,
[File/Save] (⌘+S) from the menu

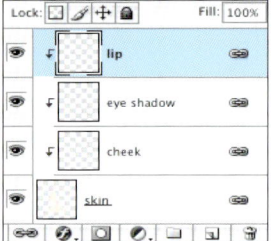

The illustration represents a neo-conservative style, popular in 2002. This style, standing out with its elegant, simple and slender look, stems from the Christian Dior Homme. The classic and modern jacket style has since become popular in the street world as well. Young men have shed their partiality towards oversized, loose clothing, and are instead clothing themselves in this refined fashion.

Color Variations

Endless color variations can be made by changing the colors in each layer. To change colors, from the menu:
[Image/Adjustments/Hue/Saturation] (⌘+U). Move the sliders to make adjustments. If the transparent areas are protected, you can color directly using the Brush Tool.

If the original colors are monochrome, when making color adjustments with "Hue/Saturation", check "Colorize".

To adjust modulations in the shading, choose [Image/Adjustments/ Brightness/Contrast]. Again, move the slider to make adjustments.

Make-up

1. Create new layers for eyeliner, blusher and lips on top of the skin layer, and create a clipping mask. A clipping mask uses the lower layers as a layer mask. The transparent areas of the lower layers are masked, and are not displayed.

When three or more layers are included in the clipping mask, all the layers are linked, and you choose from one layer from among them. From the menu: [Layer/Group with Previous] (⌘+G). By doing this the blusher and eyeliner will not be exposed from the skin color.

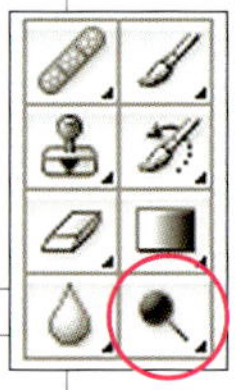

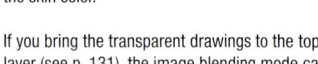

2. Here, the Dodge tool was used to create shading. Choose the brush size and drag it to partially adjust the light and dark areas. It is advisable to use a brush with a blurring effect. The Burn Tool (Selectable by right clicking on the Dodge Tool) was used to create the dark parts, while the bright parts were added using Sponge Tool.

3. Add colors to each layer so that they match the skin color.

If you bring the transparent drawings to the top layer (see p. 131), the image blending mode can be set to either "normal" or "multiply".

4. Add blurring to each area. From the menu: [Filter/Blur/Gaussian Blur]. As an approximate guide, set the eye shadow to 4.0 pixels, the lips to 1.0 pixel, and the blush to 15.5 pixels.

5. Add highlights to complete the work. For the lip highlights, make a new layer on top of the lips and paint in white. Then choose from the menu: [Filter/Blur/Gaussian Blur] and set the value at 2 pixels. The white is too strong as it is, so set the "Opacity" in the layer palette to 85%.

6. If make-up is added without shading, the eyes and lips stand out too much. To create modulations, the outline was emphasized in the direction of the shadow, and blurring added. See p. 145 for more information.

Chapter 4 : Computer Graphic Techniques

(2) Creating Textiles

Scan in your material.

You can scan in an actual material and use it to represent textiles in your fashion drawings. We will not be using the scan as it is, but adjusting it to appropriate levels of color and brightness.

1. Select [Image/Adjustments/Levels] (⌘+L)

2. In 'Input levels,' adjust the black (0), gray (1.00) and white (255) sliders so that the black slider is equally distant in the histogram (the thing that resembles a black mountain) from the white slider. If in RGB color, there will be four separate channels: RGB, R, G and B.

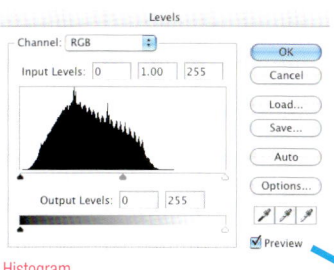

Histogram

3. The pattern should now be more clearly visible.

Repairing Image Damage

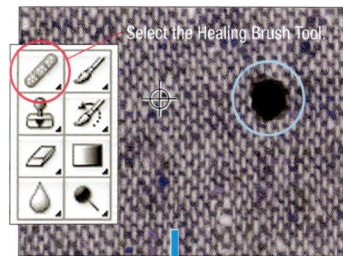

1. Hold the option key and click on the damaged part of the texture.

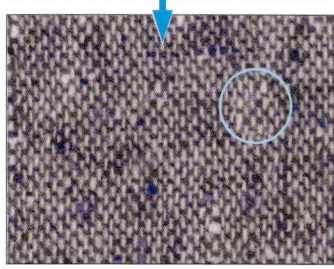

2. Release the option key and drag the brush around, painting over the damage. It will be automatically repaired by adjusting it based on data from the previously selected spot.

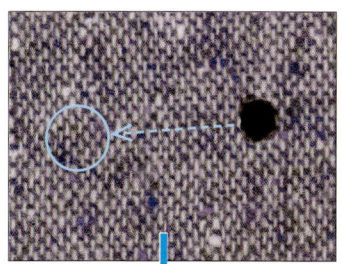

3. You can also use the Patch Tool. Select the area you wish to restore by dragging it.

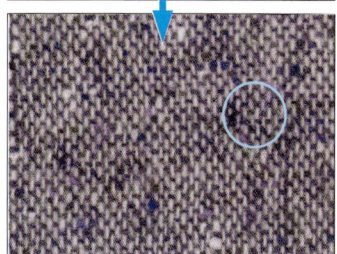

4. Drag and drop the selected area to an undamaged clean area and the selected area will be replaced by the image at the spot where you release the mouse button. The edges of the selection will be adjusted to match the surrounding area.

Expanding the Texture While Restoring It

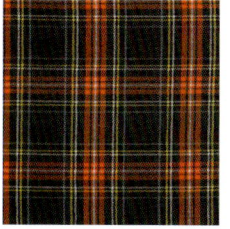 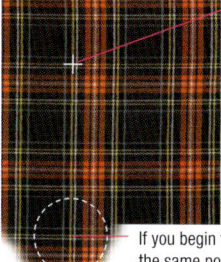

3. In this case, use the Stamp Tool. From the option bar set the mode to "normal", and opacity to 100%. 'Aligned' should be set to "Yes".
Set the copy start point to the area of the texture where the warp lines are cleanest.

1. The simplest way to expand a texture is to copy it by holding the option key while dragging. (⌘+Option)

If you begin to drag from the same point on the texture, the textures will connect cleanly.

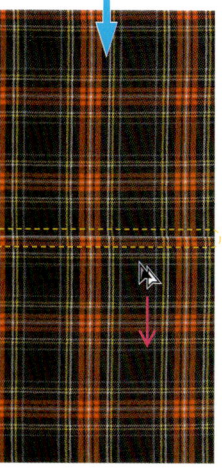 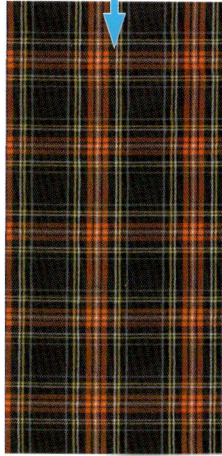

2. However, doing it this way the textures may not cleanly connect.

4. Just doing this has expanded the texture. If you check 'Aligned', even if you release the mouse button, the relative relationship between the copy-source and the mouse pointer will be preserved.

5. Do the same thing to the sides.

6. Complete.

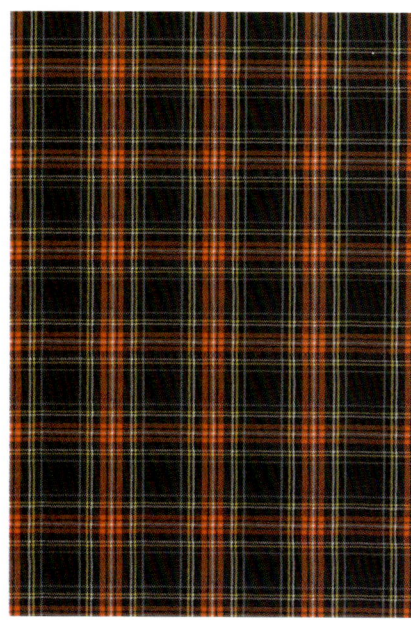

133

Representing Textiles by Using Filters

Filters are a function, which can conveniently process images in a variety of ways. There are a few included in the action palette, so feel free to use them.

● First create a file with the approximate dimensions of the item. Select [File/New] (⌘+N), and use the following settings:
Width: 45mm
Height: 45mm
Resolution: 350
Color Code: RGB
Background Contents: white

4. For a washed out effect you need to add a cloud pattern before applying the filter. Select [Filter/Render/Clouds] from the menu. Choose a shade of blue for the foreground color and white for the background.

Tweed
Creating a nubby effect
1. Select the foreground color (we will use brown this time). Select [Edit] from the menu, then [Fill] (Shift+F5).
2. Select [Filter/Noise/Add Noise] from the menu.

Amount: 50% Distribution: Uniform Monochromatic

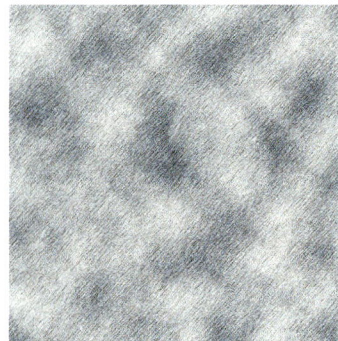

5. After inserting the cloud pattern, repeat the process explained above.
Select [Filter/Artistic/Rough Pastels] from the menu.

Stroke length: 5
Stroke detail: 4
Texture type: Canvas
Scaling: 100%
Relief: 20
Light: Bottom

Fuzzy materials
If the noise amount is put at a low setting, then it can be used to represent materials such as flannel, velvet or suede.

1. Select the foreground color (this time blue), select [Edit/Fill] (Shift+F5) from the menu.
2. Select [Filter/Noise/Add Noise] from the menu.

Amount: 50% Distribution: Uniform Monochromatic

Knit
Fuzzy texture with stitches

1. Select [Edit/Fill/Custom pattern] from the menu.
Select the third mesh pattern from the left.

2. Select [Filter/Stylize/Emboss] from the menu.

Angle: -50 Height: 10 pixels Amount: 250

3. Select [Image/Adjust/Hue and Saturation] (⌘+U) from the menu and move all sliders to adjust the color. Check the [Colorize] box and set the slider options to:
Hue: 300
Saturation: 45
Lightness: - 25

Denim
Creating unevenness and an impression of washed out vertical lines

1. Select the foreground color. Select [Edit] from the menu, then [Fill] (Shift+F5)
2. Select [Filter/Noise/Add Noise] from the menu.

Amount: 50% Distribution: Uniform Monochromatic

3. Select [Filter/Artistic/Rough Pastels] from the menu.

Stroke length: 5
Stroke detail: 4
Texture type: Canvas
Scaling: 100%
Relief: 20
Light: Bottom

4. Draw a border on top of a new layer using the Brush Tool. Set the mode to [Overlay] and the knit fabric underneath will be seen through.

Chapter 4 : Computer Graphic Techniques

Corduroy
Creating an impression of fine ribs

1. By applying a knit pattern you can make corduroy.
2. Select [Edit/Fill/Custom Pattern] from the menu and choose the third mesh from the left.
3. Select [Filter/Stylize/Emboss] from the menu.

    Angle: -100 Height: 10 pixels Amount: 250%

4. Select [Image/Adjust/Hue and Saturation] from the menu. (⌘+U) Check the [Colorize] box and set the slider options to:
Hue: 25 Saturation: 30 Lightness: - 25

Hemp
The warp and weft threads stand out. Create a crisp textured effect.

1. Select [Filter/Noise/Add Noise] from the menu.

    Amount: 60%

2. Select [Filter/Blur/Motion Blur] from the menu.

    Angle: 0 Distance: 50 pixels

3. Select [Filter/ Stylize/Emboss] from the menu.

    Angle: 90 Height: 6 pixels Amount: 150%

4. Drag and copy the background to a new layer. Set the mode to "multiply".
5. Select all the new layers (⌘+A), and select [Edit/Transform (⌘+T)/Rotate 90 degrees clockwise].
6. Merge layers. Select from the menu [Layer/Flatten image].

7. Select [Image/Adjust/Hue and Saturation] (⌘+U) from the menu and move all sliders to adjust the color. Check the [Colorize] box and set the slider options to:
Hue: 40 Saturation: 30 Lightness: 45

Crêpe de Chine
Fine creases

1. Select [Filter/Noise/Add Noise] from the menu.

    Amount: 5%

2. Select [Filter/Stylize/Emboss] from the menu.

    Angle: -180 Height: 1 pixels Amount: 200%

3. Select [Image/Adjust/Hue and Saturation] (⌘+U) from the menu and move all sliders to adjust the color. Check the [Colorize] box and set the slider options to:
Hue: 45 Saturation: 20 Lightness: 15

Herringbone
Stripes with alternating twill

1. We will be using layer styles, so first create a new layer.
2. Choose a foreground color. Select [Edit] from the menu, then [Fill] (Shift+F5)
3. Select [Layer/Layer Style/Bevel and Emboss] from the menu.

    Style: Inner Bevel Technique: Smooth
    Depth: 1% Direction: Up
    Size: 5 Pixels Soften: 0 pixels

4. Click on [Texture] in the list on the left side of the layer style dialogue box. Select the [Herringbone] pattern, second from the right in the lower row.

    Scale: 250% Depth: -1000% Link with layer

5. Select [Filter/Noise/Add Noise] from the menu.

    Amount: -100% Distribution: Uniform Monochromatic

Fur
Giving an impression of long hair

1. Create a new layer and decide on a foreground color. (This time we will use beige.) Select [Edit] from the menu, then [Fill] (Shift+F5)
2. Select [Filter/Noise/Add Noise] from the menu.

    Amount: -100% Distribution: Uniform Monochromatic

3. Select [Filter/Blur/Motion Blur] from the menu.

4. Select [Image/Adjust/Brightness and Contrast] from the menu and set the contrast to +45.

    Angle: 90 Distance: 45 pixels

5. Select [Filter/Distort/Wave] from the menu.

    Type: Sine Number of generators: 3
    Length: Minimum: 85 Maximum: 285
    Amplitude: 5.10 Proportion: 100% 100%
    Undefined areas: Wrap around edges

● Drag with the Dodge Tool to adjust the shading.

6. Duplicate the layer. While expanding and shrinking the layers (⌘+T) or applying the eraser and revealing the layers below, the texture will appear to have several layers of fur.

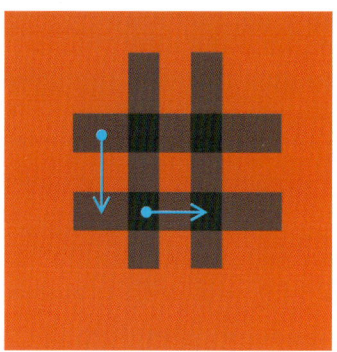

Tartan Checks

Creating and saving the smallest unit of a pattern and then using that pattern as a flood fill. The same technique is also possible with Illustrator.

1. Set the foreground color to red. Select [Edit/Fill] (Shift+F5) from the menu.

2. Use the Line tool by holding the shift key while dragging to create a thick brown line. (Height: 60 pixels, Width: 70 pixels, R: 77 G:55 B:51). Use the Rectangle Tool in the Line submenu to create a green rectangle. Next, use the copy command to duplicate it. (⌘+ Option and drag)

8. Create a new layer and set the foreground color to white. Select [Edit/Fill] (Shift+F5) from the menu. Name the layer 'noise.'
9. Select [Filter/Noise/Add Noise] from the menu.

Amount: 400%

10. Select [Filter/Artistic/Rough Pastels] from the menu.

Stroke length: 6 Stroke detail: 4
Texture type: Canvas Scaling: 100%
Relief: 20 Light: Bottom

11. Set the mode to [Overlay] and the checkerboard underneath will become visible.

3. Use the Line Tool to insert various colored lines. Set a thickness of 5 pixels, starting with dark colors- in the order of black, blue, yellow, and white. Set opacity to 80%.

4. Select [Layer/Flatten image] from the menu.

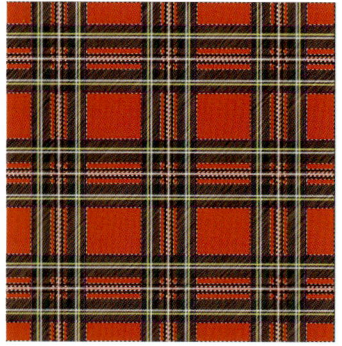

12. Go to the [Background] layer and use the Autoselect Tool to click on the red.
13. Go to the new layer 'noise' and use the delete key to erase the twill lines.
14. Return to the Background layer and add noise to the red.
Select [Filter/Noise/Add Noise] from the menu.

Amount: 4%

5. Select [Filter/Blur/Gaussian blur] from the menu. Radius: 1.0 pixels.

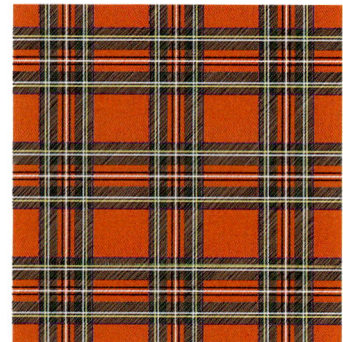

15. Select [Layer/Flatten image] from the menu and it is complete.

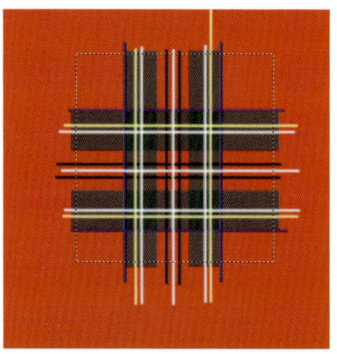

6. Make a pattern by defining a border area around the checkerboard pattern you have created, and then select [Edit/Define pattern] from the menu.

16. Filters have been used to add extra cross-wrinkles to this pattern. This method of adding cross-wrinkles is explained in detail on page 144, 'pasting a flower pattern onto a draped skirt.'

7. Select [Edit/Fill] from the menu.
Use: Pattern. Select the checkered pattern, which should have been added to the pattern thumbnail menu. (It will appear in the last space)

Mode: Normal Opacity: 100%

Chapter 4 : Computer Graphic Techniques

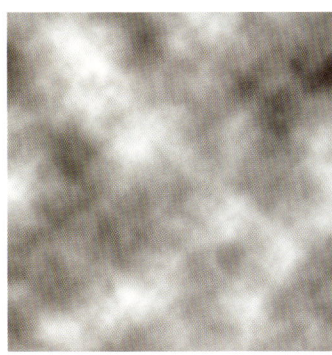

Enamel
Giving an impression of artificial polish

1. Select [Filter/Render/Clouds] from the menu.

Foreground color: Black Background color: White

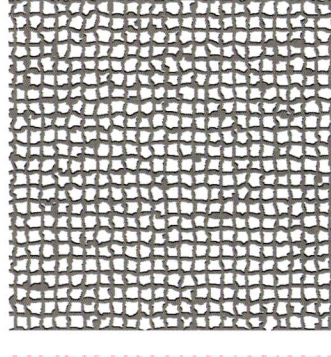

Lacy Knit
Coarsely knit fabric. Express the visible spaces between the knit stitches

1. Paint the background blue.
2. Create a new layer and paint it white.
3. Select [Filter/Texture/Mosaic Tiles] from the menu.

Tile size: 20
Grout width: 6 Lighten grout: 0

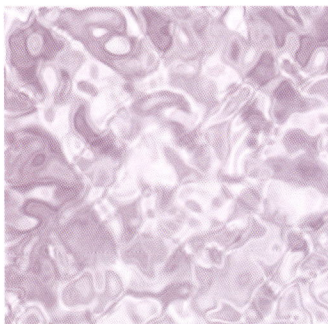

2. Select [Filter/Sketch/Chrome] from the menu.

Detail: 0 Smoothness: 10

3. Select [Image/Adjustments/Hue and Saturation] from the menu (⌘+U) and move the sliders to adjust the color. Check the [Colorize] box and set the slider options to:

Hue: 290 Saturation: 45
Lightness: 40 (315-100-45)

4. Select the threads of the weave by using the Autoselect Tool. Create a new layer and fill it with pink. Set the mode to "normal".

5. Select [Filter/Stylize/Diffuse] and [Mode: Darken only].
6. Drag the layer with the non-pink threads to the trash can on the layer palette.

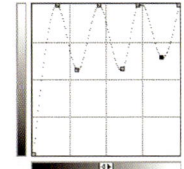

4. Go back to the menu and select [Image/Adjustments/Curves] and in each channel of RGB-red, green, and blue, drag the curve into a wave shape, as pictured above.

5. You have should now have a hologram-like enamel.

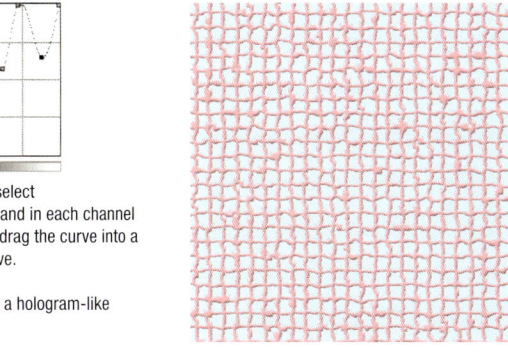

7. Select [Layer/Layer Style/Bevel and Emboss] from the menu.

Style: Inner Bevel
Technique: Chisel soft
Depth: 40% Direction: Up
Size: 5 pixels Soften: 6 pixels
Leave the shading settings at their defaults.

Washer Process
Representing creases

1. Select [Filter/Render/Clouds] from the menu.

2. Select [Filter/Sketch/Reticulation] from the menu.

Density: 12
Foreground level: 40 Background level: 5

8. From the menu, choose [Filter/Noise/Add Noise].

Amount: 20% Distribution: Uniform
Check Monochromatic

3. Select [Layer/Layer Style/Bevel and Emboss] from the menu.

Style: Inner Bevel
Technique: Smooth
Depth: 1% Direction: Up
Size: 5 pixels Soften: 0 pixels

4. Click on [Texture] in the list on the left side of the layer style dialogue box.

Select the [Satin] pattern, in the upper right.
Scale: 130%
Depth: 100%

9. Click on the eye symbol of the background and you will be able to see through to the background.

Crocodile Skin

The impression of scales

1. Select the foreground color. (This time we will use brown.) Select [Edit/Fill] from the menu (Shift + F5).

2. Create a new layer and paint it black. Set the mode to "multiply".

3. Select [Filter/Noise/Add Noise] from the menu. This time do not select monochromatic noise.

Amount: 400%   Distribution: Uniform

4. Select [Filter/Pixelate/Pointilize] from the menu. Cell size: 3

5. Select [Filter/Blur/Gaussian Blur] from the menu. Radius: 5 pixels

6. Select [Filter/Texture/Stained glass] from the menu.

Cell size: 20   Border thickness: 5
Light intensity: 1

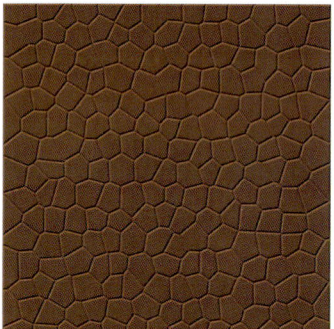

7. Select [Filter/ Stylize/Emboss] from the menu.

Angle: -56   Height: 2 pixels   Amount: 100%

8. Create a new layer and select [Filter/Render/Clouds 1] from the menu. (Foreground color: black, Background color: white) Set the mode to [Soft light].

9. Select [Image/Adjust/Hue and Saturation] from the menu (⌘+U) and move all sliders to adjust the color. Check the [Colorize] box and set the slider options to:

Hue: 260   Saturation: 25   Lightness: 40

Snake Skin

Giving the impression of fine scales and mottles

1. Paint the background with a gradient. Click on the Gradient Tool to select it. Click on the Gradient bar in the option bar and bring up the [Gradient edit] window. Click on the initial, final and in between points to set their respective colors.

Gradation type: Solid   Smoothness: 100%

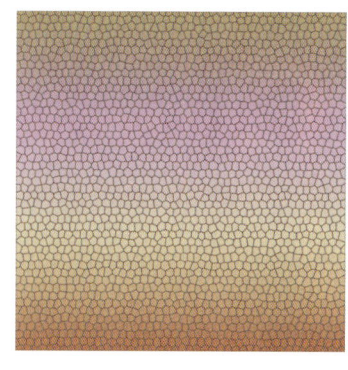

2. Select [Filter/Texture/Stained glass] from the menu.

Cell size: 6   Border thickness: 52
Light intensity: 10

3. Set the border color to the foreground color.

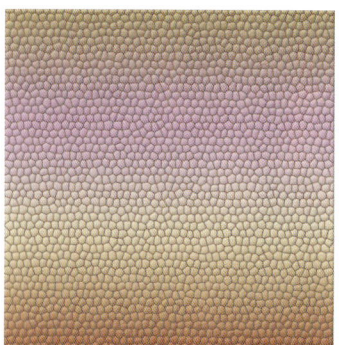

4. Copy the [Background] layer by dragging it to the new layer box.

5. Select the lines of the new layer by using the Autoselect Tool and then erase them by using the delete key.

6. On the copied layer, select [Filter/Layer/Layer Style/Bevel and Emboss] from the Menu.

Style: Inner Bevel   Technique: Smooth
Depth: 45%   Direction: Up   Size: 5 pixels
Soften: 1 pixels   Highlight mode: overlay
Opacity: 100%   Shadow mode: Normal
Opacity: 75%

7. Set the opacity of the copied layer to 50%. Set the mode to "multiply" and flatten the image.

8. Select [Filter/Sharpen/Sharpen] from the menu.

9. Select [Layer/New fill layer/Pattern] from the menu.

Mode: Color burn
Opacity: 40%
Pattern: second row far right [Clouds]
Scale: 200%

Lamé

Giving the impression of glossiness

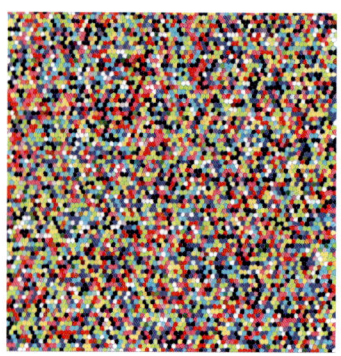

1. Set the foreground color to black and select [Edit/Fill] from the Menu.

2. Select [Filter/Noise/Add Noise] from the menu. This time do not select monochromatic noise.

Amount: 400%   Distribution: Uniform

3. Select [Filter/Texture/Stained glass] from the menu.

Cell size: 3   Border thickness: 1
Light intensity: 0

Chapter 4 : Computer Graphic Techniques

Rendering a Hand Painted Processed Textile

You can add to range of textiles by scanning in line drawings or drawing directly on the computer using the painting tools.

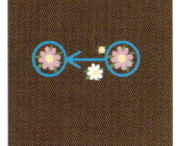

Flower Pattern

Point: Combining 2 or 3 varieties of flowers of varying sizes and colors.

1. Fill the background and create a new layer. Draw a flower using the Brush Tool. Draw three types of flowers, each on its own layer.

2. Drag and copy (⌘+Option) the flowers on each layer to increase their numbers.

3. Create yet another new layer and on it use the Brush Tool to draw the outer coloring of the leopard spots. (layer 2)

3. First cover ¼ of the target area. Flower patterns are large, so it is easiest to start with the largest flower to fill the space. Once the image has been filled with flowers, merge the layers. (Click the eye icon on the background to hide it, then select [Layer/Merge visible layers] from the menu. (Shift+⌘+E)

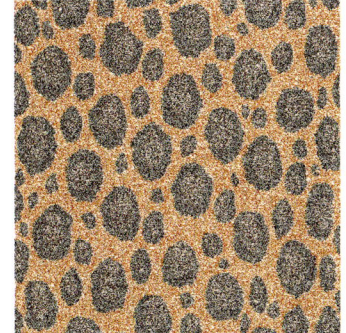

4. In yet another layer, set the foreground color to white. Select [Edit/Fill] from the menu. (Shift+F5) Set the mode to [Color burn]. (layer 3)

5. Apply some noise to the white colored layer. Select [Filter/Noise/Add Noise] from the menu.

Amount: **400%**   Distribution: **Uniform Monochromatic**

6. Copy the noise layer. Set the mode to [Hard light]. (layer 4)

Opacity: **50%**

4. Drag and copy the 1/4th area that has been filled to fill more area with flowers.

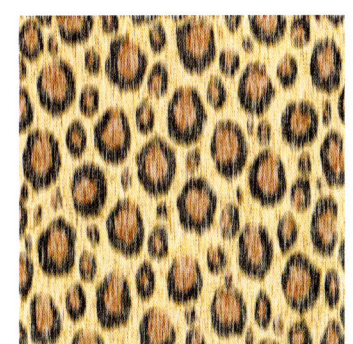

7. Process each of these 4 layers in the same way. Select [Filter/Blur/Motion Blur] from the menu.

Angle: **20**   Distance: **20 pixels**

8. You can use (⌘+F) to repeat the last applied filter setting.

5. Once the entire canvas is filled with flowers, it is complete. You can use this technique of duplicating a few small patterns to fill an area to easily create hand drawn patterns.

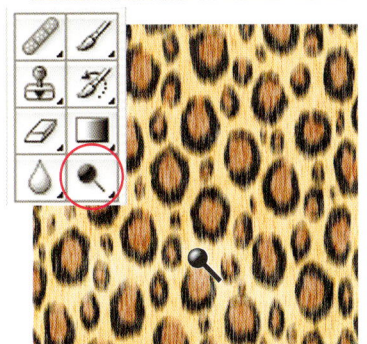

9. Use the Burn Tool on the Background to insert bright areas.

10. Flatten the image, then select [Filter/Distort/Wave] from the menu.

Type: **Sine**   Number of generators: **1**
Length: Minimum: **85**, Maximum: **285**
Amplitude: **5.10**   Proportion: **100% 100%**
Undefined areas: **Wrap around edges**

Leopard Skin Pattern
Adding fur to the spots

1. Set the Foreground color to beige. Select [Edit/Fill] from the menu. (Shift+F5)

2. Create a new layer and use the Brush Tool to draw some leopard spots. After processing they will get thicker, so draw them lightly for now. (layer 1)

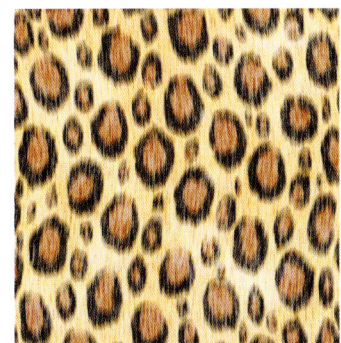

11. Select all (⌘+ A) and expand or contract the image (⌘ +T) as necessary to finish.

139

Camouflage Print
Processing a single pattern using staggered layers to produce a camouflage effect

1. Firstly, fill in the background with in beige.

2. Create a new layer and draw some camouflage with the Brush Tool. It is not necessary to worry too much about the shape.

3. Select [Select/Load selection] from the menu and identify the range of the pattern.

4. Select [Select/Modify/Contract] from the menu and enter 4 pixels.

5. Create a new layer and fill it with the color khaki.

6. Rotate the layer 90 degrees. Select [Edit/Transform/Rotate 90 degrees counterclockwise] from the menu.

7. Repeat steps 3 to 6, this time with the foreground color set to dark khaki.

Shiny Materials
Accurately projecting differences in light/dark shading

1. After painting the background with a color, create two new layers, and color one with the light color and one with the shadow color. You can leave the mode as "normal".

It is decided that the light is coming from the right. Shadow is inserted along each of the contours.

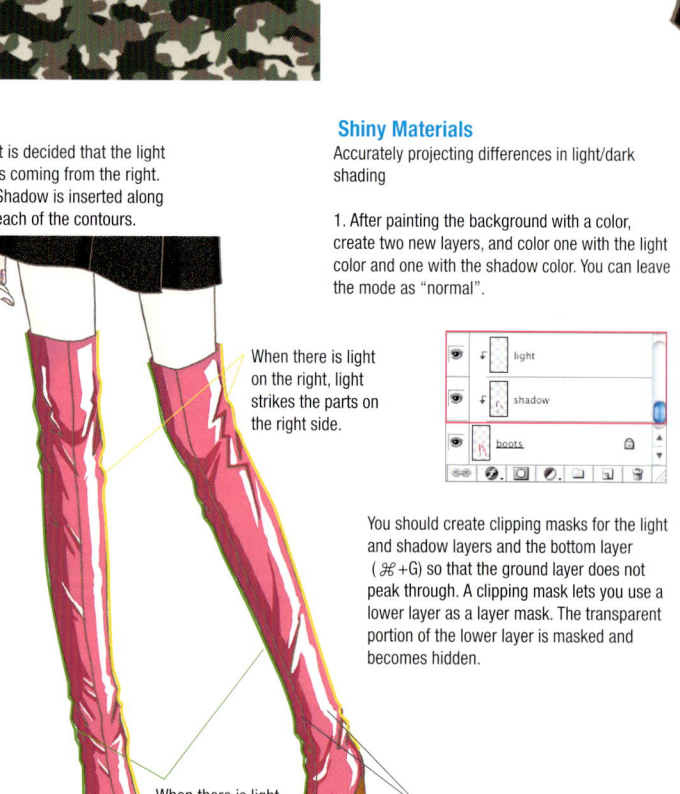

When there is light on the right, light strikes the parts on the right side.

You should create clipping masks for the light and shadow layers and the bottom layer (⌘+G) so that the ground layer does not peak through. A clipping mask lets you use a lower layer as a layer mask. The transparent portion of the lower layer is masked and becomes hidden.

When there is light on the right, there is shadow on the left side.

On shiny materials like this, differences in shading are very noticeable. Therefore it is best to try to emphasize the difference between and the background color and the other colors. The dark part can be set to black and the reflective part, to white.

2. Insert some blur into both the light and shadow layers. Select [Filter/Blur/Gaussian Blur] from the menu. Set the radius for the shadow layer at 9.5 pixels and the light layer at 7.5.

3. The illustration here is a mix from the 60s. It was popular during the 2003-04 season. The Casket tweed classic one piece dress and knee-high boots match well.

4. In order to sharpen the image, we emphasized the direction of the contours in the shadowed area and added some blur to the entire image. This method is explained in detail on page 145.

Chapter 4 : Computer Graphic Techniques

Sheer Fabrics
While considering how much translucency you wish to give to the blouse and skirt, make them appear see-through.

1. Create a see-through item
Make a new layer on top of the blouse. Create it as a clipping mask. (⌘+G) The clipping mask is used as a layer mask for the bottom layer. The transparent pixels of the bottom or base layer mask the contents of the layers above it.

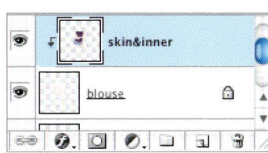

2. If you change the layer mode to "multiply," the clothes become translucent. We will blur this later, so it does not matter if it is slightly rough at this stage.

3. Remove the wrinkled parts with the eraser.

4. For the blouse, from the menu, choose [Filter/Blur/Gaussian] at radius of 9 pixels. Set opacity to 40%.

5. For the pants, from the menu, choose [Filter/Blur/Gaussian] at radius of 15 pixels. Set the opacity to 70%.

6. Create a new layer on top of both the blouse and the pants, and make them clipping masks. (⌘+G) For each, paint the highlighted wrinkles in white. Choose [Filter/Blur/Gaussian] at radius of 7 pixels.

7. In order to sharpen the image, we emphasized the direction of the contours and added a little more blur to the whole image. Details of how to do this are outlined on page 145.

This illustration is in the Bohemian style, which was popular in 2002. In those uneasy times of the world, this style came about as a romantic and gentle style, mixed with the folky layered clothing styles of the 1970s.

Making Textiles Appear Three Dimensional

When applying this to a texture, the most important thing to be aware of is the warp lines. It is best to hand draw textiles that go with the movement, creases, and the three-dimensional elements of the clothing, textiles with warp lines that are directly related to the design of striped texture (checks, borders and stripes). If the warp lines do not fit the textile it is best to use filters that emphasize the atmosphere, or flower patterns that can be drawn without matching the warp lines. In this case, it is best to set a heavy shadow, it being important to emphasize the three dimensional element of the clothing.

Drawing Checks in Free Hand for a Three Dimensional Effect.

1. Scan in your hand drawn picture and perform a color adjustment to delineate the lines. (See P130-11). Next, make a new alpha channel for your lines. (See P130-12) The checks should be drawn separately from the person's image. The knack is to draw horizontal and vertical lines and narrow checks in alternative colors. It is a good idea to trace them onto the person's image using tracing paper.

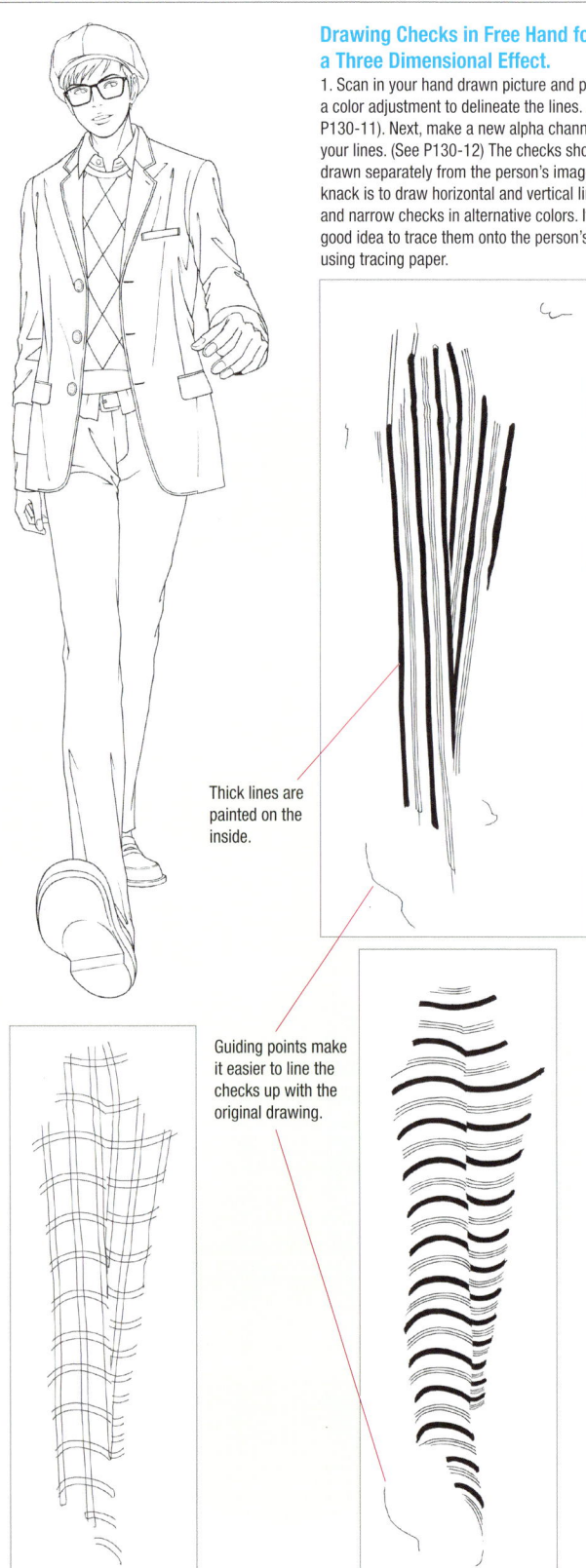

Thick lines are painted on the inside.

Guiding points make it easier to line the checks up with the original drawing.

2. Drag your newly created checkered background to a new layer box, and make a copy. The transparency should be set at 20%. The background has already been copied as a new layer, so you should whiten it out and delete it.

3. Select each layer and make copies. (⌘+C) Paste them onto the image of your person. (⌘+V).

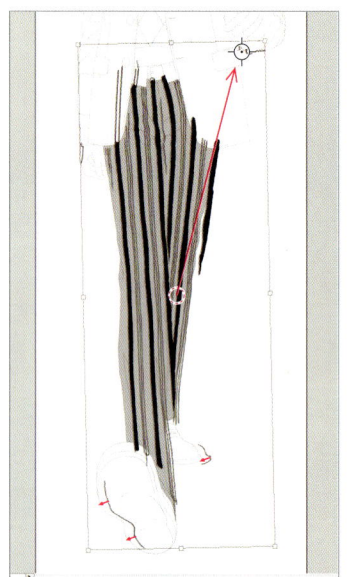

4. In case the lines should not match with the image, choose [Edit/Free transformation] from the menu. Drag and click and move within the bounding box. Next, drag the center point and match it up with the original guiding points, rotating it where necessary.

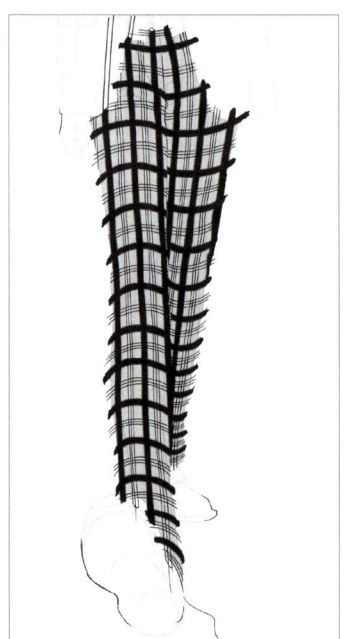

5. All the pattern layers were pasted into the original person image. You may now manipulate the RBG values.

Chapter 4 : Computer Graphic Techniques

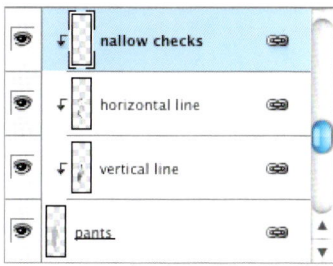

6. Create a new layer, color the pants and create a new clipping mask for the line patterns. (⌘+G) The clipping mask is used as a layer mask for the bottom layer. The transparent pixels of the bottom or base layer mask the contents of the layers above it.

7. In order to color your checked lines etc, it is necessary to make the white parts transparent and a layer for the lines.

8. Firstly, enable the Magic Eraser Tool on the option bar. Make sure that "Anti-alias" is selected. "Contiguous" should be left unchecked. Next, make the white parts of the line layers transparent, using the magic eraser.

9. Choose the line layer, and from Layer palette, select "Lock transparent pixels".

10. Adjust the color of line layers from the menu, [Image/Adjustments/Hue and Saturation] suing the sliders. (⌘+U) If you check the "Colorize" box, this will change the monotone to color.

11. Repeat the above for each of your lines.

When separating the colors of the thick and thin lines, you can do so directly with the Brush Tool, or alternatively, just select the line and fill it in.

12. To create shadows, you can make new layers on each of the items, in which case it is possible to put in other colors and patterns. Layer mode should be set to "multiply".

13. Jackets, shirts and sweaters can also be made in this way.

14. In order to sharpen the image, we emphasized the contours in the direction of the shadow and added a little more blur to the whole image. Details of how to do this are outlined on page 145.

The illustration is that of a nerd, a popular style in the early 1990s, meaning a pencil thin guy. In the fashion world, the theme of altered school styles has appeared over and over again.

143

Giving Draped Skirts a Floral Design

1. This is the line drawing. Color revisions and line revisions have already been completed, as well as changing the graphic channel and the mode to RGB. (See P130/10-13) The lines should be made transparent. (P131/27-29)

2. Fill in the skirt with a shade of gray. Make the foreground color gray. From the menu, choose Edit, and then Fill (Shift+F5). Also fill in the skin.

3. This is the pattern that will be used. It was created using the same method as described on P139.

4. Copy the flower pattern (⌘+A /⌘+C) and paste (⌘+V) onto the picture.

5. Next, use a clipping mask with the pasted textile. (⌘+G). The clipping mask is used as a layer mask for the bottom layer. The transparent pixels of the bottom or base layer mask the contents of the layers above it.

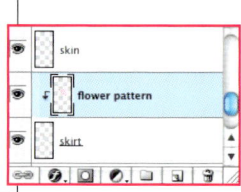

6. Create a new layer (wrinkle) on top of the skirt. Turn the skirt layer into a clipping mask. (⌘+G)

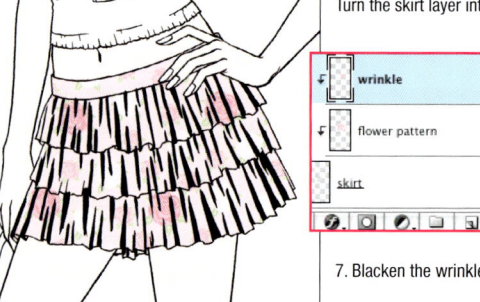

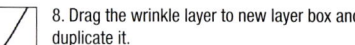

7. Blacken the wrinkles.

8. Drag the wrinkle layer to new layer box and duplicate it.

9. Choosing the wrinkle layer, from the menu select [Filter/blur/Gaussian blur] Set it to a radius of 8 pixels. Return to the layer palette, choose the copied wrinkle, and again, from the menu, [Filter/Blur/Gaussian blur] and set at the radius of 16 pixels. Mode should be set to "multiply".

10. Merge the layers and select from the menu, [Filter/Stylize/Trace Contour]

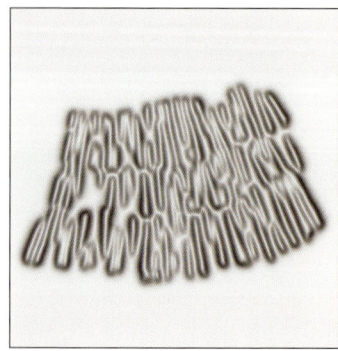

11. Create a new file from the merged Wrinkle Layer. Choose All (⌘+A), and copy (⌘+C). From the File menu, choose New (⌘+N) and paste (⌘+V). Finally, merge the entire picture.

12. Copy the image, and choose your new file. The file size and resolution should be the same as the copied layer.

13. From the menu, select [Image/Adjustments/Brightness & Contrast.]

Brightness: -25   Contrast: 55.

14. Save to the desktop. From the menu, select [File/Save] (⌘+S). The file name should be 01.

Chapter 4 : Computer Graphic Techniques

15. Return to the original style file, drag your wrinkle layer to the layer palette wastebasket, and go back to the original layer. Select it.

16. From the menu, select [Filter/Distort/Displace]. Horizontal and Vertical scales should both be set to 5%. Click "OK", and open file 01 from your desktop.

17. With this method you can make twisted wrinkles. Please refer to page 136, which has an example of twisted wrinkles in tartan checks.

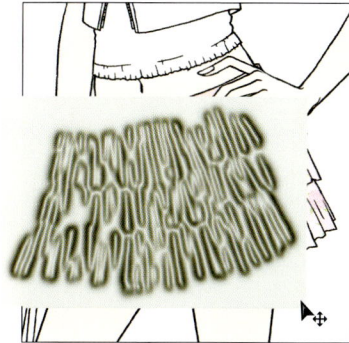

18. Copy File 01 (⌘+A, ⌘+C) and paste it on top of the skirt layer of your image.

19. Use the Move Tool and match it up with the pasted 01 file.

Wrinkle shadows appearing in the waste band are removed using the Eraser Tool.

20. The mode should be set to "normal". Set opacity to 60% and make it a clipping mask with the skirt beneath. (⌘+G)

24. This is the final image. The outer lines were set at brown and moved to the upper most layer. In order to make the skirt appear three dimensional, we avoided shadowing the other items. Overall, the picture is quite subtle, so the facial features are not unduly emphasized.

21. From the menu, choose [Image/Adjustment/Hue and Saturation] (⌘+U) and use the sliders to manipulate the image. Ensure "Edit "is set to Master.
Hue: 345 Saturation: 85 Lightness: 65

Emphasizing contours
In order to give the colors a flatter touch, it is necessary to use a slightly different sharpening technique. Here, we embossed the contradiction in blurring and the emphasis of the contours, and tried to both sharpen and soften the image.

1. Make the background non-visible (Merge the remaining layers).
2. Drag this layer to the new layer box and make a copy. In the layer Palette, choose, "Lock transparent pixels."
3. Fill in the bottom layer using the same color as the border lines, and make it a silhouette.
4. Using the Move Tool, move the bottom layer (the one you just filled in) slightly to the left, thus increasing the thickness of the lines.
5. Once again, merge the image, and drag the background into the new layer box, creating a copy. From the menu choose [Filter/Blur/Gaussian blur] with 1.6 pixels (radius). Mode should be set to "normal", and opacity to 40%.
6. Move this layer slightly to the left.
7. The overall picture becomes a lot milder when placed on this slightly blurred layer.

22. Create a new layer on top of the skirt and using the Brush Tool, create a shadow. Be sure to create a clipping mask. (⌘+G)

23. Create an additional new layer, and make it a clipping mask with the skirt, making it transparent. In this case, we used white, with a Gaussian blur, with 8.5 pixels. The transparency was set at 75%.

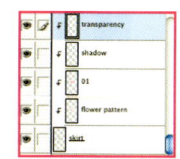

145

Final Image
Fairy Style. This was popular in spring of 2004. This style was an up-take from the romantic style of the early 2000s. In sweet floral and chiffon textiles with frills, ruffles and drapes with a feminine design, these floral and chiffon sweet textiles, like sugar coated sweets, were very popular. There were many lovely and cute girls all over town in such outfits.

Application
The 'boots' look. This style was popular among ladies from the first five years of 2000. It remains popular year after year, with only changes to the length and volume of the textile. This look not only confines the wearer to a skirt, but also other styles such as pants, pants on top of the skirt, tucking boots into pants, etc.

When drawing knit stitches along with warp lines, it is best to draw in freehand, with layers, using a slightly darker color than the color of the clothes.

Create a layer for each of the pleats of the pleat skirt, filling each one in, followed by your patterns. Finally, make it a clipping mask. We wanted to darken the heavy parts of the checks, and so with the mode set at "normal", gave it an opacity of 80%.

Long scarves were very fashionable in 2002, particularly the nearly two meter long hand knitted ones.

The fishnet tights were scanned in separately, and added as a new layer. This makes it possible to easily change the colors.

Corporation: Japan Center for Hair Dressing and Beauty Education

[2] Using Illustrator

The Illustrator Graphical User Interface (GUI)

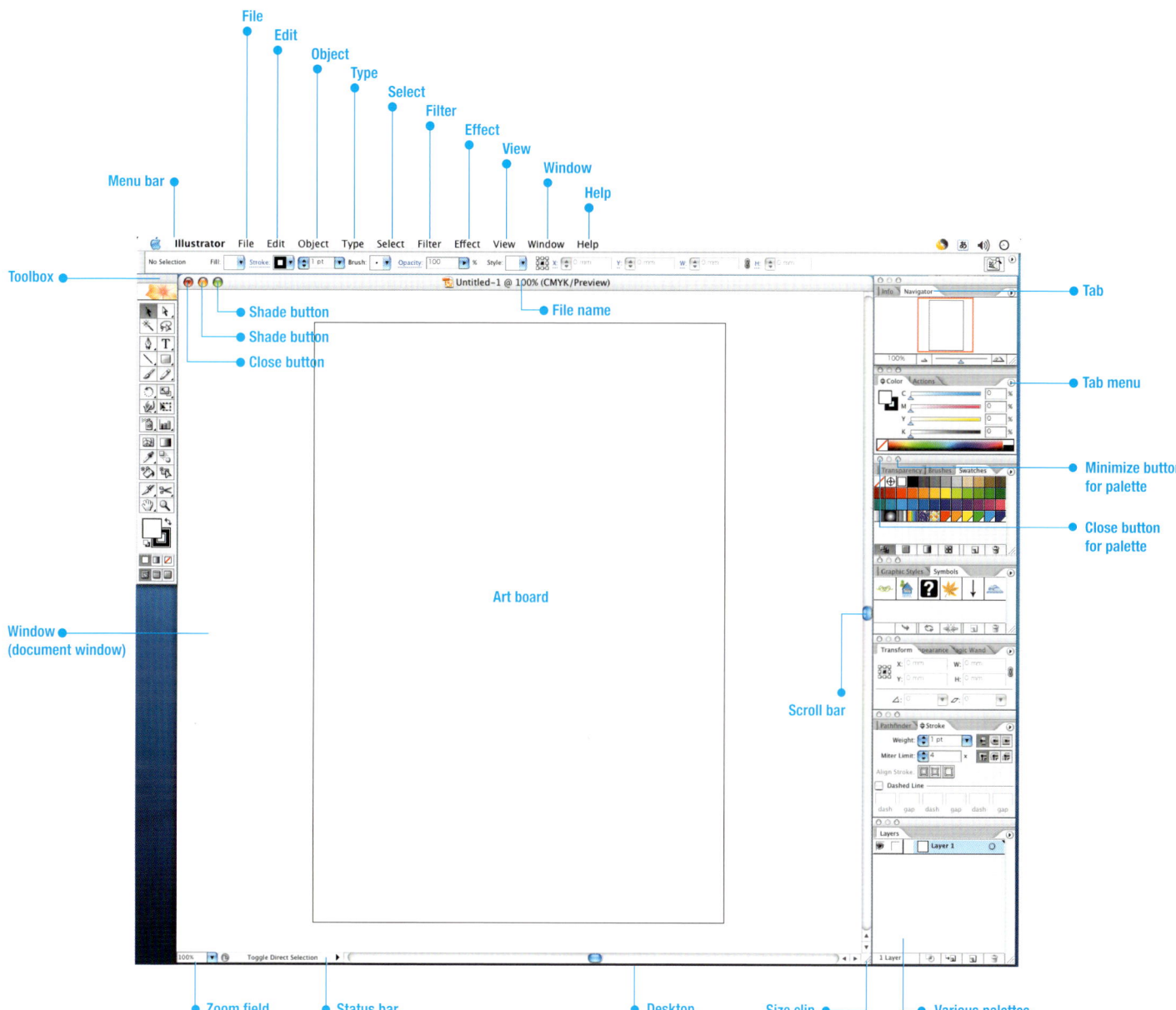

Toolbox

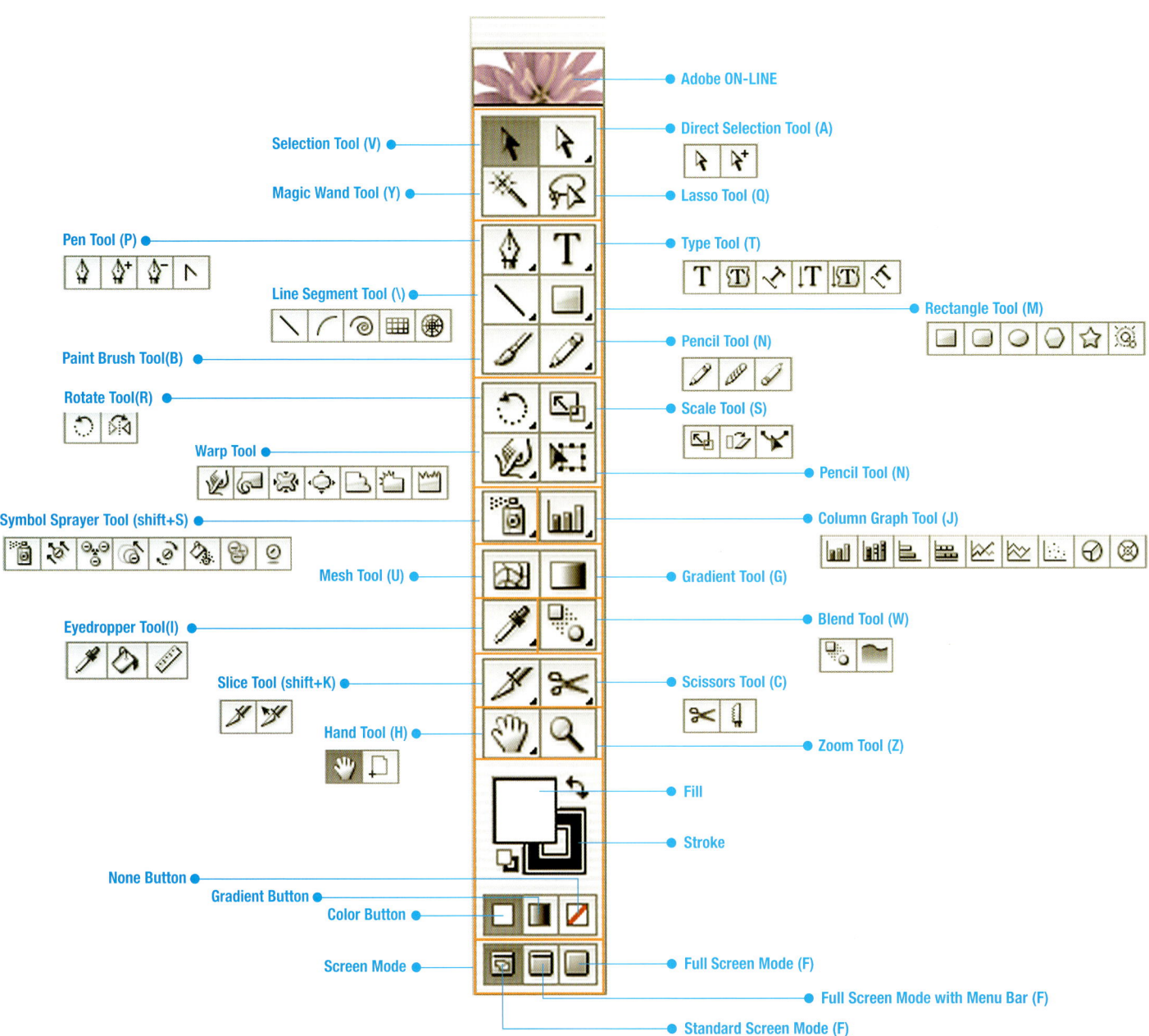

Chapter 4 : Computer Graphic Techniques

Palettes

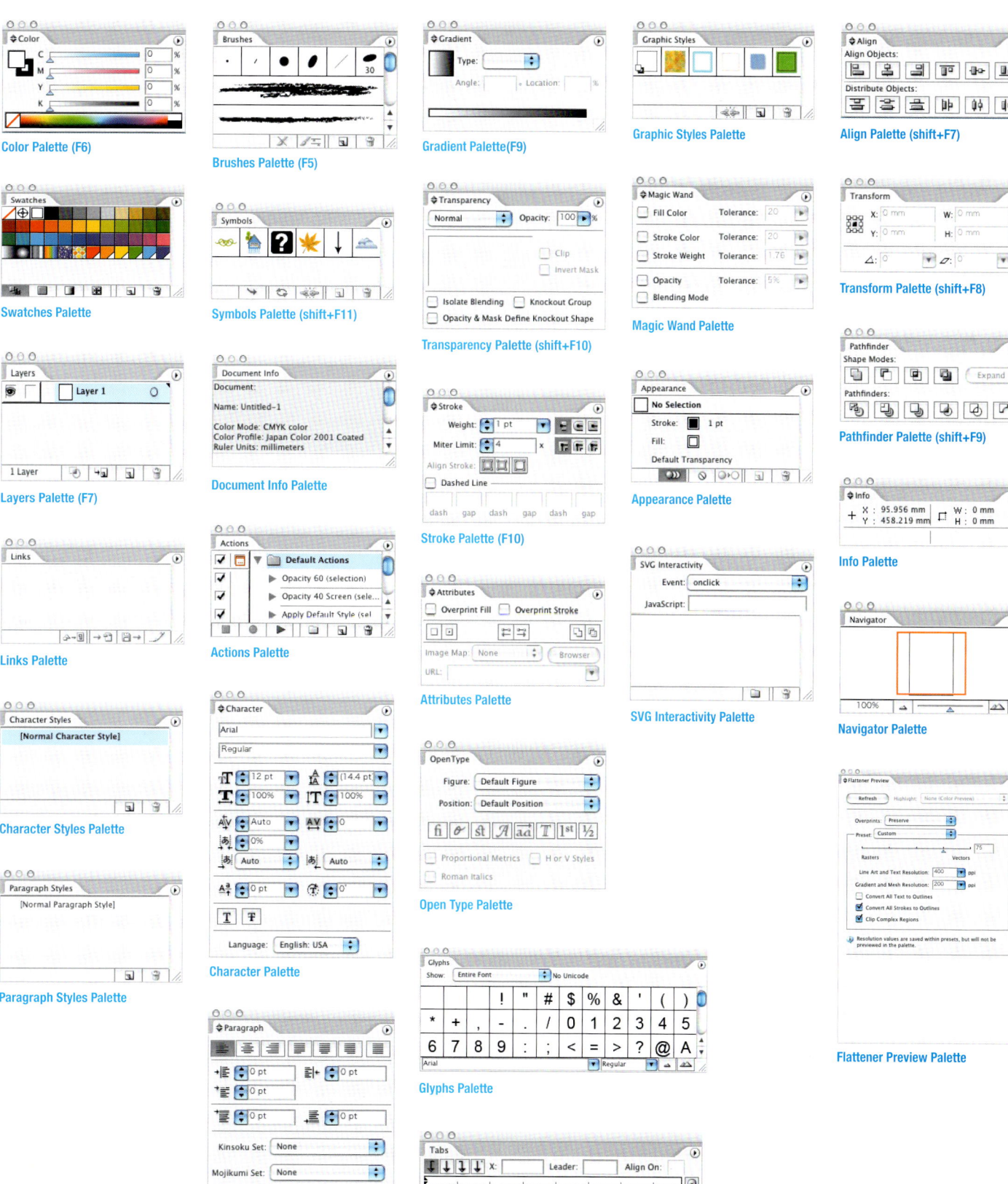

(1) Technical Drawing

The pen tool is very useful for free hand drawing as well as for drawing straight or curved lines.

Digitizing Sketches as Raster Images

First, draw the image to be scanned in pencil. See Chapter 2 (p55) for reference.

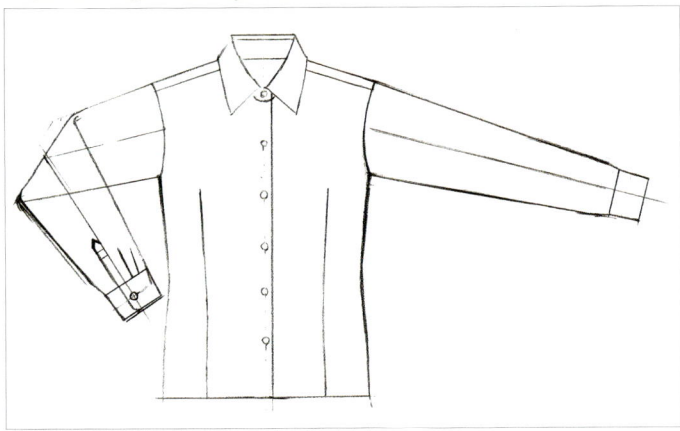

1. Scan the drawing into the computer.
2. Open Photoshop. Set the resolution to 150 and open the file in grayscale mode.
3. Save the raster image file on to the desktop. From the menu, choose [File/Save] (⌘+S). Save the image as "blouse1" in Photoshop format. Close Photoshop.
4. Open the raster image in Illustrator. When Illustrator starts up, choose [File/Open] from the menu. Choose "blouse1" from the desktop and open the file.

5. Having a ruler is useful. From the menu, choose [View/Show Rulers] (⌘+R).

6. Drag a guideline from the vertical ruler to the center of the shirt.

7. Create a new layer on top of the scanned raster image.

8. First, lock the layer "blouse1" containing the raster image.

9. The new layer is called "Layer 2." Click on the layer name to open the layer options and rename the layer "line."

10. Choose the color of the stroke from the Swatches Palette (or from the Colors Palette).

11. Set the "Fill" box to no color and the "Stroke" box to blue so that the difference between the outlining stroke and the lines of the raster image will be clearly defined. From the "Stroke Palette," Enter a stroke thickness of 1pt into the "Stroke Palette".

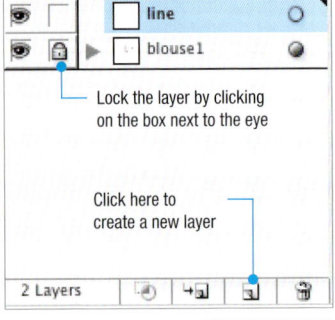

Drawing Using the Pen Tool

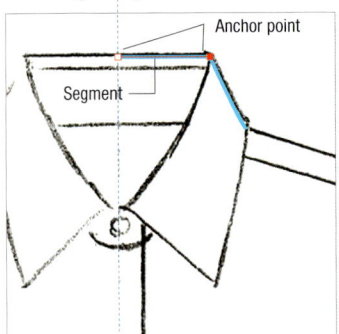

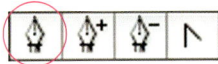

12. Straight Line
Click two anchor points and a straight line will be drawn between them.

13. Trace the outline of the right side of the blouse. First draw the symmetrical parts, then mirror them.

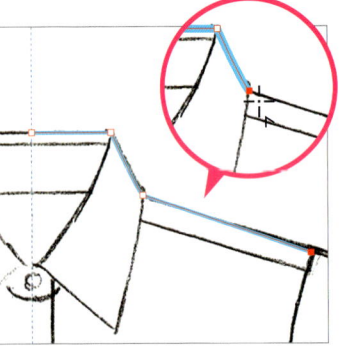

14. Curved Line
To draw a curved line first click on the end point, then drag to draw out the direction line (handle) and change the shape of the straight line. If you make a mistake, select "Undo" (⌘+Z).

Holding down the ⌘ key while using the Pen Tool activates the Direct Selection Tool. By moving the cursor to the anchor point, a mark appears. This means that "the anchor point is here." You can select and manipulate only that anchor point.

15. Combining curved lines and straight lines
To convert a curved line to a straight line, before moving on to the next point click again on the same anchor point while holding down the Option key. This will delete one handle and then when you click on the next point a straight line will appear.

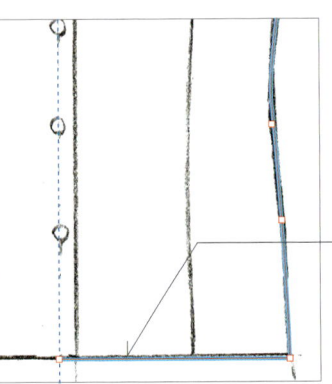

16. Continue in the same way and outline half of the blouse.

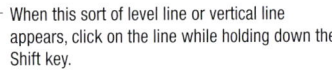

When this sort of level line or vertical line appears, click on the line while holding down the Shift key.

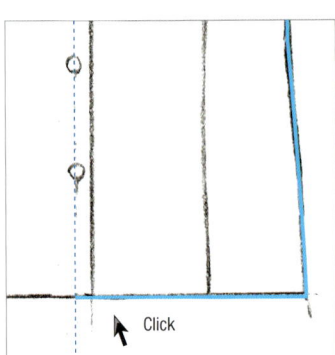

17. When you have finished, change to the Selection tool, (or press the ⌘ key while using the Pen Tool) and click anywhere on the display to end.

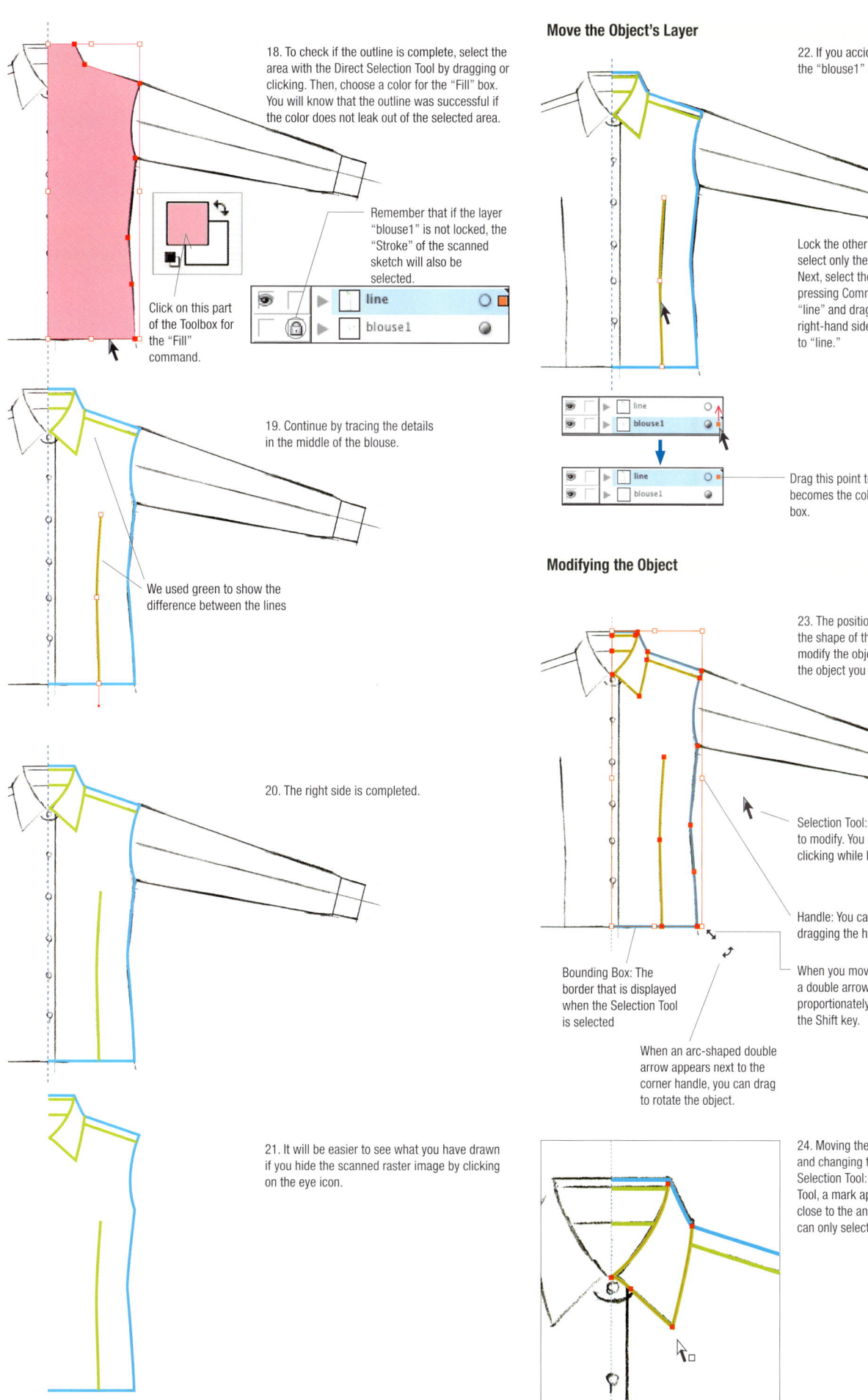

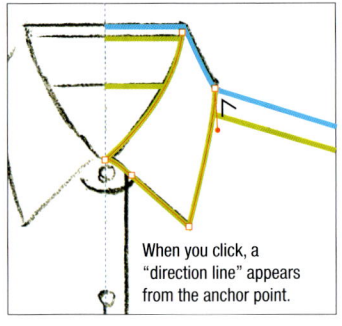

25. Select the anchor point using the "Convert Anchor Point Tool," found in the "Pen tool" sub-menu. This tool creates a direction line when you use it to click on the anchor point. Use it to increase the line's curvature.

When you click, a "direction line" appears from the anchor point.

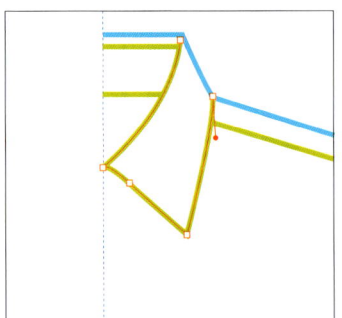

If you click on the eye of "blouse1" in the Layers Palette, you will see just the path.

Adding Asymmetrical Parts

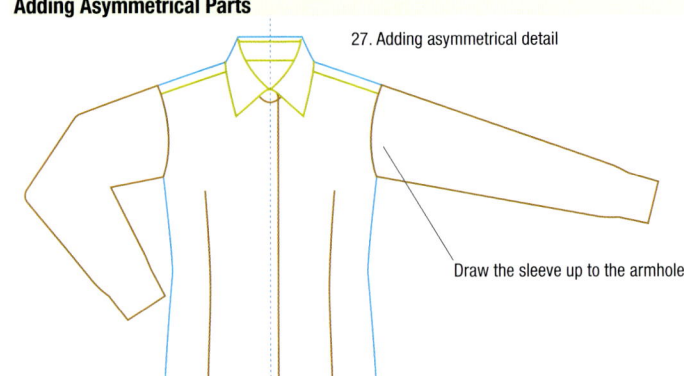

27. Adding asymmetrical detail

Draw the sleeve up to the armhole.

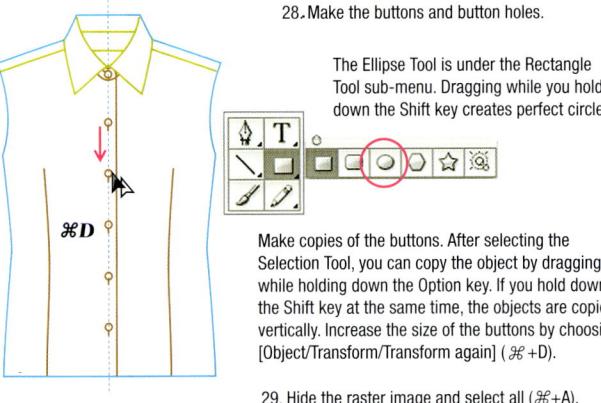

28. Make the buttons and button holes.

The Ellipse Tool is under the Rectangle Tool sub-menu. Dragging while you hold down the Shift key creates perfect circles.

Make copies of the buttons. After selecting the Selection Tool, you can copy the object by dragging it while holding down the Option key. If you hold down the Shift key at the same time, the objects are copied vertically. Increase the size of the buttons by choosing [Object/Transform/Transform again] (⌘+D).

Making a Mirrored Copy of the Object

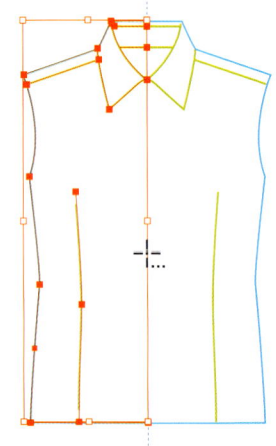

26. When the left side is completed, copy it to the right side. First, select all of the strokes (⌘+A), choose the Reflect Tool, and click on the guideline in the middle of the blouse while holding down the Option key. In the dialog box that appears, choose [Reflect Axis: Vertical/Copy] to copy to the opposite side.

The Reflect Tool is in the sub-menu of the Rotate Tool.

Choose the Reflect Tool from the Toolbox

29. Hide the raster image and select all (⌘+A). Change the stroke to black.

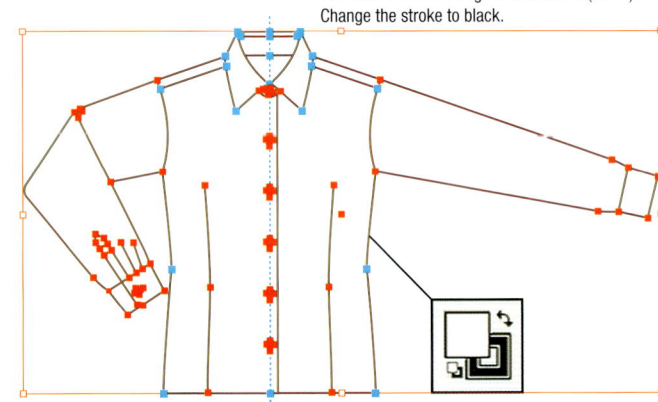

Align the left and right sides of the sleeve, while also watching the length of the warp lines in the center.

We are finished. We had drawn the blouse on the hanger as in the "hanger illustration" shown in Chapter 2, but this time drew the blouse as a flat. Rendering a top without padding as a flat allows us to clearly see the armhole and sleeve designs.

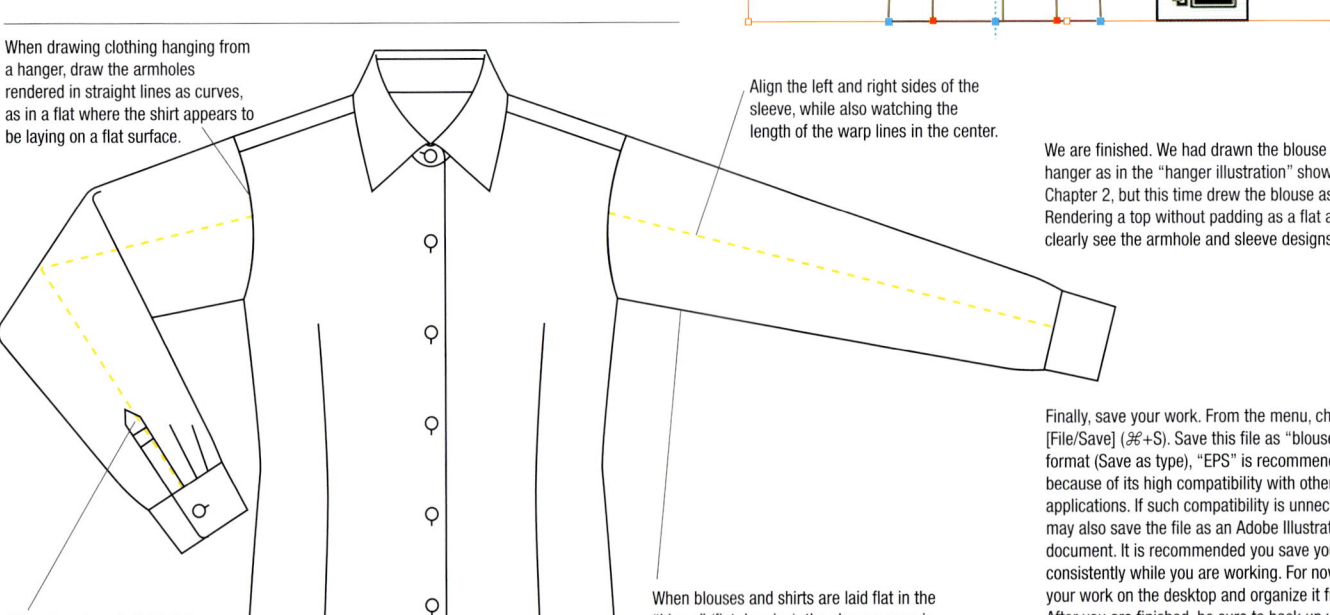

When drawing clothing hanging from a hanger, draw the armholes rendered in straight lines as curves, as in a flat where the shirt appears to be laying on a flat surface.

When the sleeve is folded, the sleeve placket should be visible. Fold the sleeve so that it does not cover the body of the blouse.

When blouses and shirts are laid flat in the "hira-e" (flat drawing), the sleeves open in the shape of a T. Be aware that the sleeves of other tops, such as jackets that have padding, will not open up in a T shape.

Finally, save your work. From the menu, choose [File/Save] (⌘+S). Save this file as "blouse2." For the format (Save as type), "EPS" is recommended because of its high compatibility with other graphic applications. If such compatibility is unnecessary, you may also save the file as an Adobe Illustrator document. It is recommended you save your work consistently while you are working. For now save your work on the desktop and organize it from there. After you are finished, be sure to back up your work.

Chaptor 4 : Computcr Graphic Techniques

(2) Color Variation for Technical Drawing
Adding various colors to the item

Coloring

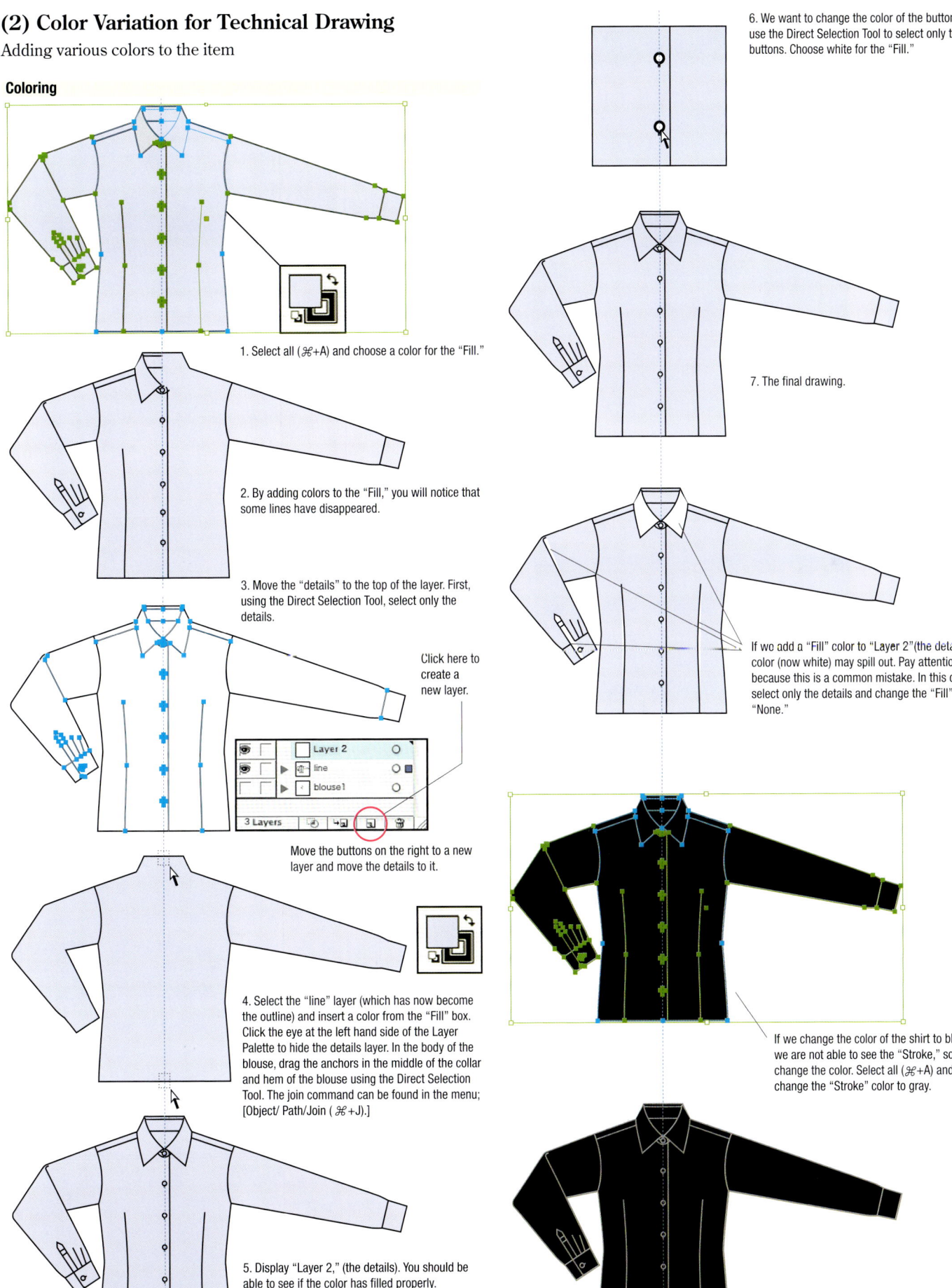

1. Select all (⌘+A) and choose a color for the "Fill."

2. By adding colors to the "Fill," you will notice that some lines have disappeared.

3. Move the "details" to the top of the layer. First, using the Direct Selection Tool, select only the details.

Click here to create a new layer.

Move the buttons on the right to a new layer and move the details to it.

4. Select the "line" layer (which has now become the outline) and insert a color from the "Fill" box. Click the eye at the left hand side of the Layer Palette to hide the details layer. In the body of the blouse, drag the anchors in the middle of the collar and hem of the blouse using the Direct Selection Tool. The join command can be found in the menu; [Object/ Path/Join (⌘+J).]

5. Display "Layer 2," (the details). You should be able to see if the color has filled properly.

6. We want to change the color of the buttons, so use the Direct Selection Tool to select only the buttons. Choose white for the "Fill."

7. The final drawing.

If wo add a "Fill" color to "Layer 2"(the details, the color (now white) may spill out. Pay attention because this is a common mistake. In this case, select only the details and change the "Fill" to "None."

If we change the color of the shirt to black, we are not able to see the "Stroke," so let's change the color. Select all (⌘+A) and change the "Stroke" color to gray.

The black shirt is finished.

153

Color Variation Painting closed paths

Go ahead and change the colors of different parts and try out various color variations. The sleeves have become closed paths, so click on the sleeves using the Direct Selection Tool. You can easily change the color of the sleeves by changing the color in the "Fill" box. Choose a color from the color picker by double clicking on the "Fill" box, or choose a color from the Swatches Palette or Colors Palette.

7. The back collar is finished. Next, fill the neckband. Make a path for the neckband fill to make sure we can see the buttons of the neckband.

This is what it looks like if you hide "Layer 2" (the details.)

8. Display "Layer 2" and the collar is complete.

9. Create paths for the cuffs in the same way.

Color Variation Painting open paths

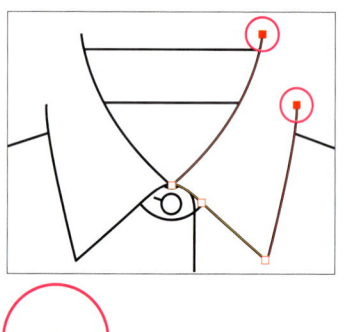

1. If you wish to make the collar and cuffs different colors, like that of a Cleric shirt, it is necessary to put the stroke of the collar on top of the fill of the collar.

2. As you can see by displaying only "Layer 2" (the details), the path of the fill part of the collar is open. First, close the path. Using the Direct Selection Tool, select both ends of the collar's open paths and join them together. (⌘+J)

3. When it closes, change the "Fill" to white and, in order to tell the difference, you should choose another color for the "Stroke."

4. When the stroke line is at a sharp angle, the angle may protrude. In this case, using the "Round Cap" button of the Stroke Palette, the corner point becomes smooth. Do the same thing to the right side of the collar.

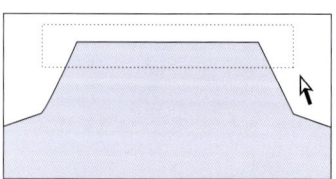

5. Make the back collar. Go back to the "line" layer and hide "Layer 2" so that the details are not visible. Drag and copy the collar section of the shirt using the Direct Selection Tool (⌘+C).

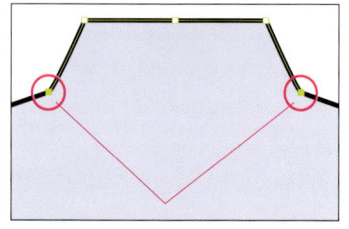

6. Cancel the temporary selection. Menu? Edit? Paste in Front (⌘+F). Select the points you wish to join by clicking on the two points with the Direct Selection Tool and choosing "Join." (⌘+J)

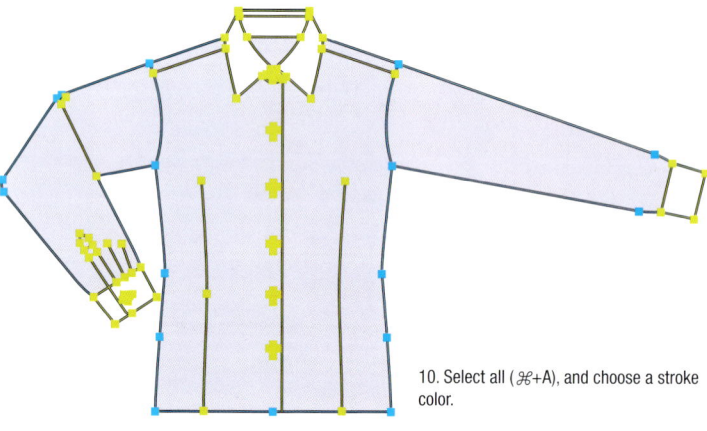

10. Select all (⌘+A), and choose a stroke color.

The Cleric shirt is complete. We have added a bit of a subdued feeling to its lines.

Chapter 4 : Computer Graphic Techniques

(3) How to Create An Original Pattern

There are many kinds of patterns. They can generally be divided into continuous patterns, such as checkers or stripes, and discontinuous patterns, such as animal prints. Here we will study how to draw arranged continuous patterns while repeating a fixed rhythm.

Flower Unit

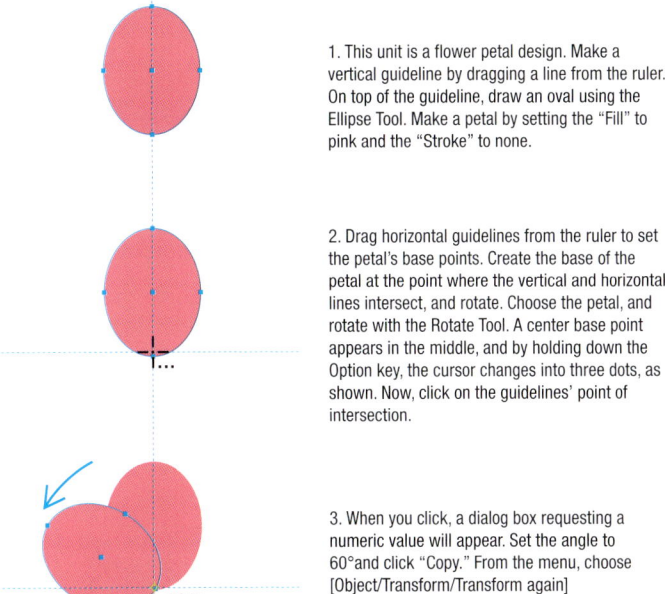

1. This unit is a flower petal design. Make a vertical guideline by dragging a line from the ruler. On top of the guideline, draw an oval using the Ellipse Tool. Make a petal by setting the "Fill" to pink and the "Stroke" to none.

2. Drag horizontal guidelines from the ruler to set the petal's base points. Create the base of the petal at the point where the vertical and horizontal lines intersect, and rotate. Choose the petal, and rotate with the Rotate Tool. A center base point appears in the middle, and by holding down the Option key, the cursor changes into three dots, as shown. Now, click on the guidelines' point of intersection.

3. When you click, a dialog box requesting a numeric value will appear. Set the angle to 60° and click "Copy." From the menu, choose [Object/Transform/Transform again] (⌘+D). Repeat this four times. We now have a flower silhouette.

4. Select all 6 petals and click on "merge," the third button from the left in the Pathfinder Palette. A string of paths is created.

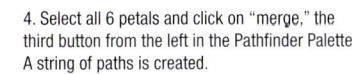

5. Next is the center section. Draw a circle by dragging the Ellipse Tool while holding down the Shift and Option keys. Set the "Fill" to light blue and the "Stroke" to yellow. The stroke can be modified in the stroke palette. Set the stroke to 6pt.

6. Create another flower of a different size. Drag with the Selection Tool to select the whole flower, and, while holding down the Option key, drag and copy.

7. Use the Selection Tool and decrease the size of the flower by dragging the bounding box. The same proportions are maintained by holding down the Shift key while dragging.

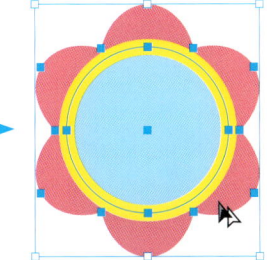

Change the color. Notice that the flower pistil stroke lines are uncolored.

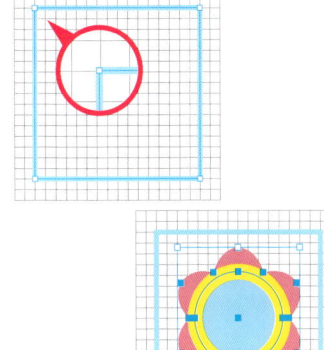

8. Make a frame. Show the grid. Adjust the size of the grid from [Illustrator/Preferences/Guides & Grid.] Set the grid size to 10mm and the subdivisions to 4 and select [Snap to Grid]. Choose the Rectangle Tool from the Tool Palette. When you click on the document window it will prompt you for numbers. Create a 50mm x 50mm frame. While it is selected, insert a "Stroke" color. Set the "Fill" to no color.

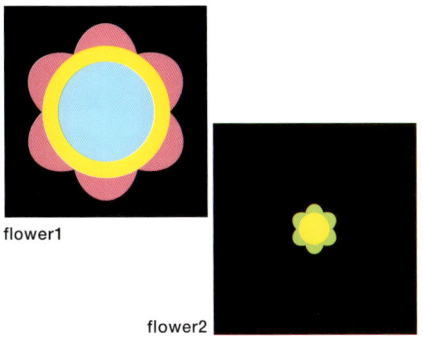

9. Use the grid to place the pattern unit in the exact center of the 50mm frame.

10. Choose a color for the frame. Select the frame with the Selection Tool and choose a color for the "Fill." Do not put a color in the "Stroke." When finished, save the pattern. From the menu go to [File/Save] (⌘+S). Name the file "flower 1."

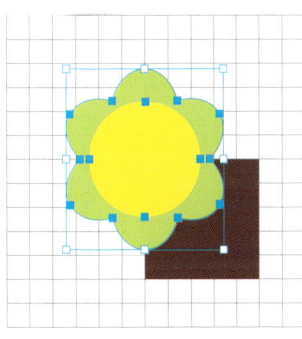

flower1

11. Make a pattern for the small flower in the same way. Save it as "flower 2."

flower2

Flower Pattern Unit Arrangement

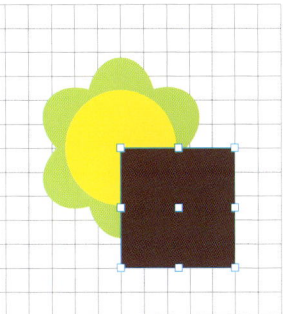

1. We will use the smaller-sized flower pattern. The stroke for both the flower petals and pistil is set to "None." From the Tool Palette, select the Rectangle Tool. When you click on the document window, you will be able to enter numbers. Create a 15 mm x 15 mm frame (inside the same layer as the flower). Add a color to the frame. Set the "Fill" to brown and the "Stroke" to "None." When the color is filled, select and drag the square and line up the top left corner with the center of the flower and bring to back. From the menu, go to [Option/Arrange/Bring to Back] (⌘+Shift).

2. Erase the portion of the pattern unit that sticks out of the frame. To get rid of protruding sections, use the Pathfinder's "crop" function. This function crops the object in front, so copy (click with the Selection Tool [⌘+C]) the square in order to bring it to the foreground. Temporarily release the selection. Next, from the menu go to [Edit/Paste in Front] (⌘+F). Doing this will copy the square to the foreground.

3. Select all and click "Crop," the fourth function from the left on the Pathfinder Palette.

4. By changing the relationship between the paths on the Pathfinder, it is possible to create various shapes.

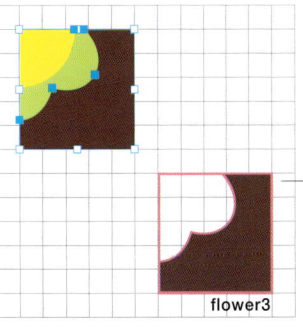

Select all (⌘+A). Click on "Crop Front Object from the Area Shape" from the Pathfinder Palette and choose a color for the "Stroke." Save this file as "flower3."

flower3

155

Creating a Pattern Unit by Free-Hand

Creating a Pattern Unit by Free-Hand

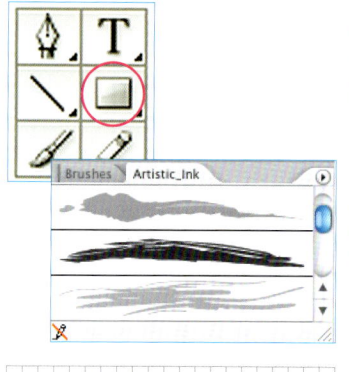

1. Making a Frame
From the Tool Palette, select the Rectangle Tool. When you click on the document window, it will prompt you for numbers. Create a 50mm x 50 mm frame.

2. Make a pattern unit using the Brush Tool. Depending on the brush you choose from the Brush Palette, you can create various brush touches.

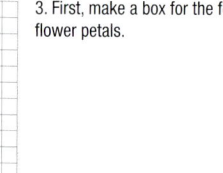

3. First, make a box for the foundation of the flower petals.

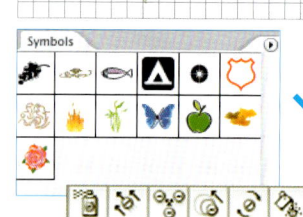

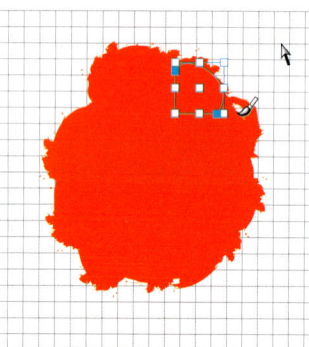

4. Draw the flower petals.

5. After you have made the brush strokes, click on the document window with the Direct Selection Tool (While using the Pen Tool, pressing the ⌘ key is also fine.) to cancel the selection enclosure. Repeat this.

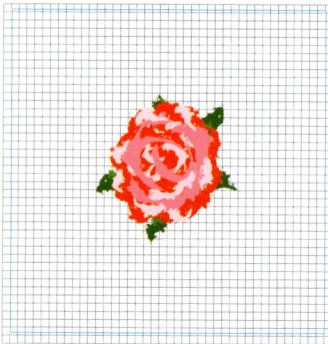

8. If you move the leaf layer to the bottom, the leaves are hidden under the flower petals.

9. You can define the flower petals you made as a symbol.
After you define the symbol, you can play around with the other pictures and symbols.

We created a few more flowers by repeating the above steps.

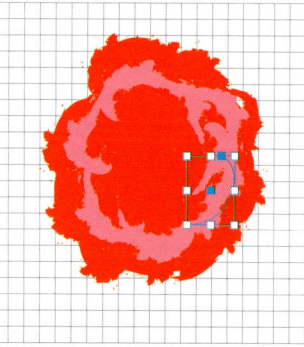

6. Next, change the color and draw more.

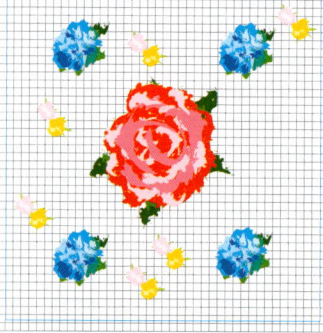

10. Place the flower in a 100mm frame. Bring it to the frame by selecting it with the Selection Tool and dragging.

11. Insert the other flowers in the same way,. Hold down the Option key when you drag to make more copies. It is better to group complicated paths as organized units.

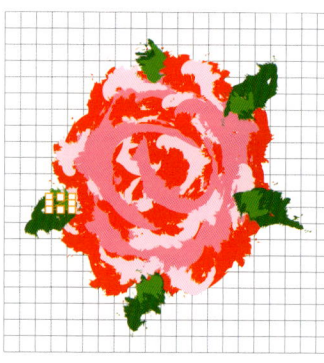

7. Create a new layer and draw leaves.

12. Paint the background. Select the 100mm squared frame and insert a "Fill" color. If you can no longer see the pattern unit because of the color of the frame, move the frame's object to the lowest layer of the list. Select the frame. From the menu go to [Object/Arrange/Send to front] (⌘+shift+[ ). When there are many layers on top of each other, it is necessary to move a layer to the bottom of the stack.

Chapter 4 : Computer Graphic Techniques

Types of Filters
Creating a Pattern Unit by Free-Hand

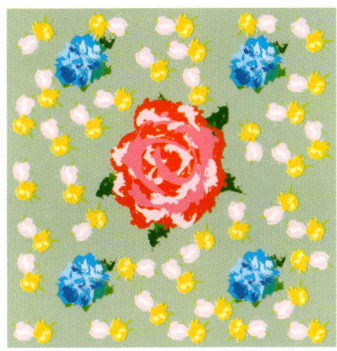

When using filters, remember to always set the color mode to RGB and rasterize the object. First, from the menu go to [File/Document Color Mode/RGB Color]. Next, select all (⌘+A) and from the menu choose [Object/Rasterize].

↑ From the menu
[Filter/Artistic/Sponge.] Save as "flower4."

↑ From the menu
[Filter/Artistic/Plastic Wrap.]

↑ From the menu
[Filter/Pixelate/Pointillize.]

↑ From the menu
[Filter/Texture/Canvas.]

Making a Pattern Unit Into a Pattern

As you can see from striped or checkered patterns, many patterns are arrangements of one repeated fixed rhythm. Use the grid to correctly place the 50mm squared pattern units.

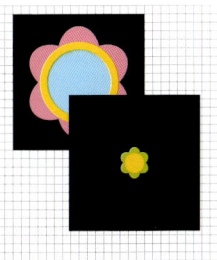

1. Open the two patterns, "flower1" and "flower2," that we made with the Shape Tool. Besides opening it from the menu bar, you can also double click on the icon.

2. In the Layers Palette of each file, select "Combine All Layers" ("Merge All"). Be careful not to let the layers separate when you are placing the pattern unit.

3. They are separated into two windows, so move "flower2" to the window of "flower1." First, from the window of "flower2" select all (⌘+A) and copy (⌘+C). Click on the display of "flower1" and paste (⌘+V). "Flower1" is pasted into "flower2's" display.

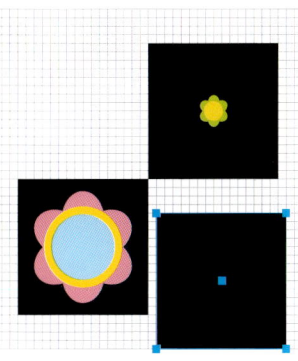

4. Try combining the two patterns. Various designs are possible by also inserting some empty space.

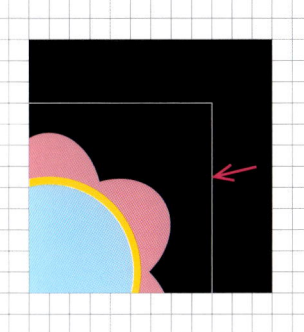

5. When you have placed the pattern unit, view it zoomed in. Even when you planned to place it neatly, there are often times when slight gaps appear. In this case, redo the foundation frame.

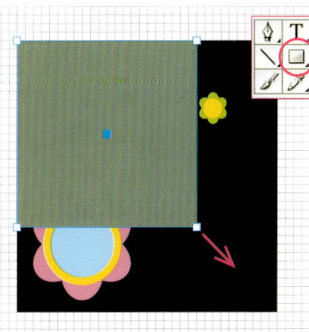

6. Select the Rectangle Tool and drag to make a rectangle of the same size. Change the "Fill", otherwise it can be confusing.

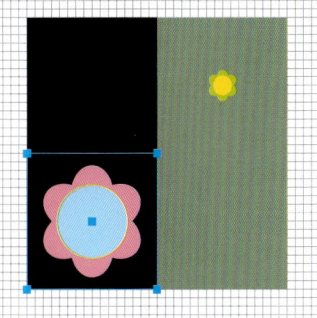

7. The frame is on top of the flower pattern, so move it back. If it is in the same layer, from the menu, go to [Object/Arrange/Send to front] (⌘+shift+[ ). If the pattern and the frame are in different layers, move the frame layer under the pattern unit's layer.

8. Select all of the pattern unit's frames and delete them.

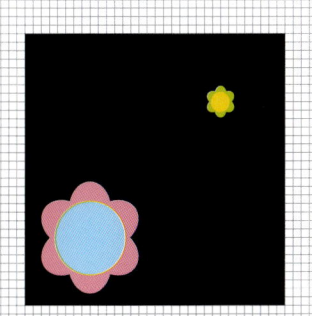

9. Change the color of the newest frame back to black.

10. We are finished. Save the document as "pattern." (⌘+S)

Pasting the Original Pattern on the Item as a Textile

- Open the files "blouse2" and "pattern."
- From the Layers Palette of the file "pattern," select "Merge All Layers." Do not let the layers separate when you are placing the pattern unit.
- Make sure that in the file "blouse2," the details and silhouette layers are separated. (Refer to p153 "(2) Color Variation for Technical Drawing."

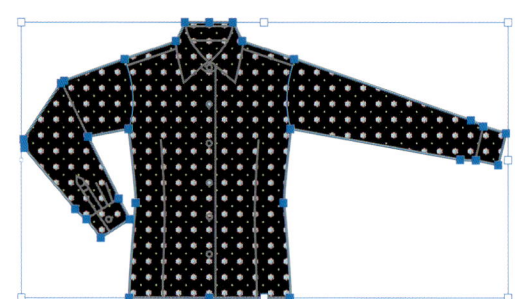

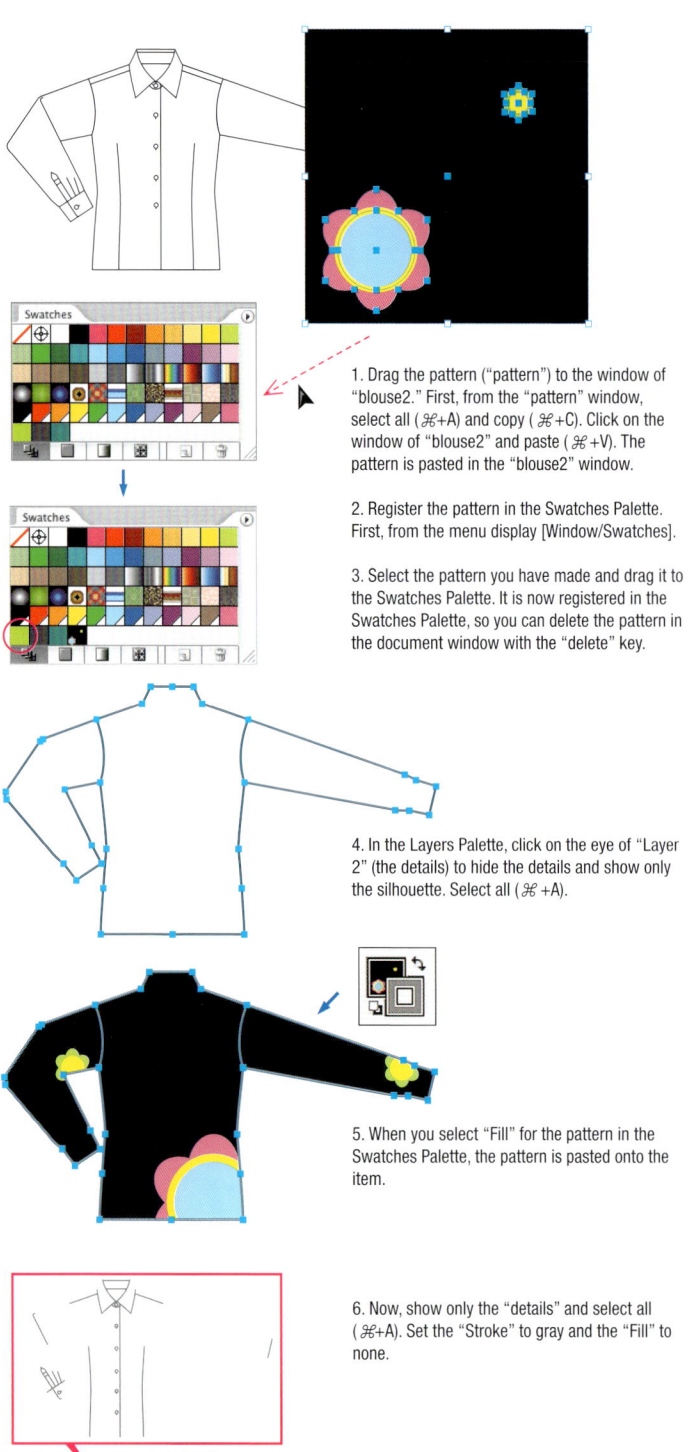

1. Drag the pattern ("pattern") to the window of "blouse2." First, from the "pattern" window, select all (⌘+A) and copy (⌘+C). Click on the window of "blouse2" and paste (⌘+V). The pattern is pasted in the "blouse2" window.

2. Register the pattern in the Swatches Palette. First, from the menu display [Window/Swatches].

3. Select the pattern you have made and drag it to the Swatches Palette. It is now registered in the Swatches Palette, so you can delete the pattern in the document window with the "delete" key.

4. In the Layers Palette, click on the eye of "Layer 2" (the details) to hide the details and show only the silhouette. Select all (⌘+A).

5. When you select "Fill" for the pattern in the Swatches Palette, the pattern is pasted onto the item.

6. Now, show only the "details" and select all (⌘+A). Set the "Stroke" to gray and the "Fill" to none.

7. Show both layers. The pattern will be too big, so reduce its size.

8. The size of the pattern can be changed. From the menu, go to [Object/Transform/Scale] and insert the percentages. For the options, check only "pattern." Check preview and adjust the percentage.

9. We want to change the color of the buttons. Select only the buttons and change the "Fill" to gray, while leaving the "Stroke" gray.

The completed image.

Place the pattern unit we made by free hand "flower4" (p157) in the same way. You can change not only the size of the pattern, but also the movement and rotation. From the menu, go to [Object/Transform/Rotate], or [Move]. This time, reduce the scale of the pattern after pasting it. We rotated it another 45 degrees.

We tried pasting "flower3" (p155) which we made in the Flower pattern unit Arrangement section. The detailed pattern offsets the white of the collar and cuffs.

References:
Mac FanSpecial26 Learn Like a Pro Photoshop & Illustrator Texture Design Technique / Mainichi Communications Inc.
Photoshop CS for Windows & Macintosh MENU MASTER / Written by X-Media / X-Media Corp.
Step Up from Zero! Adobe Illustrator CS for Windows & Macintosh / Written by Yuka Miyamoto / Ruttles Inc.

Postscript

So how did you get on?

If you repeat the exercises in the book and progress one step at a time, after one year you should have acquired a solid practical ability. I teach the content of this book over a period of one year. Nearly all students can measure their development by looking at the work they did one year earlier. Students are anxious at first that they will never succeed, and often come and ask whether I think they will really learn to draw properly. If you acquire the basics of drawing the body and dressed figure in the first six months and the more individually oriented subjects of coloring and computer graphics in the other six months, then, from the second year, you will be able to make drawings that reflect your individual ideas. Students often ask me how they should go about making works that show their individuality. Some seem to get worried when they see people around them doing work of a striking nature. But real individuality is something of a very rich character that shows through even when one is trying to master the basics. It does not emerge from a passing enthusiasm. Enthusiasm may burn brightly for a while but then fade away just as soon. If you want to go on showing individuality in the long term in this profession, you need to have a firm grasp of the basics. That is the fastest route to originality.

You should also put your own feelings into your work. Even very immature work is bound to appeal to people if it is created with a sincere input of feeling. It is important to constantly give the maximum expression to your abilities of the moment. We are not necessarily moved only by things which are technically superior. Even if a performance is not very skillful, we are moved if the performer sings with soul. Conversely, no-one pays attention to a work which is technically overdone and contains no emotion. Nevertheless it is true that if technical skill is present, it will lead to a corresponding increase in the message expressed and conveyed, and that is why it is still important to work hard at it day after day. On the other hand, people should not become discouraged because they feel they are not making progress. In every activity, cycling or playing the guitar or participating in a sport, we all start off with no ability. The way we acquire the ability is by sticking at it until we learn the knack. When we are children we are not afraid of mistakes, so no matter how many times we fall off our bicycle we get back on again. But although we accept this as natural then, after we reach adolescence, we become emotionally vulnerable and shrink back from making mistakes. When you have only made ten or twenty drawings, it is too early to start asking whether you have talent. People progress at different speeds. If after you have made 500 drawings there is still no difference from the first drawing, then you can start wondering about your talent. Until then just keep going.

Lastly, I would like to express my heartfelt gratitude to Seiki Okuda and Chieko Konaka who kept watch over the project for three years from the planning stage to the completion of the manuscript; to Yukiko Wakabayashi, who designed the book; and to the many people whom I met in the course of the project.

About the Author

Zeshu Takamura is Professor of Advanced Fashion Design and Head of the Fashion Illustration Laboratory, Faculty of Fashion Science, at Bunka Gakuen University's Graduate School in Tokyo. A graduate of the Faculty of Education of Tokyo Gakugei University and the Department of Dress Design of Kuwasawa Design School, he is active in fashion illustration, design, and research at publishers, agencies, and apparel manufacturers. His many publications include *Roots of Street Style, Fashion Design Archives,* and *Fashion Illustration Techniques: A Super Reference Book for Beginners.* www.zeshu.com

---

Fashion Design Techniques
by Zeshu Takamura

First Schiffer Publishing edition: October 2015

Copyright © 2005 Zeshu Takamura
Copyright © 2005 Graphic-Sha Publishing Co., Ltd.

This book was first designed and published in Japan in 2005 by Graphic-sha Publishing Co., Ltd., 1-14-17 Kudan-Kita, Chiyoda-ku, Tokyo 102-0073 Japan. This English edition was published in 2015 by Schiffer Publishing, Ltd.

All rights reserved. No part of this work may be reproduced or used in any form or by any means—graphic, electronic, or mechanical, including photocopying or information storage and retrieval systems—without written permission from the publisher.

The scanning, uploading, and distribution of this book or any part thereof via the Internet or via any other means without the permission of the publisher is illegal and punishable by law. Please purchase only authorized editions and do not participate in or encourage the electronic piracy of copyrighted materials.

"Schiffer," "Schiffer Publishing, Ltd. & Design," and the "Design of pen and inkwell" are registered trademarks of Schiffer Publishing, Ltd.

ISBN: 978-0-7643-5047-4

Printed in China

Published by Schiffer Publishing, Ltd.
4880 Lower Valley Road
Atglen, PA 19310 USA
Phone: (610) 593-1777; Fax: (610) 593-2002
E-mail: Info@schifferbooks.com

For our complete selection of fine books on this and related subjects, please visit our website at www.schifferbooks.com. You may also write for a free catalog.

This book may be purchased from the publisher. Please try your bookstore first.

We are always looking for people to write books on new and related subjects. If you have an idea for a book, please contact us at proposals@schifferbooks.com.

Schiffer Publishing's titles are available at special discounts for bulk purchases for sales promotions or premiums. Special editions, including personalized covers, corporate imprints, and excerpts can be created in large quantities for special needs. For more information, contact the publisher.

CG Assistant operator: Jo Ueda
Original layout and cover design: Yukiko Wakabayashi
Assistant designer: Aya Onda
Editor: Seiki Okuda (Graphic-Sha Publishing Co., Ltd.)
English edition layout: Flair
English translation management: Lingua franca, Inc.
Production and coordination: Kumiko Sakamoto (Graphic-Sha Publishing Co., Ltd.)